Is there a common European identity? If so, what kinds of history does it possess? *Narratives of Enlightenment* examines the literary and historical achievements of major figures such as Voltaire, David Hume, William Robertson, Edward Gibbon and the American historian David Ramsay in the light of eighteenth-century political and national debates in France, Scotland, England and America. Undertaking a comparative reappraisal of these writers, Karen O'Brien investigates the degree and nature of their intellectual investments in the idea of a common European civilisation. This original and incisive study intervenes from the perspective of literary criticism in contemporary debates about Enlightenments past and present, the political uses for narrative, and the European contexts of national awareness.

CAMBRIDGE STUDIES IN EIGHTEENTH-CENTURY ENGLISH LITERATURE AND THOUGHT 34

Narratives of Enlightenment

CAMBRIDGE STUDIES IN EIGHTEENTH-CENTURY ENGLISH LITERATURE AND THOUGHT

Some recent titles

Locke, Literary Criticism, and Philosophy by William Walker

The English Fable: Aesop and Literary Culture, 1651–1740
by Jayne Elizabeth Lewis

Mania and Literary Style
The Rhetoric of Enthusiasm from the Ranters to Christopher Smart
by Clement Hawes

Landscape, Liberty and Authority
Poetry, Criticism and Politics from Thomson to Wordsworth
by Tim Fulford

Philosophical Dialogue in the British Enlightenment
Theology, Aesthetics, and the Novel
by Michael Prince

Defoe and the New Sciences
by Ilse Vickers

History and the Early English Novel: Matters of Fact from Bacon to Defoe
by Robert Mayer

A complete list of books in this series is given at the end of the volume

Narratives of Enlightenment

Cosmopolitan history from Voltaire to Gibbon

KAREN O'BRIEN
University of Wales, Cardiff

PUBLISHED BY THE PRESS SYNDICATE OF THE UNIVERSITY OF CAMBRIDGE
The Pitt Building, Trumpington Street, Cambridge CB2 1RP

CAMBRIDGE UNIVERSITY PRESS
The Edinburgh Building, Cambridge CB2 2RU, United Kingdom
40 West 20th Street, New York, NY 10011–4211, USA
10 Stamford Road, Oakleigh, Melbourne 3166, Australia

First published 1997

Printed in Great Britain at the University Press, Cambridge

A catalogue record for this book is available from the British Library

Library of Congress cataloguing in publication data

O'Brien, Karen, Dr
Narratives of enlightenment: Cosmopolitan history from Voltaire to Gibbon / Karen O'Brien
p. cm. – (Cambridge Studies in Eighteenth-Century English Literature and Thought; 34)
Based partly on the author's thesis (doctoral) – St Hugh's College, Oxford
Includes bibliographical references and index.
ISBN 0 521 46533 8 (hardback)
1. Literature and history. 2. Enlightenment.
3. Intellectual life – History. I. Title. II. Series.
PN50.027 1997
907'.2–dc21 96–36667 CIP

ISBN 0 521 46533 8 hardback

For Cassy and Patrick O’Brien

Contents

Acknowledgements

For permission to quote from the Robertson–MacDonald papers, I am grateful to the Trustees of the National Library of Scotland. I am also grateful to Penguin Books for permission to quote from Geoffrey Hill's *Collected Poems*. I am grateful to the librarians and staff of the Cambridge University Library, the British Library, the Taylorian Library, the National Library of Scotland, the Edinburgh University Library, the Houghton Library, the Charleston Library Society, the Historical Society of Pennsylvania, and, particularly, to Michael Richardson of Bristol University Library and to Dr Jim Green and Mr Phil Lapsansky of the Library Company of Philadelphia.

My work on eighteenth-century literature began with a British Academy studentship and with a graduate scholarship at St Cross College, Oxford. The research for the American portion of the book was carried out at the University of Pennsylvania with the support of a Harkness Fellowship from the Commonwealth Fund of New York. A William Stone Research Fellowship at Peterhouse, Cambridge, enabled me to continue, and lectureships at Southampton and Cardiff Universities enabled me to complete the project in between full-time teaching duties.

I have been fortunate to receive a good deal of help over the years of the research and composition of this book. I am grateful to Dr Isabel Rivers of St Hugh's College, Oxford, for her 'reason, grace and (kind) sentiment' during her supervision of the doctorate upon which this book is partly based. W. H. Barber, Professor Emeritus of Birkbeck College, London, Dr John Robertson of St Hugh's College, Dr Colin Kidd of Glasgow University, Professor Mark Phillips of Carleton University, Ottawa, and Dr Christopher Kelly of Corpus Christi College, Cambridge all read chapters of this book at different stages of its development, and their comments and suggestions were gratefully received. I also wish to thank Professor Howard Erskine-Hill of Pembroke College, Cambridge, the editor of this series, for good and considered advice. Mr Brian Wormald of Peterhouse, Cambridge was enlightening on the subject of historians ancient and modern. My thanks, too, to Josie Dixon of Cambridge University Press for her help and encouragement. Needless to say, my errors are my own. Any scholar working her way towards a first book incurs longer-term debts of a less specific but no less important kind, and these I owe to Mr Paul Cheetham, Dr Helen Cooper, Dr Roy Park and Dr David Womersley. Duncan and Louise McDonald, Helen Calcraft and Stephen O'Brien have given me invaluable support. My husband Peter McDonald has helped with this project at every stage, and in far more important ways besides. My greatest debt is expressed in the dedication.

Author's note

The book ends with separate bibliographies of selected secondary studies of the five historians and an additional bibliography of general studies of the history of historical writing many of which are not cited in the notes. Primary texts, a number of which are the subject of detailed textual discussion, are cited in the notes only. Where available, I have drawn my citations from good modern editions of primary texts. The chapter on Gibbon was completed before the appearance of David Womersley's Penguin edition of *The Decline and Fall*; this preserves the volume divisions of Gibbon's text and identifies Gibbon's textual revisions, and should now be regarded as the standard modern edition.

1

Introduction: cosmopolitanism, narrative, history

This is a study of cosmopolitan approaches to the past in the work of five eighteenth-century historians, and it is concerned with their endeavours to modify or transform their readers' sense of national self-awareness through the writing of narrative history. Three of these historians, Voltaire, Hume and Gibbon, are familiar, and familiarly grouped together. The fourth, William Robertson, the Scottish historian of Scotland, Europe and its empires, was once celebrated as much as his friend David Hume, and has, after a period of neglect, received a good deal of scholarly attention in recent years. The fifth, the American historian David Ramsay, needs more introduction; he was the most talented and, also, the most sceptical of the early patriot historians of the American Revolution, and he is included in the present book because his work exemplifies the peculiar difficulties and rewards of a cosmopolitan approach to a story of national self-invention. Each historian is considered in the national and cultural contexts within which the cosmopolitan perspectives of his work acquired and tendered meaning. Robertson is accorded two chapters in view of the number and diversity of his works, and the relative shortage of secondary material about them. *Narratives of Enlightenment* has no teleological tale to tell about the rise of a historicist outlook in eighteenth-century history or the triumph of an Enlightenment meta-narrative of progress.[1] Nor is it primarily a study of lines of authorial influence, although recapitulations and adaptations of one work by another are discussed where they give insight into a historian's creative response to his cultural environment. I have examined, instead, and in a less schematic way, the play of a cosmopolitan sensibility in each of these works across the political certainties, cultural self-understandings and national prejudices which structured contemporary readings of the past. In many respects, these historians differ profoundly in their political priorities, their literary techniques, and in their very sense of the immediacy or pastness of the past. What they share is the cosmopolitan

[1] Freidrich Meinecke, *Historism: The Rise of a New Historical Outlook*, trans. J. E. Anderson (New York, 1972); Ernst Cassirer, *The Philosophy of the Enlightenment*, trans. Fritz Koellin and James Pettegrove (Princeton, 1951). For other works on the history of historical writing, see the general bibliography.

(rather than universalist) recognition that all nations are endowed with valid histories and identities which intersect with, and complete, each other, but that individual states or nations are not, in themselves, intelligible units of historical study. One corollary of this recognition was that all five historians remained, throughout the mid- to late eighteenth-century years of imperial competition and warfare between Britain and France, committed to an ideal of Europe as a harmonious system of balancing states.[2]

Cosmopolitan history

The 'cosmopolitan history' of the title of this book, then, describes both a rhetorical strategy developed and adapted by eighteenth-century historians, and a habit of thought. 'Cosmopolitanism' is no longer a term much favoured by intellectual historians: as an idea, it seems to lack intellectual content; as a category of political thought, it has no referent.[3] The term is occasionally invoked by literary and cultural historians of the eighteenth century in connection with neoclassical notions of taste, the language of bourgeois political aspirations or aristocratic consumer preferences.[4] I have revived the term for the purposes of this study because it simultaneously encapsulates an attitude of detachment towards national prejudice (often described as an 'impartial' or 'philosophical' attitude in other studies of these historians), and an intellectual investment in the idea of a common European civilisation.

Voltaire understood this civilisation in cultural rather than in political terms, and, by turns, endorsed, admonished and rebuked France's political sphere from the normative cultural domain in which he imaginatively positioned himself as a European writer. In his histories of modern France (the *Siècle de Louis XIV*, 1751 and the *Précis du Siècle de Louis XV*, 1769), he mounted a cosmopolitan critique of his own national history which he later extended and re-evaluated in his general history of the world, the *Essai sur les mœurs* (1756). David Hume acquired, in his *History of England* (1754–62),

[2] John Robertson, 'Universal Monarchy and the Liberties of Europe; David Hume's Critique of an English Whig Doctrine' in *Political Discourse in Early Modern Britain*, eds. Nicholas Phillipson and Quentin Skinner (Cambridge, 1993); Frederick Whelan, 'Robertson, Hume and the Balance of Power', *Hume Studies*, 21 (1995), 315–32; Jeremy Black, 'Gibbon and International Relations' to be published as part of the proceedings of the Royal Historical Society's bicentenary conference on Gibbon, edited by Roland Quinault and Rosamond McKitterick (Cambridge, forthcoming).

[3] The last investigation of the idea was Thomas J. Schlereth, *The Cosmopolitan Ideal in Enlightenment Thought: Its Form and Function in the Ideas of Franklin, Hume and Voltaire, 1694–1790* (Notre Dame, Indiana, 1977).

[4] For example, Gerald Newman, *The Rise of English Nationalism: A Cultural History, 1740–1830* (London, 1987); J. Pappas, 'The Revolt of the Philosophes against Aristocratic Tastes' in *Culture and Revolution*, eds. P. Dukes and J. Dunkley (London, 1990).

different though comparable kinds of European perspective by way of a historicist and revisionist approach to British constitutional history. In composing his history backwards, he began with the seventeenth century, and gradually worked his way back to the invasion of Julius Caesar; over the course of writing he tended increasingly to contextualise events within a European historical framework, and to evaluate, with subtly ironic detachment, those peculiarities and anomalies in British history cherished by so many of his British countrymen. Robertson's writing career took him from the locally specific *History of Scotland* (1759) to broader histories of Europe (*The History of the Emperor Charles V*, 1769) and its colonies (*The History of America*, 1777). He was the most insistently cosmopolitan of all eighteenth-century historians, in part because he felt that persistent tensions between Scottish and English cultural and political identities could only be resolved through a reappraisal of their common European frame of meaning. Where Hume exposed the parochial and wayward behaviour of past generations of English and Scots, Robertson sought to transcend national and denominational prejudices in Britain by drawing attention to common patterns and affinities between the British and continental European journeys to modernity and empire. Edward Gibbon, whose vast *History of the Decline and Fall of the Roman Empire* (1776–88) is necessarily approached selectively in the present study, incorporated into his story of the protracted decay of Rome and Byzantium a partial and incomplete narrative of that same European journey towards the 'safer and more Enlightened age' of the present. The genesis and growth of this more enlightened Europe out of its classical past is, I shall argue, one important theme of *The Decline and Fall* as a whole which arises, not so much from political concerns, as from Gibbon's deep imaginative interest in his own consciousness as a modern historian endeavouring to assimilate the great sweep of a previous civilisation. Lastly, David Ramsay brought a Humean tone and sceptical temperament to bear in his *History of the American Revolution* (1789), a work which provided the first serious analysis of the Revolution and the events leading up to the adoption of the American federal constitution. Ramsay's authorial posture of cosmopolitan detachment from the passions of the Revolution was not, in any way, a sign of residual emotional loyalty to Britain, but a pragmatic and politically engaged way of facing up to an unknown and (possibly) unstable future for the independent American nation.

Cosmopolitanism is thus a point of orientation for these historians, and, frequently, an impetus to irony at the expense of the partialities and accidents which lie behind those reassuring stories which nations tell to themselves. It is also, in the work of some eighteenth-century historians, an identity-prescription for their readers: Europe, it is implied, must remain part of the structure of their self-awareness as French, British or American subjects or citizens. Our understanding of the forms and expressions of national self-awareness available to men and women in the eighteenth century has been deepened by recent literary and historical scholars, and this study engages with some of the ideas and debates generated by their work.[5] In rediscovering and documenting cultural manifestations of Britishness, American-ness or Frenchness, these scholars have tended to construe national awareness as a kind of patriotic allegiance to the state and, in the process, to assume (whether tacitly or explicitly) that cosmopolitanism either antedated or impeded the growth of a fully-fledged national consciousness among some of the more educated sections of society. A national self, it is often held, needs a negative counter-image of the 'other' to give it definition and psychological purchase. In Britain, for example, a growing sense of a Protestant, robust, masculine British self is said to have affirmed itself in opposition to a projected image of a Catholic, superstitious, effete French other.[6] Yet, as I shall argue, such straightforward antinomies of patriotism and cosmopolitanism appear to dissolve when tested against the work of some of the eighteenth century's most prestigious and popular national historians. It was, at least in this period, possible to fashion an image of national selfhood which derived, not from an idea of the 'other', but from the interplay of likeness and difference within the family of Christian churches and nations. Our sense of what it might have meant to be French, British or American in the eighteenth century can be enriched and complicated by examining the peculiar modes of national self-consciousness to be found in the work of the historians discussed in this study, including those, such as Montesquieu and John Millar, given briefer treatment in individual chapters.

Modes of national self-awareness imply or include concrete political ideas about what a state has been and should be; the journey, however, from political ideas to modes of awareness is an imaginative one, entailing, in the case of narrative history, a process of literary implementation. Most of the works of history in this study belong, in part, to the history of political thought in so far as they present the past as a potential arbitrator between different political theories and programmes. Indeed, all of the historians except Gibbon hold (by nineteenth-century and modern standards) comparatively instrumental views of their historical material in relation to general political inquiry. But their histories also inhabit the discursive

[5] In addition to Newman's book, Raphael Samuel, *Patriotism: The Making and Unmaking of British National Identity* (3 vols;. London, 1989); Keith Michael Baker, *Inventing the French Revolution: Essays on French Political Culture in the Eighteenth Century* (Cambridge, 1990); John Lucas, *England and Englishness: Ideas of Nationhood in English Poetry, 1688–1900* (London, 1991); Linda Colley, *Britons: Forging the Nation, 1707–1837* (New Haven, 1992); Jack P. Greene, *The Intellectual Construction of America: Exceptionalism and Identity from 1492 to 1800* (Chapel Hill, NC, 1993); Kathleen Wilson, *The Sense of the People: Politics, Culture and Imperialism in England, 1715–1785* (Cambridge, 1995).

[6] 'Britishness was superimposed over an array of differences in response to contact with the Other, and above all in response to conflict with the Other' (Colley, *Britons*, 6). More recently, Michele Cohen, *Fashioning Masculinity: National Identity and Language in the Eighteenth Century* (London, 1996).

medium of extended narrative which demands a literary management of ideas quite different from the logic of theoretical or practical political argument. For this reason, the present study has attempted to combine and integrate the analytical techniques of intellectual history and literary criticism. It pays attention to the (often virtuoso) literary handling of moments in the past important to the political self-understanding of eighteenth-century readers – the executions of Charles I and Mary, Queen of Scots, for example, the attempt by the Emperor Julian the Apostate to reinstate the pagan republic of Rome, or the Revocation of the Edict of Nantes. It examines the application in these histories of heroic, tragic and sentimental vocabularies, modulations in register and tone, and structuring metaphors and metonymies – as they serve, not merely as textual ammunition in a war of ideas, but to enlarge their readers' range of responses to the emotional and moral, as well as political lessons of history. There was, of course, nothing new in the eighteenth century about the idea of history as a literary medium employing politically suasive literary techniques; but the firmly empirical manner with which most of these historians approached theoretical questions about politics and nationhood, and their peculiarly eighteenth-century alertness to their audience, give unusual literary depth and complexity to their historical practice. For Hume, especially, but also for Voltaire, Robertson, Gibbon and Ramsay, it was their readers' responses to their own history and, by extension, to histories of their own history (rather than to abstract ideas about laws and governments) which constituted the national community itself. In subsequent years, in the later work of Edmund Burke and of the British nineteenth-century historians inspired by his work, this idea would acquire the force of prescription (as they might have said, 'must constitute', 'is the only thing which *can* be said to constitute ... the national community').[7] Eighteenth-century historians had a more dynamic sense of historical writing as an arena in which both historian and reader exercise political, emotional, and aesthetic choices; together they create, not an imagined, but an interpretive community engaged in a rhetorical arbitration of their own history.

In examining the fundamentally literary way in which eighteenth-century historians approached the historical operation, the modern critic might be tempted to celebrate this period as something of a golden age prior to the dissociation of the literary from the historical sensibility.[8]

[7] On Burke's nineteenth-century historical legacy, see J. W. Burrow, *A Liberal Descent: Victorian Historians and the English Past* (Cambridge, 1981).

[8] A number of critics do this, including Suzanne Gearhart, *The Open Boundary of History and Fiction: A Critical Approach to the French Enlightenment* (Princeton, 1984) and Leo Braudy, *Narrative Form in History and Fiction: Hume, Fielding and Gibbon* (Princeton, 1970). For an overview of recent debates on the question of narrativity and history, see Andrew P. Norman, 'Telling it like it was: Historical Narratives on their own Terms', *History and Theory*, 30 (1991), 119–35.

Hayden White's vision of history as a neutral series of data which the historian emplots as tragedy or comedy according to his political, emotional and aesthetic preferences no longer scandalises.[9] Eighteenth-century historians might be said, according to this model of an undissociated sensibility, to have been wiser structuralists than their more scientifically minded nineteenth-century successors, since they recognised the exclusively textual nature of history. The gap between eighteenth-century literature and narrative history inevitably seems to close once the critic resorts to structuralist or post-structuralist notions of textuality. Indeed, eighteenth-century theorists of history were themselves slow to define any basic ontological difference between the respective referents of literature and history; 'sober' History calms Tragedy in the final book of *The Dunciad* promising her that she will, in time, join her in exposing retrospectively the 'barb'rous Age' of dulness.[10] In a similar spirit, Adam Smith, in his lectures on rhetoric and *belles lettres* (noted down by a student in 1762–3), commented: 'For what is it which constitutes the essential difference betwixt a historicall poem and a history? It is no more than this that the one is in prose and the other in verse.'[11] Although Gibbon and Voltaire, in particular, thought deeply about the way in which the historian imposes form upon his primary data, few historians registered the generic proximity of history to fiction as a threat to the epistemological validity of their work. Some writers of history, such as Oliver Goldsmith and Catharine Macaulay, went so far as to employ the epistolary form traditionally associated with the novel in their historical works, while others, including the five historians at the centre of this study, were open and eclectic in their responses to the relatively new form of the novel.[12] Eighteenth-century novelists, meanwhile, adapted strategies of textual authentication from history, calling their works histories (*The History of Tom Jones, A Foundling*, *Clarissa: or the History of a Young Lady*) and setting them out in (often parodic) relation to the truth-claims of narrative non-fiction. On the whole, the familiar wisdom that history was little challenged by the novel before Walter Scott, seems broadly true.[13] By the third decade of the nineteenth century, things had certainly changed and (the other) Macaulay could

[9] Hayden White, *Metahistory: The Historical Imagination in Nineteenth-Century Europe* (Baltimore, 1973).

[10] *The Dunciad*, IV, 39–40 in volume V of *The Twickenham Edition of the Poems of Alexander Pope*, eds. John Butt et al. (11 vols.; London and New Haven, 1739–69).

[11] *Lectures on Rhetoric and Belles Lettres*, ed. J. C. Bryce , *The Glasgow Edition of the Works of Adam Smith*, IV (Oxford, 1983), 117.

[12] Catharine Macaulay, *The History of England from the Revolution to the Present Time, in a Series of Letters* (volume I only completed, London, 1778); Oliver Goldsmith, *A History of England in a Series of Letters from a Nobleman to his Son* (2 vols; London, 1764).

[13] This wisdom is, however, complicated by Mark Phillips, 'Macaulay, Scott and the Literary Challenge to Historiography', *Journal of the History of Ideas*, 50 (1989), 117–33, and by Fiona Robertson, *Legitimate Histories: Scott, Gothic and the Authorities of Fiction* (Oxford, 1994).

speak of history as a province 'under the jurisdiction' of those 'two hostile powers', reason and imagination; after the equilibrium of the eighteenth century, history is, Macaulay complains, no longer an integrated field of study: 'Instead of being equally shared between its two rulers, the Reason and the Imagination, it falls alternately under the sole and absolute dominion of each. It is sometimes fiction. It is sometimes theory.'[14]

Macaulay's diagnosis of a loss of literary innocence in history after Walter Scott may explain, but does not assist, continuing investigations, since White's *Metahistory*, of the fictional and theoretical affinities of eighteenth-century narrative history. The problem turns for modern theorists (as it did, to a degree, for Macaulay) on the relationship between the literary enunciation and ordering of information in a work of history, and its aspirations to verifiable referentiality. However, rather than resorting to modern notions of textuality, we come closer to comprehending the kind of literariness at work in these histories if we rephrase the problem in eighteenth-century language. Eighteenth-century historians understood the relationship between history and literature in evolutionary rather than in generic or referential terms. Adam Smith's consideration of historical writing starts from the contemporary commonplace that 'the Poets were the first Historians of any'; what follows from this, Smith explains, as societies start to undertake increasingly sophisticated economic activities and acquire more developed tastes, is that prose succeeds poetry, novels succeed romances, and civil history takes over from fabulous and biographical narratives.[15] The eighteenth century, Smith argues in the twenty-third lecture, is an age of prose and commerce. The substantial difference between traditional literary forms and more modern kinds of historical writing lies in the originating mode of consciousness; the modern historian displays and contributes to the advanced state of his age. A highly defined generic sense of narrative history was thus precluded, in this period, by a residual sense of its continuity with other literary kinds, by an idea of the historical contingency of more or less sophisticated forms of historical representation, as well as by a more general understanding of history as (epideictic or deliberative) rhetorical performance.

The rhetorical model, in particular, helps to explain the nature of the presence of eighteenth-century historians in their own texts both as political persuaders and orchestrators of their readers' aesthetic responses. History was also understood in this period, in related but non-rhetorical ways, as a form of spectacle designed to awaken the imagination and stimulate the sensibility. Addison set out, early in the century, what he expected from a true historian:

[14] Thomas Babington Macaulay, 'History' (1828) in *Miscellaneous Writings and Speeches* (London, 1882), 133.

[15] *Lectures on Rhetoric*, 104 and 111–13.

He describes everything in so lively a manner, that his whole History is an admirable Picture, and touches on such proper Circumstances in every Story, that his Reader becomes a kind of Spectator, and feels in himself all the Vanity of Passions, which are correspondent to the several Parts of the Relation.[16]

Voltaire's St Bartholomew massacre, Robertson's Balboa high on a peak in Darien and Gibbon's great canvases of Constantinople or Arabia – all of these meet Addison's almost Romantic prescription for a history of sublime or moving special effects. Yet, unlike the fully spectacular Romantic histories of Thomas Carlyle or Francis Parkman, the spectatorships of writer and reader never quite converge, and the voice of the historian communicates to an interested, but never entirely complicit, audience the emotionally edifying distance between history's observer and its participants. This double distance is often, but not always, registered as irony. Irony is often assumed to be the governing characteristic of Enlightenment history, and its primary mode of engagement with fortunate faults of the past.[17] The present study regards the trope of irony as one among many rhetorical strategies available to eighteenth-century historians, an index, rather than a condition of their persuasive authority. This persuasive oratorical presence is, according to a literary critical way of reading, a textual effect known as a 'voice'; it is also, according to a more historical way of reading, a function of the historian's social authority often secured elsewhere in the public or political sphere. This book has identified, at the risk of seeming to reconstruct originating authorial intentions, continuities between the authorial voices in the histories and public careers of the historians. In some cases (particularly those of Voltaire, Robertson and Ramsay), the prominent public lives of the historians form one important context within which the histories are to be read, supplying both rhetorical ethos and hidden referent to the text. Gibbon, too, although not particularly prominent in his public career as a Member of Parliament, was intrigued by the apparent interaction between his own inability to make speeches in the House and his oratorical volubility in *The Decline and Fall.*[18] Whatever their professional or gentlemanly fortunes, all of the historians discussed here adopted an authorial posture of cultural centrality and spokesmanship unavailable to women writers. For this reason, no detailed consideration has been given to the century's two most successful female historians, Catharine Macaulay, the historian of England, and Mercy Otis Warren, an early historian of the American Revolution.[19] These women

[16] *The Spectator*, ed. Donald F. Bond (5 vols.; Oxford, 1965), III, 574.

[17] For example, White, *Metahistory*, 67.

[18] *The Letters of Edward Gibbon*, ed. J. E. Norton (3 vols.; London, 1956), nos. 294, 297, 498 where Gibbon reflects on his own muteness in public and his lack of verbal oratorical gifts.

[19] Catharine Macaulay's major work is the *History of England* (8 vols.; 1763–83). It is fully discussed in Bridget Hill, *The Republican Virago: The Life and Times of Catharine Macaulay* (Oxford, 1992);

writers advocated radical reform rather than cosmopolitan and enlightened national self-understanding; and they claimed social authority in their work as the female bearers and arbitrators of moral standards rather than as experienced and philosophically well-travelled adjudicators of political causes and contests.

Narratives of Enlightenment

The historians in this study sometimes referred to themselves, and are often discussed today, as 'philosophical' historians. The term has many applications, including the notion of a second-order awareness and discussion, in these histories, of the epistemological procedures at work in the evaluation of sources and the perception of causes and effects. The nature of each historian's interest in such 'philosophical' questions is considered in the separate chapters. Here again, however, my own rhetorical understanding of these works takes priority; this 'philosophy' operates in these histories not in opposition to rhetoric (as the potential basis for a new science of history, for example) but as a discursive adjunct to the construction of narrative. Eighteenth-century historians were wary of drawing analogies between their work and the natural or mathematical sciences. Even Voltaire, who, in a number of his non-historical works, searched for quasi-Baconian or Newtonian natural laws of history, shared a common conviction that historical interpretation deals mainly in phenomenal probability and is best achieved by way of narration. This point is not a new one, and would not need labouring but for the fact that, in recent years, the Enlightenment has so often been held responsible for generating giant interpretive myths, those 'master' or 'meta-narratives' which, it is said, western Europeans still tell themselves in order to understand their past, their future, and their right to control other nations.[20] The notion of the Enlightenment as a source of meta-narratives (about political and inner emancipation, about international harmony and the coming of a 'universal cosmopolitan condition') derives from Kant's essay on an 'Idea for a Universal History from a Cosmopolitan Point of View' (1784). A scientific extrapolation of the secret mechanism of emancipation from the outward chaos of events can and should be, according to Kant, the historian's greatest gift to his readers. ('Post')modern theorists, who generally find Kant's universal history ideologically suspect, declare themselves politically hostile and philosophically incredulous towards the meta-narratives which

Mercy Otis Warren, *History of the Rise, Progress and Termination of the American Revolution* (completed 1791, published 1805), ed. Lester Cohen (2 vols.; Indianapolis, 1988).

20 Most famously, Jean-François Lyotard, *Le Différand* (Paris, 1983). For an overview of these ideas, see Kerwin Lee Klein, 'In Search of Narrative Mastery: Postmodernism and the People without History', *History and Theory*, 34 (1995), 275–98.

they detect at the precognitive level beneath many eighteenth- to twentieth-century versions of history. The cosmopolitanism of eighteenth-century histories might, according to this 'post'modern critique, be said to partake of the Kantian aspiration to narrative mastery; not a mode, but a tale told by western men about the coming of liberty and global dominance to western Europe. Eighteenth-century histories can easily fall prey to such circular accusations, just as any historical narrative which gains currency and claims general interpretive validity might be said to operate as a master or meta-narrative. Yet none of the works studied here grounds its claim to validity in a universal, unchanging logic of nature or spirit as all meta-narratives are said to do. Rather, these histories endorse the tendency, praised by Richard Rorty in a rejoinder to Lyotard's theory of meta-narratives, of modern societies towards 'Cosmopolitanism without Emancipation'.[21] In eighteenth-century terms, this entails a philosophically informed and politically principled scepticism towards the grand narratives of their forebears and contemporaries – towards the exclusivity and chronology of Christian universal history, for example, the party myths of the English Whigs, the providential certainties of Scottish Presbyterian traditions, or the promises made by the American declarers of independence about the coming of life, liberty and happiness in America. Where their predecessors and contemporaries looked for constancies and continuities in the past, these historians tended to disaggregate history into periods and stages, specifying the forms of polity, culture and even consciousness which differentiated one era from the next.

The 'Enlightenment' of my title, then, implies no hidden logic or triumphant inevitability behind the narrative histories of Voltaire, Hume, Robertson, Gibbon and Ramsay. Nor, by extension, does it indicate a general thesis about the existence or nature of a European Enlightenment or 'Enlightenment project'. At present, the term 'Enlightenment' makes its most frequent and unconsidered appearances in modern critical theory where it often functions as a negative pole in the definition and discussion of 'postmodernity'. Meanwhile, amongst historians and literary scholars, the old historiography of the pan-European Enlightenment has given way to a more complicated picture of the intellectual life of the period as a site of political and cultural contestation.[22] It is within the context of these eighteenth-century debates, and without recourse to a general thesis about

[21] Responding to Lyotard's 'Histoire universelle et différences culturelles', *Critique*, 41 (1985), 559–68, Rorty remarks 'We see no reason why either recent social and political developments or recent philosophical thought should deter us from our attempt to build a cosmopolitan world society', *Objectivity, Relativism and Truth: Philosophical Papers*, I (Cambridge, 1991), 213.

[22] The last major overall study was Peter Gay, *The Enlightenment: An Interpretation* (2 vols.; London, 1967, 1970). Roy Porter and Mikulas Teich's *The Enlightenment in National Context* (Cambridge, 1981) was indicative of a new, more locally contextual trend.

the Enlightenment, that I have tried to render intelligible the central idea, shared by all of the historians examined here, that they were living in an age more enlightened than the past. This idea registers, in some instances, as a glow of confidence in the historian's own age and country, but is more often received as a soberly responsible recognition of the benefits and limitations of living in a modern world less spectacular, heroic or culturally innovative than that which has gone before. Narrative representations of the past, as Hayden White has explained, generate 'the illusion of a centred consciousness capable of looking out on the world, apprehending its structure and processes'.[23] The eighteenth-century idea of the present as an age more enlightened than the past renders literal this illusion of an encompassing consciousness, although, in all of these historical works, this modern clarity is vulnerable to a sudden and disorientating access of illusoriness. Despite the claims once made for the nascent historicism of these historians, there is never an illusion of unmediated access to the past, and always a sense of discontinuity between the past and the modern world.[24] The idea of the 'modern' is, in this period, enriched by its older frame of reference within the moral and cultural disputations of the ancient/modern debate now replayed historically in the works of these writers.[25]

Above all, the 'Enlightenment' of my title is intended to suggest the elaboration of a common descriptive model for the history of Europe through separately periodised ancient, medieval, early modern and enlightened modern stages. A new and quickly canonical reading of European history as the transition from medieval, feudal to modern, commercial social systems is shared and developed in these histories. The contours of this first-order (rather than meta-) narrative of the development of modern Europe will be familiar to many students of this period, although few have credited Voltaire with a role in its formation. The medieval feudal-agricultural period is characterised politically by an absence of (all but aristocratic) liberty, legally by local and oppressive aristocratic jurisdictions, and culturally by expressive but crude forms of art. Voltaire, Hume and Robertson demonstrate how this medieval world was inwardly eroded by the incorporation of cities, the development of new technologies, the expansion of domestic and overseas markets, the improved prestige and scholarship of the legal profession, and the relative decline of aristocratic

23 White, *The Content of the Form: Narrative Discourse and Historical Representation* (Baltimore, 1987), 36.

24 Meinecke, *Historism.*

25 For example, Hume, 'Of Commerce' (1754) in *Essays, Moral, Political and Literary*, ed. Eugene F. Miller (Indianapolis, 1985). This debate and its consequences for historical writing are discussed in Joseph Levine, *Humanism and History: Origins of Modern Historiography* (Ithaca, NY, 1987) and *The Battle of the Books: History and Literature in the Augustan Age* (Ithaca, NY, 1991), and in my review article on the latter in *The Age of Johnson*, ed. P. J. Korshin, 5 (1993), 467–76.

wealth. Gibbon's narrative incorporates and engages critically with their readings of medieval history, but remains reluctant, for reasons which I will explore, to assimilate the Roman Empire to a comparable model of historical phases. In none of the accounts of this period (not even those of Voltaire or Gibbon) is the Catholic Church simply identified as an agent of oppression, nor, at any stage, is the journey towards the more enlightened age of the present characterised as a straightforward process of secularisation.

A number of the historians identify (but do not name) an early modern period of transition in the fifteenth to sixteenth centuries when strong, centralising monarchies win out in many countries over warring aristocratic or religious factions. By describing (and generally welcoming) strong monarchy as a post-medieval phase of development, Voltaire, Hume and Robertson set themselves apart from most of the seventeenth-century historians and scholars upon whose researches they drew.[26] Their retrospective preference for unified sovereign power as the prerequisite for the development, in any given European state, of either representative institutions or, at least, a proper rule of law, tends to subvert the legal and historical terms within which contemporary constitutional debates were generally conducted. They also identify a final modern stage in which increased commercial activity facilitates greater access to property and hence liberty (formalised, in Britain, in representative institutions) for ever increasing numbers of people. In the works of Ramsay, Robertson and Hume, the imperial activities of modern European states are interpreted as an aspect of this commercial phase; they extend, but also, paradoxically, imperil, the political order which this phase installs. Robertson speculates that Spain's empire was acquired prematurely before that country had reached a state of political and commercial readiness. Ramsay fears that the territorial empire which his country is about to acquire in the continent of North America may bring dangers to the new American political order never encountered in the colonial history of the old world.

National contexts

The cosmopolitan approach to questions of national history in the writings of Voltaire, Hume, Robertson, Gibbon and Ramsay updated and put a new polemical spin on older, humanist notions of the European inheritance of a common cultural identity from the ancient Roman world (the *translatio*

[26] With notable exceptions such as Robert Brady, *A Complete History of England from ... the Romans ... to ... Henry III* (1685, continuation 1700); see J. G. A. Pocock, *The Ancient Constitution and the Feudal Law: A Study of English Historical Thought in the Seventeenth Century* (2nd edn; Cambridge, 1987) and Chantal Grell, *L'histoire entre érudition et philosophie: étude sur la connaissance historique à l'âge des lumières* (Paris, 1993).

studii). The motivations and consequences of this cosmopolitan outlook are interpreted in the present book not as an epiphenomenon of the Enlightenment, but within national structures of debate. Chantal Grell has shown how, in France, Voltaire's refusal of the conventions of seventeenth-century dynastic French history in his first major history, the *Siècle de Louis XIV*, enabled him to generate, in this and subsequent works, a periodised and globally applicable narrative model of history.[27] My chapter on Voltaire explores the literary and ideological backgrounds to these innovations, and explains how Voltaire's rejection of traditional dynastic and public law-based discourses of French nationality opened the way for a new critical and cosmopolitan reading of French and, later, global history according to aesthetic rather than political norms. Voltaire's historical works are contextualised within the fierce constitutional debates of the Regency and the reign of Louis XV, and are interpreted both as an intervention in those debates and as an attempt to situate imaginatively a civil jurisdiction for narrative history outside the national political arena.

The greater part of this study is concerned with British historical writing, and specifically with the internal dialogue between Scottish and English forms of historical self-understanding during the years immediately following the last Jacobite uprising of 1745. The cosmopolitanism of Hume, Robertson and Gibbon is interpreted in the context of the forms of national historical consciousness available in mid-eighteenth-century England and Scotland. National self-awareness in this period was, as a number of historians have shown, quite different from anything we would now understand by 'nationalism' or 'national identity'. It was, as Jonathan Clark has explained, 'a legal and religious conceptual structure' which was articulated primarily as allegiance to one's country, and which 'turned only to a small degree on the later preoccupations of ethnicity and language'.[28] Like other writers of the period, the British historians in this study established and contested their sense of Britain's destiny and identity within the medium of legal, constitutional and religious discourses, and their cosmopolitan overviews of their own national history emerged from a second-order appraisal of this medium of debate.

Three events, the 'Glorious' Revolution of 1688–9, the Anglo-Scottish Union of 1707, and the Act of Settlement of 1701, rendered the larger question of allegiance deeply problematic. Early eighteenth-century (non-Jacobite) historians of Britain, in particular, felt that they were responding to a cultural demand for an explanatory and legitimating emplotment of British history after a period of dynastic and constitutional discontinuity. Whig historians throughout the century had to reckon with Clarendon's

27 *L'histoire entre érudition et philosophie*, 218–19.

28 J. C. D. Clark, *The Language of Liberty 1660–1832; Political Discourse and Social Dynamics in the Anglo-American World* (Cambridge, 1994), 46.

royalist *History of the Rebellion*, which was published in 1702–4 at the beginning of the reign of his granddaughter Anne, and whose factual substance was soon after co-opted to Tory and Jacobite readings of modern history.[29] Hume's own difficult reckoning with Clarendon, in the seventeenth-century portion of his *History of England*, is discussed in chapter three. However, the complex *narrative* substance of Clarendon's history – a web of personal miscalculations and disloyalties, a national story of deviation from righteousness and providential deliverance, and a style self-consciously accountable to the lost continuities of English history, recording, as Christopher Ricks has phrased it, his dismay at the way in which 'the continuities of his own prose are so often obliged to incarnate discontinuity' – could not readily be assimilated by any historian writing after 1688.[30] Even before the publication of Clarendon's history, William III's own propagandists had tried to reclaim the language of deep continuity and providence for their own reading of England's and Scotland's historical destiny.[31] A point of continuity between their sense of the past and the next generation was provided by another great posthumous history, Gilbert Burnet's *History of his Own Time*, written between 1683 and 1715, and published with enormous commercial success in 1724 (volume I) and 1734 (volume II).[32] Burnet's history records the triumph, in 1688–9, and precarious survival, during the reign of Anne, of Whig and Protestant ideals as they were expressed or debased in the fallible personalities of monarchs, clerics and statesmen. Hume was among the many subsequent historians of the Restoration captivated by Burnet's providential comedy of manners.

In generic terms, Clarendon's and Burnet's histories belong to the Renaissance tradition of the statesman's posthumous memoir which served to vindicate the author's life while offering examples of conduct to future statesmen. Henry St John, Viscount Bolingbroke's *Letters on the Study and Use of History*, written for Clarendon's descendant Lord Cornbury and first printed for public consumption in 1752, also belong, as Philip Hicks has pointed out, to this tradition of posthumous memoir.[33] Bolingbroke served in Queen Anne's Tory ministry, and, after a period in exile in France

[29] On the reception and popularity of Clarendon's history, see Laird Okie, *Augustan Historical Writing: Histories of England in the English Enlightenment* (Lantam, MD, 1991), 21.

[30] Christopher Ricks, 'The Wit and Weight of Clarendon' in *Essays in Appreciation* (Oxford, 1996), 54.

[31] Tony Claydon, *William III and the Godly Revolution* (Cambridge, 1996) reappraises the language of the Revolution and provides a new interpretation of Gilbert Burnet.

[32] On the reception of Burnet, Laird Okie, *Augustan Historical Writing*, 23.

[33] Philip Hicks, 'Bolingbroke, Clarendon, and the Role of the Classical Historian', *Eighteenth-Century Studies*, 20 (1987), 445–71. On Bolingbroke generally, see Isaac Kramnick, *Bolingbroke and his Circle: The Politics of Nostalgia in the Age of Walpole* (Cambridge, MA, 1968); David Womersley, 'Lord Bolingbroke and Eighteenth-Century Historiography', *The Eighteenth Century: Theory and Interpretation*, 28 (1987), 217–34. The notion of 'nostalgia' has, however, been overturned by

during which he was involved in an unsuccessful attempt to place the Pretender on the British throne, spent a portion of the 1720s and 1730s rallying Tory and disaffected Whig opposition to Walpole's ministry. The *Letters*, written in the late 1730s, retain the knowing and intimate sense of audience characteristic of the kind of classical history which teaches wisdom by examples, but project, at intervals, a much fuller, more nationally serviceable narrative history beyond the generic limits of memoir. History, Bolingbroke explains in the second letter, is something more than recorded experience:

> Experience is doubly defective; we are born too late to see the beginning, and we die too soon to see the end of many things. History supplies both these defects. Modern history shows the causes, when experience presents the effects alone: and ancient history enables us to guess at the effects, when experience presents the causes alone.[34]

History, Bolingbroke argues, enables us to imagine experience narratively, or, rather, places us in a narrative relationship to our collective experience. Readers already familiar with Bolingbroke's sketches of British history in his 1730s opposition paper the *Craftsman*, probably expected the *Letters* to provide another patriotic narrative sketch of the experience of liberty in England.[35] Yet the *Letters* contend that proper history 'serves to purge the mind of those national partialities and prejudices that we are apt to contract in our education, and that experience for the most part rather confirms than removes'.[36] After this purging process, Bolingbroke suggests, we can be re-educated into a more rational attachment to our country and into a cosmopolitan recognition of other nations: 'surely the love of our country is a lesson of reason, not an institution of nature. Education and habit, obligation and interest, attach us to it, not instinct.'[37] Bolingbroke's cosmopolitan *Letters* on history, which include a sketch of the origins, in the sixteenth century, of the European system of balancing states, are attuned to a wider sense of audience and engaged with broader cultural debates than their classical and epistolary format at first suggests. Although they exerted only limited influence over Hume, Robertson and Gibbon, the *Letters* at least accustomed their readers to a new cosmopolitan mode of address, and to a kind of history in which the 'legal and religious conceptual structure' of British nationhood is more the subject of philosophical inquiry than of historical elaboration.

The European perspectives and sceptical tone of the *Letters* are informed

Christine Gerrard's *The Patriot Opposition to Walpole: Politics, Party, and National Myth, 1725–42* (Oxford, 1994).

34 *The Works of Lord Bolingbroke* (4 vols.; London, 1967), II, 186.

35 See Isaac Kramnick, 'Introduction' to *Lord Bolingbroke: Historical Writings* (Chicago, 1972).

36 *Works*, II, 183. 37 Ibid., 183.

by Bolingbroke's (at once Jacobite and country Whig) conviction that the real significance of the Glorious Revolution lay, not in the acquisition of liberty (he argued that, in any case, political liberty had been the birthright of Englishmen since Anglo-Saxon times), but in Britain's sudden strategic involvement with the dynastic politics of Europe. As he explained in his 'Plan for a General History of Europe', the year 1688 was, in a bad sense, England's European moment.[38] Most of the Whig and some of the Tory historians writing in the early part of the century regarded this moment as the most important confirmation of the country's distinctiveness, the point at which the nation departed or even escaped from the common pattern of European historical development.[39] Indeed, the sense of being outside Europe so strongly suffuses the political debate of the period, that historians of our own time have tended to describe the British 'Enlightenment' in its own terms, not as a continental process of intellectual transformation, but as a unique enterprise engaged in implementing the legal rights and religious tolerance gained at the Revolution.[40] Many of the histories of Britain before Hume's characterised themselves in classical terms as lessons in the nation's distinctive political culture; readers might learn prudent statecraft or, at least, wise public conduct by contemplating the historical workings of Britain's balanced constitution. The preface to the compilation *Complete History of England* (1706), for example, pointed out that 'the Original of our Laws and Customs is a part of Knowledge ... requisite to Men of Learning or of publick Employment, [and] necessary to the Understanding of our Constitution, Rights, and Liberties'.[41] Most of the histories of Britain before Hume's, from John Oldmixion's radical Whig *Critical History of England* (1724) to Thomas Carte's scholarly, Jacobite *General History of England* (1747–55) were, indeed, centrally preoccupied with the country's constitution, rights and liberties.[42] In particular, the notion of historically transcendent Saxon liberties, which ultimately won out as a Whig argument despite Bolingbroke's appropriation of the idea in the 1720s and 1730s, set the parameters for popular histories of Britain; these tended to be structured by dialectics of liberty and prerogative, parliaments and kings, the nation and the Norman feudal yoke.[43]

[38] Ibid., 337.

[39] For example, the pious and Whig third volume by White Kennett of the composite *Complete History of England* (see note 41 below) and Laurence Echard's broadly Tory *History of the Revolution and the establishment of England in the year 1688* (1725). See generally, Jeremy Black, 'The European Idea and Britain, 1688–1815', *The History of European Ideas*, 17 (1993), 439–60.

[40] For example, Roy Porter, *The Enlightenment* (London, 1990), 54.

[41] *A Complete History of England with the lives of all the Kings and Queens thereof from the earliest account of time to the death of ... William III* (3 vols.; London, 1706), I, i.

[42] The story of Carte's history, which was supported financially by the mainly Jacobite Society for an History of England which included Gibbon's father Edward, is told by Okie in *Augustan Historical Writing*, 135–54.

[43] Kramnick, *Bolingbroke and his Circle*; R. J. Smith, *The Gothic Bequest: Medieval Institutions in British*

The most internationally minded and sophisticated of the histories structured according to this pattern was also the most popular: Paul de Rapin-Thoyras' *Histoire d'Angleterre*, written between 1707 and 1724 and published in English translation between 1721 and 1731, provided the Whigs with a secular and scholarly account of the origins of the nation's mixed and liberal constitution.[44] Rapin himself was a figure exemplary of England's late seventeenth-century European moment. A Huguenot lawyer, he left France for England after the Revocation of the Edict of Nantes, fought for William of Orange at the Battle of the Boyne, and, on the proceeds of a pension from the new king, set up home in the Dutch Republic among an international community of exiled scholars to write, in French, a narrative history of England. His history repeatedly draws attention to those moments in the past when England's political development was stimulated and its culture enhanced by contact with foreigners. Rapin tells us, for example, that under the yoke of the Romans the ancient Britons 'assume the Politeness of the Conquerors' and cultivate their 'Arts and Sciences'.[45] The invading Saxons bring with them the representative forms of government characteristic of other continental Germanic peoples.[46] Later, King Alfred wages war on the cultural front against ignorance by 'inviting into his Dominions Foreigners that were eminent in their Professions'; 'his aim', Rapin remarks, 'was to stir up the Emulation of the English, and provoke them to use their Endeavours to come out of the state of gross ignorance they were in'.[47] Rapin's history peters out after the flight of James II, but his views on the invasion of 1688 may be deduced from his description of the Norman Conquest; his William I is almost a type for William III – a military hero who pushes the insular English people into an international arena:

> God, no doubt, was pleased to make use of this Conqueror, to render the English Nation more Illustrious than ever. The English, hitherto almost unknown to the rest of the World, began after this Revolution to make a considerable figure in Europe.[48]

The year 1066 (or is it 1688?) is, in a good sense, England's European

Thought, 1688–1863 (Cambridge, 1987); Jeremy Black, 'Ideology, History, Xenophobia and the World of Print in Eighteenth-Century England' in *Culture, Politics and Society in Britain, 1660–1800*, eds. Jeremy Black and Jeremy Gregory (Manchester, 1991).

44 *Histoire d'Angleterre* (10 vols.; 1724–7). Rapin's work is discussed in Duncan Forbes, *Hume's Philosophical Politics* (Cambridge, 1975), 233–40.

45 *The History of England as well Ecclesiastical and Civil*, trans. Nicholas Tindal (2nd edn, 2 vols.; 1732), I, 19.

46 'A Dissertation on the Government, Laws, Manners, Customs and Language of the Anglo-Saxons', *History of England*, I, 147.

47 *History*, I, 96.

48 Ibid., I, 164. This connection between the two Williams is made in a similarly covert way for opposite political ends in Pope's 'Windsor Forest' (1713).

moment. Rapin's *History of England* is cosmopolitan to the extent that it underscores, at key points in the narrative, England's entanglements with the rest of Europe at the levels of strategy, intellectual culture and political ideas. It is elsewhere politically and morally engaged with the distinctive and exemplary manifestations of English personal and political liberty.

During the first half of the eighteenth century, Rapin's history played a role in the political education of the nation. The immense popularity of Rapin's work – the fact that it was extracted or cannibalised in numerous pamphlets and articles (not least, in the *Craftsman*), and the expressed desire of so many successor historians to rival or surpass its achievement – could be regarded today as a complicating factor in our understanding of national self-awareness in this period. Recent historians have constructed a persuasive narrative of emergent cultural nationalism during the period from the second to the fourth Georges, crediting the extra-parliamentary oppositions to Walpole and, later, to Bute and to North with a formative role in the elaboration of a 'Rule Britannia' style of patriotism.[49] This patriotism, it is argued, engendered new ethno-centric ways of reading the nation's history and literature, along with a revived Protestant sense of special destiny which was eventually deployed by governments themselves during the Napoleonic wars. The popularity of Rapin in the first half of the century, and the eventual and enduring success of Hume's *History of England*, are not easily reconciled to this modern narrative of emergent national awareness except, perhaps, as evidence for the persistence of older elite, cosmopolitan ways of characterising the nation's history.[50] Instead, it is, I think, more accurate to see Hume's work, and, indeed, the works of Robertson and Gibbon, not as an evasion, but as a *response* to the new manifestations of cultural nationalism, the anti-French or anti-Spanish myths, and the patriotic rhetoric of political protest which surrounded them. The dissatisfied feeling, evident in Rapin's history, that both traditional and new accounts of British nationhood were too insular and ahistorical is echoed by many writers of the period. In the young Edmund Burke's excellent *Essay towards an Abridgement of English History*, written around the same time as the first volume of Hume's history but never published, this feeling registers as hostility specifically to the reports of England's uniqueness educed by legal historians from its heritage of common law:

49 In addition to the historical work of Newman, Colley and Wilson, see, on the literary side, Marilyn Butler, 'Romanticism' in *Romanticism in National Context*, eds. Roy Porter and Mikulas Teich (Cambridge, 1988); Michael Dobson, *The Making of a National Poet: Shakespeare, Adaptation and Authorship, 1660–1768* (Oxford, 1992); Howard Weinbrot, *Britannia's Issue: The Rise of British Literature from Dryden to Ossian* (Cambridge, 1993); Gerrard, *The Patriot Opposition to Walpole*.

50 The story of the popularity of Hume's *History* in the late eighteenth and nineteenth centuries is told by Graeme Paul Slater, 'Authorship and Authority in Hume's History of England' (Oxford D.Phil, 1990).

> the truth is, the present system of our laws, like our language and our learning, is a very mixed and heterogeneous mass; in some respects our own; in more borrowed from the policy of foreign nations, and compounded, altered, and variously modified, according to the various necessities, which the manners, the religion, and the commerce of the people, have at different times imposed.[51]

In rejecting the ahistorical (one might almost say anti-historical) attachment of some contemporary legal historians to England's immemorial, or, at least, ancient constitutional peculiarity, Burke discerns a tendency in British cultural life which he would later help to accelerate; the discovery of inherent value in history itself. In recognising this tendency, the present study tries to convey the mischievous or melancholy flavour of the histories of Hume, Robertson and Gibbon as they attribute complexities rather than assign value to the processes of the past.

In America, David Ramsay's starting-point for *The History of the American Revolution* was also his sense of dissatisfaction with both traditional accounts of colonial American distinctiveness and new versions of American nationhood. Ramsay's intellectual dealings with American colonial histories and imported European historical works, his reception of local canons of political thought, and his responses to the leading theoretical defenders of American independence are all discussed in detail in chapter 7. This chapter also inevitably encounters the larger question of an American Enlightenment; it avoids the old paradigm of an Enlightenment imagined in Europe and realised in America, and retains the emphasis of much recent scholarship upon the growing anglicisation of American culture in the years running up to the Revolution.[52] Ramsay's sophisticated evaluation of the Revolution took place within a discursive framework in which the similarities and continuities between European and American history were ideologically contested. His own patriotic vision of an America not so much repudiating as repeating and improving upon European history represented a politically conservative contribution to that Enlightenment debate. His cosmopolitan vision of a future America taking up her station among the international fraternity of civilised states was made possible by the imperial ideas and social theory of Burke, Robertson and Adam Smith.

Eighteenth-century British writers in general held a peculiarly cosmopolitan image of their colonial and trading empires as peaceful and mutually beneficial consumer communities.[53] It was an idea, or, rather, an ideal,

[51] Edmund Burke, 'An Essay towards an History of the Laws of England', *An Abridgement of English History; from the Invasion of Julius Caesar to the End of the Reign of King John*, *Works* VI (1803), 555. Burke is thinking particularly of Matthew Hale, *The History of the Common Law of England* (1713).

[52] For example, Henry Steele Commager, *The Empire of Reason: How Europe Imagined and America Realized the Enlightenment* (New York, 1977).

[53] Kathleen Wilson has spoken of the 'illusion of cosmopolitanism that actually strengthened English ethnocentricity' in 'The Empire of Virtue: The Imperial Project and Hanoverian Culture' in *An Imperial State at War*, ed. Lawrence Stone (London, 1994), 136. See also, T. H.

which withstood even the sombre awareness of slavery; as the anti-slavery poet William Cowper remarked, shortly after the American Revolution, 'the band of commerce was design'd / T'associate all the branches of mankind. ... / Tis thus, reciprocating each with each, / Alternatively the nations learn and teach'.[54] In Robertson's works, there is a cosmopolitan appreciation of empire as a culturally and economically beneficial international system of interplay and emulation. This combines in his histories with a new underlying taxonomy of economies, political systems and forms of social organisation according to which the developmental levels of different peoples are assessed and compared. Peoples at lower levels of social development, such as Native Americans or the immigrant colonists in the Americas, can, in this scheme of things, be said to require the tutelage of a more advanced European government. The genesis of this style of social analysis in the work of Hume, Smith and others, and its narrative adaptation in the histories of Robertson and Gibbon are treated at length in chapters 5 and 6. For American writers, the idea of developmental stages in history provided a model for the repetition and improvement of Europe in the new world.[55] Ramsay felt sure that America had reached a stage of maturity sufficient for independent nationhood, but he feared that his country's vast and unpredictable geography, its social investment in slavery, and the regional divisions between its states might lead it down a dangerous historical road not taken in the old world. It was these fears which necessitated in his work a sceptical and cosmopolitan approach towards the cultural and intellectual content of new American nationhood, but which also rendered it so little congenial to his newly independent American audience. At the end of this final chapter, a closing Afterword notes the persistence in later British historical writing of a cosmopolitan tone little favoured in post-revolutionary America and post-Napoleonic France. It also reflects briefly upon the uses of the idea of developmental stages and cosmopolitan perspectives in nineteenth-century histories of empire – a context in which the old European cosmopolitanism of the eighteenth century seemed to qualify as much as to support historical narratives of Enlightenment.

Breen, 'An Empire of Goods: The Anglicisation of Colonial America, 1690–1776', *Journal of British Studies*, 25 (1986), 467–99.

[54] 'Charity', (1782), lines 83–4, lines 119–20 in volume I of *The Poems of William Cowper*, eds. Charles Ryscamp and John Baird (3 vols.; Oxford, 1980–95) and my 'Protestantism and the Poetics of Empire' in *Culture, Politics and Society in Britain*, II, ed. Jeremy Black (Manchester University Press, forthcoming).

[55] The model of history can be seen at work, for example, in Noah Webster, 'On Morality' (1785), *A Collection of Essays and Fugitive Writings on Moral, Historical, Political and Literary Subjects* (Boston, 1790); Benjamin Franklin, 'Remarks concerning the Savages of North America' (1783) in *Works* II (2 vols.; London, 1793); Benjamin Rush, 'The Manners of the German Inhabitants of Pennsylvania' (1786) in *Essays, Literary, Moral and Philosophical* (Philadelphia, 1798).

2

Voltaire's neoclassical poetics of history

Before his apotheosis as the personification of the Enlightenment, Voltaire was known to French, British and American readers, perhaps primarily, as a historian of France and the world.[1] Before he became demonised, in nineteenth-century eyes, as the prophet of atheism, Voltaire's histories were perused by appreciative and unperturbed readers throughout the continent and its colonies.[2] Voltaire's histories have not recovered today from the low reputation to which they sank after the French Revolution, and the last book-length study of these works is now nearly forty years old.[3] Without wishing to make excessive claims for their merit and influence, this chapter will attempt to assess

[1] All citations in the notes from the collected works of Voltaire refer either to *Oeuvres complètes de Voltaire*, ed. Louis Moland (52 vols.; Paris, 1877–85) [hereafter *Moland*] or, where texts are available, to *The Complete Works of Voltaire* (Institut et Musée Voltaire, Geneva, 1968– in progress) (hereafter *Works*). All citations which refer to the letters of Voltaire are from *Correspondence and Related Documents*, ed. Theodore Besterman, *Works*, LXXXV–CXXXV (1968–77), hereafter Best. D.

All citations in the text of this chapter from *L'Histoire de Charles XII* are from Voltaire, *Oeuvres historiques*, ed. René Pomeau (Paris, 1957). This text is taken from the 'Kehl' edition, *Oeuvres complètes de Voltaire* (70 vols.; Kehl, 1774–89), and differences between this and earlier texts are noted. All citations from *Le Siècle de Louis XIV*, from the *Précis du Siècle de Louis XV*, and from the *Histoire de l'Empire de Russie sous Pierre le Grand* are also from the Pomeau edition of the *Oeuvres historiques*. These texts are also based on the 'Kehl' edition. Citations from the *Essai sur les mœurs et l'esprit des nations* are taken from the edition of René Pomeau (2 vols.; Paris, 1963). This text is based on the 'Kehl' edition. In all cases, textual differences in earlier editions will be noted and discussed. Citations from *La Philosophie de l'histoire* are from the edition by J. H. Brumfitt in *Works*, LIX (1969). This is based upon the separately published edition (Amsterdam (Geneva), 1765). Spelling in all of the above twentieth-century editions is given in modern form.

Bibliographical details are drawn from Georges Bengesco, *Voltaire: bibliographie de ses oeuvres* (4 vols.; Paris, 1882–90). This must be supplemented by Theodore Besterman, 'Some Eighteenth-Century Voltaire Editions unknown to Bengesco', *Studies on Voltaire and the Eighteenth Century*, 64 (1968), 7–150. The first three volumes of the new, multi-volume biography of Voltaire are invaluable guides to the 'historical' period of his writing life. These are: René Pomeau, *D'Arouet à Voltaire, 1694–1734* (Oxford, 1985); René Vaillot, *Avec Mme du Châtelet, 1734–1749* (Oxford, 1988); René Pomeau, Christiane Mervaud *et al.*, *De la Cour au Jardin, 1750–1759* (Oxford, 1991).

The journal *Studies on Voltaire and the Eighteenth Century* is here after cited as *SVEC*.

[2] For an exhaustive study of the popularity of Voltaire's histories and other works in Britain, see A. M. Rousseau, 'L'Angleterre et Voltaire, *SVEC*, 145–6 (1976).

[3] J. H. Brumfitt's *Voltaire, Historian* (Oxford, 1958, revised, 1970) is still the fullest study of his historical works.

the distinctive and original contribution made by Voltaire's histories to cosmopolitan history in the eighteenth century. Most of these works belong roughly to the middle period of his career during which time he enjoyed a measure of official sanction and approval from Louis XV, who appointed him historiographer royal in 1745, and from Frederick II of Prussia.[4] Voltaire's major histories include *L'Histoire de Charles XII* (1731), *Le Siècle de Louis XIV* (1751 and after) and the *Essai sur les mœurs* (1754 and after), all of them many times reissued, revised and translated during his lifetime. Together, these works represent a sustained and wide-ranging exploration of the literary, cognitive and thematic potential of historical narrative. As literary works, they make new commitments to form and style which exceed and displace older rhetorical theories of purpose and expression. As meta-historical investigations of the cognitive problems of retelling the past, they contribute something to contemporary French philosophical debate, although their engagement with these rather involved epistemological matters was not the primary source of their appeal in the very dissimilar philosophical and religious environments of Britain and America where such questions were differently framed and differently answered. It was the thematic concerns of Voltaire's histories, which centred upon the evolution and existence of a unique, common European civilisation, that particularly attracted an international readership. Voltaire was the first historian to articulate in detail an Enlightenment narrative of the rise of Europe as it was hastened by the growing wealth and independence of the middle orders of society. He was the first to explain the political utility of this common sense of European identity, and the first to show how this sense of identity had a more solidly political basis than the older Renaissance notion of a shared classical heritage. Despite all this, Voltaire was never entirely at ease with the narrative enterprise of history; in all of his works, the desire to explain competes with besetting scepticism about the possibility of historical explanation, the earnest endeavour to research conflicts with a disingenuous contempt for serious historical scholars, and the cosmopolitan historian of France sometimes gives way to the champion of French cosmopolitanism. The result is a historical writing more complex and contradictory than he may have intended. I intend to discuss, in turn, the cognitive, literary and thematic aspects of Voltaire's histories in the hope of restoring to (sometimes unenvisaged) complexity a historian often dismissed as an unthinking apostle of progress.[5]

[4] Vaillot, *Avec Mme du Châtelet*, 246–7.

[5] For a very different kind of attempt to rehabilitate Voltaire's histories, see Freidrich Meinecke *Historism: The Rise of a New Historical Outlook*, trans. J. E. Anderson (New York, 1972).

Reconstruction

Seventeenth-century French intellectuals regarded history primarily as the site of cognitive questions which ultimately had to do with the nature and value of all factual data. Many sceptics, or 'pyrrhonists' of the period, motivated by both scientific and anti-religious ('libertin') principles, doubted the reliability and usefulness of historical knowledge. By undermining the epistemological foundations of narrative and scholarly history, they lowered the prestige of this previously buoyant Renaissance discipline.[6] Descartes' rationalist solutions to this scepticism had the effect of further disgracing history, along with scholasticism, as outmoded forms of cognition. Towards the end of the century, however, the fortunes of the discipline revived somewhat, and Pierre Bayle's celebrated *Dictionnaire historique et critique* (1697) did a great deal to re-establish history as a discrete field of knowledge capable of delivering truths whose status could not be determined by Cartesian methodology.[7] Voltaire grew up intellectually during a period of reconstructive historical thinking during which interest had at last begun to shift from the ontological to the anthropological value of historical knowledge.[8] By then the pyrrhonian debate had been channelled into evidentiary questions and away from the problem of the ultimate value of historical inquiry. As a young man, Voltaire would have encountered the famous scholarly debates in the 1720s between scholarly and pyrrhonian members of the French Académie des Inscriptions over the reliability of information about the very earliest history of Rome.[9] One academician, Nicholas Fréret, in an essay entitled 'Réflexions sur l'étude des anciennes histoires', made an important contribution to the debate by arguing that the problem of historical scepticism sprang from a persistent false analogy between history and the mathematical sciences. He defined history as a separate cognitive field, and laid down the principles for an empirical method in historical inquiry.[10]

Voltaire's early intellectual endeavours were directed towards similar ends. As well as forging a successful writing career as a poet and playwright, the young Voltaire schooled himself as a metaphysician; he mounted a challenge to the mathematical certainties of French rationalist

[6] Richard H. Popkin, *The History of Scepticism from Erasmus to Descartes* (revised edn, Berkeley, California, 1979); Blandine Barret-Kreigel, *La défaite de l'érudition* (Paris, 1988).

[7] Haydn Mason, *Pierre Bayle and Voltaire* (Oxford, 1963).

[8] On this shift, see Günther Pflug, 'The Development of Historical Method in the Eighteenth Century', *History and Theory*, 11 Beiheft (1971), 1–23.

[9] On this debate, see Carlo Borghero, *La certezza e la storia: Cartesianesimo, Pirronismo e Conoscenza Storica* (Milan, 1993), 357–75.

[10] Nicholas Fréret, 'Réflexions sur l'étude des anciennes histoires, et sur le degré de leurs preuves', *Histoire de l'Académie Royale des Inscriptions et Belles Lettres*, VI (Paris, 1717), VI (1729), 146–89. The whole debate is printed in this volume.

philosophy in the name of English scientific empiricism (for example, the *Eléments de la philosophie de Newton*, 1738). His collection of essays on English culture, the *Lettres philosophiques* (1734) did much to publicise the work of Newton and Locke in France. He praised them both for having found reasonable empirical resolutions to the problem of pyrrhonism, even describing Locke's *Essay concerning Human Understanding* as a form of history: 'Tant de raisonneurs ayant fait le roman de l'âme, un sage est venu qui en a fait modestement l'histoire.'[11] Although Voltaire sometimes contrived to make Newton, in particular, sound like the prophet of all kinds of moral and historical inevitabilities, he always tried to preserve this early commitment to reasonable empiricism in the historical domain.[12] As he later remarked, 'Je ne veux ni un pyrrhonisme outré, ni une crédulité ridicule.'[13]

Despite improvements in the philosophical fortunes of history in the first decades of the eighteenth century, this form of writing still lacked prestige and credibility when Voltaire started to publish his major histories in the 1750s. The subject was little esteemed, for example, by the editors of the *Encyclopédie*. D'Alembert and Diderot prefaced their work with a table of human knowledge (1751) which arranged 'history' (sacred, ecclesiastical and civil) under the taxonomic heading of 'memory', along with natural history, the arts and crafts. The table thereby separated history from the more advanced mental category of 'reason' under which it grouped philosophy and the mathematical sciences, implicitly downgrading its cognitive function. When Voltaire came to write the 'Histoire' entry for the *Encyclopédie*, along with other 'H' articles, he observed, in implicit protest, that natural history is a physical science rather than a subset of history, and devoted most of the piece to refuting the notion that history is an unreliable form of human knowledge.[14]

Voltaire never resolved to his own satisfaction the problem of historical knowledge in his histories. Even in the last revisions to the *Essai sur les mœurs*, carried out at the end of his life, he continued to tinker with words and phrases conveying notions of facticity and causality. His pyrrhonian predecessors had tried to detach history from narrative by arguing that the narrative piecing together of the past entailed unwarranted reification of the primary factual data. In most of Voltaire's historical works, the problem hovers in abeyance, and these doubts are suspended in the rhetorical medium of narrative. He settles willingly for a traditional presentation of history as a branch of demonstrative rhetoric, and he apportions praise or blame according to unusually broadly conceived

[11] 'Sur M. Locke', *Lettres philosophiques* (1734), *Moland*, XXII, 122.

[12] For example, *Le Philosophe ignorant* (1766), *Works*, LXII (1987), 86.

[13] 'Le Pyrrhonisme de l'histoire' (1768), *Moland*, XXVII, 235.

[14] In the article 'Histoire', Voltaire mentions 'l'*histoire naturelle*, improprement dite *histoire*, … qui est une partie essentielle de la physique' (*Works*, XXXIII, 164).

political and cultural imperatives. Even so, when he composed his political and cultural narratives of France and the world, Voltaire had few fully realised French narrative histories upon which to draw. There were some exceptions. History had survived the *crise pyrrhonienne* as a narrative art in the semi-fictionalised *histoires galantes* of fashionable authors such as Varillas and Saint-Réal. Voltaire found 'sublime' Saint-Réal's *Conjuration des Espagnols contre la République de Venise en l'année 1618* (1674), an elegant neo-Machiavellian study of psychological and political motive whose character study set pieces probably influenced the *Histoire de Charles XII* (and, incidentally, inspired Thomas Otway's tragedy, *Venice Preserved*).[15] Voltaire was impressed by the ability of these *historiens galants* to give shape to historical data within a single critical perspective. Their work, however, was really an anecdotal outgrowth of humanist history written in the voice of experienced *hommes d'état*; Voltaire, although he shared this commitment to history as a branch of rhetoric, sought a more representative voice and questioned the value of anecdotes. These *histoires galantes*, moreover, had few scholarly ambitions. They bear witness to the fact that the *crise pyrrhonienne* in historical thought had effected a marked dissociation of philosophical historiography from the information-gathering side of history. On the scholarly side, late seventeenth- and early eighteenth-century France had played host to an extraordinary flowering of historical learning, including the pioneering work of the clerical scholars of the Benedictine Congregation of St Maur in the study and criticism of primary sources, and in new techniques in lexicography, diplomatics and palaeography.[16] The leading figure in this enterprise, Jean Mabillon, showed some interest in the narrative presentation of history, including, for example, the role of cultural forces in the shaping of events.[17] In general however, these scholars were not concerned to establish additional veracity for their researches on a philosophical basis, and were otherwise annalists dealing only with the seriality of events.

Despite these developments, there was one form of narrative history which had continued untroubled and unabated throughout the seventeenth and early eighteenth centuries. This was the chronological history of France, a compendious and compliant genre whose traditions and royal patronage (as Chantal Grell has shown in her excellent study of eighteenth-century history in France) enabled it to withstand most philosophical and

[15] Voltaire to Pierre Joseph Thoulier d'Olivet (6 January, 1736), Best. D980. See Andrée Mansau, *Saint-Réal et l'humanisme cosmopolite* (Paris, 1976), 440–2. Voltaire later remarked that, for all his merits, Saint-Réal was not really a historian: Voltaire to Pierre Jean Grosley (22 January, 1758), Best. D7599.

[16] David Knowles, *Great Historical Enterprises: Problems in Monastic History* (London, 1963); Blandine Barret-Kreigel, *Jean Mabillon* (Paris, 1988).

[17] Jean Mabillon, *Annales Ordinis S. Benedicti Occidentalium Monachorum Patriarchae* (6 vols.; Paris, 1703–39). See, in particular, the Praefatii to volume II (1704) and volume III (1706).

scholarly innovations.[18] Two of the most significant histories of France to precede Voltaire's *Siècle de Louis XIV*, Mézeray's *Histoire de France* (1643–51), and Daniel's *Histoire de France* (1713), appeared at the beginning and end of Louis XIV's personal reign.[19] Although constantly lambasted by Voltaire, these two works anticipate his histories in their refusal to surrender broad sweeps of developmental narrative to the ravages of Pyrrhonism. However, like most traditional dynastic histories of the nation, Mézeray's work rarely rises above the annalistic, in spite of its stylishness. Daniel's *Histoire* announces its ambition to avoid scepticism, and to produce 'un tissu et une suite de faits véritables', as well as the intention to include, 'les Coûtumes, les Usages, les Loix, la Jurisprudence, la manière du Gouvernement Civil et Militaire', although, in practice, it does not keep either of these promises.[20]

Voltaire's solution to the poverty of national history and to the philosophical depreciation of history was, I shall argue, to effect a closer *rapprochement* between history and literature. He was, by the time he came to compose his narrative histories, an acknowledged master in the genres of epic and tragedy. He executed and interpreted his plays and poems according to the neoclassical principles of criticism elaborated in the late seventeenth century, and soon conceptualised his histories in similar ways. Boileau, Le Bossu, Bouhours and other neoclassical critics of the preceding century had elaborated a theory of literature which cogently defended its integrity and social utility, and so protected it from devaluation by philosophers and moralists.[21] By arranging his histories within identifiable literary structures (not excluding the *Essai sur les mœurs*), Voltaire hoped to annex similar prestige to history. Voltaire also imported from neoclassical theory the notion of 'vraisemblance' which encapsulated the moral and aesthetic requirement that literature should treat only of the natural and probable, and never of the fantastic, trivial or debased. The notion of vraisemblance provided a convenient means of reconciling the narrative and cognitive demands of the medium of history, and acted as a means of arbitrating both oddities in his source material and potential inconsisten-

[18] Chantal Grell, *L'histoire entre érudition et philosophie: étude sur la connaissance historique à l'âge des lumières* (Paris, 1993).

[19] On French national history in this period, see Orest Ranum, *Artisans of Glory: Writers and Historical Thought in Seventeenth-Century France* (Chapel Hill, NC, 1982); Erica Harth, *Ideology and Culture in Seventeenth-Century France* (Ithaca, 1983), 129–79.

[20] Gabriel Daniel, *Histoire de France depuis l'Etablissement de la monarchie Françaises dans les Gaules* (3 vols.; Paris, 1713), I, i; I, xiv. For a different view of Mézeray, see Phyllis K. Leffler, 'From Humanist to Enlightenment Historiography: A Case Study of François Eudes de Mézeray', *French Historical Studies*, 10 (1977–8), 416–38.

[21] N. Boileau-Despréaux, *L'Art poétique* (1674), R. Le Bossu, *Traité du poëme épique* (1675), and Dominique Bouhours, *La Manière de bien penser dans les ouvrages de l'esprit* (Paris, 1687). The classic secondary study is René Bray, *La Formation de la doctrine classique en France* (Paris, 1927); see also, Gordon Pocock, *Boileau and the Nature of Neoclassicism* (Cambridge, 1980).

cies in his narrative. Voltaire also embraced the ethical function performed by neoclassical literature; like poetry, history must assert civilised standards, and harmonise moral, social and aesthetic values. Given the secondary status which neoclassical criticism assigned to mock genres, mock epic (the collapse of epic into satire instigated by a voice comically aware of the gap between the grandeur of the poem's structure and the low stature of its subject) cannot be taken as the paradigm for Voltaire's historical work, let alone Enlightenment history as a whole (as Hayden White has assumed).[22] Voltaire constantly struggled to sustain history as a serious genre, and to resist the satirical treatment which much of his material appeared to require.

Epic beginnings

Before turning to Voltaire's major histories, some understanding of the literary roots of his historical method can be gained from an examination of his earlier engagement with historical epic in poetry and prose. His first historical production was an epic poem about the life of Henri IV, published first as *La Ligue* (1723), and then recast as *La Henriade* (1728). These were succeeded in 1731 by Voltaire's first prose history, the highly accomplished *Histoire de Charles XII* of Sweden. Many features of Voltaire's historical method were worked out in this transition from poetry to prose. This development was also facilitated by Voltaire's meditation on the problems of poetics, national culture and changing standards of taste in the (English) *Essay upon the epick poetry of the European nations.*[23] In all of these can be detected the neoclassical roots of Voltaire's historical practice. The *Henriade* narrates the story, in Alexandrine couplets, of the religious wars of late sixteenth-century France up to the point when the victorious Henri de Navarre is about to accede to the throne. The poem updates for the eighteenth century the traditional myth of Henry IV as a peace-loving, tolerant philosopher king.[24] In structure and tone it conforms to neoclassical rules for epic poetry, beginning *in medias res*, maintaining a consistently formal register, and blending decorousness and plausibility ('vraisemblance'). The deeper historical drama in the poem is enacted by abstract types (with names such as 'Discorde', 'Fanatisme', 'Politique', 'Vérité'). Like his precursor epic and mock-epic poets, such as Chapelain and

[22] Hayden White, *Metahistory: The Historical Imagination in Nineteenth-Century Europe* (Baltimore, 1973), 50–1.

[23] Voltaire, *An Essay upon the civil wars of France, extracted from curious Manuscripts, and also upon the epick poetry of the European nations from Homer down to Milton* (London, 1727). On this, see also David Williams, 'Voltaire's "True Essay" on Epic Poetry', *Modern Language Review*, 88 (1993), 46–57.

[24] Grell, *L'histoire entre érudition et philosophie*, 219.

Boileau, Voltaire situates the substance and meaning of history in supra-historical types.[25] There are, however, some innovations. Voltaire's idealised hero, Henri de Navarre, is a social improver as well as a warrior king. In the *Essay upon the epick poetry*, Voltaire argues that epic poetry, as well as having universal appeal, must mirror the peculiarities and meet the specific needs of its country of origin. Much of the *Essay* is an evaluation of epic poets, including Homer, Milton and Camöens, in national context, and it demonstrates that, although all great epic poems are and must be obedient to certain formal principles, their content and mode of formal adaptation are culturally determined. For example, he finds Milton's 'Idiom ... wonderfully heighten'd, by the Nature of the Government, which allows the *English* to speak in Publick'.[26] Thus, in conformity with his own critical principles, Voltaire attempted to adapt the rules of epic poetry in his own epic poem *La Henriade* to the cultural imperatives of his French audience by reminding them, at a time of heated religious and social debate, of their innate gifts for order and conciliation.[27]

Voltaire's next foray into the genre of historical epic took the form of a short narrative history of the life of King Charles XII of Sweden (1682–1718), a man who thought he was Alexander the Great and set out to conquer Poland, the Baltic states and Russia. The product of the extreme severity of the Swedish climate, Charles believed (at least, according to Voltaire's account) that his self-mastery would lead inevitably to mastery of Eastern Europe and Central Asia, but he suffered defeat at the hands of Czar Peter I, was held captive by the Ottomans at Bender, and was eventually killed during the siege of a minor Norwegian fortress. The facts of the case are so patently the stuff of mock epic (Fielding, who translated an account of the life of Charles by G. Adlerfeld, exploited its comic potential in the eponymous protagonist of *Jonathan Wild* who modelled himself on the Swedish king) that most critics have assumed this to be the generic orientation of Voltaire's work.[28] However, the text is, in fact, rather more remarkable for its reluctance to seize the mock epic opportunities presented by the primary material, or to exploit the potentially comic gap between Charles' epic self-image and the defeated or even bizarre

[25] Voltaire, *La Henriade*, ed. O. R. Taylor, *Works*, II, (1970). David Maskell, *The Historical Epic in France, 1500–1700* (Oxford, 1973).

[26] *Essay upon the epick* (1727), 122–3.

[27] See also O. R. Taylor, 'Voltaire's Apprenticeship as a Historian: *La Henriade*' in *The Age of the Enlightenment: Studies Presented to Theodore Besterman*, eds. W. H. Barber, J. H. Brumfitt, R. A. Leigh, R. Shackleton and S. S. B. Taylor (Edinburgh, 1967).

[28] Henry Fielding (trans.), *The military history of Charles XII. King of Sweden, written by the express order of his Majesty, by G. Adlerfeld* (3 vols.; London, 1740). The view of *L'Histoire de Charles XII* as mock epic has been expressed in sophisticated ways by Lionel Gossman, 'Voltaire's Charles XII: History into Art', *SVEC*, 25 (1963), 691–720; Hayden White, *Metahistory*, 62–4; Suzanne Gearhart, *The Open Boundary of History and Fiction: A Critical Approach to the French Enlightenment* (Princeton, 1984), 57–94.

circumstances in which he frequently finds himself. When, for example, Charles is dragged away by his legs and arms from the residence in Bender which he had vainly attempted to defend against the overwhelming strength of the sultan's forces, Voltaire barely comments. Similarly, when Charles dies in petty circumstances, hit in the eye by a stray bullet on a minor campaign, Voltaire resists the temptation to dwell upon this apparent piece of poetic justice ('A petty fortress, and a dubious hand', in Johnson's poetic retelling of this story).[29] Instead, Voltaire follows this episode with a set-piece moralising passage describing how virtues pushed to excess can become destructive vices. The emphasis is placed more strongly upon the inhumane consequences of such vices than upon Charles' comic defeat: 'homme unique plutôt que grand homme; admirable plutôt qu'à imiter. Sa vie doit apprendre aux rois combien un gouvernement pacifique et heureux est au-dessus de tant de gloire' (272–3). While it is certainly the case, as one critic has suggested, that the Swedish king 'personifies the [deluded] view that history is essentially epic in nature', Voltaire does not expose Charles' epic pretensions by means of a generic descent into mock epic, and the conventions of humanist biography are retained with knowing gravity.[30]

Voltaire's critique of Charles is thrown into relief by his admiring presentation of the reforming and patriot Czar Peter I of Russia. In the *Histoire de Charles XII*, the climactic event of the history, a titanic encounter between Charles and Peter at the Battle of Poltava (1709), is dramatically enlarged as the confrontation between two great styles of monarchy: 'l'un [Charles] glorieux d'avoir donné des Etats, l'autre [Peter] d'avoir civilisé les siens; Charles aimant les dangers et ne combattant que pour la gloire; Alexiowitz ne fuyant point le péril, et ne faisant la guerre que pour ses intérêts' (161). Peter is the history's displaced centre of seriousness, and subsequent revisions to the book shift the balance of interest further in his direction.[31] Peter subsequently featured as the hero of Voltaire's more blatantly hagiographic *Histoire de L'Empire de Russie sous Pierre le Grand* (1759–63) where he is portrayed as a secular, progressive ruler, and symbol of Russia's potential modernity. The moral centre of *L'Histoire de Charles XII* is thus to be found at the margin of the plot, in the person of Peter, and does not simply emanate from the disguised moral voice of the mock-epic historian. Unlike Charles' barbaric false heroics, Peter's ruthlessness is excused since, understood properly in national context, it is indispensable to his programme of reform in Russia. *L'Histoire de Charles XII* retains many

[29] Samuel Johnson, 'The Vanity of Human Wishes', line 220 in *Poems*, ed. E. L. McAdam and George Milne (New Haven, 1964).
[30] Gearhart, *The Open Boundary*, 76.
[31] In the 1739 Amsterdam edition of *L'Histoire de Charles XII*, Voltaire added a section at the end of book I on Peter's reforms in Russia.

of the tonal and structural features of *La Henriade*. The work demonstrates Voltaire's quest for an authorial point of view which absorbs neoclassical seriousness into the present tense, but which remains committed to the organising, authoritative proficiency of traditional genre. Prose epic is still, for Voltaire, appropriate to the presentation of national history, but only in cases where rulers have enacted their epic history in ways suited to the peculiarities and demands of their nation and time. Peter the Great personifies an epicity properly adapted to modern Russia; Charles XII compels his country to take part in an outdated heroic saga. Voltaire works within a neoclassical aesthetic which places upon literature the demands of universal ethical validity, but which is also amenable to the historical particularities of its subject-matter.

In the years which followed, Voltaire ventured into more ambitious historical territory. The moral complexities of his new material, and its greater intractability to unified narrative exposition soon led to a doubling of voice in Voltaire's histories – one part engaged with events as constituents of an epic or a tragedy, the other providing a moralising commentary from a more distanced perspective. By this manœuvre, Voltaire continued to forestall the collapse of history into mock-epic without abandoning a sense of critical distance. Of the *Siècle de Louis XIV*, he remarked:

> J'envisage encore le siècle de Louis XIV comme celui du génie, et le siècle présent comme celui qui raisonne sur le génie.[32]

One part of the authorial voice, he claims, is fully engaged with the part epic, part tragic age of Louis XIV ('le siècle . . . du génie'), and the other is situated in a distanced present, possessing the rational clarity of the modern critic but not the creativity of genius ('celui qui raisonne sur le génie'). By comparison with the *Siècle de Louis XIV*, the *Histoire de Charles XII* and the *Histoire de l'Empire de Russie sous Pierre le Grand* (1759–63) suffer artistically from a lack of such a split voice; the modernity of the authorial perspective is too completely identified with Peter and the progress of his national epic adventure. In the *Histoire de Charles XII*, Voltaire investigated the generic pertinence of epic to recent events, and this had led him to an implicit periodisation of heroic and modern forms of historical behaviour. French historians of his era, as Grell has shown, used only rudimentary schemes of historical periodisation, and Voltaire was more energetic than most in seeking to divide history up into distinct epochs.[33] The *Siècle de Louis XIV* opens with a famous passage singling out the four great ages of the arts in human history: ancient Greece, ancient Rome, Renaissance

[32] *Défense de Louis XIV* (1769), *Oeuvres historiques*, 1294.
[33] Grell, *L'historie entre érudition et philosophie*, 44–9.

Italy and, best of all, the reign of Louis XIV. By clear implication, the authorial commentator is situated in the separate and inferior period of the present. This idea of present-day France is consistent with the commonplace neoclassical notion of declension; as soon as a civilisation reaches its apex, it must inevitably fall into decline. However, Voltaire's first major history also incorporates, in an innovative way, the idea of a distinct critical voice, engendered by this separately periodised modernity, which speaks from the cultural realm to the political sphere of history, tradition and law. The nature of this voice will merit further investigation, but it will first be necessary to say something of the origins of Voltaire's idea of the cultural authority of the historian.

The notion of the emancipation of art from tradition was a paradoxical and persistent feature of French neoclassicism. Since Malherbe early in the seventeenth century, neoclassical theorists had been concerned with the elaboration of artistic rules which might stand independently of their classical origins. The process reached an extreme point when, in 1687, Charles Perrault delivered a famous address in praise of 'Le Siècle de Louis le Grand' in which he celebrated the unity of inspiration behind his times and its artistic superiority over the classical past upon which it had hitherto relied.[34] With this speech, the age-old quarrel of the ancients and the moderns entered a new phase, as the moderns tried to accelerate the detachment of French classicism from the classics, in the name of a cultural nationalism which the ancients found both presumptuous and historically ignorant. The quarrel was still rumbling on when Voltaire first came to Paris in the late 1710s, and, in some respects, the *Siècle de Louis XIV* is a retrospective evaluation of the debate. As in England, the French quarrel in the early eighteenth century turned on the merits of Homer and the extent to which art could be said to have progressed since his times.[35] The modern camp included those, such as Homer's none-too-faithful verse translator Houdart de la Motte, who thought that the past, and past epic poets, were largely unintelligible and not worth meticulous attention, and those, such as the Abbé Terrasson, who proclaimed, by extravagant analogy with mathematical rules, the liberation of art from tradition.[36] As a scientist of art, Terrasson believed that art was reducible to mathematical laws and could therefore be expected to progress as rapidly in the eighteenth century as physics had done in the seventeenth. Voltaire,

[34] Charles Perrault, 'Le Siècle de Louis le Grand' (delivered 1687) printed in volume I of *Parallèle des Anciens et des Modernes en ce qui regarde les arts et les sciences* (4 vols.; Paris, 1688–97).

[35] The classic account is Hippolyte Rigault, *Histoire de la querelle des anciens et des modernes* (Paris, 1856). The most important recent account of the debate in England contains a good deal of information about France: Joseph M. Levine, *The Battle of the Books: History and Literature in the Augustan Age* (Ithaca, New York, 1991).

[36] Antoine Houdart de la Motte, 'Discours sur Homère' (1713), *Oeuvres* (11 vols.; Paris, 1753–4), I; Jean Terrasson, *Dissertation critique sur l'Iliade d'Homère* (2 vols.; Paris, 1715).

though he generally preferred to see himself as occupying the middle ground between the two camps, once expressed some enthusiasm for this idea: 'Peut-être arrivera-t-il bientôt dans la manière d'écrire l'histoire ce qui est arrivé dans la physique.'[37] In England, meanwhile, the debate was reversed, as the scholarly side of the argument fell to the moderns, with ancients such as Temple, Swift and Pope, struggling in different media, and with differing degrees of irony, to preserve the pristine authority of the classics. The greater willingness of both sides in the French debate to acknowledge that, for good or ill, Homer was the product of a more primitive period in history, had its origins in their self-confident recognition of the national uniqueness and novelty of French cultural modernity. The French moderns, whatever their scholarly limitations, set a new, irreverent tone in cultural debate. Their extrapolation of aesthetics from tradition licensed a new spirit of critical freedom which coincided with a relaxation in the demands of official ideology towards the end of the reign of Louis XIV and during the Regency which followed. The French modern confidence in the universal validity of certain aesthetic rules – rules which Homer, in his understandable primitive ignorance, did not know how to follow – was not, as Pope scornfully suggested in *An Essay on Criticism* (1711), merely a mirror-image in the artistic domain of absolutist monarchical law ('But *Critic Learning* flourish'd most in *France*: / The Rules, a Nation born to serve, obeys', lines 712–13), but the insistent recognition of cultural norms *wider* than political structures. Voltaire found liberating this post-classical neoclassicism with its exuberant periodisation of modern civilisation. In the *Siècle de Louis XIV*, he would also try to situate himself as a writer in this normative modernity from which to scrutinise history, politics and tradition. His critical position, like that of other moderns, would be secured in the aesthetic sphere. Much of the *Siècle de Louis XIV* is a panegyric of the French state in its great age of absolutism, yet, as Perrault had demonstrated, the artistic assessment of a state can also imply the existence of cultural rules over and above the decisions of an absolute monarch.[38]

'Le Siècle de Louis XIV'

Voltaire's preoccupation with the relationship between history, good kingship and good art led him to produce a history of France which is both

[37] 'Nouvelles considérations sur l'histoire' (1744), *Oeuvres historiques*, 46–9. Voltaire attacked the modern camp in a satirical poem 'Le Bourbier' (1714), *Moland*, X, 75–7. However, he summarised the debate impartially in an article in *Questions sur l'Encyclopédie* (1770–2), *Moland*, XVII, 225–40. See David Williams, 'Voltaire: Literary Critic', *SVEC*, 48 (1966).

[38] A similar argument, from a very different perspective, has been made about the French Enlightenment as a whole by Reinhart Koselleck, *Critique and Crisis: Enlightenment and the Pathogenesis of Modern Society* (Oxford, 1988).

highly crafted at the aesthetic level, and engaged, at the discursive level, in a complex appraisal of the role of aesthetics in political life. During composition and revision of the *Siècle de Louis XIV*, additional complications arose as Voltaire wrestled with the problem of how to achieve form in historical writing while resisting the unwelcome stasis and closure which it seemed to impose. Voltaire became increasingly aware of his own authorial location in a separately periodised critical modernity. He conferred upon his subject-matter, one of the great epochs of human civilisation, the coherence of a work of art whose constituent parts have the quality of universal types. However, the temporal perspective mandated by his self-conscious authorial subjectivity inevitably competes with and contextualises this perfected world of types. The context into which the authorial voice transposes the sealed age of Louis XIV is not primarily an ironic one, and a double authorial perspective is strenuously maintained, identified partly with his age and partly with the less brilliant reign of Louis XV. By avoiding both sustained irony and nostalgia, Voltaire is able to generate a secondary critical account of eighteenth-century French modernity and nationality. The *Siècle* is directly engaged with eighteenth-century political controversy, and is partly intended to provide a critique of the legal–theoretical foundations of these contemporary debates, particularly as they had been expounded by Montesquieu. Throughout the work, nationality is shown to be more essentially a matter of cultural identity than of legal history or political boundaries. Throughout the *Siècle de Louis XIV*, Voltaire makes neoclassical history a weapon with which to engage and even disable contemporary political debate about the nature of the French state.

Although a portion of the *Siècle de Louis XIV* had appeared in 1739, and Voltaire had started the work at least as far back as 1735, the first major text did not come out until 1751, followed by a significantly revised and expanded edition in 1753.[39] In 1756 this was incorporated as the final part of the *Essai sur les mœurs* in the Geneva collected works; further alterations were made in 1761–3, and the last major series of authorial revisions was added in 1768.[40] Voltaire drew upon a wide range of secondary source material, including a number of regency histories of Louis XIV's time, but also relied heavily upon the oral recollections which he had meticulously

[39] Voltaire started work in earnest in 1735. See Vaillot, *Avec Mme du Châtelet*, 42. However, he referred to the projected work as early as 1732: Voltaire to Jean Baptiste Nicholas Formont (*c.* 12 September 1732), Best. D526. He also outlined his plans in a letter to Dubos (30 October, 1738), Best. D1642.

[40] For details of the 1739 portion of *Le Siècle de Louis XIV*, see Bengesco, *Bibliographie*, I, 341. I have based my observations throughout upon the George-Conrad Walther edition (2 vols.; Dresden, 1753) (Bengesco, no. 1186). Significant revisions to the first edition (2 vols.; Berlin, 1751) are noted. For ease of access, all quotations are cited in the first instance from *Oeuvres historiques* and I have given a second reference to the Walther edition immediately after this in my text. On the printing of *Le Siècle de Louis XIV*, see Pomeau and Mervaud, *De la Cour au Jardin*, 51, 61, 69, 73.

collected in England and in France while still a young man.[41] Voltaire insisted throughout that the work was more than a mere annalistic or military history ('point . . . une simple relation des campagnes, mais plutôt une histoire des mœurs des hommes'). The work is divided into two separate halves; the first is, in fact, a briskly narrated chronological history of the period, military campaigns and all, and the second contains all the material relating to the 'mœurs' of the age. The history begins, appropriately enough, with an artistic event: the founding by Richelieu of the Académie Française (618: 1753, I, 189). The first part of the history moves from an overview of the age of Richelieu to the chaotic mid-century years of the Frondes under the regency of Anne of Austria. Once Louis' personal reign begins in earnest in 1661, Voltaire supplies quite detailed military histories of his conquests in the Netherlands and Germany through to the War of the Spanish Succession. The second part of the *Siècle* contains a substantial selection of anecdotes relating to Louis' private life and court, and then deals at length with the internal politics of France during his reign, followed by economic, artistic and scientific developments, and the religious controversies surrounding Jansenism, Quietism and Huguenot persecution. All editions have, as an appendix, catalogues of significant artists and other personages of the period. The chronological portion of the work is artistically crafted as a tragic drama, in which the protagonist, Louis XIV, at first rises to the height of success ('comble de sa grandeur') in 1688, and then overreaches himself to the point when, after the Battle of Blenheim, his mistress, Mme de Maintenon is at last obliged to tell him that he is no longer invincible ('qu'il n'était plus invincible') (759, 834: 1753, I, 254; 1753, I, 377). He eventually dies *en philosophe*, a little the wiser for his sufferings.[42]

Louis' heroic tragedy is incorporated into a larger epic tale of France's greatness and defeat in its most glorious era. This era appears to have the coherence of a work of literature, being sealed off from the events which precede and follow it. The period before Louis' reign is rendered wholly in terms of negatives; this is a time of gothic barbarity ('barbarie gothique'), without regular laws ('lois . . . fixes') – not so much pre-modern as the

41 On Voltaire's sources, see Gustave Lanson, *Voltaire*, trans. Robert Wagoner (London, New York and Sydney, 1966), 97–8; J. H. Brumfitt, *Voltaire Historian*, 59–60; Larissa Albina, 'Voltaire et ses sources historiques', *Le XVIIIè Siècle*, 13 (1981), 349–59; M. S. Rivière, 'Voltaire and the Fronde', *Nottingham French Studies*, 26 (1987), 1–18; Rivière, 'Voltaire's use of Larrey and Limiers in *Le Siècle de Louis XIV*: History as a Science, an Art and a Philosophy', *Forum for Modern Language Studies*, 25 (1989), 34–53; Rivière, 'Voltaire's use of Dangeau's *Mémoires* in *Le Siecle de Louis XIV*: the paradox of the historian-raconteur', *SVEC*, 256 (1989), 97–106; Pomeau and Mervaud, *De la Cour au Jardin*, 76–7. On Voltaire's oral sources, see Pomeau, *D'Arouet à Voltaire*, 236; Vaillot, *Avec Mme du Châtelet*, 72.

42 For a more systematic reading of *Le Siècle* as a classical tragedy, see M. S. Rivière, 'Voltaire's concept of dramatic history in *Le Siècle de Louis XIV*', *SVEC*, 284 (1991), 179–98.

opposite of modern when a total lack of Enlightenment ('défaut de lumières') permeates all aspects of life (619, 634: 1753, I, 7; 1753, I, 43). In the 1739 chapters of the *Siècle de Louis XIV*, there were originally some references to the existence of men of talent prior to Louis XIV's personal reign, but these are suppressed in 1751 for starker effect. History before Louis XIV is redefined as absence ('point d'académies, point de théâtres réguliers', 635: 1753, I, 44). Voltaire evokes, not historical evolution, but positive and negative manifestations of order. Like Perrault before him, Voltaire identifies and celebrates discontinuities between the age of Louis XIV and the chaos which came before. Louis himself is mainly functionally related to the form of the history through his body politic. He is a shadowy figure, more of a principle than a personality, with little private moral presence in the work. This artistic conflation of the king as protagonist and the actions of the state resembles the *Histoire de ... Pierre le Grand*: 'Enfin Pierre naquit, et la Russie fut formée' (388).

Voltaire depicts Louis XIV's France as a state self-consciously reinventing itself as an ordered and unified work of art. Economic, military and legal reforms under Louis XIV, as well as improvements in technology and communications, are described as modernisations contributing to the formal unity of the state: 'l'Etat devient un tout régulier dont chaque ligne aboutit au centre' (980: 1753, II, 147). Allegiance to this reforming state by its subjects is a matter of good taste, and all those able to perceive the formal harmoniousness of the state ('un tout régulier') wish to participate by vying with each other in the service of their sovereign (979: 1753, II, 147). Voltaire praises Louis' administration as an interventionist, mercantilist, centralised government of the talented. He regards developments in manufactures and trade as the most significant factors behind France's economic success, and Louis' chief minister, Colbert, a figure often disparaged in the eighteenth century, is rehabilitated as the pioneer of protectionist economics and promoter of commerce in luxury goods – a judgement Voltaire was not subsequently inclined to revise even after personal contacts with French physiocrats such as Turgot. Meanwhile, artistic life in France flourishes under Louis' personal governance, and the national language acquires purity and stability ('la langue commençait à s'épurer et à prendre une forme constante', 1003: 1753, II, 179). The prestige of the nation is enhanced by the growing international influence of French culture; in 1752, Voltaire added a passage underlining this point:

> Sa langue [France's] est devenue la langue d'Europe. ... L'esprit de société est le partage naturel des Français; c'est un mérite et un plaisir dont les autres peuples ont senti le besoin. (1017: 1753, II, 205)

Indeed, as this national history evolved over a number of stages of revision, Voltaire showed increasing signs of the cosmopolitan historical sensibility which would develop more fully in the *Essai sur les mœurs*. For example, in 1757, he added a chapter entitled 'Des beaux-arts en Europe' which projects an image of Europe as an increasingly civilised, culturally interdependent system of states.

Cultural constructions of monarchy

Voltaire's retelling of the myth of the Sun King, in terms slightly more cosmopolitan but no less ardent than Louis' original propagandists, came as a surprise to contemporary audiences. The myth had been in decline since the Regency when it was dismantled by aristocratic critics of absolutism, and its rehabilitation in the middle of the century appeared to some to insinuate unfavourable comparisons with Louis XV's troubled and lack-lustre monarchy.[43] Nevertheless, Louis XV is not, in fact, the concealed satirical target of the *Siècle de Louis XIV*. Rather, Voltaire, as historiographer royal, aims to approach the ages of Louis XIV and Louis XV by means of a new narrative representation and endorsement of the institution of monarchy. The *Siècle de Louis XIV*, with its splendid tableaux of war abroad and lavish peace at court, stages a return to the baroque idea of history as spectacle, while inviting its eighteenth-century audience to contemplate the political nature of their own spectatorship. A convinced monarchist, Voltaire reminds his readers that they are formed as nation by the spectacle of the king; monarchy confers upon them a unity of gaze and purpose, but it also assigns to them an active role as arbiters of taste in the theatre of the state. In presenting the age of Louis XIV as a distinctive and separate work of time's art ('heureux ouvrage', 619: 1753, I, 7), Voltaire breaks with traditional dynastic representations of monarchy, and suggests that the shared history of France is best approached through cultural rather than through political, legal or religious traditions. Voltaire's approach both reflects and accelerates the general desacralisation of the iconography of the French monarchy during the eighteenth century. The monarchy had not altogether lost its sacred and mystic aura by this time, but naturalistic images of the king had started to prevail over eucharistic models.[44] As a defender of strong kingship as a bulwark against both aristocratic power and the constitutional claims of the *parlements*, Voltaire wanted to do something more than simply revive old notions of the royal *mystique du sang*. His cultural defence of monarchy entails a polemical rejection of the traditional discourses of French politics, and enables him to postulate the existence within the state of a critical cultural sphere in which monarchy is both appreciated and regulated.

[43] N. R. Johnson, 'Louis XIV and the Age of the Enlightenment: The Myth of the Sun King from 1715 to 1789', *SVEC*, 172 (1978).

[44] Roger Chartier, *Les origines culturelles de la Revolution française* (Paris, 1990), chapter 6.

The background to Voltaire's cultural polemic is complex. Since the early sixteenth century, the debate about the French state had separated into two general strands: constitutionalist theories which posited that the king was subject to both the positive and fundamental laws of the kingdom, and absolutist theories in which the king is said not to be legally bound by any law, or only bound by fundamental laws.[45] These jurisprudential arguments often entailed a re-evaluation of the long-term impact of the occupation of Roman Gaul by the Franks, and the consequent relationship between France's heritage of Roman law and its Frankish, German legal tradition. All this had some affinities with and some bearing upon the elaboration of a common law interpretation of English history in seventeenth-century England.[46] The constitutionalist arguments had persisted throughout the seventeenth century. Louis XIV, however, did not require or encourage a juristic defence of his kingship, and preferred to associate himself with the idea of dynastic blood right ('mystique du sang').[47] With the resurgence of the influence of the parlements and the aristocracy during the Regency, juristic scholarship enjoyed the faint beginnings of a revival. The debate about the nature of the French constitution was reoriented towards the origins and nature of feudal custom and law. The constitutionalist argument was now largely appropriated by oppositional 'Germanist' theorists – proponents of a limited and mixed regime of king, parlements and nobility, in accordance with the best Frankish traditions. In 1727, the Comte de Boulainvilliers stated the Germanist-aristocratic case in its baldest form in his *Histoire de l'ancien gouvernement de France*; the Franks who had conquered Gaul had imposed an oligarchic constitution which eventually enshrined aristocratic feudalism as its system of government. The contemporary nobility and parlements continued to be, in this interpretation, essential parts of the machinery of the French constitution.

Royalists like Voltaire (who was much influenced by his friend the Marquis D'Argenson who circulated in manuscript the polemical 'Considérations sur le gouvernement ancien et présent de la France', *c.* 1739, but published in 1764), regarded the vestiges of aristocratic feudal jurisdictions in France as oppressive, and saw strong monarchy as the best means of maintaining equality among French subjects.[48] That the juristic, as opposed to the mystic case for absolute monarchy, was not ideologically bankrupt by the early eighteenth century is demonstrated by the popularity

[45] Nannerl O. Keohane, *Philosophy and the State in France: The Renaissance to the Enlightenment* (Princeton, 1980); Donald Kelley, *Foundations of Modern Historical Scholarship: Language, Law, and History in the French Renaissance* (New York, 1970).

[46] J. G. A. Pocock, *The Ancient Constitution and the Feudal Law* (revised edn, Cambridge, 1987).

[47] Ranum, *Artisans of Glory*.

[48] Keohane, *Philosophy and the State in France*, 376–88; J. Q. C. Mackrell, *The Attack on Feudalism in Eighteenth-Century France* (London, 1973).

of Dubos' 'Romanist', royalist riposte to Boulainvilliers, the *Histoire critique de l'établissement de la monarchie françoise dans les Gaules* (1734).[49] In Dubos' account, the Franks are said to have acceded peacefully to Roman power in Gaul, taking over at the same time Roman laws, civility and the constitutional principle of allegiance to a single emperor or monarch. Feudalism is, in this version, a later usurpation of power by the nobility whose authority, therefore, has no legal basis in French history.

On the opposing side, it was the nobleman Montesquieu who ultimately gained respectability and currency for the Germanist-aristocratic thesis. His scholarly contribution to the debate was followed by the adoption of a Germanist outlook by the *Encyclopédie*, and a flourishing eighteenth-century tradition of aristocratic apologetics.[50] Montesquieu's analysis of the origins of the French constitution and feudal law in *De l'Esprit des lois* (books 28, 30, 31) is unusually sophisticated; he describes France as a state from its very origins a monarchy limited by the constitutional power of the nobility and their institutions, although he does concede that the rigours of aristocratic feudal power had, at various points in French history, become excessive. French legal history, in Montesquieu's reading, authorises a limited monarchy in which the nobility functions as an intermediate power ('pouvoir intermédiaire'), and in which the parlements perform the role of repository of the laws ('corps dépositaire des lois').[51] Thus, Montesquieu implies, there is a case for strengthening the role of the second estate and the parlements in the name of a wider, historically sanctioned tradition of French national liberty.

Voltaire's response to the Germanist/Romanist historical debate is somewhat contradictory. His accounts of early post-Roman France have a number of Romanist elements.[52] Elsewhere, however, he insists that the Frankish barbarians completely destroyed the civilised urban culture which the Gauls had derived from Rome (*Essai*, I, 338). In 1753, yielding to a request from the Duchess of Saxe-Gotha, Voltaire published a two-volume summary of the history of the Holy Roman Empire, the *Annales de l'Empire*, in which he gave serious attention to the question of the Frankish conquest of Gaul, and the subsequent establishment of the feudal system in France. Here, he explicitly refutes Dubos' 'peaceful takeover' thesis; the Franks are

[49] Thomas E. Kaiser, 'The abbé Dubos and the historical defence of monarchy in early eighteenth-century France', *SVEC*, 267 (1989), 77–102.

[50] The standard work is Elie Carcassonne, *Montesquieu et le problème de la Constitution Française au XVIIIè Siècle* (Paris, 1926). See also Iris Cox, 'Montesquieu and the history of French Laws', *SVEC*, 216 (1983).

[51] C. de Secondat, Baron de Montesquieu, *De l'Esprit des lois* (2nd edn, Paris, 1757), Books 20, 22. The concept of a depository body ('corps dépositaire') denotes a function within a state and need not necessarily be performed by parlements.

[52] On 30 October, 1738, Voltaire wrote to Dubos to congratulate him on having clarified the question of French origins (Best. D1642).

said to have overrun Gaul, and not to have been invited in as welcome successors to the Romans ('non pas en alliés du peuple, comme on [i.e. Dubos] l'a prétendu, mais après avoir pillé les colonies romaines').[53] In all these entanglements it is at least clear that Voltaire thought that the French civil state had improved over its history through the gradual social participation and power of the commons, in alliance with the sovereign against feudal structures and aristocratic privilege. This bourgeois–royalist narrative of history would later be endorsed, in different circumstances, by Voltaire's more scholarly successors in the Scottish Enlightenment. Montesquieu, as Voltaire realised, represented the most intelligent obstacle to this interpretation since he had successfully combined historical jurisprudence with a sociology of checks and balances. For this reason, in the *Siècle*, the *Essai* and in other works, Voltaire's objective was not so much to refute the Germanist-aristocratic thesis, as to rob it of all political significance.

In 1769, at the behest of Louis XV's Chancellor Maupeou, who was then engaged in a programme to bring the troublesome parlements to heel (and ultimately, in 1771, to suppress them), Voltaire published a *Histoire du Parlement de Paris* which, despite its royalist polemical bias, continued to insist on the fact of a Frankish invasion of Gaul.[54] Voltaire plundered Boulainvilliers' *Histoire de l'ancien gouvernement* for this work, as the annotations all over his surviving copies show.[55] The result is a surprisingly fair-minded history of the Paris parlement, but one which insists upon the discontinuity between the historical parlement and its modern successor institution. Even the word 'parlement' has changed its meaning beyond all recognition: 'et les noms et les choses ont subi les mêmes vicissitudes'.[56] In all of Voltaire's accounts of the period, the constitution of medieval France is said to be nothing more than a licensed form of brigandage. He finds no legitimacy in any historical–juristic thesis whether Romanist or Germanist: 'La jurisprudence était celle de la férocité et de la superstition' (*Essai*, I, 339). In so far as Voltaire expounds a *thèse royale* in his reading of French history, it is one without juristic content.[57] The French sovereign is

[53] *Annales de l'Empire, depuis Charlemagne* (2 vols.; Bâle, 1753), *Moland*, XIII, 220. See Pomeau and Mervaud, *De la Cour au Jardin*, 189–90, 207. For Voltaire's own annotations to J. B. Dubos, *Histoire critique de l'établissement de la monarchie française dans les Gaules* (3 vols.; Amsterdam, 1734), see *Corpus des notes marginales de Voltaire*, eds. L. Albina, T. Voronova, S. Manévitch *et al.* (Berlin, 1979–), II, 161–92.

[54] *Histoire du Parlement de Paris par M. l'abbé Bigore* (2 vols.; Amsterdam, 1769), *Moland*, XV, 446. The text was altered and expanded successively in 1769 (Bengesco, *Bibliographie*, no. 1248), 1770 (Bengesco, no. 1251) and 1775 (Bengesco, no. 1253n.).

[55] *Corpus des notes marginales*, I, 433–97.

[56] *Histoire du Parlement de Paris*, *Moland*, XV, 448.

[57] Peter Gay identifies two broad strains in eighteenth-century French political thought, the 'thèse nobiliaire' and the 'thèse royale', around which he groups, respectively, the Germanist and Romanist juristic theses. In so far as he de-emphasises the legalistic content of Voltaire's 'thèse royale', these broad outlines are helpful, although he has a tendency to place Voltaire in the

identified culturally with the urbanised world of the Roman Empire, and monarchy emerges, in Voltaire's reworking of Dubos, as the sign and achievement of civilisation.[58] Modernity and monarchy are thus seen as interdependent:

> il est vrai que cet esprit philosophique qui a gagné presque toutes les conditions excepté le bas peuple, a beaucoup contribué à faire valoir les droits des souverains.
>
> (*Siècle de Louis XIV*, 1001: added after 1753)

Voltaire's royalism has often been caricatured as a preference for 'Enlightened despotism'. This notion erroneously implies that Voltaire naively supposed that good sovereigns are not limited but self-limiting, whereas, although Voltaire recognised no constituted intermediate powers in the French state – such as the nobility or the church – which might set legal limits to the power of the monarch, he did believe that the crown was, in practice, culturally rather than legally limited. Peter Gay sees Voltaire's liking for monarchy as pragmatic, a matter of geographical suitability in some states, though not necessarily in others.[59] René Pomeau regards Voltaire's royalism as a matter of doctrine based on a clear set of principles – 'l'antichristianisme, un activisme autoritaire, un humanisme libéral' – and on a conviction that nothing else can control France's factional, sectarian and feudal tendencies.[60] Neither interpretation rings entirely true for Voltaire's histories themselves which elaborate no doctrine of monarchy as such, but do articulate an aesthetic preference for monarchy, and a neoclassical vision of the sovereign imposing fixed rules and coherent form upon the state.[61] Voltaire regards these rules or 'positive laws' as necessary social fictions; their legitimacy is not derived from tradition or nature, but from empirical observation of their tendency to civilise and promote justice.[62] A general social 'esprit philosophique' and monarchy mutually advance each other. In the *Siècle*, Voltaire shows that Louis XIV was restrained in his actions by the very aesthetic understanding of politics

Dubos camp, and to underestimate the flexibility of Voltaire's historical case for monarchy: *Voltaire's Politics: The Poet as Realist* (2nd edn, New Haven, 1988), 87–116. For a somewhat different critique of Gay's book, see Robert S. Tate, 'Voltaire and the Question of Law and Order in the Eighteenth Century: Locke against Hobbes' in *Studies in Eighteenth-Century French Literature Presented to Robert Niklaus*, eds. J. Fox, M. Waddicor and D. Watts (Exeter, 1975).

58 Voltaire did not succeed in his aim of putting an end to juristic debate about the French constitution. Around this time, his fellow historian, Gabriel Bonnot de Mably set about constructing a legal-historical case for democracy in France. See Keith Michael Baker, *Inventing the French Revolution: Essays on French Political Culture in the Eighteenth Century* (Cambridge, 1990), chapter 4.

59 *Voltaire's Politics*, 101–2.

60 Pomeau ed., *Politique de Voltaire* (Paris, 1963), 36.

61 Pomeau finds Voltaire's preference both doctrinal and aesthetic (*Politique de Voltaire*, 41).

62 'On a dit dans l'Essai sur les mœurs, qu'il n'y a point en rigeur de loi positive fondamentale; les hommes ne peuvent faire que les lois de convention.' ('Remarques pour servir de supplément à l'*Essai sur les mœurs*' (1763) in *Essai*, II, 936.)

which he had himself generated, and that it was this, rather than adherence to a constitution, which caused him to observe a regular system of laws. Voltaire thus situates himself within the tradition of state panegyric which Louis himself had fostered, but which had, in turn, strategically celebrated a system in which arbitrariness could have no place. (Voltaire himself wrote a panegyric poem to Louis XV after the French victory at Fontenoy in 1745).[63]

Montesquieu and despotism

Voltaire fully appreciated the political dangers of presenting the French monarchy in an aestheticised way without any pleasing illusions about the legal constraints placed upon it. He acknowledged the troubling fact that there was no *categorical* difference between monarchy and despotism, and he once asked himself, 'Où est la ligne qui sépare le gouvernement monarchique et le despotique?'; to this question, the only answer which Voltaire could supply was that the difference was largely a matter of style.[64] The question appears in Voltaire's *Commentaire sur l'Esprit des lois* (1777), a compilation of many of his previous comments on Montesquieu, and culmination of years of reflection upon Montesquieu's generic distinctions between republics, monarchies and despotisms. Although direct contacts between the two men were limited, Montesquieu represented for Voltaire both an admired ally in the cause of justice and anti-clericalism, and a persistent imagined intellectual opponent.[65] Voltaire derived energy for his historical writing from his urge to refute what he saw as Montesquieu's hopelessly abstract sociology of laws by putting it to the test of history; all of his later histories, whether explicitly or implicitly, represent an engagement with *L'Esprit des lois*. In his intellectual opposition to Montesquieu, Voltaire would later come to represent an alternative strand of influence in British and American historiography.[66]

In the *Esprit des lois*, Montesquieu begins with a taxonomy of the three basic forms of government (despotic, republican – both in its democratic and aristocratic forms – and monarchic); each form has a nature and an animating principle (fear, virtue and honour respectively). Voltaire persis-

[63] Voltaire, 'Poëme de Fontenoy', *Moland*, VIII, 371–95.

[64] Voltaire, 'Commentaire sur l'Esprit des lois' (1777), *Moland*, XXX, 430. See also *Pensées sur le gouvernement* (1752), *Moland*, XXIII, 530 ('Il n'y a point d'Etat despotique par sa nature').

[65] There is a generous biographical note on Montesquieu in *Le Siècle de Louis XIV*, 1187–8. Voltaire came to Montesquieu's defence during a pamphlet war over *De l'Esprit des lois* (*Remerciement sincère à un homme charitable* (1750), *Moland*, XXIII, 457–61). See also Robert Shackleton, 'Allies and Enemies: Voltaire and Montesquieu' in *Essays on Montesquieu and the Enlightenment* (Oxford, 1988).

[66] Hugh Trevor-Roper identifies a split in the respective influences of Voltaire and Montesquieu, the former politically radical in his legacy, the latter conservative ('The Historical Philosophy of the Enlightenment', *SVEC*, 27 (1963), 1667–87).

tently, even wilfully, misinterpreted this. He misunderstood Montesquieu's analysis of the principles of public behaviour in different types of government, and insisted that this should be replaced with strictly empirical questions (not 'is virtue the category of political behaviour which enables the functioning of republican government?' but 'are people in republics in fact virtuous?').[67] His notes and comments are full of objections to (what he sees as) Montesquieu's abstract and schematic account of political motivation, including a long footnote to the *Siècle de Louis XIV* (862–3: added after 1753). Voltaire especially disliked the caricature of eastern despotisms which provides the negative pole in Montesquieu's normative discourse of limited government. Voltaire pointed out, in the *Essai* and elsewhere, that the Ottoman system, in particular, though not conformable to Montesquieu's notion of tempered monarchy ('gouvernement monarchique tempéré'), is nevertheless culturally limited in ways which he chooses to ignore (*Essai*, I, 833).[68]

Book 19 of *De l'Esprit des lois* examines, in an innovatory way, the complex interrelationship between 'mœurs' (a term which includes customs, traditions and manners) and laws. This discussion, as chapter 16 previously explains, is predicated upon a distinction between man's dual role as a citizen (regulated by laws) and as a private individual (influenced by custom). Voltaire points out in *La Défense de mon oncle* (1767), written as a vindication of *La Philosophie de l'Histoire*, that such a distinction is artificial, since the effectiveness of the laws of any society depends upon more general patterns of cultural behaviour: 'Le vrai savant est celui ... qui juge d'une nation par ses mœurs plus que par ses lois, parce que les lois peuvent être bonnes et les mœurs mauvaises.'[69] Law is a matter of 'opinion' ('l'opinion a fait les lois'), and by 'opinion' Voltaire means the sum total of what a society believes about itself ('Remarques', *Essai*, II, 935). This is a relatively participatory view of law-making, and it provides Voltaire with another explanation as to how monarchy can be limited *de facto* as well as *de jure*: 'Il y a partout un frein imposé au pouvoir arbitraire, par la loi, par les usages, ou par les mœurs' (*Essai*, II, 809). Voltaire responds to Montesquieu's sociology of laws with his own idea of an 'esprit du temps' or 'esprit général' which dissolves the boundary, in a way the *Esprit des lois* does not, between institutional structures and the activities of society at large. Voltaire reckons all institutional arrangements to be customary, facilitated by particular habits ('usages'), and by the current state of the collective 'esprit général'. Changes in custom and taste, as the *Essai sur les mœurs*

[67] For examples of this, see *Pensées sur le gouvernement, Moland*, XXIII, 531; *Idées républicaines* (1762), *Moland*, XXIV, 427; *Commentaire sur l'Esprit des lois, Moland*, XXX, 426–7.

[68] See also *Commentaire, Moland*, XXX, 417; Judith N. Shklar, *Montesquieu* (Oxford, 1987), 114–18.

[69] *La Défense de mon oncle* (1767), ed. José-Michel Moureaux, *Works*, LXIV (1984), 229.

would later argue at some length, are thus key indicators of historical development.

Perfection postponed

The *Siècle de Louis XIV* incorporates a theory of culturally limited monarchy articulated in more detail elsewhere in Voltaire's writings. This theory challenges contemporary legal–historical as well as abstract sociological descriptions of the French constitution in the name of a type of egalitarian royalism. It also embodies an implicit claim for the authority of the historian who addresses political rulers from the very cultural domain in which their power is legitimated. The historian both shapes the national past into an artistic whole, and engages in the second-order creation of a role for aesthetics in politics. In the *Siècle de Louis XIV*, the national past is subjected to a further tier of evaluation as, with each stage of revision, the author superimposes a more self-consciously international perspective. Although the identification of a cosmopolitan 'esprit philosophique' with the age of Louis XIV is a feature of the earlier texts, later revisions suggest a growing tendency to see the seventeenth century as part of a much longer progress of civilisation, especially when the work is eventually appended to the *Essai* in later editions of the collected works.[70] The closure and formal perfection of the age of Louis XIV is, in all texts, slightly compromised by the bathos of the last chapter which treats of acrimonious seventeenth-century disputes about the alleged atheism of the Chinese. This absurdity is cited as an example of the degree to which the public rationality, or an 'esprit philosophique' still needed to develop (267: 1753, II, 336).

Further revisions to the text indicate Voltaire's growing interest in religious strife as an obstacle to the period's attempts at modernisation. The chapters on religious affairs dramatise a conflict between an 'esprit raisonable', characteristic of the age at its best, and a wilfully anachronistic 'esprit dogmatique' bedevilling different groups of sectarians. In this section of the work, Voltaire is often obliged to postpone rather than to celebrate the modernity he wishes to locate in the age of Louis XIV. Jansenism makes an appearance as a backward-looking and fanatical form of sectarianism, and Voltaire finds this variant of Catholicism, not fundamentally incompatible with civil order, but embarrassing to a rational state. In the closing sections of the *Siècle* (which cover the period shortly after Louis XIV's reign), there is a passage relating how, in 1725, Jansenist enthusiasts disgraced themselves by going into a frenzy over supposed

[70] In the *Collection complète des Oeuvres de M. de Voltaire* (17 vols.; Geneva, 1756) it makes up chapters 165–215 of the *Essai sur l'histoire générale et sur les mœurs et l'esprit des nations.*

'miracles' at the tomb of a revered Jansenist deacon; Voltaire loftily declares such fanaticism outmoded if harmless:

> Ces sottises auraient eu des suites sérieuses dans des temps moins éclairés. Il semblait que ceux qui les protégaient ignorassent à quel siècle ils avaient affaire. (1087: 1753, II, 310)

The modernity of the age of Louis XIV is more seriously called into question by the Revocation of the Edict of Nantes (which had guaranteed Protestant toleration in France), the repression of the Protestants which preceded it, and the Protestant revolt in the Cévennes which followed. Voltaire is fascinated and appalled by the disastrously inflexible character both of the French Protestants and of the Jesuit-inspired repressive action of the state. Although he carefully distances Louis XIV from personal responsibility for the state oppression, Voltaire finds on both sides a failure of Enlightenment, and a perverse unwillingness to subordinate religious to civil interests. The Huguenots' demand for political autonomy seems to him seditious and unreasonable (their 'esprit dogmatique' inevitably engenders an 'esprit republicain'). He finds the Huguenots anachronistic in their unsocial asceticism: 'Les fêtes magnifiques d'une cour galante jetaient même de ridicule sur le pédantisme des huguenots' (1048–9: 1753, II, 246). State oppression, too, is an anachronistic act, aggravated by the ultramontane proselytising of Louis' Jesuit advisers. The ironic consequence of this intolerance is the exodus from the country of a vast pool of expertise in arts and manufacturing, causing still further delays in the country's process of modernisation. The age of reason now appears to be some way off: 'Cette raison ... est un des grands ouvrages du temps, et ce temps n'était pas encore venu' (1063: added after 1753). Here, for the first time, Voltaire finds a dark correlation (never fully articulated in any of the texts of the *Siècle*) between the artistic perfections of Louis XIV's state and its cruelty:

> On voyait alors des scènes bien différentes: d'un côté, le désespoir et la fuite d'une partie de la nation; de l'autre, de nouvelles fêtes à Versailles; Trianon et Marly bâtis; la nature forcée dans tous ces lieux de délices, et des jardins où l'art était épuisé. (930–1: 1753, II, 68)

Voltaire is usually more indulgent towards ceremonial display in the high places of Louis XIV's France, but here he detects culpable shallowness in its oblivious baroque artistry.

For the most part, the *Siècle de Louis XIV* converts history into a spectacle discontinuous with the natural order. Under the subsequent, less dazzling administrations of Fleury in France and Walpole in Britain, affairs return to their natural order ('Les affaires politiques rentrèrent insensiblement dans leur ordre naturel', 886: 1753, I, 471). The sequel to this work, the

Précis du Siècle de Louis XV (1769), documents this 'natural order' of history in a largely unembellished account of events from the death of Louis XIV to the present.[71] Throughout the work, Voltaire applies a detached cosmopolitan perspective to recent events in his country. Once again, French history is analysed within a broad European context, and again French modernity is compromised by anachronistic episodes – in this case, the stabbing of Louis XV by the Jansenist fanatic Damiens, and the romanticised Jacobite Rebellion of 1745.[72] Some of the most significant achievements of the period are said to have taken place during the financial revolution of the Regency; even John Law's catastrophic financial system is said to have had beneficial long-term effects upon monetary and commercial behaviour ('un système tout chimérique enfanta un commerce réel', 1307). The era of Louis XV is one of relative artistic decline. Voltaire expresses the conventionally neoclassical fear that, once the nation's language and the arts have been perfected in one epoch, they will inevitably be corrupted in the next: 'La langue fut portée, sous Louis XIV, au plus haut point de perfection dans tous les genres ... Il est à craindre aujourd'hui que cette belle langue ne dégénère, par cette malheureuse facilité d'écrire que le siècle passé a donnée aux siècles suivants' (1570). The rehearsal of neoclassical ideas of declension in the chapter entitled 'Des Progrès de l'esprit humain dans le siècle de Louis XV', has led some critics to assume that the work's predecessor, *Le Siècle de Louis XIV*, should be read as a satirical commentary on the twilight period in which Voltaire was living. However, since both ancients and moderns had recognised a distinction between the arts and other aspects of progress, and, since Voltaire had shown the great epoch of Louis XIV to have been an exceptional case within the normative evolution of the philosophical spirit of mankind, such inferences are not necessary.[73]

The narrative of Europe

Voltaire's most ambitious historical work, the *Essai sur les mœurs et l'esprit des nations et sur les principaux faits de l'histoire depuis Charlemagne jusqu'à Louis XIII*

71 *Précis du Siècle de Louis XV* (2 vols.; Geneva, 1769). This evolved out of the chapter 'Tableau de l'Europe depuis la paix d'Utrecht jusqu'en 1750' which featured in all editions of *Le Siècle de Louis XIV*. It also incorporates adapted portions of the *Histoire de la guerre de mil sept cent quarante et un* (1755), ed. J. Maurens (Paris, 1971). The *Précis* first appeared as an appendix to the 1768 edition of *Le Siècle de Louis XIV* (4 vols.; Geneva, 1768). The *Précis* was the indirect result of Voltaire having been made Historiographe de France in 1745, and having undertaken to write about Louis XV's campaigns. See Vaillot, *Avec Mme du Châtelet*, 209.

72 *Précis*, chapter 24. See Laurence Bongie, 'Voltaire's English High Treason and a Manifesto for Bonnie Prince Charles', *SVEC*, 171 (1979), 7–29; F. McClynn, 'Voltaire and the Jacobite Rising of 1745', *SVEC*, 185 (1980), 7–20.

73 On discontinuities between artistic and political progress, Bernard de Fontenelle, *Digression sur les anciens et les modernes* (1688), ed. Robert Shackleton (Oxford, 1955), 161–76.

(this title was first used in 1769) supplies the wider historical context within which the account of the age of Louis XV is to be understood. The *Essai* explores the complex, and sometimes contradictory relationship between the arts, the philosophical spirit, and the evolution of civilisation in Europe. Moreover, it attempts to do so in ways which will erode national partialities; local cultural achievements such as the *Siècle de Louis XIV*, which was appended to this work, appear as (particularly impressive) variations on the theme of international evolution. Despite its declared ambition to supply an overview of the development of civilisation, the *Essai* is essentially an agglomeration of a number of national histories held together by a (sometimes fragile) narrative thread. At the outset, Voltaire approaches them as he might a collection of national epic poems, identifying a small number of constant formal elements and many national variants. The unity of these national histories, Voltaire explains in the summary 'Résumé de toute cette histoire' (1756), is to be found, not at the level of master narrative, but in the pre-cognitive drive to civilisation inherent in all men and women:

> Au milieu de ces saccagements et de ces destructions que nous observons dans l'espace de neuf cent années, nous voyons un amour de l'ordre qui anime en secret le genre humain, et qui a prévenu sa ruine totale. C'est un des ressorts de la nature, qui reprend toujours sa force: c'est lui qui a formé le code des nations.
> (II, 808: 1756, XVI, 149)

Man's creative love of order, which has affinities with the historian's own artistic quest for form in variety, fashions and sustains the delicate and slow process of civilisation: 'Il est aisé de . . . conclure . . . avec quelle lenteur la raison humaine se forme' (II, 87: 1756, XII, 315). The *Essai* does not, as is often supposed, sound the drum of the march of reason. When Voltaire speaks of progress, he uses the very unusual unreflexive verb 'se civiliser' to signify that the civilising process is voluntary and not mechanical: 'Avec quelle lenteur, avec quelle difficulté le genre humain se civilise, et la société se perfectionne!' (II, 724: 1756, XIV, 231). The process is silent, whereas the forces of destruction and regression are associated with noise: 'Le commerce et l'industrie de ces villes a réparé *sourdement* le mal que les princes [Edward III and Philippe de Valois] faisaient avec tant de fracas' (my italics, I, 721: 1756, XII, 125).

Voltaire's complementary task as a creative historian is to piece together remnants of order in an often chaotic past, and to reveal the constant elements in history while revelling in the infinite diversity of peoples and ages. In the 'Résumé' (1756) of the *Essai*, Voltaire explains that this simultaneous search for order and variety springs from the contrasting functions in history of nature and custom:

L'empire de la coûtume est bien plus vaste que celui de la nature; il s'étend sur les mœurs, sur tous les usages; il répand la variété sur la scene de l'univers: la nature y répand l'unité; elle établit partout un petit nombre de principes invariables: ainsi le fonds est partout le même, et la culture produit des fruits divers. (1756, II, 810)

Voltaire's second major history is, then, in part, an *essai* in Montaigne's sense of the word: a detached, often sceptical and episodic evaluation of the cultural eccentricities and natural propensities of mankind.[74] Yet the *Essai* also transcends the Renaissance preoccupation with peculiar human customs in its search for a coherent narrative of the development of European civilisation in relation to the rest of the world. This narrative is secured in Voltaire's idea of nature and natural law, although this, in turn, derives from a precarious metaphysic which history puts to the test. With each new revision of the text of the *Essai*, Voltaire runs increasing epistemological difficulties, and he confesses himself unable to shore up the work against the old, familiar pyrrhonian enemy. Nevertheless, he persists in his original aim of supplying his readers with a normative historical perspective from which to re-evaluate national, and, ultimately, European diversities and prejudices.

The 'Essai sur les mœurs'

Originally a response to his mistress's request for a history which eschewed mere chronology of kings and queens, the *Essai* eventually grew into a grand summary of world history from the time of Charlemagne to the dawn of the age of Louis XIV. In the 1769 Geneva edition of his works, Voltaire placed at the front of the *Essai* a preliminary discourse on the natural history of primitive societies entitled *La Philosophie de l'histoire*. This work, the first ever to use the term 'the philosophy of history', makes explicit many of the themes of nature and natural law in the *Essai*, although its presence also overmagnifies their importance to the *Essai* as a whole. Voltaire began work on the *Essai* in the 1740s, publishing portions of the chapters on the crusades in the early 1750s. The first authorised text appeared in 1754, and the work reached its basic form in the edition printed in the 1756 Geneva works under the title *Essay sur l'histoire générale et sur les mœurs et l'esprit des nations*. I shall base my interpretation upon this edition, noting the successive revisions of 1761, 1769, 1775, as well as those which appeared in the posthumous 'Kehl' edition of 1785.[75] Modern

[74] Voltaire greatly admired Montaigne. See his letter to Louis Elisabeth de La Vergne, comte de Tressan (21 August, 1746), Best. D3453.

[75] For a detailed bibliography of the *Essai*, see Pomeau ed, *Essai*, pp. lxvii-lxxiii. The Pomeau edition is based upon the 'Kehl' posthumous 1785 edition which incorporates Voltaire's final revisions. I have cited in my text the Pomeau edition for ease of access, followed by a second reference to the 1756 text of the *Essai* to be found in the Cramer *Collection complète des oeuvres de*

critics, basing their readings upon the Kehl edition, have tended to assume that the *Essai* was conceived as a militantly ironic exposure of human folly and cruelty in history.[76] In its 1754–6 incarnations, the *Essai* is not, as is generally supposed, a *Candide*-like satire on human depravity writ large, but a developmental narrative which tells calmly of the material and cultural changes which brought about the rise of modern European societies out of the ruins of feudalism. Although Voltaire polemically dissociates the modern world from the medieval, he does not simply consign the Middle Ages to darkness, but shows that they, too, undergo a transformational process set in motion by the growth of towns, the (generally benign) influence of the Church, and the trauma of the Crusades. The rise of a civilised European system of states comes about through the establishment of powerful monarchies, and the eventual decline in the influence of the Church and the nobility. Voltaire's concept of world history is quite generous, embracing the Middle and Far East, though rarely Africa. Nevertheless, the narrative largely follows the trajectory of Europe and the triumph of its norms within an international framework. Although Voltaire describes other civilisations as they develop in ways wholly independent of Europe, his narrative shifts of perspective are usually strategic manœuvres in which Europe remains his main subject. It was this, only sporadically ironic, account of the rise of modern Europe which was read, translated and reviewed throughout Britain and North America, and which shaped international opinion of Voltaire as a historian. Gibbon, Robertson and Hume read and absorbed the early versions of the *Essai* long before a more bitterly satirical, older Voltaire had reshaped the text into a more blatant contest between reason and unreason.

The *Essai* provided its readers with the outlines of an Enlightenment narrative of the rise of Europe; many of its essential features would later be elaborated by British and American historians attempting to construct a satisfactory history of their own civilisation. The story of the *Essai* opens in China and India. The initial perspective is widened before the narrative proper begins with the reign of Charlemagne (not, in Voltaire's view, a golden age), and a backward glance at the destruction of the Roman Empire. Voltaire, like the Gibbon of the notorious chapters 15 and 16 of *The Decline and Fall*, identifies Christianity as a major cause of the weakening and collapse of the Roman Empire. As the narrative travels through the chaos of the early Middle Ages, Voltaire shows the Church gradually grasping at power. On balance, however, he sees this institution as a force for civilisation ('on sentait qu'elle . . . était faite pour donner des leçons aux

M. de Voltaire (17 vols.; Geneva, 1756). The *Essai* makes up volumes XI to XIV of this edition. See also *De la Cour au Jardin*, 196–9; 298–300.

[76] This, in a sophisticated way, is the thrust of much of the interpretation in J. H. Brumfitt, *Voltaire, Historian* (revised edn, Oxford, 1970).

autres'), and even as a kind of intermediate power in the states where it operates ('un frein qui retienne les souverains', I, 492, 529: 1756, XI, 263, 306). The Crusades and the ravages of Genghis Khan form part of a post-classical pattern of barbarian incursions world-wide. In this context, the Crusades are merely the last explosion of barbarian restlessness, temporarily disrupting the underlying tendency of European societies, from the thirteenth century onwards, towards synthesis, civility and urbanisation. The rigours of aristocratic and church-sponsored forms of feudalism are steadily attenuated as chivalry harmonises social relations and monarchy gains ground. By the fourteenth century, in Italy and elsewhere, municipal incorporation has led to advances in the arts and sciences, and to the recovery of natural rights lost during the destruction of the Roman Empire: 'les hommes ne rentrèrent que par degrés et très difficilement dans leur droit naturel' (I, 777: 1756, XII, 187). The cultivated civil society of the Ottoman Empire during this period holds out future possibilities for Europe.

By the early sixteenth century, monarchy is on a secure footing throughout the western and eastern worlds, and this, along with the increased wealth and stability brought by burgeoning commercial activity in the towns, leads to greater and more centralised internal order in the states, as well as increases in the technical sophistication and cost of warfare (II, 163–5: 1756, XIII, 36–9). This is accompanied by a cluster of artistic achievements (the word 'Renaissance' was not in use in the eighteenth century), reaching a crescendo in François I's France, which are, however, partly overshadowed by religious strife. Religious turmoil, in turn, has its origins in the gap, which had been widening since the early fifteenth century, between the learned and hence powerful clergy, and the intellectually disadvantaged laity (I, 69: 1756, XII, 98). Paradoxically, then, it is when clerical learning and power are at their height, during the papacy of Leo X, that Luther first lifts a corner of the veil which has shrouded the populace in ignorance (II, 217: 1756, XIII, 94). The 'monument' of the Church of Rome totters under the weight of this last straw (II, 251: 1756, XIII, 125). The Reformation is the ideological fruition of long gestated passions. Voltaire betrays a mild distaste for the somewhat buffoon-like Luther, and argues that, with hindsight, even legitimate resistance to the tyranny of Rome was not worth all the subsequent years of religious war in Europe. The discoveries and colonial enterprises in the Americas, which would be discussed at greater length in later editions of the *Essai*, are given brief, ironic presentation as further evidence of this persistent streak of barbarity in the Europe of the fifteenth to seventeenth centuries. The effect of the Reformation is to loosen the bonds of civil order established earlier in the sixteenth century. The ensuing disorder culminates (at least, to a French way of thinking) in the St Bartholomew Massacre, and again in the assassination of Henri IV of France. Even in the earliest texts of the *Essai*, Voltaire emphasises that Europe at this time is in the grip of an epidemic of irrational hatred ('fureur épidémique'), and public life has become a bizarre mixture of polish and fanaticism ('mélange de galanterie et de fureurs'); none of this can be said to represent an advance on the previous century (II, 541, 494: 1756, XII, 364, 281). The English, who have enriched their country through commerce, and redistributed some of their wealth, belatedly suffer a civil war along the lines of the continental religious wars (II, 466, 661: 1756, XIII, 328; XIV, 156).

By the sixteenth century, Voltaire starts to refer to the 'esprit' of the people (at this stage, it is generally one of fanaticism). As the seventeenth century unfolds, an 'esprit général' begins to evolve among the European nations. The emergence of this general spirit, however capricious and ill educated it may be, brings with it the prospect of more participatory kinds of societies in which public opinion and cultural priorities play a shaping role. By the later seventeenth century, commerce has enhanced the political role of the 'esprit' of the people, and the world seems, quite suddenly, to have outgrown religious wars. For England, this is a period of real cultural achievement: 'L'esprit de la nation acquit sous la règne de Charles II une réputation immortelle, quoique le gouvernement n'en eût point' (II, 689: 1756, XIV, 190). Rome, during the Counter-Reformation, and Holland, in its golden age, reach similar cultural heights. The European portion of the *Essai* ends with France poised to undergo a great expansion of national spirit in the age of Louis XIV. The history closes with the rejection of Christianity by China and Japan, while Persia and the Ottoman empire echo the cultural advances of the age.

Voltaire allocates a considerable amount of textual space to events outside western Europe. These, although they cannot be seen as mere tricks of perspective, function primarily as a referential framework within which the apparently normative character of the rise of the West is both comprehended and rendered problematic. Voltaire's accounts of other, non-western civilisations are appreciative, but not fully developmental. China is a particularly curious case, representing both a utopia and – since it is a society which has advanced as far as it can go – a haunting image of cultural atrophy (I, 216: 1756, XI, 19). What puzzles Voltaire is that Europe, unlike China, seems able to perpetuate its own processes of advancement, yet, with its frantic missionary and colonial activities, it lacks the Chinese genius for self-sufficiency. In praising the great isolationist civilisations, China and Japan (who finally banish Europe from their midst at the very end of the *Essai*), Voltaire attacks the greed of Europe, and its perverse desire to transmit its culture to other parts of the globe:

Nos peuples occidentaux ont fait éclater dans toutes ces découvertes une grande supériorité d'esprit et de courage sur les notions orientales ... Mais la nature leur avait donné sur nous un avantage qui balance tous les nôtres: c'est qu'elles n'avaient nul besoin de nous, et que nous avions besoin d'elles.

(II, 325: 1756, XIII, 207)

Many of Voltaire's non-western chapters (especially those on the Spanish depredations in the Americas) are similarly instrumental to his moral message that the East – a world in which stasis and isolation, rather than furious activity and cultural interaction, are the norms – is essential to the self-understanding of the West.

Voltaire's self-reflexivity also informs the European portions of the narrative where he is, on occasion, suspicious of his own tendency to seek out signs of cultural sophistication and civility, and wary of the imaginative seductions of periods simultaneously glittering and barbaric (for example, II, 494: 1756, XIII, 364). He is enthralled and horrified by the courts of François I and the Emperor Charles V which are at once chivalric, courteous and violently factious. In a final revision, he remarks: 'Cette politesse brillait même au milieu des crimes: c'était une robe d'or et de soie ensanglantée' (II, 135). Despite such *frissons*, Voltaire stops well short of the kind of critique of the moral snares of civilisation which Jean Jacques Rousseau mounted around the same time.[77] At bottom, Voltaire sees no actual connivance between aesthetic and inhumane pursuits, and he objected to this strain in the argument of the *Discours sur ... l'inegalité* in a letter to Rousseau himself: 'Avouez que le badinage de Marot n'a pas produit La St Barthélemi, et que la tragédie du Cid ne causa pas les guerres de la Fronde.'[78]

Revision

With his perception of his own artistic practice sharpened by Rousseau, Voltaire remained acutely aware of the moral difficulties of salvaging an artistically coherent narrative from the past without giving up to irony a sense of progress in European history. There are moments of savage irony – the sections on the Crusades and the New World discoveries, for instance- but these are contained and absorbed within the larger developmental structure. After 1756, the text of the *Essai* was substantially expanded, with new information and evidence, and also with added remarks and asides, many of these acerbic, satirical, and suggestive of growing doubts about the inherent value of history.[79] These revisions

[77] For intimate evidence of Voltaire's hostility to Rousseau, see George R. Havens, *Voltaire's Marginalia on the Pages of Rousseau* (New York, 1966).

[78] Voltaire to Rousseau (30 August 1755), Best. D6451.

[79] The 1756 text of the *Essai* is a more straightforwardly expanded version of the 1754 texts (Pomeau, *Essai*, pp.lxviii–lxxi), with additional information on feudal government, artistic and legal developments in the Middle Ages, and on the East (including Genghis Khan).

reveal a changing Voltaire, more inclined to subordinate history to his moral crusade against 'l'infâme', more pessimistic about human nature, and more virulently hostile to the clergy. In the last quarter century of his literary career, Voltaire showed a new preference for shorter textual formats as vehicles for effective propaganda. Accordingly, many of the revisions to the *Essai* have the effect of reducing long developmental sections to sharp, arresting anecdote, and breaking the evolutionary thrust of the narrative. For example, in the 1756 text, he argues that, throughout the Middle Ages, fundamental changes occurred in Europe which steadily increased the sum of human liberty. However, in a textual revision of 1769, he supplements this with a remark that, even by the late fifteenth century, very little had actually happened to mitigate the barbarousness of the times: 'Les mœurs ne furent pas meilleurs ni en France, ni en Angleterre, ni en Allemagne, ni dans le Nord. La barbarie, la superstition, l'ignorance couvraient la face du monde, excepté en Italie' (II, 10). Gradually, Voltaire comes to see the Middle Ages as the opposite, rather than the precursor of modern Europe.

Later texts tend to distil the ironic character of individual episodes in history. Even when discussing the Crusades, already characterised as an absurd, futile act of fanaticism, Voltaire intensifies, in a revision of 1761, the irony of the crusaders' attack on Constantinople: 'Ainsi les chrétiens dirigèrent leur croisade contre le premier prince de la chrétienté' (I, 581). The narrative is constantly undercut by these new verbal flounces about the futility of it all; François I's France is suddenly dismissed as barbarous, and humanists such as Pico della Mirandola are now held up for ridicule as examples of the blind ignorance of Renaissance Italy (II, 202 (1769); II, 89 (1761)). With each incremental set of revisions, the satirist steadily gets the better of the historian. The historical narrative of the *Essai* is subtly remoulded into a contest between the archetypes of reason and fanaticism. In another instance of this process, Voltaire originally attributed the desire of the crusaders to crusade to religious prejudice, avarice and restlessness; in 1761, however, this behaviour is redescribed in archetypal terms: 'Cette fureur épidémique parut alors pour la première fois, afin qu'il n'y eût aucun fléau possible qui n'eût affligé l'espèce humaine' (I, 560).

As he retouched the *Essai*, Voltaire became more preoccupied with the ironies of causality in history, and less interested in its (ultimately relatively civilised) outcome. Narrative connectives are traded for a satirical sense of necessity. The rudimentary causal coherence, which Voltaire originally found in the history of the world, starts to look like a Panglossian fantasy. Voltaire now sees only an unpredictable game of consequences (the word he uses to convey this is 'enchaînement'). François I's death of the new world disease, syphilis, is presented, in 1761, as an example of this ironically treacherous 'enchaînement':

C'est ainsi que les événements sont enchaînés: un pilote génois donne un univers à l'Espagne; la nature a mis dans les îles de ces climats lointains un poison qui infecte les sources de la vie; et il faut qu'un roi de France en périsse. (II, 201)

The term 'enchaînement' conveys an idea of human helplessness in the face of meaningless fatality: 'il paraît un enchaînement fatal des causes qui entrainent les hommes comme les vents poussent les sables et les flots' (II, 794: 1756, XIV, 319). The use of the term 'enchaînement' also carries with it an indirect attack on Catholic providential history of the kind most famously exemplified by Bossuet's *Discours sur l'histoire universelle* (1681). Bossuet uses the term 'enchaînement' to denote the divine order in which God simulates logical cause–effect relationships in order to give man a sense of the moral intelligibility of the world. Or as Bossuet phrases it:

ce mesme Dieu qui a fait l'enchaisnement de l'Univers ... a voulu aussi que le cours des choses humaines eust sa suite et ses proportions.[80]

Voltaire's use of the word 'enchaînement' suggests a parodic reworking of theocentric universal history. Bossuet's God, by acting directly upon human passions, produces a historical order identical to the providential order, whereas Voltaire's 'enchaînement' reveals a moral sequence discontinuous with or in ironic relation to the historical one.[81]

Epistemological problems once again

With each revised stage of the *Essai*, the balance of authority shifts away from history and towards the narrator who submits his material to his own rational and moral mediation. In 1756, Voltaire had acknowledged that a selective evaluation of the past would deprive some parts of history of their significance: 'vous attachant toujours aux événements et aux mœurs, vous franchissez tous ces espaces vides pour venir aux temps marquées par de grandes choses' (II, 785: 1756, XIV, 308). As later versions of the *Essai* metamorphose history into moral typology, the past seems to lack content; it oscillates between empty spaces ('espaces vides') and moments of moral illumination. The additional moralising and satiric asides bestow only sporadic and contingent value upon the content of history, and Voltaire appears to have reverted to the epistemological preoccupations of his youth. His partial solution to the problem was, in 1769, to prefix to the *Essai* an anthropological study of early human civilisations, *La Philosophie de*

[80] Jacques-Bénigne Bossuet, *Discours sur l'histoire universelle à Monseigneur le Dauphin: pour expliquer la suite de la Religion et les changemens des Empires* (Paris, 1681), 437. The work gives an overview of the rise and fall of empires before and after Christ up until the reign of Charlemagne.

[81] For a less pessimistic account of 'enchaînement, however, see Voltaire's article 'Chaîne des événements', *Dictionnaire philosophique portatif* (1764 and after), eds. R. Naves and Julien Benda, (Paris, 1954).

l'histoire. This innovative pseudo-history of man in the ancient world identifies the natural and constant aspects of human behaviour with regard to language, social interaction and religious belief.[82] Originally published separately in 1765, *La Philosophie* provides, in its new position, a comprehensive statement on the natural determinants of human civilisation as a kind of theoretical underpinning for the history of variations in human custom in the *Essai.* Nevertheless, *La Philosophie* and the *Essai* need to be read separately if Voltaire's ideas of history are not be subordinated to his mechanist sociology of early man. This need for separate reading is, at one level, implicit in the distinction which Voltaire makes in *La Philosophie* between nascent (or natural) reason and cultivated reason. He evaluates primitive societies according to how far they have realised natural, moral and rational human potentialities. All societies progress from primitive reason ('raison commencée') to advanced reason ('raison cultivée') through a sequence of religious and political forms: at the religious level, from intuitive monotheism, to superstitious polytheism, and then to sophisticated monotheist belief in a rewarding and punishing god; at the political level, from theocracy to republicanism or monarchy.[83] In advancing cultures, cultivated reason brings an unconscious return to the intuitions of primitive reason; this, for example is the essence of the achievement of ancient Greece and Rome.[84] By representing reason as a potentiality released through personal and collective development, Voltaire tries to put history back on a semi-empirical footing. Even so, the historical twist which he gives to natural moral law, does not, finally, enable him to extricate this work from the mechanistic and uniform character of his youthful Newtonianism.

The later texts of the *Essai* continue to preserve a degree of emphasis upon human diversity and unpredictability. Natural impulses are, Voltaire argues, the foundation of ethical behaviour throughout the world (do as

82 *La Philosophie de l'histoire* (1765), *Works*, LIX. This work was added, after some alterations, as a preface to the *Essai* in the Cramer edition of 1769 as volume VIII of the *Collection complète des Oeuvres de M. de Voltaire* (45 vols.; Geneva, 1768–96). On Voltaire's contribution to the development of anthropology, see Michèle Duchet, *Anthropologie et histoire au siècle des lumières* (Paris, 1971). Also, Grell, *L'histoire entre érudition et philosophie*, 100–5.

83 The whole discussion of early forms of religious belief owes something to Voltaire's early acquaintance, Bolingbroke; the sections on the Pentateuch echo the sceptical tone of the fourth letter of Bolingbroke's *Letters on the Study and Use of History* (first published, 1752). The vexed question of Bolingbroke's influence on Voltaire is addressed by Rousseau, 'L'Angleterre et Voltaire', *SVEC*, 147 (1976), 820–23. Voltaire's response to Bolingbroke can also be gauged directly from his *Défense de milord Bolingbroke* (1752), *Moland*, XXIII, 547–54, and his *Examen important de milord Bolingbroke* (1766 and 1767), ed. Roland Mortier, *Works*, LXII (1987), 127–362, as well as from the numerous references in the *Essai.* In the *Examen*, Voltaire, writing as an imagined Bolingbroke, ventriloquises him as a scathing satirist against many tenets of Judaeo-Christianity – a clear indication that, by this time, the balance between former pupil and master had shifted in Voltaire's favour.

84 *Works*, LIX, 180.

you would be done by, do not steal from your neighbour, respect your parents, and so on), but this is not, as he reiterates at the end of *La Philosophie*, an adequate basis for a historical study of different cultures.[85] Even in this theoretical work, he stresses the discontinuity between moral laws which are naturally intuited ('lois ... naturelles, communes à tous') and political laws which are artificial, arbitrary ('lois purement civiles, éternellement arbitraires'), and best judged according to their social utility (a pragmatism closer to Hume than to Newton).[86] Nature, since it is incapable of modification, is a condition of stability; human variety and identities are culturally generated. Even in *La Philosophie de l'histoire*, perhaps the most mechanistic of his writings on human history, Voltaire allows room for a cultural history of individual and national variety, and for difference at the level of manners, customs and positive laws. The movement of Voltaire's historical concerns away from the political and cultural towards ethical and metaphysical questions is consistent with a general shift in his public persona during this period. From his years as a courtier and socialite in Paris and Berlin, through a period of crisis, and a recuperation of dignity and moral authority at Ferney, Voltaire's personal preoccupations had changed enormously. His early cosmopolitanism, which reflected both his social aspirations and his affection for modern European civilisation, gave way to a universalism of humanitarian concern. The ethical preoccupations of *La Philosophie de l'histoire* and the later texts of the two major histories are of a piece with his public campaigns for the Calas family, Sirven and La Barre. More than any other historian in this study, Voltaire projected himself as the final signified of his own works. The authority of this extra-textual self correlates with the defiant stylishness of these histories; his style is offered as evidence of civility, an exemplary act of aesthetic ordering by the autonomous and self-aware 'esprit philosophique' of its creator. For this reason, perhaps, Voltaire's personality proved and continues to prove more seductive to his French, British and American readers than the brand of cultural history which he invented.

[85] *Works*, LIX, 274–5.
[86] *Works*, LIX, 274.

3

European contexts in Hume's *History of England*

David Hume's *History of England* (1754–62) earned him rapid and unwelcome recognition as the Voltaire of British history, not least from Voltaire himself who found the work as philosophical, rational and cosmopolitan as his own.[1] Commentators as astute as Horace Walpole and Samuel Johnson thought that Hume had tried to imitate Voltaire, although Hume denied it, rightly feeling that his work presented British readers with a new kind of national history, at once more sophisticated and more uncomfortable than anything to be found in the *Siècle de Louis XIV*.[2] Modern critics have tended to confirm Hume's estimation of his own achievement as the first philosophically independent history of the Enlightenment age. They have, however, tended to praise the *History*'s analysis of the changing historical fortunes of the British constitution and British politics at the expense of the cosmopolitan dimension celebrated by Voltaire. For Hume's *History of England* seemed to his contemporaries to speak to a European audience on European themes, and to provide a historiographical model for other national narratives. The *History*, which covers the period from the invasion of Julius Caesar to the accession of William III, was written (like a witch's spell, quipped one reviewer) in reverse order: the two volumes on the seventeenth century appeared (as a kind of *Siècle des Stuart*) in 1754 and 1756, the two on the Tudor period in 1759, and the medieval and pre-

[1] Voltaire's review of Hume's *History* in the *Gazette Littéraire* (2 May, 1764) can be found in the *Oeuvres complètes*, XXV, 169–73. Hume wrote to Abbé le Blanc in 1755, 'In this Countrey, they call me his [Voltaire's] Pupil, and think that my History is an Imitation of his Siecle de Louis XIV. This Opinion flatters very much my Vanity; but the Truth is, that my History was plan'd, and in a great measure compos'd, before the Appearance of that Agreeable Work', *The Letters of David Hume*, ed. J. Y. T Greig (2 vols.; Oxford, 1932) [hereafter cited as *Letters*], no. 113. Hume did mention his 'historical projects' to Lord Kames as early as 1747, *Letters*, no. 54. Hume was, however, librarian to the Advocates' Library in Edinburgh from 1752 to 1757 where he had access to a copy of the *Siècle de Louis XIV*. See Brian Hillyard, 'The Keepership of David Hume' in *For the Encouragement of Learning: Scotland's National Library, 1689–1989*, eds. Patrick Cadell and Ann Matheson (London, 1989).

[2] Walpole remarks that 'his [Hume's] style, which is the best we have in history, and his manner, imitated from Voltaire, are very pleasing', *Horace Walpole's Correspondence*, ed. W. S. Lewis (48 vols.; New Haven, 1937–83), XXXV, 214. Boswell quotes Johnson as saying 'Hume would never have written History, had not Voltaire written it before him', *Boswell's Life of Johnson*, ed. G. B. Hill, revised L. F. Powell (6 vols.; Oxford, 1934–50), II, 53.

medieval pair in 1761.[3] All of these were considerably revised during Hume's lifetime; the posthumous 1778 edition incorporated his last revisions and has remained the standard text ever since. The Stuart volumes, in many ways the most artistically accomplished portion of the *History*, originally appeared under the title the *History of Great Britain*. The work became the *History of England* with the publication of the Tudor volumes as Hume came, more and more, to describe Scotland and Wales along an English axis. This might, at first sight, suggest a narrowing of national concerns during the composition of the history. In fact, the reverse is the case, since the diversities of British history came to matter less to Hume than his desire to bring them into focus under the perspective of a more general history of the rise of modern liberty. For this reason, I will be concentrating upon the earliest texts of the *History* as they respond to Hume's altering interests and priorities.

Among the modern critics of the *History of England*, Duncan Forbes has placed the greatest emphasis upon the cosmopolitan nature of Hume's vision of history: 'It is the European dimension of the progress of civilization', he remarks, 'that gives Hume's *History of England*, as a whole, such thematic unity as it has' – a 'Europocentricity', which, as Forbes points out elsewhere, is 'only thrown into relief when all Hume's writings on politics are considered together'.[4] Indeed, as Forbes implies, Hume's endeavour was to take the political and constitutional materials of British history (as they had been researched and reordered by so many of his predecessor historians of Britain), and insert them into a social, national and ultimately European fabric of causation.[5] Hume's philosophical grasp of this wider

[3] I will be basing my observations and quotations upon the earliest texts of Hume's volumes in order to show how the work evolved during its first composition. The first Stuart volume, *The History of Great Britain, Volume One, containing the reigns of James I and Charles I* (1754), is most readily available in Duncan Forbes' Penguin edition (Harmondsworth, 1970) and will be cited from this edition. The second Stuart volume, which came out under the title *The History of Great Britain containing the Commonwealth, and the reigns of Charles II. and James II* (1756, dated 1757) will be cited from this first edition. The two Stuart volumes were the most heavily revised, notably in an edition of 1759. The two Tudor volumes appeared in 1759 under the title *The History of England under the House of Tudor*. The two medieval volumes appeared in 1761 (dated 1762) under the title *The History of England from the Invasion of Julius Caesar to the Accession of Henry VII*.

The above texts appear as the first citation in the text of my chapter. I also supply, both to indicate revisions and to facilitate access, a second citation in my text from a modern reprint of the final 1778 version of Hume's work, *The History of England*, ed. William B. Todd (7 vols.; Indianapolis, 1983). In this edition, volumes I and II coincide, respectively, with the first and second medieval volumes, volumes III and IV with the first and second Tudor volumes, and volumes V and VI with the two Stuart volumes. The most important treatment of Hume's revisions is Graeme Paul Slater's 'Authorship and Authority in Hume's *History of England*' (Oxford D.Phil, 1990).

[4] Duncan Forbes, 'The European, or Cosmopolitan Dimension in Hume's Science of Politics', *British Journal for Eighteenth-Century Studies*, 1 (1978), 59; Forbes, 'Introduction' to *The History of Great Britain*, 23.

[5] On Hume as a political and constitutional historian in dialogue with his seventeenth- and

fabric enabled him to gain an apparently detached perspective on the peculiarities and parochialisms of British history, and the deep structure of his stylistically and generically eclectic historical narrative is much illuminated by the political theory of the *Essays*, many of which were published before or around the time of the *History*. This chapter will build on Forbes' findings about the cosmopolitan theme of Hume's *History*, and explore the ways in which Hume developed his own unique form of historical cosmopolitanism, not only in partnership with the philosophical politics of the *Essays*, but more significantly, perhaps, as a consequence of accepting, over six volumes, the constraints of narrative, and so being brought into dialogue with other literary forms. It will be necessary, at least initially, to resist the tendency of many Hume scholars to map the philosophical coordinates of the *Essays* onto the very different landscape of the *History*. In the process, we will gain insight into the ways in which Hume based his authority as a cosmopolitan historian upon his own artistic accountability to the contingencies of character and action. By comparison, Voltaire's own brand of historical cosmopolitanism will (as Hume would no doubt have concurred) appear to have been too easily won from the aesthetic ordering of history.

In order to understand the evolution of Hume's cosmopolitan perspectives, it is necessary to approach the volumes of the *History* in order of publication, starting with the Stuart period and ending with the Middle Ages. The two Stuart volumes, especially in their earliest unrevised form, are not in any obvious sense cosmopolitan in perspective or context. In their minute and absorbing analyses of the motives and actions of great men, these volumes appear, rather, to belong to the kind of classical history which examines and prescribes prudent statecraft; they are Tacitean in their ruthless dissection of individual and collective depravity, yet Thucydidean in their depiction of politics as discourse-in-action.[6] It is not until the narrative of the seventeenth century is supplemented with the Tudor and medieval portions of the *History*, that its place (albeit an untypical, even deviant one) in the developmental patterns of European history becomes fully apparent. Subsequent revisions to the Stuart volumes further acknowledge the modifying presence of the history of European civilisation embedded in the Tudor and medieval sections. Nevertheless, the fact that the Stuart volumes (which contain many of the most dazzling literary performances of the *History*) were first printed as a separate entity should caution us against reading them too closely in conjunction with the

eighteenth-century precursors, see Duncan Forbes, *Hume's Philosophical Politics* (Cambridge, 1975); Victor Wexler, *David Hume and the History of England* (Philadelphia, 1979); Laird Okie, *Augustan Historical Writing: Histories of England in the English Enlightenment* (Lantam, MD, 1991).

[6] On Hume's *History* and the notion of prudent statecraft, see Nicholas Phillipson, *Hume* (London, 1989), 76–82.

narrative of European progress in the other volumes. Hume came to a comparative European perspective by way of a search for an impartial and historicist approach to British constitutional history. This search can be seen at its earliest and most strenuous stage in the volumes dealing with the contentious and divisive history of seventeenth-century Britain.

Impartiality and artistry

Hume often stated that he had been spurred on to write the history of seventeenth-century Britain by his observation that none of his predecessors had sufficiently divested themselves of Whig or Tory partialities to produce a work unclouded by party prejudice. After an initial period of admiration, Hume even came to regard the sophisticated work of Rapin de Thoyras as tainted by party bias.[7] 'No man has yet arisen', he remarked disingenuously in the closing pages of the *History*, 'who has payed an entire regard to truth, and has dared to expose her, without covering or disguise, to the eyes of the prejudiced public' (227: VI, 532). The failure of the public to recognise and applaud the non-partisan character of his own 'regard to truth' was a source of great exasperation to Hume.[8] The detachment from, or, at least, alternation between Whig and Tory party perspectives in Hume's *History* has dominated critical discussion of this work, and it is not my purpose to contribute to this debate.[9] Although Forbes' description of Hume as a 'sceptical Whig', rather than a Tory or any other kind of Whig, is now widely accepted, even this designation does not adequately capture the evolutionary nature of his political thinking.[10] The many asides and digressions in the *History* on the way in which constitutional arrangements were conventionally understood at given points in history, are often taken together by modern interpreters to suggest that Hume felt that Britain had possessed not one, but a series of constitutions. For Hume, the key to understanding why the British people behaved in particular ways at particular times often lies in the country's constitution as it was then understood or (as was the case for much of the seventeenth century) contested. Less remarked upon is the way in which Hume links this notion of successive British constitutions to an evolutionary account of the very language of politics. Hume repeatedly alerts his readers to the anachronistic fallacies of both Whig and Tory readings of the past.

[7] Duncan Forbes, *Hume's Philosophical Politics*, 233–40.

[8] For example, 'Of My Own Life' (1777), *Essays Moral, Political and Literary*, ed. Eugene F. Miller (Indianapolis, 1985), xxxvii.

[9] On party positions in the *History*, see Forbes, *Hume's Philosophical Politics*; David Wootton, 'Hume, "The Historian"' in *The Cambridge Companion to Hume*, ed. David Fate Norton (Cambridge, 1993), 296–307.

[10] Forbes, 'Sceptical Whiggism, Commerce and Liberty' in *Essays on Adam Smith*, eds. A. S. Skinner and Thomas Wilson (Oxford, 1975).

One example of this is the case of Archbishop Laud, universally berated by Whig historians and polemicists for his narrow, intolerant spirit. By way of implicit rebuke to such unthinking Whig attitudes, Hume points out that, at that time, the conception religious 'toleration' had only just been added to the apparatus of European political thought, and that it is too much to expect that an English state under pressure should have made toleration an official practice: 'The maxims . . . of his administration were the same which had ever prevailed in England, and which had place in every other European nation, except Holland. To have changed them for the modern maxims of toleration, would have been esteemed a very bold and dangerous enterprise' (589–90: V, 575, expanded with a reference to Montesquieu's ideas on the state management of toleration). Hume's discussions of the conceptual evolution of terms such as 'toleration', 'constitution' and 'party' greatly influenced Robertson's work on the history of civil and religious liberty, although, unlike Robertson's, Hume's main focus tends to be upon language as the prison house, rather than the mobiliser of political action.

At first, Hume's political impartiality consists in a provocative dismantling of first Whig (in the first Stuart volume) and then Tory shibboleths (in the second). Stability of perspective is gained when, in the later part of these volumes and in the subsequent Tudor and medieval instalments, Hume begins to contextualise the story of British peculiarity within a more general European framework. Hume's philosophical perspective is also secured in two additional and more important ways in the Stuart volumes, and this sets them apart from the rest of the *History*. The first has to do with Hume's endeavour to generate a social history of religious enthusiasm in the seventeenth century. This takes place within a mock-epic reconstruction of the progress of religious and civil liberty in this period, and is inspected from an authorial position which combines Augustan satirist with social philosopher. Hume's second means of securing historical authority is effected by appropriating the detached yet feeling voice of the sentimental novelist or tragedian.[11] In both cases, the generic suppleness of Hume's *History*, and his careful artistic management of historical data serve ultimately political ends. Both perspectives enable Hume to precipitate an unusually complex (in Hume's vocabulary 'impartial') encounter between his British readers and the political meaning of their history.

Private sentiments and public consequences

Some years ago, J. C. Hilson suggested that Hume's *History* belonged, in part, to the genre of sentimental historiography described by contemporary

[11] On Hume in relation to fiction, see Leo Braudy, *Narrative Form in History and Fiction: Hume, Fielding and Gibbon* (Princeton, 1970).

Scottish rhetoricians such as Adam Smith, Lord Kames and Hugh Blair.[12] 'Sentimental historiography', Hilson explained, '... is essentially a spectatorial experience for both historian and reader; and the ideal spectator is both impartial and sympathetic, rational and feeling.'[13] Hilson cites a letter from Hume to William Mure which illustrates the way in which Hume envisaged a conjunction of impartial and sympathetic responsiveness in both his male and female readers: 'The first Quality of an Historian is to be true and impartial; the next to be interesting. If you do not say, that I have done both Parties Justice; and if Mrs Mure be not sorry for poor King Charles, I shall burn all my Papers, and return to Philosophy.' Some years later, Hume recalled that he too 'had presumed to shed a generous tear for the fate of Charles I'.[14] Hilson then goes on to give one of the best literary evaluations of the *History* to date, and to explain in scholarly detail how Hume's approach to character analysis was – in the precise, Scottish sense of the word – sentimental (rather than ironic or sceptical, as is often assumed). His test cases include Charles I in his last days, and Mary, Queen of Scots.

Hilson's diagnosis of the sentimental infectiousness of Hume's *History* is persuasive, and is corroborated by the special interest which Hume himself took, in his letters and essays, in the most sentimentally appreciative portion of his audience, the ladies.[15] Hilson saw this sentimental approach to history as a peculiarly eighteenth-century updating of the traditional, classical view of character as a good or bad exemplar of virtue and prudence in action. Beyond this, Hilson did not give any explanation as to how the sentimental aspects of Hume's *History* might relate to its wider reappraisal of British political history. He might have suggested, for instance, that the detached yet sympathetic stance of the sentimental historian is for Hume the literary corollary of the political impartiality of the constitutional historian. However, any modern critic who tries to connect the *History*'s literary and political methodologies in this way would quickly run into difficulties as soon as he or she came to consider more closely Hume's attitudes towards sympathy in art and life. In the same year as the publication of Hume's Tudor volumes, Adam Smith brought out his treatise on the moral and social function of sympathy and imagined spectatorship, the *Theory of Moral Sentiments*. Hume compiled an abstract of this work in which he singled out Smith's central notion that 'there is a

[12] J. C. Hilson, 'Hume: The Historian as Man of Feeling' in *Augustan Worlds: Essays in Honour of R. A. Humphreys*, eds. J. C. Hilson, M. M. B. Jones and J. R. Watson (Leicester, 1978).

[13] Ibid., 209.

[14] Hume to William Mure (24 October 1754), *Letters*, no.102. On Hume's encouragement of a female audience for history, see Wootton, 'David Hume, "The Historian"', 282; 'Of My Own Life', *Essays*, xxxvii.

[15] 'There is nothing which I would recommend more earnestly to my female readers than the study of history' ('Of the Study of History' (1741), *Essays*, 563).

pleasure which attends all sympathy'.[16] In a letter to Smith of the same year, Hume makes a revealing critique of this tenet of the *Theory of Moral Sentiments*:

> And indeed, as the Sympathetic Passion is a reflex Image of the principal, it must partake of its Qualities, and be painful when that is so ... It is always thought a difficult Problem to account for the Pleasure, receivd from the Tears and Grief and Sympathy of Tragedy; which would not be the Case, if all Sympathy was agreeable. An Hospital would be a more entertaining Place and a Ball.[17]

Hume, unlike Smith, finds that sympathy (or 'empathy' in modern terminology) in response to actual or artistic spectacle may be a painful, even unsettling experience. For this we may infer that, when Hume does provoke the readers of the *History* to a sentimental response, he sometimes envisages, not so much a confirmation of their sympathetic yet detached position, as a certain disruption to the amiable narrative flow of his text. We shall see below the precise ways in which Hume deploys and manipulates the disruptive potential of sentimentally moving incidents and characters. It may be noted at this stage that the function of sentiment within the political narrative of the *History of England* is not simply to enhance the author's and readers' simulation of detached spectatorship. Hume's sentimental vocabulary evokes interpretive possibilities often discontinuous with the larger political narrative of the *History*.

Hume remarked in a letter of around 1756: 'With regard to the politics and the character of princes and great men, I think I am very moderate. My views of *things* are more conformable to Whig principles; my representations of *persons* to Tory prejudices. Nothing can prove that men commonly regard more persons than things, as to find that I am commonly remembered among the Tories.'[18] Forbes found this remark unhelpful and 'superficial', and other historians have generally agreed.[19] Yet, in their essential drama of persons and things, the Stuart volumes do undeniably conform to this scheme: the monarchs, especially James I and Charles I, but also Charles II (in the earlier textual versions of this section) and James II are treated with broadly Tory sympathy for their various predicaments and for their absolutist view of the royal prerogative; even so, over and above the royal and aristocratic personalities of the volumes, Hume whiggishly, though cautiously, welcomes a larger scheme of 'things' in which the English people

[16] For this abstract and the case for Hume's authorship, see David R. Raynor, 'Hume's Abstract of Adam Smith's *Theory of Moral Sentiments*', *Journal of the History of Philosophy*, 22 (1984), 51–75. Hume's discussion of this section of the *Theory* (I.i.2.6) appears on page 67 of the abstract.

[17] Hume to Smith (28 July 1759), *Letters*, no. 169.

[18] Hume to John Clephane (?1756), *Letters*, no. 122. For a different discussion of this letter in relation to the *History*, see Donald W. Livingston, *Hume's Philosophy of Common Life* (Chicago, 1984), 263.

[19] Forbes, *Hume's Philosophical Politics*, 292.

demand and eventually obtain a liberal constitution. The readers' responses are continually exercised in the history by this tension between the demands of 'persons' and 'things.' This is not simply a case of readers being invited to split public and private judgements about monarchs. Hume goes so far as to disable the politically partial responses of his readers through his presentation of the central dilemma of the Stuart era: the bad 'fit' between the private and public selves of the monarchs and the economic, social and constitutional inevitabilities in which they find themselves. Hume often insisted that all the revisions he later made to the Stuart volumes were to the Tory side.[20] There are a number of examples of this (for example the excision of a passage in the 1754 volume discussing 'public hatred' of Buckingham and Charles I's reluctant complicity with him), although there are also a number of cases of revisions in a Whig direction (258). Hume, in fact, carried out many of the revisions in order to heighten the contrast between his Tory perspectives on (particularly the first two) Stuart monarchs and his eventual, if reluctant Whig concession as to the desirability of the 1688–9 settlement.[21] The effect is further to disorientate readers seeking to extrapolate a party position from the narrative.

No character better exemplifies the bad fit between monarchs and their times, or is drawn with more apparently Tory warmth than King Charles I. He combines the virtues and graces of a private gentleman with the self-discipline and dutiful paternalism of a public ruler: 'A kind husband, an indulgent father, a gentle master, a stedfast friend; to all these eulogies, by his conduct in private life, he was fully intitled. As a monarch too, in the exterior qualities he excelled; in the essential, he was not defective' (328: V, 220). Charles' chief fault is his failure to modify his inherited (and, in Hume's view, historically legitimate) ideas about his royal prerogative in the light of changing circumstances: 'In every other age, or nation, this monarch had been secure of a prosperous and a happy reign. But the high idea of his own authority, with which he had been imbued, made him incapable of submitting prudently to the spirit of liberty, which began to prevail among his subjects' (329: V, 221 italicises 'began'). It is Charles' imprudence, rather than any egregious act of royal tyranny (as certain Whigs would have it), which sets him on a collision course with the Commons, and precipitates his personal tragedy.

20 'Of My Own Life', *Essays*, xxxviii; Hume to Gilbert Elliot (12 March 1763), *Letters*, no. 203; Hume to Elliot (21 February 1770), *Letters*, no.439. In this last letter Hume remarks, 'I either soften or expunge many villanous seditious Whig Strokes, which had crept into [the *History*].' Slater ('Authorship and Authority', 225–34) finds many instances of Hume's softening of attitude towards (particularly the first two) Stuart monarchs.

21 A number of historians have pointed out that Hume's whiggism has affinities with that of pro-Walpole Whig theorists and propagandists earlier in the century who emphasised the *newness* of English constitutional liberties since 1688. See Isaac Kramnick, *Bolingbroke and his Circle: The Politics of Nostalgia in the Age of Walpole* (Chicago, 1972).

As the tragedy unfolds, Hume embellishes Charles' role as a sentimental hero by permitting himself to enter into the king's feeling heart. When, for example, in the winter of 1645, Charles finds himself unable to pay the wages of his loyal officers, Hume imagines that 'the affectionate duty . . . of his more generous friends, who respected his misfortunes and his virtues, as much as his dignity, *must have wrung his heart* with new sorrow' (my italics, 610: V, 479). Hume's eulogising of Charles' dignity and tender loyalties to his family and friends reaches a crescendo during the scenes of his trial and his last farewell to his children (675–80: V, 535–9). Although Clarendon's *History of the Rebellion* is an intimate source for these sections, Hume sets out to exceed even this most Tory of predecessors in the fervour of his royalism. For example, Clarendon mentions that, on his way to his trial, Charles was publicly insulted when 'one [person] spit in his face; which his Majesty, without expressing any trouble, wiped off with his Handkerchief.'[22] Hume reports the same incident in a more emotive tone, multiplying the number of soldiers involved and emphasising Charles' devout heroism: 'Some of [the soldiers] were permitted to go to the utmost length of brutal insolence, and to spit in his face, as he was conveyed along the passage to the court. To excite a sentiment of piety, was the only effect which this inhuman insult was able to operate upon him' (678: V, 537). Hume had to rely on sources other than Clarendon for the execution itself, since the earlier historian had omitted all details of that event. '[Clarendon] himself', Hume later explained in the essay 'Of Tragedy', 'as well as the readers of that age, were too deeply concerned in the events, and felt a pain from subjects, which an historian and a reader of another age would regard as the most pathetic and most interesting.'[23] Thus, Hume's description of the execution and its aftermath, despite some recognisably Clarendonian touches (when, for example, Hume says that this act 'had thrown an indelible stain upon the nation'), acquires the 'pathetic and interesting' elements of a sentimental tragedy: 'The very pulpits were bedewed with unsuborned tears' (682: V, 541). Hume mediates the tragedy through the spectatorship of the English people suddenly united in sorrow: 'It is impossible to describe the grief, indignation, and astonishment, which took place, not only among the spectators, who were overwhelmed with a flood of sorrow, but thro'out the whole nation' (682: V, 540–1). Hume's pathetic rendition of the martyrdom of Charles I was much imitated in the eighteenth century, not least by the more overtly sentimental Tory historian Oliver Goldsmith.[24]

[22] Edward Hyde, First Earl of Clarendon, *The History of the Rebellion and Civil Wars of England, Begun in the Year 1641* (3 vols.; Oxford, 1702–4), I, 196.

[23] 'Of Tragedy' (1757), *Essays*, 223–4.

[24] Oliver Goldsmith, *The History of England* (4 vols.; London, 1777), III, 314. Goldsmith copies and embellishes Hume's words.

In addition to extending, in a certain direction, the emotional range of narrative history, Hume's sentimental register has an important function for the political analysis in the work. The execution of Charles I gives rise to some general reflections on the people's right of resistance to their sovereign (685–7: V, 544–6). Hume concludes that it is always better for the happiness of the realm for elites not to say too much about the people's right of resistance, and to inculcate instead a 'doctrine of obedience' supported by a mystique of monarchy. He admonishes his readers that 'that illusion, if it be an illusion, which teaches us to pay a sacred regard to the persons of princes' is so 'salutary' for the peace of the nation, that it should almost never be shattered by executing the king (686: V, 545). In his account of the life of Charles I and the other Stuart monarchs, Hume may indeed be suggesting that sentimental attachment to monarchy might fulfil, in the eighteenth century, the function once performed, in the seventeenth, by this 'sacred regard' to kings. As well as appearing moved by the events he describes, Hume embraces the sociological cunning of sentiment in order to engage his readers' affections for the monarchy.

Few of Hume's contemporaries needed reminding, either in pious or in sentimental language, that the execution of Charles I was a stain on the national past. Catharine Macaulay provoked outrage when, a few years later, she suggested otherwise.[25] The purpose of Hume's Tory-sentimental tragedy of Charles I is, rather, to provide his readers (especially the Whigs among them) with a satisfactory means of integrating their responses to the private and public events of this period. The emotional trauma of Charles' story is replayed in the language of sentiment; this language both registers and absorbs its disruptive political significance. The most recalcitrant Whigs are thus invited to respond to Charles as a 'good' man, which is to say, a man, as any Whig might recognise, whose private virtues nourished his sense of public duty (however misjudged) (684: V, 542). Hume's model of a sympathetic monarch is severely tested, however, when he writes about Charles II and James II. For, although Hume remains Tory 'as to persons' in his essentially generous treatment of the later Stuarts, he ultimately finds them neither good enough nor tragic enough to elicit a fully sentimental response. James II's lack of goodness consists in his elevation of private inclination over public requirements. At first sight, Hume's presentation of James II does, at least, appear to have the makings of another sentimental drama of royal virtue traduced. Like his father, James' 'conduct was irreproachable' in 'domestic life' (434: VI, 520). James' private affections run deep, despite his seeming inability to excite these feelings in others. For example, when, in the days immediately before

[25] Bridget Hill, *The Republican Virago: The Life and Times of Catharine Macaulay, Historian* (Oxford, 1992), 33–4.

his dethronement, his daughter Anne deserts him, paternal feelings rather than state considerations are uppermost in James' mind:

> He burst into tears, when the first intelligence of [Anne's defection] was conveyed to him. Undoubtedly he forsaw in this incident the total expiration of his royal authority: But the nearer and more intimate concern of a parent laid hold of his heart; when he found himself abandoned in his uttermost distress by a child, and a virtuous child, whom he had ever regarded with the most tender affection.
>
> (428: VI, 513)

James' mistake, however, is to make his private self and circle ('his own temper' and 'those persons, with whom he secretly consulted') the 'springs of his administration' (377–8: VI, 452). His public persona, far from being grounded in his private virtues (as Charles I's had been), is a 'mask' which he wears and drops by turns (398: VI, 477).

Hume sentimentalises James II sufficiently to enable his readers to re-evaluate Whig prejudice against him, though Hume's diagnosis of the failure of James' monarchy is, ultimately, a Whig one; James II lacks a sense of public responsibility, and is never inhibited from trampling upon his people's religious sensibilities (392: VI, 470). Further to intensify this Whig reorientation of the second Stuart volume, Hume redirects the sentimental vocabulary towards James' suffering people. The violent repression of Monmouth's rebellion is vividly reported. Hume retells the story of a young woman from Bridgwater who pleaded with one of James' brutal henchmen, Colonel Kirke, for the life of her captured brother: '[she] flung herself at Kirke's feet, armed with all the charms, which beauty and innocence, bathed in tears, could bestow on her' (386: VI, 462). Kirke ('the tyrant', 'the wanton savage') demands her virginity as the price of her brother's life; this granted, he hangs the brother in front of her (386: VI, 462–3). She then suffers the sentimental fate of all ruined maids by descending into madness: 'Rage and despair and indignation took possession of her mind, and deprived her for ever of her senses' (386: VI, 463). 'The whole country', adds Hume, lest his readers think that this was merely an isolated incident, 'innocent as well as guilty, were exposed to the ravages of this barbarian' (386: VI, 463).

Hume's presentation of Charles II has similarities with that of James II. Hume is admiring, even indulgent towards the domestic Charles, and in 'private life', Charles II has many of the virtues of his brother: 'He was an easy generous lover, a civil obliging husband, a friendly brother, an indulgent father, and a good natured master' (371: VI, 446–7). Hume is untroubled by Charles' carefree promiscuity; he admires, and echoes in passing, Dryden's analogy of Charles II as King David imparting 'vigorous warmth ... / To Wives and Slaves' (453: VI, 543). Like his brother, too, Charles is 'much fitted for private life, preferably to public', and his royal self is so completely absorbed into the private man that his very private virtues and affections are corrupted: 'he had a heart not very capable of sincere friendship, and he had secretly fostered a very bad opinion and distrust of mankind' (158: VI, 189). Hume derives this last observation from Gilbert Burnet's *History of his Own Time* (the first part of which was published in 1724): '[Charles II] had a very ill opinion both of men and women ... He thought that no body did serve him out of love: And so was quits with all the world, and loved others as little as he thought they loved him.'[26] Burnet's famous pen portrait of Charles II as a hypocrite, dissembler, and thoroughly modern Tiberius is explicitly rejected by Hume (373: VI, 448). In other respects, however, Hume's depiction of Charles II is deeply indebted to Burnet. Burnet's favourite word for describing Charles is 'easy': 'He was affable and easy, and loved to be made so by all about him. The great art of keeping him long was, the being easy, and the making of every thing easy to him.'[27] Hume expands this as a still fuller portrait of a monarch engagingly, but dangerously at ease with his throne: 'Strongly desirous by his natural temper to be easy himself, and to make every body else easy'; 'It was the charms of this sauntering easy life, as much as any force of passion or appetite for pleasure, which, during the latter part of his life, attached Charles to his mistresses' (256: VI, 309). In Dryden's *Absalom and Achitophel*, it is the common 'pamper'd' people, who are 'debauch'd with ease' whereas Achitophel/Shaftesbury is 'Prodigal of Ease'.[28] Hume reverses these ascriptions of ease, contrasting the frenetic activity and bigotry of Shaftesbury and the people with the languid indifference of Charles. Where Burnet signifies by the word 'ease' Charles's mask of hypocrisy, Hume encapsulates in this word the usurpation of the public by the private sphere.

Further to reinforce this point, Hume contrasts Charles' inappropriate 'ease' with the purposeful activity of his rival Louis XIV: 'Lewis availed himself of every opportunity to aggrandize his people, while Charles, sunk in indolence and pleasure, neglected all the noble arts of government' (248: VI, 299). Hume follows Voltaire closely (even, on occasions, to the extent of echoing phrases from *Le Siècle de Louis XIV*) in representing Louis XIV as a moderniser who brings the benefits of centralised financial and military administration to his country. Nearly all of Voltaire's and Hume's predecessors, including Montesquieu, had condemned Louis XIV as the personification of despotism or universal monarchy. Like Voltaire, however, Hume applauds Louis' success in taming the 'mutinous spirit' of the nobility, subjugating the parlements, and promoting industry and

[26] Gilbert Burnet, *History of his Own Time* (Dublin, 1724), 55.

[27] Ibid., 54.

[28] John Dryden, *Absalom and Achitophel* (1681) in *Poems*, ed. James Kinsley (4 vols.; Oxford, 1958), I, lines 47 and 168.

bravery among his people: 'His finances were reduced to order: A naval power created: His armies encreased and disciplined: Magazines and military stores provided: And ... the magnificence of his court was supported beyond all former example' (181: VI, 216–17). This echoes a passage in *Le Siècle de Louis XIV*: 'La discipline fut rétablie dans les troupes, comme l'ordre dans les finances. la magnificence et la décence embellirent sa cour'.[29] From Charles II's indolent and lack-lustre court, Hume glimpses across the water the brilliant but cruel Versailles of Louis XIV.

It is a measure of Hume's scholarly earnestness as a historian that he was willing, in later versions of the second Stuart volume, to alter the balance of his parallel lives of the easy Charles and ambitious Louis in the light of new evidence. Hume's rummagings among documents at the Scots College in Paris produced some disturbing revelations about Charles' secret dealings with Louis XIV, and about his religious attitudes. James II's memoirs came as a particular surprise, as Hume explained to the Earl of Hardwick:

> I see from these Memoirs, that I have in one particular somewhat mistaken K. Charles's Character. I thought that his careless negligent Temper had rendered him incapable of Bigotry; and that he floated all his Life between Deism and Popery: But I find, that Lord Halifax better knew his Sentiments, when he says, that the King only affected Irreligion in order to cover his Zeal for the Catholic religion.[30]

Hume's own researches were further supported by the publication of John Dalrymple's *Memoirs of Great Britain and Ireland* (1771) which adduced documentary evidence to 'prove' that Charles II secretly planned to make Catholicism the state religion. Thereafter, Hume set about making piecemeal revisions to the *History* emphasising Charles' connivances with France, his attachment to the Catholic faith, and, most seriously, his conspiratorial plan 'for changing the religion and subverting the constitution of England' (1983, VI, 308, 448, 286). Charles II had been a favourite figure with Tory opponents of Walpole who contrasted the boorish Hanoverians ('Still Dunce the second reigns like Dunce the first') with the elegance of the merry monarch.[31] Despite his declared policy of making revisions 'invariably to the Tory side', Hume was obliged to compromise the artistic unity of his portrait of Charles II in a more whiggish and, indeed, Burnetian presentation of this monarch. In so doing, Hume could no longer retain the original dialectic between his mild Tory sympathies

[29] *Siècle de Louis XIV*, ed. Pomeau, 977. On the image of Louis XIV in the period, see N. R. Johnson, 'Louis XIV and the Age of Enlightenment: The Myth of the Sun King from 1715–1789', *SVEC*, 172 (1978).

[30] Hume to Hardwick (23 July, 1764), *Letters*, no. 245. On Hume's discoveries about Charles II, see also nos. 178 and 248.

[31] Ronald Hutton, *Charles the Second, King of England, Scotland and Ireland* (Oxford, 1989), 446.

with Charles II and his Whig sense of the general direction of British history during the Restoration period.

Whig inevitabilities

In both the early and later editions of the second Stuart volume, Hume argues that Charles II and James II failed to perceive the general drift, not only of domestic developments, but also of European affairs as a whole. Charles' idleness or partiality in foreign policy leads his country into two (in Hume's view futile) Dutch wars, and to neglect its proper international role as the bulwark against France and arbitrator of the balance of power in Europe. Charles' refusal to intervene constructively in favour of the Dutch in the peace negotiations between France and Holland in 1677 is cited as one of several examples of his stupidity in foreign policy: 'It is certain, that this was the critical moment, when the King both might with ease have preserved the ballance of power in Europe, which it has since cost this island an infinite profusion of blood and treasure to restore ... This opportunity being neglected, the wound became incurable' (255: VI, 308). Hume's perception of the general shape and destiny of Europe in this period, as well as his berating of Britain's failure to support the Dutch interest, is overtly indebted to William Temple's *Memoirs of what Past in Christendom from the war begun 1672* (1692). Temple, who was the English ambassador to the Hague in the late 1660s and architect of the triple alliance between England, Holland and Sweden, is the Whig hero of the European sections of the narrative. Hume's admiration for Temple as an author 'unpolluted by that inundation of vice and licentiousness, which overwhelmed the nation' is exceeded only by his esteem for the private man 'full of honour and humanity' (454: VI, 544). Temple's *Memoirs* are used to illustrate Charles' blindness in foreign policy (later editions only, VI, 220–1). Hume's reading of Dutch history is Orangist rather than republican in orientation, and lays Whig ground for the coming of William of Orange (whose bravery in battle is enthusiastically noted). This reading also springs from Hume's assessment of the balance of European affairs on the eve of the eighteenth century (241: VI, 291). Temple had worked for and Hume still advocated a model of European stability based on mutually balancing, autonomous states. Without this system of balance, Hume had earlier argued, human nature itself, and the wider sympathies of which it is capable, becomes distorted in an atmosphere of international competition.[32]

Throughout the Stuart volumes, Hume invites his readers (particularly

[32] 'Of the Balance of Power' (1752), *Essays*, 340–1; John Robertson, 'Universal Monarchy and the Liberties of Europe: David Hume's Critique of an English Whig Doctrine' in *Political Discourse in Early Modern Britain*, eds. Nicholas Phillipson and Quentin Skinner (Cambridge, 1993).

those Whigs among them still stubbornly hostile to the Stuart monarchs) to reintegrate their sense of the public history of this era with their sensitivity to the private dilemmas of its kings. Hume points to some of the Whig inevitabilities embedded in the deepest level of the history of the seventeenth century, as well as giving a general outline of the European process of modernisation. From the outset, and throughout all the upheavals it describes, the *History* points forward to an eventual denouement of Protestant, constitutional monarchy and political liberty. The resolution of the seventeenth-century story is a comic one, although the story which it brings to a conclusion is closer in tone to a bombastic mock epic of national liberty than to a triumphant Whig history of progress. The resolution, as Hume's summaries of the reign of James I and of the Glorious Revolution make clear, will guarantee neither stability nor the 'best system of government' for Britain (226; VI, 531; also 304: VI, 367). Although Hume agrees with the Whigs that the 1688–9 settlement has indeed 'put the nature of the English constitution beyond all controversy', he stipulates that these events in fact arose from a series of accidents and an 'unavoidable situation of affairs', and owe nothing to the guiding wisdom of those heroes of the Whig pantheon, the members of the Convention parliament who put the settlement together (443–4: VI, 531).

On many occasions, Hume presents these accidents and unavoidable affairs in a mock-epic or even burlesque mode. Like Samuel Butler's *Hudibras* (which Hume compliments at length on its 'just and inimitable wit'), the Civil War is imagined as a kind of diminutive *Pharsalia* (454: VI, 544). Hume exacts bitter humour from the disparity between ancient history and its seventeenth-century re-enactments. He measures the distance between such British republicans as Pym, Hamden and Vane and Roman heroes such as Cato, Brutus and Cassius:

> Compare only one circumstance, and consider its consequences. The leizure of these noble antients was totally employed in the study of Grecian eloquence and philosophy; in the cultivation of polite letters and civilized society: The whole discourse and language of the moderns were polluted with mysterious jargon, and full of the lowest and most vulgar hypocrisy. (418: V, 304)

The Scots, meanwhile, are Athenians in reverse de-civilising the rest of the world: 'Never did refined Athens so exalt in diffusing the sciences and liberal arts over a savage world ... As the Scotch now rejoiced, in communicating their barbarous zeal, and theological fervour, to the neighbouring nations' (449: V, 333). James II, in his last days as king of England, cuts a rather pathetic figure as a despotic Roman emperor:

> It is indeed singular, that a Prince, whose chief blame consisted in imprudences and misguided principles, should be exposed, from religious antipathy, to such

treatment, as even Nero, Domitian, or the most enormous tyrants ... never met from their family and friends (428: VI, 513)

The classical analogues of English history, particularly cherished by radical Whigs and country party polemicists, are assimilated to a comic epic whose machinery is risible, but whose outcome is nevertheless a happy one.[33] There will be more to say about the mock-heroic component in Hume's history of liberty when I come to discuss the presentation of religious enthusiasm.

Patterns of generic allusion are, of course, only one of the ways in which Hume explains the larger inevitabilities of seventeenth-century British history. Although Hume's characters often seem to have stepped out of the histrionic world of mock epic (James I deludes himself that he is a continental kind of absolute prince; the Scots believe that 'the mild, the humane' Charles I is as bad as 'the treacherous, the cruel, the unrelenting' King Philip II of Spain), he does explain that this is partly because they are compelled to act upon a new and unfamiliar stage (83: V, 19; 366: V, 258). Hume describes this changing stage towards the beginning of the Stuart volumes: economic developments have enlarged and secured the wealth of the commons to the detriment of an impoverished monarchy (107: V, 39); as well as attaining a more cultivated way of living, sections of the commons have also benefited from the intellectual ferment of Counter-Reformation Europe and acquired independent and liberal habits of thought (82: V, 18). The changes taking place in early seventeenth-century England add up to a 'general, but insensible revolution' in habits of thought which will later precipitate a political one (82: V, 18). For a brief moment the age of James I is a golden era, at least for one section of the population: 'Could human nature ever reach happiness, the condition of the English gentry, under so mild and benign a prince, might merit that appellation' (230: V, 135).

Hume's portrait of the early seventeenth century consciously adapts (and moves back chronologically) Clarendon's elegy for the idyllic early years of the reign of Charles I: 'this Kingdom ... enjoy'd the greatest Calm, and the fullest measure of Felicity, that any People in any Age, for so long time together, have been bless'd with; to the wonder, and envy of all the other

[33] Frank M. Turner, 'British Politics and the Demise of the Roman Republic, 1700–1939' in *Contesting Cultural Authority*: *Essays in Victorian Intellectual History* (Cambridge, 1993). Towards the end of his life, Hume contemplated further qualification to the happy ending for Britain in 1688–9 by striking out the words 'and happy' from the closing reference to 'that singular and happy Government which we enjoy at present'. He changed his mind, however: 'but as the English Government is certainly happy, though probably not calculated for Duration, by reason of its excessive Liberty, I believe it will be as well to restore them', Hume to William Strahan (3 March, 1772), *Letters*, no.472.

parts of Christendom.'[34] Having echoed his point about the happiness of England, Hume retains Clarendon's emphasis upon the unprecedented heights of personal and artistic polish attained in this era (227: V, 132).[35] Hume adds that those 'violent extremes' in manners, which would later set England apart from the rest of Europe, had not yet emerged. He chooses to ignore Clarendon's organising metaphor of good and ill husbandry. For Clarendon, England and Scotland are a garden 'planted' with arts and sciences, and later ruined by the 'ill husbandry' of Charles I and his favourites: 'the Kingdoms, we now lament, were alone look'd upon as the Garden of the world'.[36] Clarendon hopes that, with humility and wisdom, the English might return to their Caroline pastoral. By contrast, Hume's organising mechanism for the section in the *History of Great Britain* on the golden days of James I is a slippery kind of syntax combining praise and prolepsis, for example, the sentence: 'Great riches, acquired by commerce, were more rare, and had not, as yet, been able to confound all ranks of men, and render money the chief foundation of distinction' (228: V, 132). Jacobean England is rich, but not too rich, monarchical but not oppressive, cultivated but not self-indulgent (226–30: V, 132–5). The price of greater liberty, Hume tells us, will be the destruction of the ideal equilibrium which this liberty had itself helped to create: 'By the changes, which have since been introduced, the liberty and independence of individuals has been rendered much more full, intire and secure; that of the public more uncertain and precarious' (226: V, 128–9). Hume thus repositions Clarendon's pastoral moment within a wider fabric of ironic inevitabilities.

The social history of fanaticism

Hume willingly devotes a large part of the Stuart and Tudor volumes to the social and religious forces which ruined this Jacobean country-house world and erected something more eccentric and less stable in its place. By the time of Charles I, religious excess has become the distinguishing feature of the British people: 'of all the European nations, the British were, at that time, and till long after, sunk into the lowest and most odious bigotry' (264: V, 164 specifies this 'bigotry' as the 'religious spirit'). This popular bigotry is still very much in evidence during the Popish Plot in the late 1670s: 'In all history, it will be difficult to find such another instance of popular frenzy and bigoted delusion' (296: VI, 348). Hume regards religious fanaticism as the most distinctive characteristic of the nation, and often relates degrees of zeal to stages of social development in different parts of the country. For example, although the fanaticism of Scotland

[34] Clarendon, *History of the Rebellion*, I, 58. Slater ('Authorship and Authority', 130–4) has found a number of other echoes of Clarendon in Hume.

[35] Ibid., I, 59. [36] Ibid., I, 59, 53.

appears similar to that of England in the 1630s, Hume reports that it in fact emanates from a far lower level of social development: 'The same horror against popery, with which the English puritans were possessed, was observable among the populace in Scotland; and among these, as being more uncultivated and uncivilized, seemed rather to be inflamed into a higher degree of ferocity' (360: V, 252). The turbulence of the highlanders, who 'were the people the most disorderly and least civilized' in the country emanates from a still lower developmental level (292: VI, 329). Britain's Irish colonial subjects are even further behind ('a wild nation'), despite the best efforts of James I and Charles I 'to cure that sloth and barbarism to which they had ever been subject' (427: VI, 313 amends this to the more scientific 'a rude people'). This barbarism manifests itself as religious extremism (460: V, 343). The kingdoms of Britain are all distinguished by their propensity to fanaticism. This propensity is, however, measured according to a rudimentary scale of social development although, ironically, it is frequently those parts of the country occupying the earlier stages of social development (Scotland and Ireland) which draw England down to their level of barbarousness (449: V, 333).

Hume's philosophical interest in the religious impulse in human nature both antedated and developed alongside the composition of the *History*. In his dissertation on *The Natural History of Religion* (1757), Hume explored the natural causes and social agency of religious belief.[37] A similar though more rhetorically strategic separation between the moral and social dimensions of religious behaviour can be found in the draft preface to the second Stuart volume:

> The proper Office of Religion is to reform Men's Lives, to purify their Hearts, to inforce all moral Duties, and to secure Obedience to the Laws and civil Magistrate. While it pursues these useful Purposes, its Operations, tho' infinitely valuable, are secret and silent; and seldom come under the Cognizance of History. That adulterate Species of it alone, which inflames Faction, animates Sedition, and prompts Rebellion, distinguishes itself on the open Theatre of the World. [38]

Hume decided not to print this preface, but his investigation, in the *History*, of those aspects of religiously motivated behaviour which 'come under the Cognizance of History' does, at first sight, appear to be perfectly consistent with this wider philosophical project. Many critics have been happy to assume that Hume's *History* simply extends the philosophical line of inquiry set out in *The Natural History of Religion* as an investigation of the behavioural patterns of the British people in their historical context.[39] British history, in

[37] *The Natural History of Religion* in *Philosophical Works* eds. T. H. Green and T. H. Grose (London, 1889), IV.

[38] Ernest Campbell Mossner, *The Life of David Hume* (second edn, Oxford, 1980), 306–7.

[39] For example, Livingston, *Hume's Philosophy of Common Life*, chapter 8.

this interpretation, provides Hume with a set of local manifestations of the natural workings of the human instinct for belief. Hume himself peppers the earlier texts of the *History* with statements to this effect: 'History addresses itself to a more distant posterity than will ever be reached by any local or temporary theology; and the characters of sects may be studied, when their controversies shall be totally forgotten' (96: subsequently cut). Two kinds of perspective appear to converge in the *History*: Hume's cosmopolitan notion of Britain's deviance from the European path towards more civil and submissive forms of religious behaviour; and his philosophical analysis of the social operation of extreme forms of religious belief.

Despite its philosophical stipulations, a closer inspection of the *History of England* reveals the cracks in its philosophical armour caused by the local generic conditions of British history. Although it is Hume's stated intention to explore the historical operation of deviant forms of religious belief, philosophically understood, in practice, however, his text is often strained between the different generic poles of history and philosophy. This strain manifests itself in two ways. The first is the tension between Hume's philosophic voice, which anatomises religious fanaticism, and his satiric voice, which castigates it as a national vice. The second is the way that Hume's accounts of the motives behind fanatical action vary from socially specific explanations to highly abstract remarks about the sources of fanaticism in human nature. Hume's contradictory presentations of religion-in-action are, nevertheless, a source of complexity, rather than of confusion for the *History*. The tensions and contradictions in Hume's natural, social and national histories of religion are commensurate with the tensions between the typical and the exceptional in his vision of British history as a whole.

Hume's representations of religious fanaticism in the Stuart volumes grew out of older traditions of religious satire in England. Such satires, from Ben Jonson's stage character Zeal-of-the-Land Busy to Swift's mechanical operators of the spirit, were directed at the excesses of Protestant non-conformist zeal, usually known as 'enthusiasm.' As well as knowing these, Hume would also have been familiar with traditions of satire against Catholic credulous 'superstition', most recently adapted in Voltaire's acerbic vignettes of Jansenist, Quietist and Jesuit folly in the *Siècle de Louis XIV*. Hume was himself an inventive and entertaining satirist of both superstition and enthusiasm. Despite Hume's declaration, in a letter to his French translator, that he had 'always kept from . . . all Satyre and Panegyric', he allowed his satiric impulses, especially when dealing with religious matters, to run unchecked through many sections of the *History*.[40] His relish for satire is most clearly in evidence when he has the

[40] Hume to Abbé le Blanc (12 September 1754), *Letters*, no. 94.

chance to dramatise encounters between these two forms of religious extremism, as, for example, when Archbishop Laud tried to impose a new liturgy upon the Scottish people. Laud prescribed a ceremony for the consecration of new churches in both Scotland and England which Hume satirised at length as a preposterous piece of high theatre (333–4: V, 224–6). In the quotation below, Hume describes the moment when, in one particular enactment of this ceremony, the bishop came to prepare the sacrament:

> After the reading of many prayers, he approached the sacramental elements, and gently lifted up the corner of the napkin, in which the bread was laid. When he beheld the bread, he suddenly let fall the napkin, flew back a step or two, bowed three several times towards the bread; then he drew near again, and opened the napkin, and bowed as before.
>
> Next, he laid his hand on the cup, which had a cover upon it, and was full of wine. He let go the cup, fell back, and bowed thrice towards it. He approached again; and lifting up the cover, peeped into the cup. Seeing the wine, he let fall the cover, started back, and bowed as before. Then he received the sacrament and gave it to others. (334: V, 225–6)

Words and phrases such as 'gently', 'flew back a step or two', and 'peeped' mischievously capture the histrionic solemnity of the occasion. The humour of the passage does not fully encapsulate Hume's generally hostile, but complex, appraisal of Laud, but it reinforces his political attack on the Laudian church by showing his readers the comic outer edges of its ritualised portentousness.

The Scottish response to the introduction of Laud's ecclesiastical innovations is no less amusingly recounted: 'the surplice was a rag of popery; and each motion or gesture, prescribed by the liturgy, was a step towards that spiritual Babylon, so much the object of their horror and aversion' (147: V, 69). The Assembly of the Church of Scotland, resenting the increased power given by Laud to the Scottish episcopacy, thunder from their pulpits 'an accusation against the bishops [representing them] as guilty, all of them, of heresy, simony, bribery, perjury, cheating, incest, adultery, fornication, common swearing, drunkenness, gaming, breach of the sabbath, and every other crime, which had occurred to the accusers' (369: V, 261). Hume's satiric method often involves, as it does here, mimicking the extravagant and undisciplined language of enthusiasts. Like Swift, Hume associates formless speech with uncivil madness (Swift quoted approvingly an Irish prelate who said that 'if the wisest man would at any time utter his thoughts, in the crude, indigested manner, as they come into his head, he would be looked upon as raving mad').[41] Hume's favourite

[41] 'Some Thoughts on Freethinking' in *The Prose Writings of Jonathan Swift*, eds. Herber Davis *et al.* (16 vols.; Oxford, 1939–74), IV, 49.

technique is a kind of demented enumeration; this he applies, for example, to the manic ambition of the young Cromwell, the very personification of enthusiasm: 'His active mind, superior to the low occupations, to which he was condemned, preyed upon itself; and he indulged his imagination in visions, illuminations, revelations ... He preached, he prayed, he fought, he punished, he rewarded. This wild enthusiasm ... still propagated itself; and all men cast their eyes on so pious and so successful a leader' (II, 46, 47: VI, 56, 58).

Like Swift, Hume is irresistibly attracted to the bizarre energies of enthusiasm, and fascinated by their origins in an exorbitant and deranged sense of the self. This selfish enthusiasm is, for Hume, typical of the Scottish mentality, as well as characteristic of enthusiasts in general: 'by nourishing in every individual, the wildest raptures and extasies of devotion, it consecrated, in a manner, every individual' (368: V, 260). Cromwell is the supreme example of a gigantic self created out of the raw materials of enthusiasm and ambition. As such, Cromwell does not belong to Hume's scheme of the good or bad 'fit' between private men and public affairs. Cromwell, as Hilson pointed out, has no private self separate from the public enthusiast.[42] For Hume, Cromwell 'was at bottom as frantic an enthusiast as the worst of [his followers]' (90: VI, 109). All Hume says about Cromwell's private life is that it 'is exposed to no considerable censure, if it does not rather merit praise' (91: VI, 110). Hume gives a compelling account of Cromwell in his last days when his confidence in his public self breaks down, and he is left terrified by his own lack of inner resources, wearing out his body with worry. A short quotation can only give a limited idea of the artistry of Hume's sketch of the decay of Cromwell:

> Society terrifyed him, while he reflected on his numerous, unknown, and implacable enemies: Solitude astonished him, by withdrawing that protection, which he found so necessary for his security.
>
> His body also, from the contagion of his anxious mind, began to be affected; and his health seemed very sensibly to decline. (87: VI, 105)

We are reminded of Dryden's Achitophel ('A fiery Soul, which working out its way, / Fretted the Pigmy-Body to decay', lines 156–7), and also of Clarendon's description of Cromwell, the Great Dissembler upon which Hume draws heavily. Clarendon's obituary portrait of this 'brave wicked man' provides Hume with his main elements; a man afraid of strangers and solitude who looses his 'serenity of mind', and so frets away his body, a man of some virtues and more vices, a man whose very hypocrisy has something 'magnanimous' about it.[43] Hume selects and rearranges Clar-

[42] Hilson, 'Hume: The Historian as Man of Feeling', 217.
[43] *History of the Rebellion*, III, 504, 506.

endon's observations into an altogether less sympathetic portrait of an enthusiast consumed by his own overreaching enthusiasm. Despite this, Hume's presentation of Cromwell retains, throughout the second Stuart volume, some vestiges of Clarendon's individualised 'brave wicked man', and Cromwell is never entirely lost as person to Hume's general phenomenology of enthusiasm.

Hume's satire of enthusiasism had a social as well as philosophical purpose. From the time of the Restoration, Anglican apologists, acutely aware of the dangerous sincerity of Protestant extremism, had developed satirical modes of ridiculing non-conformists into social compliance.[44] Swift's *A Tale of a Tub* belongs to this tradition, even though his relatively coercive notions of social compliance do not. Hume follows this tradition of Anglican polemic to the extent that he sees enthusiasts as sincere rather than hypocritical (with the exception of his Clarendonian Cromwell). He may have been particularly influenced by the way in which Swift linked his sense of the solipsism engendered by puritan fanaticism to a vision of the social chaos which it produces. At the beginning of the section on the Commonwealth, Hume remarks that 'every man had framed the model of a republic; and, however new or fantastical, he was eager of recommending it to his fellow citizen, or even of imposing it by force upon them' (1: VI, 3). What follows from these acts of excessive interpretive individualism is the dissolution of the social order: 'The bands of society were every where loosened; and the irregular passions of men were encouraged by speculative principles, still more unsocial and irregular' (2: VI, 4). However, Hume does not embrace either Swift's or Pope's sense of the collective inverted logic beneath apparent social disorder, such as the bizarre coherence of the world of the dunces, or the rigorous ingenuity of the aeolists or the mechanical operators of the spirit. Nor, except for a few comments such as those quoted above, does Hume share the Augustans' passionate concern with the abuse of unrestrained private judgement. Satirists from Dryden to Swift saw the threat of the usurpation of the state by dissenters as, in origin, a problem of excessive independence in scriptural interpretation (as Dryden quipped, 'But, since our Scots in prophecy grow higher / The Text inspires not them; but they the Text inspire').[45] Hume's satirical animus is generally expended against the *collective* pathologies of religious fanaticism, whether Protestant or Catholic, and, unlike his predecessors, he rarely spends time locating this collective fanaticism in individual abuses of reason. For Hume, religiously motivated group behaviour has a momentum of its own which requires no internal

[44] George Williamson, 'The Restoration Revolt against Enthusiasm', *Studies in Philology*, 30 (1933), 571–603; Phillip Harth, *Swift and Anglican Rationalism: The Religious Background of A Tale of a Tub* (Chicago, 1961).

[45] Dryden, 'The Medall', *Poems*, ed. Kinsley, I, lines 165–6.

psychological explanation; it belongs to those wider patterns of collective action analysed by Shaftesbury and Voltaire, and it also has to do with the 'national character' of the British people.

The social operation of enthusiasm

Hume invited his readers to dissociate themselves through laughter from the worst excesses of their fanatical past, while at the same time seeking to provide them with a satisfactory social analysis of fanaticism as an essentially natural phenomenon. In the process, his *History* offered them a more rigorous and comprehensive account of the social operation of religious impulses than anything they might have encountered before. Hume was not, in fact, the first writer to attempt this feat nor the first to combine it with a measure a ridicule. Among his predecessors, Hume may have been familiar with Meric Casaubon's *A Treatise concerning Enthusiasme, as it is an effect of Nature* (1655, revised 1656), which introduced a bemused philosophical tone in the investigation of different forms of enthusiasm (religious enthusiasm, though not discussed explicitly, is, of course the covert subject of Casaubon's text). William Temple mentions this work in an essay 'Of Poetry' (which Hume may also have known), and goes on to call for 'a clear Account of Enthusiasm and Fascination from their natural Causes'.[46] Temple's request was, in some measure, granted by Shaftesbury in the famous 'Letter Concerning Enthusiasm' (1708). Shaftesbury's essay anatomises the causes of enthusiasm, among them intolerance and persecution, and advances some urbane remedies of his own for this problem, including Horatian ridicule: 'Good-humour is not only the best security against enthusiasm, but the best foundation of piety and true religion.'[47] In addition to his theorisation of the social purposiveness of laughter, Shaftesbury diagnoses some general social phenomena arising from religious frenzy. One of these, which clearly interested Hume, was the phenomenon of popular 'panic':

> One may with good reason call every passion panic which is raised in a multitude and conveyed by aspect or, as it were, by contact of sympathy. Thus popular fury may be called panic when the rage of the people, as we have sometimes known, has put them beyond themselves; especially where religion has had to do. And in this state their very looks are infectious. The fury flies from face to face; and the disease is no sooner seen than caught.[48]

Hume almost certainly had this passage in mind when he wrote of the mass

[46] Temple, 'Of Poetry', *Miscellanea: The Second Part* (London, 1690), 7.
[47] Anthony Ashley Cooper, Earl of Shaftesbury, 'A Letter Concerning Enthusiasm' in *Characteristicks*, ed. John M. Robertson (2 vols.; London, 1900), I, 17.
[48] Ibid., I, 13.

hysteria surrounding the supposed 'Popish Plot' in the 1670s, 'an event, which would otherwise appear prodigious and altogether inexplicable' without reference to a notion of a popular 'panic':

> While in this timorous, jealous disposition, the cry of a *plot* all on a sudden struck [the people's] ears: They were wakened from their slumber; and like men affrightened and in the dark, took every figure for a specter. The terror of each man became the source of terror to another. And an universal panic being diffused, reason and argument and common sense and common humanity lost all influence over them. (275: VI, 333)

Hume, following Shaftesbury, refers the problem of religious motivation in popular action to a more general psychology of group behaviour. A Shaftesburian note of patrician ridicule of the people is sounded, but there is also insight into the social mechanics of religious hysteria. Hume may also have been indebted for this insight to Temple's ruminative essay 'Of Popular Discontents', and there is some verbal evidence for Hume's close acquaintance with this piece.[49] Temple's essay explores the origins of popular commotions, whether secular or religious in motivation, in man's 'natural Propension' to restlessness.[50] Like Hume, Temple noted that popular restlessness can often be fomented by the public speculations of more educated men: 'From this original fountain issue those Streams of Faction, that with some course of Time and Accidents, overflow the wisest Constitutions of Government and Law.'[51] Although he gave a somewhat different account of its causes and effects, Temple, like Hobbes before and Hume after him, believed that the Civil War was a war of political and religious opinion in which popular discontent, however unprovoked, took on a momentum of its own.[52]

Despite his patronage of Swift, Temple never entirely approved of satire. He was among those writers before Hume searching for a new, more philosophical vocabulary through which to approach the issues of popular enthusiasm and unrest.[53] Although he may have been attracted by Temple's project, Hume was not willing to dispense altogether with an exasperated satirical tone when describing the historical operations of

[49] William Temple, 'Of Popular Discontents', *Miscellanea: The Third Part* (London, 1701). Temple speculates about a 'Perfect Scheme of Government' which might remedy these social ills. Yet he quickly realises that no perfect government could ever be framed to last: 'Could we suppose a Body Politick, framed perfect in its first Conception or Institution, yet it must fall into Decays, not only from the Force of Accidents, but even from the very Rust of Time' (p. 20). Hume might have had this passage in mind when writing the essay on 'The Idea of a Perfect Commonwealth' (1752): 'It is needless to enquire, whether such a government would be immortal . . . Perhaps, rust may grow to the springs of the most accurate political machine, and disorder its motions' (*Essays*, 528–9).

[50] 'Of Popular Discontents', 17.

[51] Ibid., 10–11.

[52] Ibid., 38; Thomas Hobbes, *Behemoth; or, the Long Parliament* (written late 1660s, published 1682).

[53] A. C. Elias, *Swift at Moor Park: Problems in Biography and Criticism* (Philadelphia, 1982), 156.

fanaticism, or to espouse a completely causally integrated mode of philosophical explanation. Summarising the events of the Civil War, Hume does not disguise his vexation at the senseless stupidity of the people, and unleashes a string of irritable-sounding abstract nouns where a philosopher might have been expected to supply connectives:

> No people could undergo a change more sudden and entire in their manners than did the English nation during this period. From tranquillity, concord, submission, sobriety, they passed in an instant to a state of faction, fanaticism, rebellion, and almost frenzy. The violence of the English parties exceeded any thing, which we can now imagine. (117: VI, 141)

Hume's almost burlesque vision of the Civil War reminds us again of *Hudibras* ('When *civil* Fury first few high, / And men fell out they knew not why.'). In the preceding pages, Hume carefully documents the causes and motives which precipitated the 'sudden and entire' change in the people's manners, and yet, in the final analysis, he declares himself bewildered by it all. The political, social and economic historian of manners and motives gives place, here and throughout the *History*, to the baffled philosophical inquirer into the mysterious mechanics of human nature. Satire and burlesque protect the philosophical integrity of this bafflement. For Hume, fanaticism, whether superstitious or enthusiastic, is its own motive; it must be confronted in the past both with and without reference to other systems of explanation.

Hume does remind his readers on several occasions that the human passion of religious fanaticism may sufficiently explain a particular incident. Of the superstitious Gunpowder plotters he remarks: ''Twas bigotted zeal alone, the most absurd of prejudices masqued with reason, the most criminal of passions covered with the appearance of duty, which seduced them into measures, that were fatal to themselves' (95: V, 31). Early in the reign of Charles I, Hume comments upon the way in which enthusiasm usurps every other motive for action among the English: 'above all, the spirit of enthusiasm, being universally diffused over the nation, disappointed all the views of human prudence, and disturbed the operation of every motive, which usually influences society' (329: V, 221). This has something in common with Voltaire's bewildered and testy asides about the 'fureur épidémique' which periodically infected the French nation in the seventeenth century. Voltaire's own enthusiastic review of the *History* praises the medical detachment with which Hume speaks of such epidemical diseases: 'on découvre un esprit supérieur à sa matière, qui parle des faiblesses, des erreurs, et des barbaries, comme un médecin parle des maladies épidémiques'.[54] Nevertheless, if one looks closely at Voltaire's

[54] Voltaire, *Moland*, XXV, 173.

own examination of Protestant enthusiasm in the *Siècle de Louis XIV*, one senses a very different kind of historical intelligence at work. In the chapter on the Huguenots at the time of the Revocation of the Edict of Nantes (which Hume adapts and echoes in the second Stuart volume), Voltaire identifies an 'esprit dogmatique', which had for centuries nourished their sense of separateness, and eventually given rise to a more subversive sense of political identity (the 'esprit républicain'). Adapting Shaftesbury's ridicule, in the *Letter Concerning Enthusiasm*, of the Huguenots' compulsion to martyrdom, Voltaire satirises the obstinacy and pedantry of these persecuted people.[55] However, Voltaire's satiric voice is greatly attenuated by his detailed interest in the historical background to the persecutions – the economic and legislative changes, and the power struggles which both fostered the dogmatic mentality of the Huguenots, and ultimately aggravated their persecution. Fanaticism, in both its Protestant and Catholic forms is, in fact, a less disruptive and more readily explicable social force in Voltaire's work than in Hume's *History*. In contrast to *Le Siècle de Louis XIV*, the peculiar abstraction of Hume's account of fanaticism in British history tends to disrupt the causally integrated fabric of the narrative. In addition to the historian's evolutionary perspective, the reader encounters the satirist's vision of chaos, and the philosopher's case history of human passions. If Hume does not reconcile these different perspectives in the Stuart volumes, it is, perhaps, because he would not wish to resolve the unpredictable and unstable forces in Britain's past into a deceptively closed artistic whole.

Some time after the publication of the *History*, during the popular agitation surrounding Wilkes' election to a parliamentary seat in Middlesex, Hume was again reminded of the unique fractiousness of the English:

> This exceeds the Absurdity of Titus Oates, and the popish Plot; and is so much more disgraceful to the Nation, as the former Folly, being derivd from Religion, flow'd from a Source, which has, from uniform Prescription, acquird a Right to impose Nonsense on all Nations and all Ages: But the present Extravagance is peculiar to Ourselves, and quite risible. [56]

It is, of course, the final irony of the *History* that English extravagance, particularly of the enthusiastic kind, nearly always enlists on the side of

[55] Shaftesbury, *Characteristicks*, I, 20–1; Voltaire, 'Du Calvinisme au temps de Louis XIV', *Le Siècle de Louis XIV*, ed. Pomeau, chapter 36. 'Près de cinquante mille familles, en trois ans de temps, sortirent du royaume, et furent après suivies par d'autres. Elles allèrent porter chez les étrangers les arts, les manufactures, la richesse' (*Siècle*, 1055). Compare Hume: 'Above half a million of the most useful and industrious subjects deserted France; and exported, together with immense sums of money, those arts and manufactures, which had chiefly tended to enrich that kingdom' (393: VI, 471).

[56] Hume to Blair (28 March 1769), *Letters*, no. 427.

liberty. The Independents, for example, are among the first inventors of the social policy of religious toleration: ' 'tis remarkable', Hume comments, 'that so reasonable a doctrine owed its origin, not to reasoning, but to the height of extravagance and enthusiasm' (571: V, 443). Hume's earlier essay 'Of Superstition and Enthusiasm' (1741) explains the mechanism whereby enthusiasm tends to promote liberty, whereas superstition generally promotes political passivity. Although this essay converges with the *History* on this point, I have excluded it from my discussion until now because, as I hope to have shown, the *History* approaches the subject of religious extremism in a quite different way: first, the *History* does not maintain so strenuous a distinction between superstition and enthusiasm; secondly the *History* investigates pathologies of group behaviour common to both superstitious and enthusiastic systems of belief, as well as to group behaviour in general. In the last analysis, Hume's *History* does not abandon the conclusion of the earlier essay that enthusiasm is, in the long term, a paradoxical friend to civil liberty; and he believes that the wise British legislator should always try to placate the dangerously enthusiastic spirit behind the British people's worship of liberty by giving ground to some of their demands. For instance, the Glorious Revolution, 'by deciding many important questions in favour of liberty', is praised for exhibiting some of this pragmatic wisdom (443: VI, 581).

Tudor antecedents

The two Tudor volumes which followed the Stuart volumes in 1759 provide, in many respects, a retrospective reorientation of the *History of England* (as the *History of Great Britain* now became). The same year, Hume brought out a revised and corrected edition of the Stuart volumes. The Tudor volumes have, of course, a thematic purpose of their own, although this is driven in part by the need to provide an explanatory context for the volumes which follow. The Tudor volumes do not emulate the psychological, sociological and generic complexity of their predecessors with the result that they are, by comparison, both more accessible and less artistically accomplished. They solidify the achievement of the earlier part of the history, and a number of unresolved themes in the Stuart volumes find their moorings in the narrative of Tudor England. One such theme is the nature and paradoxical libertarianism of Protestant enthusiasm. Another is the political, and hence cultural divergence of seventeenth-century Britain from the path taken by most of the rest of Europe towards civilised absolute monarchy. In order to emphasise the exceptional nature of seventeenth-century developments in Britain, Hume presents the Tudor period as one of underlying stability and (by contemporary European standards) normality.

It is in the Tudor volumes that Hume consciously searches for continuities between British and European history; even the Reformation (the implied source of British peculiarity in the Stuart volumes) is reinterpreted in its European context. After an audacious opening passage on the dangers of permitting churchmen to proselytise (or, as he puts it, to go in search of 'customers'), Hume paints a picture of the early sixteenth-century Catholic Church in Britain, as in the rest of Europe, at a new pinnacle of glory (I, 117–18: III, 135–7). At this very moment, Luther emerges, trailing behind him Hume's usual retinue of enumerative adjectives ('a man naturally inflexible, vehement, opinionative') and a group of followers who denounce the Catholic Church as 'abominable, detestable, damnable; foretold by the sacred writ itself as the source of all wickedness and pollution' (I, 120, 122: III, 139, 141). Although he attributes the European Reformation to a complex concurrence of incidents, Hume singles out one particular cause behind this extravagant enthusiasm; the dissemination of printing which, paradoxically, fosters the very taste for novelty and learning from which the Catholic Church was also drawing renewed glory (I, 121: III, 140). The new opinions circulated by the Reformers generate a Europe-wide popular 'panic', and the people are 'agitated, even in the most opposite directions' (I, 184: III, 211). Hume satirises the reformers as coarse and fanatical, and none more so than those of his native Scotland (II, 420: IV, 22). Nevertheless, once the initial process of Reformation in England gets under way, Hume alights upon the central irony of the country's fanatical history:

> So absolute was the authority of the crown, that the precious spark of liberty had been kindled, and was preserved, by the puritans alone; and it was to this sect, whose principles appear so frivolous and habits so ridiculous, that the English owe the whole freedom of their constitution. (II, 527: IV, 145–6)

As a prospectus for the Stuart volumes, this seems somewhat simplified, and the ironies of Hume's history of enthusiasm in the seventeenth century are not, in fact, anchored in this single structuring paradox. Hume, bewildered by what he regarded as the incomprehending stupidity which had greeted the first instalment of the *History*, perhaps takes fewer literary risks with his ideas in the second.

Despite his guarded admiration for the tradition of liberty kept alive by puritan sects, Hume is nostalgic for the Renaissance civilisation of Catholic Europe of which England once partook, and which 'facilitated the intercourse of nations, and tended to bind all the parts of Europe into an immense republic', as well as diffusing 'a general elegance of taste, by uniting it with religion' (I, 118: III, 137 replaces 'republic' with 'into a close connection with each other'). England is part of this civilisation by the early sixteenth century, experiences its economic, political and cultural revolutions during the Tudor dynasty, and yet, to Hume's evident disappointment, withdraws into a cultural world of its own by the 1630s. By characterising the Tudor age as the era in which Britain most fully participated in and shaped the destiny of the European fraternity of states, Hume retrospectively marks out the Stuart age as the one in which Britain acquired its deviant distinctiveness. The Stuart volumes do not consistently subject the peculiarities of British history to a comparative or cosmopolitan gaze. However, in the light of the wider context provided by the Tudor, and, subsequently, the medieval volumes, commentators, such as Duncan Forbes, have tended to read the Stuart volumes in this cosmopolitan dimension.[57] It is more accurate to say that the presence of the Tudor and, later, the medieval volumes effects a cosmopolitan reorientation of the Stuart sections of the *History*.

This process of reorientation towards a more comparative, European outlook for the *History*, gets underway with Henry VII and continues throughout the Tudor instalment. The process can be seen most clearly in the Henry VII section where Hume is in constant dialogue with one of the richest of all his sources, Francis Bacon's *The Historie of the Reigne of King Henry VII* (1629). As Hume's footnotes demonstrate, a great many of the observations in this section stem from a conscious decision to agree or disagree with Bacon, and, by looking back over his source, we are able to see the direction which his Tudor history is taking. Hume is, on occasions, unable to resist the influence of Bacon's marvellously bluff, Senecan style, as, for example, when he tells his readers how Perkin Warbeck grew 'tired of the savage life, which he was obliged to lead, while *skulking* among the wild Irish' (my italics, I, 43: III, 53). Bacon's Henry VII is a politic, energetic and tight-fisted prince: 'this Salomon of England, for Salomon also was too heavy upon his people in exactions'.[58] For Bacon, Henry is England's first great legislator, economic reformer and expert in foreign affairs. Hume starts out by disagreeing with Bacon's finding that Henry granted his parliament as many privileges as he withdrew.[59] Hume concedes that Henry's reign was 'a kind of epoch in the English constitution', but for precisely the opposite reason that the crown gained an unprecedented degree of prerogative (I, 61: III, 74). Hume's Henry VII is an accidental despot. The statesmanship so admired by Bacon is really, in his account, the executive heavy-handedness of a king suddenly unimpeded by other powers. Henry's absolutism is, for Hume, the outcome, not of 'the King ever having an eye to might and multitude' (as Bacon would have it), but of a more impersonal economic revolution which, in England as in the

57 Forbes, 'The European, or Cosmopolitan Dimension in Hume's Science of Politics', 58.

58 Bacon, *Henry VII*, 231–2. Slater ('Authorship and Authority', 153–6) gives an interesting account of how Hume smooths out Bacon's style and so alters his meaning.

59 Ibid., 234–5.

rest of Europe, steadily shifts resources away from aristocracies and towards kings (I, 66: III, 80).[60] Hume dismantles Bacon's praise of Henry's economic policies item by item (I, 63–5: III, 79). Where Bacon finds in Henry's fiscal reforms wise public policy sometimes carried to avaricious excess, Hume sees a private 'ruling passion' of 'avarice' (I, 54: III, 66). For Bacon, Henry's private self is mainly absorbed into the royal bureaucrat, and has few of these passions.

Bacon's bureaucrat is distracted throughout much of his reign by the problem of the legitimacy of his administration, and his narrative is structured by Henry's long and infuriating duel with the false claimant to his throne, Perkin Warbeck. The drama ends in execution for Warbeck ('this little Cockatrice of a King'), bringing to an end 'one of the longest Playes of that kind that hath beene in memorie'.[61] Hume's account of the Perkin affair is colourless by comparison, and his structuring devices are different. And, unlike Bacon's, Hume's 'reign of Henry VII' is set within a larger narrative of European transformation in the early sixteenth century. Just outside the frame of Henry's moderately distinguished regime, Hume descries the fall of Constantinople, the spread of printing and learning, the New World discoveries, and the rise of other absolute monarchies. Bacon insists upon the European stature and renown of his politic prince; Hume finds this stature an accident of the wider changes taking place in Europe at the time. By the time he came to write the Tudor portion of the *History*, Hume's belief in the personal efficacy of monarchs in national affairs was waning. Bacon considers Henry's administration to be the first serious exercise of modern statecraft by a gifted monarch. Hume sees the beginnings of a Tudor revolution in government, albeit he attributes this less to the energy of the king, than to general alterations in European affairs. This is a revolution which does not get properly under way until the reign of Henry's son, Henry VIII: 'here … commences the useful, as well as the more agreeable part of modern annals' (I, 67: III, 82). For Hume, modern history begins with Henry VIII.

Hume's increasingly restricted idea of the role of royal 'persons' in relation to international, economic and social 'things' continues throughout the Tudor volumes. The consolidation of royal absolutism under Henry VIII is facilitated by the king's authoritarian personality, although it does not spring from any deliberate plan of his own: 'And tho' in all his measures [Henry VIII] was really driven by his ungoverned humour, he casually held a course, which led more certainly to arbitrary power, than any which the most profound politics could have traced out to him' (I, 186: III, 214). Henry VIII is the reverse of Charles I, a 'great' but not a 'good' monarch,

[60] Ibid., 216.
[61] Ibid., 194–5.

since by 'greatness' Hume means an intuitive matching of private passions to the tendency of the times (I, 278: III, 322). Under the moderate and intelligent supervision of Wolsey, Cranmer and the Cecils, the Tudor dynasty maintains and consolidates its power. Only Elizabeth I is accorded a more interventionist role in the narrative, and this is a consequence, not of her personality or sex, but of her mastery of both: 'the true method of estimating her merit, is to lay aside all these considerations [of personality and sex], and consider her merely as a rational being, placed in authority, and entrusted with the government of mankind' (II, 715–6: IV, 353). Unlike her father and grandfather, she is able to carry out her designs because she has assimilated her royal self to the prevailing public rationality. By playing down the personal aspects of Elizabeth's style of government, Hume, of course, signals his independence from the kind of 'Good-Queen-Bess-ery' common to the eighteenth-century historians of this period (Bolingbroke in his *Letters on the Study and Use of History*, for example). Hume's interest in character has not entirely waned. He devotes a great deal of space in the Elizabeth chapters to Mary, Queen of Scots. No doubt he had an eye to Robertson's competitor volume on sixteenth-century Scotland, which was due to go to press the same year as the Tudor volumes. Nevertheless, as we shall see in the next chapter, Hume's main interest, at this stage of the composition of the *History*, was in those characters with publicly serviceable private qualities, and Mary was, for him, the great contrary example of a sovereign ill suited to her times.

In the Tudor volumes, the dynamic between 'persons' and 'things', which had infused such artistic complexity into the Stuart volumes, is pared down to a more unilinear narrative of the formation of the English state. After the preparatory reign of Henry VII, Hume identifies a number of evolutionary processes at work during the sixteenth century, some of which reach stability under Elizabeth I. First, there is the European system of military and economic balance between states, born of the rivalry between Spain and France in the early sixteenth century. Robertson would later elaborate, in his *History of Charles V*, the story here outlined by Hume. In Hume's account an ideal equilibrium of European power is achieved during the early days of Henry VIII, with England holding the scales:

> There has scarcely been any period, when the ballance of power was better secured in Europe, and seemed more able to maintain itself without any anxious concern or attention of the princes. Several great monarchies were established; and no one so far surpassed the rest as to give any foundation, or even pretence, for jealousy. (I, 74: III, 88)

Despite this situation, Henry VIII fails to press his 'inestimable advantage' as European ringmaster, and is reproached by Hume for his short-sightedness (I, 110: III, 128). This European order is later upset during the closing years of the Tudor dynasty, but remains for Hume a desirable goal of modern foreign policy.

Accompanying these developments in the European state system, Hume finds, in this period, a steady increase in royal authority made possible by a comparative decline in the wealth of the aristocracy, and consolidated by the unification of church and state during the Reformation: 'in the interval between the fall of the nobles and the rise of [the commons], the sovereign took advantage of the present situation, and assumed an authority almost absolute' (II, 737: IV, 384). Hume is very favourable towards England's unusual Reformation by due course of law. Despite some satirical strokes at the expense of the more zealous reformers, he regards the Reformation as a constitutional event of great, though not deliberate wisdom:

> The acknowledgement of [Henry VIII's] supremacy introduced there a greater simplicity in the government, by uniting the spiritual with the civil power, and preventing disputes about limits, which never could be exactly determined between contending parties ... And on the whole, there followed from these revolutions many beneficial consequences; tho' perhaps neither foreseen nor intended by the persons who had the chief hand in conducting them.
>
> (I, 181: III, 206–7 replaces 'parties' with the less anachronistic 'jurisdictions')

Edward VI completes, and Mary does little to overturn these constitutional alterations. By the end of the reign of Elizabeth, a normative constitutional position has been reached in which the queen has become absolute head of church and state. This picture of Elizabeth as an absolute (though not, it is carefully pointed out, despotic) monarch came as a surprise to many eighteenth-century readers, yet, Hume insists, her regime was both legitimate and acceptable to her people (II, 728: IV, 370). In a passage strongly reminiscent of his earlier essay 'Of the Original Contract' (1748), Hume explains that Elizabeth's subjects 'entirely acquiesced in her arbitrary administration' because they felt the legitimating force of established governmental practice (II, 716: IV, 354). Furthermore, he finds Elizabeth's moderate style of absolute government typical of monarchs of her day: 'the power of the prince, though really unlimited, was exercised after the European manner, and entered not into every part of the administration' (II, 728: IV, 370). Elizabeth's reign is thus a constitutional non-event, an exercise in 'business as usual' by a European monarch remarkable only for her sagacity and skill. Hume's description, at the end of the Tudor volumes, of a stable but economically underdeveloped Elizabethan England prepares the way for the ensuing narrative of an economically dynamic but politically insecure Stuart England. The achieved stability of the Tudor order is thus imaginatively established before the nation's great leap in the seventeenth century into a peculiarly English chaos of enthusiasm and liberty.

Medieval contexts

Published in 1761 [dated 1762], Hume's two medieval volumes provide a still deeper context for this process of national formation, while generating perspectives and methodologies of their own. The largest story which they have to tell is imposition, consolidation and erosion of a form of political and social life which Hume calls the 'feudal' system. This system had to be explained in detail to the readers, as Nicholas Phillipson has pointed out, if they were to understand the magnitude of the Tudor revolution in government.[62] Feudalism was a form of social organisation shared with the other gothic nations of Europe, and, in examining its slow decline, Hume encounters a process typical of other European polities, with plenty of local English peculiarities. With the focus upon the European dimension of the feudal order, Hume makes a conscious contribution to the investigations currently being carried out by Scottish contemporaries, such as Lord Kames and Adam Smith, into feudalism as a particular stage of social development.[63] Hume's sociological vocabulary, which is concentrated in the three appendix sections (on Anglo-Saxon government, on the feudal and Anglo-Norman regime, and on the later Middle Ages) sits awkwardly at times with his routine accounts elsewhere in the volumes of kings and great ones. The general effect, however, is to anchor England's aberrant recent past more firmly than ever in the deep currents of an earlier European history.

Hume's narrative of feudal elaboration and erosion in England undoubtedly owes something to Voltaire's *Essai*, the first historical work to treat this subject on an international scale. Hume had spotted the *Essai* on a friend's desk during the composition of the medieval volumes and asked to borrow it.[64] Hume's narrative of the mitigation of feudalism through technological developments, and municipal incorporation, and his focus upon the Catholic Church (in spite of all its superstitious follies) as a force for legal order has much in common with Voltaire's work. Hume lays far greater emphasis than Voltaire upon the role of the newly rediscovered corpus of Roman law in promoting more impartial legal structures and professions, even in countries such as England where the traditional legal system persisted and grew (II, 441: II, 520). Hume's unusually complex narrative of the rise of the post-feudal centralised state in England – with its new forms of property, commerce, and more vigorous arts and sciences – has been paid the tribute of many modern assessments.[65] It is not my purpose

62 Phillipson, *Hume*, 135.

63 On eighteenth-century Scottish studies of feudalism, see chapter 4.

64 Hume to Gilbert Elliot, Lord Minto (1 May 1760), *Letters*, no. 64.

65 On the nature and context of Hume's analysis of 'feudalism', see R. J. Smith, *The Gothic Bequest: Medieval Institutions in British Thought, 1688-1863* (Cambridge, 1987), chapter 3. See also Wexler,

to add anything more to recent accounts of Hume's analysis of feudalism, except to point out that they mostly concentrate upon the appendix chapters to the *History*, and so exaggerate the overall thematic coherence of the medieval volumes. The long read through the whole of these volumes dispels any impression of this kind of unity. In between moments of sociological generalisation, the reader often encounters a historian frustrated by the intractable nature of his material: 'The ancient history of England is nothing but reversals: Every thing is in fluctuation and movement: One faction is continually undoing what was established by another' (II, 264: II, 311). Hume is worried by the evidential problems of the Anglo-Saxon and medieval periods, and dubious about their intrinsic interest as subjects for history. His relief is palpable when, in a coda to the second volume, he takes his leave of his *History* and waves his readers on to the Tudor era:

> Thus have we pursued the history of England thro' a series of many barbarous ages; till we have at last reached the dawn of civility and science, and have the prospect, both of greater certainty in our historical narrations, and of being able to present to the reader a spectacle more worthy of his attention. (II, 439: II, 518)

Although Hume soon modifies this by adding that the 'spectacle' of these barbarous ages is not 'altogether unentertaining and uninstructive', his developmental narrative of feudal erosion is often halted by the moments of senseless disorder which England's medieval history seems to entail (II, 440: II, 518). Hume's medieval Europe has little autonomous life. He is not greatly interested in its arts or chivalry (as Gibbon would later be), but sees it merely as an inversion of the outward-looking, commercially-minded and centralised states of his own era (I, 262: I, 296). Like the medieval sections of Voltaire's *Essai*, an evolutionary narrative of the decline of feudalism competes with a horrified pathology of barbarousness. At times, the lessons Hume draws from the Middle Ages seem weakly prudential: 'and if the aspect in some periods seems horrid and deformed, we may thence learn to cherish with greater anxiety that science and civility, which has so close a connexion with virtue and humanity' (II, 440: II, 518).

The discursive character of the appendices belies a generally annalistic structure. Following Rapin's example, Hume presents the Anglo-Saxon age in chronicle format. Hume has nothing positive to salvage from the Norman Conquest. This is surprising, since, during the eighteenth century, historians had started to assimilate the Conquest to a cosmopolitan narrative of British adaptability and multi-ethnicity. Rapin, who applies an insistently European perspective to the whole of his medieval narrative,

David Hume and the History of England, chapter 4; John W. Danforth, 'Hume's *History* and Economic Development' in *Liberty in Hume's History of England*, eds. Donald Livingston and Nicholas Capaldi (Dordrecht, 1990).

welcomes the Conquest as Britain's moment of accession to continental culture and prestige: 'The *English*, hitherto unknown to the rest of the World, began after this Revolution to make a considerable figure in *Europe*. This may be said to be the first Step by which *England* is arrived to that height of Grandeur and Glory, we behold it in at present.'[66] Temple, whose *Introduction to the History of England* gives an elegant account of English history to 1066, shares Rapin's sentiments on this subject:

> *England* [after the Conquest] grew much greater both in Dominion and Power abroad, and also in Dignity and State at home ... Besides, by this Conquest we gained more Learning, more Civility, more Refinement of Language, Customs, and Manners, from the great Resort of other Strangers, as well as Mixture of *French* and *Normans*.[67]

Defoe used this new strain of British cosmopolitanism to witty effect in his satire 'A True-Born Englishman' (1701): 'Thus from a Mixture of all Kinds began, / That Het'rogeneous Thing, an Englishman' (lines 334–5). A solemn tone in cosmopolitan readings of the Conquest persisted, however, as can been seen later in the century in Burke's unpublished *Abridgement of English History*:

> The English laws, manners, and maxims, were suddenly changed [by the Conquest]; the scene was enlarged; and the communication with the rest of Europe being thus opened has been preserved ever since in a continued series of wars and negotiations.[68]

Albeit cautiously, Burke welcomes the fact that the Conquest put an end to Saxon insularity. Hume, however, rejects such cosmopolitan interpretations of this event. Although he acknowledges that William wisely 'bore the semblance of the lawful prince, not of the conqueror', he emphasises the immediate sufferings and oppressions of the English rather than any long-term gains (I, 169: I, 192). Hume itemises the political and cultural weaknesses of the Anglo-Saxons ('the people had in a good measure lost all national pride and spirit') which had left them vulnerable to foreign take-over (I, 164: I, 187). His analysis is, in some respects, similar in its preoccupations to Milton's account, in his *History of Britain*, with the political and moral decline of the Anglo-Saxons which ultimately left them prey to 'so easie a Conquest' by the Normans.[69] The Conquest becomes, in Hume's closing review of his *History*, the lowest 'point of depression' in the

[66] Paul de Rapin-Thoyras, *The History of England*, trans. Nicholas Tindal (4 vols.; London, 1732–45), I, 164.

[67] Temple, *Introduction to the History of England* (London, 1695), 313, 315.

[68] Edmund Burke, *An Essay Towards an Abridgement of English History* (*c.* 1757), *Works* (10 vols.; London, 1803–12), 369.

[69] Milton's history was readily available to eighteenth-century readers since it formed part of volume I of the compilation *Compleat History of England* (3 vols.; London, 1706).

dark ages after the Roman Empire, after which the wheels of history begin to rotate upwards again (II, 441: II, 519). The 'science and civility' which some eighteenth-century historians had associated with the coming of the Normans is thus deferred in Hume's *History* until the eve of the Tudor era (II, 439: II, 519).

In the pages following the Conquest, Hume's medieval Britain progresses only with faltering steps. Robertson, in his *View of the Progress of Society in Europe* (1769), would later describe the twelfth to the fifteenth centuries as a period of rapid, even exponential development in Europe. In particular, he would rehabilitate the Crusades as an event fortunate in its outcome if not in its fanatical motivation, and a decisive moment in the development of inter-European trading and cultural links. Hume, by contrast, is close to Voltaire in dismissing the Crusades as 'the most signal and most durable monument of human folly, that has yet appeared in any age or nation' (I, 209: I, 234). Hume silently follows the contours and, on occasions, the vocabulary of Voltaire's account. For instance, when he comes to describe the conquest of Jerusalem in 1099, he responds directly to Voltaire's comments on the primary sources. Most of the contemporary accounts, Voltaire notes, state that, after a general massacre of non-Christians in the city, the crusaders burst into tears as soon as they approached the holy sepulchre. Voltaire doubts whether such contradictory behaviour was humanly possible: 'Il est très vraisemblable qu'ils y donnèrent des marques de religion; mais cette tendresse qui se manifesta par des pleurs n'est guère compatible avec cet esprit de vertige, de fureur, de débauche, et d'emportement. Le même homme peut être furieux et tendre, mais non dans le même temps' (1963, I, 566). Hume appears to engage with and revise this account by accepting the evidence of the sources, and drawing attention to this incident as an example of the paradoxes of barbarism:

> And their devotion, enlivened by the presence of the place where [Christ] had suffered, so overcame their fury, that they dissolved in tears, and bore the appearance of every soft and tender sentiment. So inconsistent is human nature with itself! And so easily does the most effeminate superstition ally, both with the most heroic courage, and with the fiercest barbarity! (I, 221–2: I, 250)

Hume's account of this event retains Voltaire's horrified emphasis upon the 'fury/fureur' of the Latins, but improves upon his philosophical analysis of the pathology of the superstitious mind. Neither historian anticipates the historicising readings of the Crusades which would later be developed in the works of Robertson and Gibbon.

To a large extent, Hume's medieval volumes describe the years preparatory to the continental-style regime of the Tudors, but they also reflect, in the episodes of the Conquest, the Crusades and elsewhere, a negative image of modernity. The argumentative heart of the *History* remains the Tudor volumes, the *terminus ad quem* of the Middle Ages and the most internationally comparative section of the work. The Tudor volumes become, once the *History of England* is completed, the measure of England's divergence, in the seventeenth century, from the more usual, and perhaps more desirable, tendency of European states to develop civilised, absolute monarchies after a late medieval period of defeudalisation. The hasty account of the Glorious Revolution at the very end of the *History* takes on the burden of a happy ending anticipated only in the last few hundred pages, marking, for good or ill, an irrevocable break with the political forms of the past: 'it gave such an ascendant to popular principles, as has put the nature of the English constitution beyond all controversy' (443: VI, 531). These closing pages offer an implicit revision to Hume's earlier essay on a similar subject, 'Whether the British Government Inclines more to Absolute Monarchy or to a Republic' (1741) which predicted that, if things became any worse in Britain, 'we shall, at last, after many convulsions, and civil wars, find repose in absolute monarchy, which it would have been happier for us to have established peaceably from the beginning'.[70] The *History of England* offers no conjectured road back down to the constitutional repose of Elizabethan England, and Hume, with his wry and qualified appreciation of the Revolution Settlement, is no longer sure that, even if there were such a road, he would be in any hurry to take it: 'we, in this island, have ever since enjoyed, if not the best system of government, at least the most entire system of liberty, that ever was known amongst mankind' (443: VI, 531). Only a European sensibility such as Hume's can gauge the oddity of such a system of liberty, but it also takes a philosopher to accept the sociological wisdom of a form of government which, however flawed, can accommodate the desire of the British people to behave as oddly as they please.

[70] *Essays*, 53.

4

William Robertson to the rescue of Scottish history

William Robertson enjoyed, in his day and for much of the nineteenth century, a reputation as a historian little inferior to Hume. Recent scholarship has gone some way towards reinstating Robertson as a figure of central importance both to the cultural life of eighteenth-century Scotland and to the historical enterprises of Enlightenment Europe.[1] The coincidence of these two spheres of Robertson's importance is not accidental, but helps to explain the nature and former scale of his reputation. By the mid-eighteenth century, when Robertson first ventured into the historical field, narrative history in Britain had attained a degree of prestige and popularity which made it inevitable that any social group in the country seeking prominence would want to be able to boast a successful historian in their midst. One such group, Scotland's clerical and professional elite, was particularly desirous of cultural recognition in Britain as a corollary of the greater participation in British society made possible by the Union of 1707, and also by the relative economic buoyancy, and atmosphere of university reform and religious liberalisation in the country during this period. The ferment of intellectual activity in the university towns of mid-eighteenth-century Scotland, now known as the Scottish Enlightenment, generated achievements in the fields of moral philosophy, social analysis, political economy and history. This activity entered an intense phase at the point when Hume was writing his *Essays* and *History*. However, the historian whom the Scottish literati tended to regard as their cultural spokesman was the more orthodox, eventually eminent and highly remunerated minister and principal of the University of Edinburgh, William Robertson.[2]

[1] See, for example, the forthcoming volume of essays, *William Robertson and the Expansion of Europe*, ed. Stewart J. Brown as part of Cambridge University Press' Ideas in Context series. The Thoemmes Press is about to bring out a complete edition of Robertson's historical and lesser works with critical introductions. However, very little has as yet been published on Robertson as a historian.

[2] It is not my purpose in this chapter to supply details of Robertson's life and career; these have been admirably discussed by Richard B. Sher, *Church and University in the Scottish Enlightenment* (Princeton, 1985). Dugald Stewart supplied the first biography, along with many of Robertson's letters in *Biographical Memoirs of Adam Smith, LL.D., of William Robertson, D.D. and of Thomas Reid, D.D.* (Edinburgh, 1811), and further information on his background along with a sociology of his

Robertson spent his career in Scotland and dedicated himself, implicitly in his histories and directly in his professional life, to local voluntary societies, and to church and university reform. In particular, he led the 'Moderate' reforming wing of the Church of Scotland in its long and successful campaign to fashion what they saw as a less morally austere, more politically reasonable ecclesiastical establishment. As the principal of Edinburgh University, he promoted religious tolerance in his community and the new kinds of moral and social philosophies in his own institution.

The intellectual world which Robertson and Hume shared with Adam Smith, the literary critic Hugh Blair, the social philosopher Adam Ferguson, the autobiographer Alexander Carlyle, and many other prominent church and university men was at once unionist, cosmopolitan and intensely proud of post-Union Scotland. This culture has, in recent years, been influentially represented as partaking of an 'Addisonian' social idiom, which is to say that it placed special emphasis upon the qualities advocated in Addison's *Spectator* of urban politeness, sociability and moderation in all things.[3] It was both an expression of new-found self-confidence in the social and intellectual life of Scotland, and a bid for respectability and prestige in Britain as a whole, particularly after the 1745 Jacobite Rebellion had rendered Scotland suspect in English eyes. Robertson's historical works are of a piece with the quest for personal and Scottish prestige which informed his public life, and they distil and refine his wider cultural objectives of moderation, tolerance and politeness. They are buttressed by the self-confidently provincial identity of his aristocratic, professional and clerical Whig circles. However, they also give some hint of the cost of deep anxiety at which such provincial self-confidence was sometimes bought. Robertson was the most insistently cosmopolitan of all eighteenth-century historians, in part because he felt that enduring tensions between Scottish and British identities could only be recuperated within an encompassing European perspective. In this chapter, a detailed reading of Robertson's *History of Scotland* (1759) as an attempt to stabilise the precarious identity of united Britain, by diverting it into still broader channels, will exemplify some aspects of the national predicament faced by him and his Scottish contemporaries. Robertson's cosmopolitan history is of a different cast to Hume's. Hume ironises the provincial peculiarity of the English by gradually subjecting their wayward historical performance to the cold gaze of a European eye; 'I am, however, sensible,' he confessed

ideas can be found in Charles Camic, *Experience and Enlightenment; Socialization for Cultural Change in Eighteenth-Century Scotland* (Edinburgh, 1983).

3 See Nicholas Phillipson, 'The Scottish Enlightenment' in *The Enlightenment in National Context*, eds. Roy Porter and Mikulas Teich (Cambridge, 1981) and 'Culture and Society in the Eighteenth-Century Province: The Case of Edinburgh and the Scottish Enlightenment' in *The University in Society*, ed. Lawrence Stone (2 vols.; Princeton, 1974).

in a letter to a Scottish friend, 'that the first Editions [of the *History*] were too full of those foolish English Prejudices, which all Nations and all Ages disavow'.[4] Robertson, however, seeks, with an ever widening gaze, the common patterns and cultural affinities in the histories of the European nations and their colonies in order to transcend the national and religious prejudices of Britain. In these patterns he finds the organising hand of God hidden behind European social processes of evolution and convergence. With each new history, he approaches these evolutionary processes with greater diagnostic precision. Robertson's mature histories, *The History of the Reign of the Emperor Charles V* (1769) and *The History of America* (1777), precipitate a complex encounter between the social theory of the Scottish Enlightenment and the histories of Britain and Europe to which it is applied, tested, and ultimately found wanting. Robertson's first work, *The History of Scotland*, lacks this complicating dimension of social theory, but is otherwise indicative of the advantages of a cosmopolitan perspective to an ambitious Scottish historian writing himself in from the margins of British literary culture.

Apprenticeship

In 1756, Robertson collaborated with Hugh Blair, Adam Smith and other aspiring literati on a short-lived magazine entitled the *Edinburgh Review* whose object was to give an account of books published in Scotland and, more generally, to promote higher standards in Scottish learning and literature.[5] The magazine folded after only two issues, and, as it happened, the last thing to appear in its pages was a letter from Smith to the editors in which he tried to reformulate the publication's objectives. The magazine, worried Smith, had allowed itself to become too parochially Scottish in its literary interests; it needed to be, not simply more broadly British, but more European in focus: 'you should observe', Smith added by way of qualification, 'with regard to Europe in general the same plan which you followed with regard to England, examining such performances only, as tho' they may not go down to the remotest posterity, have yet a chance of being remembered for thirty or forty years to come'.[6] Smith then praised warmly the France of Voltaire and the *Encyclopédie*, which seemed to him to abound in such potentially durable productions. Robertson, at least, had

[4] Hume to Gilbert Elliot (21 February 1770), *Letters*, no. 439.

[5] *The Edinburgh Review; containing an account of books and pamphlets that have been published in Scotland* (2 numbers; 1755–6). For a full account of this project, see Richard Sher, *Church and University*, 68–72. Robertson's pieces included reviews of David Moyses, *Memoirs of the Affairs of Scotland*, a collection of poems published by Dodsley, a catalogue of bishops to the year 1688, a printing of some of Louis XIV's letters and William Douglass' *Summary, Historical and Political … of British Settlements in North America*.

[6] *Edinburgh Review*, ii, 59.

anticipated Smith's point that even works of local interest ought to be considered within a European frame of reference. Reviewing some rather lack-lustre *Memoirs of the Affairs of* [sixteenth-century] *Scotland*, compiled by one David Moyses, he complained that the work falls short of the 'real objects of history' in ignoring large-scale political developments and 'the influence of foreign connections' in this period.[7] Robertson then rounded off the review with a discreet manifesto for his own projected history:

We cannot, on this occasion, forbear expressing our wishes, that some person of candor and abilities would condescend to the labour of clearing this mysterious passage in our history.[8]

A good history of the sixteenth-century Scotland – the important period during which the 'principles' were 'fixed, and the ends ascertained' of the country's political parties – would, Robertson disingenuously suggests, be consonant with the vision of Scottish culture promulgated by the magazine as a whole, and the man would be performing a public service who undertook to write it.[9]

Robertson was well under way with his history of Scotland by the following year, and was writing letters to his friend David Dalrymple (later Lord Hailes) requesting research material. By 1758 he was able to send him a completed fragment, not subsequently revised, on one of the most controversial topics of all, John Knox.[10] When Robertson's *History of Scotland* did appear in 1759, it embodied cultural aspirations for Scotland similar to those of the *Edinburgh Review* and, more generally, of the Moderate clergymen, literati and their patrons who made up his Edinburgh circle. In addition to supporting warmly the Union and the Glorious Revolution of 1688–9, Robertson looked forward, in the closing pages, to the coming economic and cultural improvement of Scotland under the leadership of the nation's educated and professional elites.[11] The period preceding the Union, Robertson argued in the closing section of the *History of Scotland*, had been one of decline partly because of a failure of cultural leadership in the country: clergymen were at that time 'more eminent for piety than for learning', and, presumably, were unable to write elegant sermons of the type praised by the *Edinburgh Review*; lawyers, Lords of Articles and parliamentarians similarly failed to furnish Scotland with

[7] Ibid., i, 26. [8] Ibid., i, 25. [9] Ibid., i, 14 (misprint for 24).

[10] For Robertson's research requests see National Library of Scotland, *Newhailes Papers*, MS 25294, f. 7, ff. 37–8, ff. 55–6, ff. 57–8. The fragment is in the same collection, NLS, MS 25294, f. 76.

[11] On the social milieu of Enlightened Scotland, see Nicholas Phillipson, 'Culture and Society in the Eighteenth-Century Province'; Roger L. Emerson, 'The Enlightenment and Social Structures' in *City and Society in the Eighteenth Century*, eds. Paul Fritz and David Williams (Toronto, 1973) and 'The Social Composition of Enlightened Scotland; the Select Society of Edinburgh, 1754–1764', *SVEC*, 114 (1973), 291–329; R. A. Houston, *Social Change in the Age of Enlightenment: Edinburgh 1660–1760* (Oxford, 1994).

speeches of taste and refinement.[12] The *History of Scotland* thus indirectly factors into its closing aspirations for the Scottish nation a role for its clergyman-author in future social improvements.

This unobtrusive claim to cultural leadership, made good in Robertson subsequent career, was not, in fact, unusual in a work of this type. As David Allan has shown in a recent study of the Scottish Enlightenment and its antecedents, Scottish writers and their readers habitually regarded erudition as a qualification for social leadership.[13] However, Robertson, like his fellow Edinburgh reviewers, adds to this leadership requirement a new qualification: stylistic polish on an English model, and the elimination from prose of all recognisably Scottish vocabulary and grammar. He intended his own elegant English prose to set the linguistic standard for Scotland, and to contribute to the correction of Lowland peculiarities of dialect. Two years later he even joined the 'Society for Promoting the Reading and Speaking of the English Language in Scotland'.[14] Robertson's determination to remove all Scotticisms from his prose (even though he would never have been mistaken for an Englishman in his speech) was common to many of Scottish writers of his time, and he welcomed advice on this score from Horace Walpole and fellow Scotticism-eliminator, David Hume.[15] Many of the revisions to the *History of Scotland* were in fact directed to this end.

Robertson's history was well received. Letters and reports of praise poured in from both sides of the border from Walpole, Garrick, Prince Edward and William Warburton, as well as Hume, the Scottish MP Gilbert Elliot and other Scottish friends and acquaintances.[16] The work went through an impressive total of fourteen editions before his death. Robertson had been well aware from the outset of the close connection between the anglicised polish of his writing, his own fame, and the success of his and his friends' promotional activities on behalf of Scotland. The Union, he too much protested in the closing paragraph of his history, had placed the Scots on an equal footing with the rest of England, 'and every

[12] *The History of Scotland, during the Reigns of Queen Mary and King James VI. till his accession to the crown of England: with a review of the Scottish history previous to that period, and an appendix containing original papers* (2 vols.; London, 1759), II, 259. All quotations in this chapter will be taken from this second edition (a slightly corrected version of the first edition of 1759 with an added dissertation on the murder of Darnley). The history was only slightly revised during Robertson's lifetime, and differences between the second edition and the fourteenth edition 'with the author's last emendations and additions' (2 vols.; London, 1794) are noted.

[13] David Allan, *Virtue,Learning and the Scottish Enlightenment* (Edinburgh, 1993).

[14] See Davis D. McElroy, *Scotland's Age of Improvement: A Survey of Eighteenth-Century Literary Clubs and Societies* (Pullman, Washington, 1969), chapter 3.

[15] Walpole to Robertson (4 February 1759), *Horace Walpole's Correspondence*, ed. W. S. Lewis (48 vols.; Oxford, 1937–83), XV, 41–5. Hume to Robertson (8 February 1759), *New Letters of David Hume*, eds. E. C. Mossner and R. Klibansky (Oxford, 1954), no. 27.

[16] These letters of approbation are preserved in the National Library of Scotland, *Robertson–MacDonald Papers*, MS 3942, ff. 5–24.

obstruction that had retarded their pursuit, or prevented their acquisition of literary fame, was totally removed'(II, 260). This was something of a reminder to his English audience not to succumb to the anti-Caledonianism common among them since the 1745 Jacobite Rebellion. Hume was generously delighted that Robertson had won in England the acceptance which he craved for himself and for Scotland: 'The town will have it that you was educated at Oxford', Hume reported, 'thinking it impossible for a mere untravelled Scotchman to produce such language'.[17] Hume has been identified as the most likely author of a warm review of the work which appeared in the London-based *Critical Review* the same year.[18] Robertson was no doubt gratified by this timely puff; as his somewhat jaded friend, the diarist Alexander Carlyle noted, he was an ambitious cleric, and the *History of Scotland* combined a personal programme for self-aggrandisement with his cultural promotion of Scotland.[19] Within the next few years, Robertson was amply rewarded with the principalship of Edinburgh University, and the title of Historiographer Royal of Scotland, a post in the gift of Lord Bute.[20]

Robertson went on to write two more major and one minor historical works, remaining committed throughout his successful career to the traditional Scottish humanist idea of history as the exemplification of active and responsible social leadership. Even so, the subject-matter of his subsequent histories – Europe from the Middle Ages to the sixteenth century, the discovery and conquest of the Americas, and pre-British India – took him far beyond the Protestant, provincial concerns of his environment. Where historians such as Sher and Allan have seen a symmetry between Robertson's institutional roles in church and university and his historical activities, it is also possible to discern a growing disparity between them. Robertson's increasingly international historical perspectives disrupt as much as they confirm the new provincial self-confidence of

[17] Hume to Robertson (8 February 1759), *New Letters*, no. 27.

[18] David Raynor, 'Hume and Robertson's *History of Scotland*', *British Journal for Eighteenth-Century Studies*, 10 (1987), 59–63.

[19] *The Autobiography of Dr. Alexander Carlyle of Inveresk, 1722-1805*, ed. John Hill Burton, with an introduction by Richard B. Sher (Bristol, 1990), 304: 'Robertson's conversation was not always so prudent as his conduct; one instance of which, his always asserting that any minister of state who did not take care of himself, when he had an opportunity, was no very wise man; this maxim shock'd most young people, who thought the doctors standard of public virtue was not very high'.

[20] For details, see Sher, *Church and University*, 93–119. See also, Jeremy Cater, 'The Making of Principal Robertson in 1762: Politics and the University of Edinburgh in the Second Half of the Eighteenth Century', *Scottish Historical Review*, 49 (1970), 60–84; James Lee McKelvey, 'William Robertson and Lord Bute', *Studies in Scottish Literature*, 6 (1969), 238–47. Robertson's correspondence with Lord Bute over the matter of the position of Historiographer Royal can be found in *The Jenkinson Papers: 1760-66*, ed. N. S. Jucker (London, 1949). Denys Hay, 'The Historiographers Royal in England and Scotland', *Scottish Historical Review*, 30 (1951), 15–29 explains the nature and history of the post.

his Whig, Presbyterian colleagues. His growing interest in the uniqueness and interconnectedness of Europe was by no means encouraged by or calculated to satisfy his British patrons and audience. Robertson was granted the position of Historiographer Royal (with its attendant stipend of £200 a year) on the understanding that he would produce a history of England. He indicated that he would comply with this condition, and, in 1761, received a letter from Lord Cathcart conveying Bute's pleasure at his willingness to undertake the project.[21] Robertson did not proceed with the history; he may have been uneasy about placing himself in direct competition with his fellow historian of England and friend, David Hume, although, once Hume had finished, he clearly felt that this was no obstacle.[22] He told Horace Walpole, as early as 1759, that he intended to avoid narrow political controversy, and to broaden his field to include all of European history up to the sixteenth century.[23] Hume found the project too broad and ambitious, and recommended safer biographical projects, but Robertson ignored the advice of his friends and pressure from his patrons, and went on to expand his work on sixteenth-century Scotland onto the European scene.[24] Robertson's gamble on his choice of literary career paid off and his reputation steadily gained solidity. Although many of Robertson's contemporaries did aim to renegotiate, on more favourable terms, cultural relations between the Scottish province and the English metropolis, Robertson played to a more international audience. Like Adam Smith in his letter to the *Edinburgh Review*, Robertson sought to display from his provincial position a European historical sensibility.

Whether deliberately or not, Robertson followed in all its essentials Voltaire's career path as a historian – from national to (mainly) European history, and then to pseudo-scientific pieces on the social evolution of early man. An honorary member of the Philosophical Society of Edinburgh since 1745, Voltaire was widely published and read in Scotland. Republication and translation of his works began when the Scottish press first started to expand in the 1750s, and Voltaire's histories were dominant in their category of the Scottish book trade until the end of the century.[25]

[21] Cathcart to Robertson (21 August 1761), NLS, *Robertson–MacDonald Papers*, MS 3942, f. 48.

[22] Robertson to Elliot (7 April 1761), NLS, *Minto Papers*, MS 11009, ff. 149–52.

[23] Robertson to Walpole (20 February, 1759), *Horace Walpole's Correspondence*, XV, 46: 'The events are great and interesting ... The field is wide and I shall have many books to read, but as I shall not be plagued with the endless controversies which perplexed me in my last work, I am not dismayed at mere labour.'

[24] Hume to Robertson (7 April 1759), *New Letters*, no. 28.

[25] Keith Marshall, 'France and the Scottish Press, 1700–1800', *Studies in Scottish Literature*, 13 (1978), 1–14; Alison K. Howard, 'Montesquieu, Voltaire and Rousseau in Eighteenth-Century Scotland; a checklist of editions and translations of their works published in Scotland before 1801', *The Bibliotheck*, 2 (1959), 40–63. The latter should be consulted for details of reviews and extracts in Scottish magazines only since it has been supplanted, in Voltaire's case, by the bibliography of A. M. Rousseau, 'L'Angleterre et Voltaire', *SVEC*. 145–7 (1976). More

The *Scots Magazine* started printing extracts of Voltaire's *Siècle de Louis XIV* in 1752, the same year as the first untranslated Scottish edition of the work; the first extracts from his *Essai* did not appear until 1757, some three years after the publication in England of the first substantial edition, and the first Scottish translation only appeared the following year. There were Scottish editions of nearly all of Voltaire's historical works, including his histories of Russia, Charles XII of Sweden, and of the War of 1741. Robertson, a very able linguist, probably read all or most of these in French at some stage, and paid fulsome, if double-edged, tribute to Voltaire's historical skill and scholarship in the final note to his 'A View of the Progress of Society in Europe'.[26] There was a copy of the *Siècle de Louis XIV* in the Advocates' Library in Edinburgh, and Robertson had certainly read this or another edition by the time he came to participate in the *Edinburgh Review* venture. Reviewing a collection of Louis XIV's letters, he commented:

> If the *Siècle de Louis XIV.* had not awakened the curiosity of the public so much as to render every particular of the reign of that prince interesting, this collection had remained forever in the cabinet where it was lodged. [27]

As he indicated in this review, he was persuaded by Voltaire's and Hume's presentation of Louis XIV as a civilised absolute monarch who, far from being the despot of Whig demonology, presided over a 'free state' and often governed in the best interests of his country.[28] In a more general way, Hugh Blair, although critical of Voltaire in his unpublished lecture notes, publicly praised the *Siècle de Louis XIV* in his *Lectures on Rhetoric and Belles Letters* (which he began delivering at the same time as the publication of the *History of Scotland*) for introducing to the world a species of historical composition which pays 'a more particular attention than was formerly given to laws, customs, commerce, religion, literature, and every other thing that tends to show the spirit and genius of nations'.[29] As well as showing similar interest in the institutional and cultural characteristics of particular nations, both Robertson and Voltaire were concerned to situate their national stories within the larger structures of Europe and the world; both did this, not primarily in order to verify ontological propositions about human nature and the functioning of societies (in Montesquieu's manner), but in order to confer upon national histories the validity of belonging to a wider pattern of history.

generally, Henry W. Meikle, 'Voltaire and Scotland', *Etudes anglaises*, 2 (1958), 193–201 and J. H. Brumfitt, 'Scotland and the French Enlightenment' in *The Age of Enlightenment*, ed. W. H. Barber (Edinburgh, 1967).

[26] Smith to Robertson (October 1788), *The Correspondence of Adam Smith*, eds. E. C. Mossner and I. Simpson Ross (Oxford, 1987), no. 282: 'You are, I imagine, by far the best modern linguist among us.'

[27] *Edinburgh Review*, ii, 18. [28] Ibid., ii, 21.

[29] Blair, NLS, *Lecture Notes*, MS 850 and MS 250. *Lectures on Rhetoric and Belles Lettres*, ed. Harold F. Harding (2 vols.; Illinois, 1965), II, 288.

Deciding where to begin and how to end

Robertson prefaced the *History of Scotland* with an extensive essay on Scottish medieval history, which examines the country's political formation within the context of developments in the other European countries – a narrative and scholarly feat admired by Hume, among others.[30] Prior to the publication in 1768 of the *Précis du Siècle de Louis XV*, editions of the *Siècle de Louis XIV* contained, by way of an appendix, an extensive 'Tableau de l'europe, depuis la paix d'utrecht jusqu'en 1750', which displays a similar propensity for grand overviews of the development of Europe. Robertson divides the history of Scotland into four eras, dismissing the first three, and declaring his intention to concentrate upon the last (from the death of James V to the Union of the Crowns) because, like the age of Louis XIV which Voltaire considered in the context of the other three great ages of man, it alone influenced the course of history in neighbouring European states: 'The first ages of Scottish history are dark and fabulous. Nations, as well as men, arrive at maturity by degrees, and the events, which happened during their infancy or early youth, cannot be recollected, and deserve not to be remembered' (I, 1). In addition to a possible debt to Voltaire, Robertson's somewhat bland scheme of history here (dark ages not recoverable, infancy and maturity) may also owe something to the work of his old university teacher Charles Mackie, who was Professor of Universal History at Edinburgh. In a lecture delivered to the Philosophical Society in 1741, Mackie had meditated upon problems of evidence in early Scottish history; citing Marcus Terentius Varro's well-known division of history into three periods, the obscure, the fabulous and the historical, Mackie had warned that Scottish records and traditions rarely sufficed for a properly 'historical account' of the nation's distant past.[31] Robertson might also have been interested by the way in which Mackie linked the problem of evidence in early Scottish history to the problem of national bias: 'Writers have often been blinded by passion and strong prejudice arising from a regard to their country or their religion, or both.'[32] Robertson's relegation of earlier Scottish history to the lower division of antiquarian subject-matter is, of course, silently polemical, since studies of earlier periods in Scottish history were often the locus for overtly nationalistic myth-making. Around this time, as Colin Kidd has shown, Scottish scholars were conducting a frontal assault upon the traditions and myths once associated with Scotland's heroic and independent national

[30] David Hume, *History of England* (6 vols.; Indianapolis, 1983), I, 455.

[31] Charles Mackie, 'A Dissertation on the Sources of Vulgar Errors in History' (1741), Edinburgh University Library, *Lectures and Notes*, MS La. ii. 37. See L. W. Sharp, 'Charles Mackie, the First Professor of History at Edinburgh', *Scottish Historical Review*, 41 (1962), 23–45.

[32] MS La. ii 37 (14).

past.[33] Robertson aligns his history with, but keeps a politic distance from, this modernising intellectual enterprise.

Robertson decided to begin his narrative proper at the point where Scotland's history had left the realm of the obscure or fabulous, and where it could be said to have a number of political features in common with the rest of European history. Like Voltaire and Hume, Robertson regarded the arrival of the idea of the balance of power as a key event in the history of European interrelations. At the beginning of his story, he notes the arrival, in the mid-sixteenth century, of a balanced, diplomatic 'system' in which Scotland, gradually becoming an international player, 'took her station' (I, 76). Scotland becomes a legitimate object of study at the point at which it becomes a piece in the European chess game. Even so, Scotland still appears to require a certain amount of special pleading as a subject for history:

> [Scotland's] situation in the political state of Europe was so important, its influence on the operations of the neighbouring kingdoms was so visible, that its history becomes an object of attention to Foreigners. (I, 5)

Robertson's objective was to absolve Scottish history from provincialism through narrative cosmopolitan contextualisation. Robertson places his history, in part, at the service of the Whig literati's programme for promoting Scotland, although the execution of the narrative takes many risks with the national self-confidence upon which this promotion depended. The *History of Scotland* undertakes a paradoxical enterprise both to celebrate and redeem the province's history. It is not simply a chapter in the history of the consolidation of moderate Scottish provincial self-confidence in the eighteenth century, nor does it succumb entirely to the generalising pressures of cosmopolitan history.

In the prefatory essay to the *History of Scotland*, Robertson sets out the European terms of reference within which he will interpret the narrative of sixteenth-century Scotland. Despite the fact that, in the early part of the century, Scotland had already 'emerged from her obscurity' and 'began to have some influence upon the fate of distant nations', the narrative concentrates upon Scotand's failure (atypical, from a European point of view) to evolve stable post-feudal political institutions, most notably a strong, centralised monarchy. Ill-equipped for the early modern period, Scotland nevertheless finds itself suddenly drawn into a European pattern of ideological, religious and dynastic upheaval (I, 76–7). Scotland's failure, in the late Middle Ages, to modernise along the European lines described in the prefatory essay exacerbates its experience of violence and fragmentation in the sixteenth century. Highly centralised, even despotic monarchy

[33] Colin Kidd, *Subverting Scotland's Past: Scottish Whig Historians and the Creation of an Anglo-British Identity, 1689–c. 1830* (Cambridge, 1993).

in Scotland, Robertson implies, might have eased the transition from feudal oligarchy to a modern balanced political constitution. Colin Kidd has argued that it was an article of faith with Scottish Whig historians that 'nations had to pass through the valley of the shadow of despotism if they were to attain civil liberty'.[34] Scotland's problem in the early modern period is, in Robertson's diagnosis, that it does not even enter the unhappy valley, let alone find its own way up to civil liberty. Robertson finds no internal remedy for Scotland's descent, in the sixteenth century, into civil and religious strife; after 'universal licence and anarchy prevailed to a degree, scarce consistent with the preservation of society', a resolution occurs only with the chance accession of a Scottish monarch, James VI, to the English throne (II, 174).

The story ends with a cultural, economic and political disaster for Scotland, the Union of the Crowns, which leads to the withering away of the country as a distinctive, independent nation in the seventeenth century. Robertson is confident that the Union of 1707 has halted this decline, and he represents Scotland as somewhat passively acceding at this point to the more just, balanced English constitution. Scotland's national peculiarities are then slowly eroded as both countries come to share the same standard of 'taste' and enter, as it were, a neoclassical community of cultural and political aesthetics (II, 259). The closing pages of the history suggest that, after the Union, Scotland embarked upon a path of historical Enlightenment along which 'commerce advanced in its progress, and government attained nearer to perfection' (II, 253). The acquisition of political rights after 1688 awakens in the Scottish people a form of *esprit philosophique* as 'their mind began to open' (II, 253). The section on post-Union Scotland welcomes the development of polite civil activity and culture with no signs of regret for the nation's loss of political independence:

> adopted into a constitution, whose genius and laws were more liberal than their own, they [the Scots] have extended their commerce, refined their manners, made improvements in the elegancies of life, and cultivated the arts and sciences. (II, 254)

Robertson's enthusiasm for the Union, however, stems, less from political deference to England, than from a preoccupation with Britain's international prestige. It is largely on these grounds that he welcomes the Union of the Crowns:

> Thus were united two kingdoms, divided from the earliest accounts of time, but destined, by their situation, to form one great monarchy. And by this junction of its whole native force, Great Britain hath risen to an eminence and authority in Europe which England and Scotland could never have attained.
>
> (II, 249; 1794 text, II, 299 adds 'while separate' after 'Scotland')

[34] Ibid., 182.

Scotland's post-Union success is predicated upon the necessity of discontinuity in its history. In some ways, the closing section resembles the meditation of a Voltairean sensibility upon the necessary discontinuity between the pre-modern and the modern. Nevertheless, though Robertson is also welcoming and implicitly advocating creative activity in the social and cultural spheres (the modern commercial analogue to active valour and virtue in the settings of ancient or Renaissance republics), he gives some intimation of the failure on the part of the Scottish people to take their political obligations seriously enough to preserve their society. In other words, side by side with the Enlightenment historical celebration of the repudiation of the pre-seventeenth-century world by the modern, Robertson betrays civic moralist anxieties about the lack of historical precedents in Scotland upon which the modern citizen is to draw. He is, by implication, not entirely confident that the modern Scottish citizen can act effectively for the social and cultural improvement of his country in the face of such an impoverished history.

The literary uses of civic moralism

In the last lines of the *History of Scotland*, Robertson restates his belief that the Union has facilitated the cultural revival of Scotland:

> And the Scots, after being placed, during a whole century, in a situation no less fatal to the liberty than to the taste and genius of the nation, were at once put in possession of privileges more valuable than those which their ancestors had formerly enjoyed; and every obstruction that had retarded their pursuit, or prevented their acquisition of literary fame, was totally removed. (II, 260)

Behind the obvious assertive reflexivity of this passage is a more general equation between cultural activity, liberty and social participation. Writing is the exemplification of active citizenship, even when it is confined, as it was in post-Union Scotland, to civil rather than political areas of national activity. Robertson was heir to a fertile and enduring stoic and humanist tradition in Scotland which endorsed the role of an active, often martial citizenry in the defence of Scotland's liberty and commonweal. The civic-stoic tradition, as it was adapted in Scotland from Machiavelli and classical sources, embodied a double moral and political prescription for disinterested patriotism or civic virtue and a mixed constitution. Traditional notions of Scottish liberty had acquired Stoic nuances in the sixteenth century, most notably in the work of the statesman and humanist George Buchanan whose *Rerum Scoticarum Historia* (1582) makes frequent appearances in Robertson's footnotes to the *History of Scotland.* Buchanan had developed a theory of Scotland's ancient constitution which emphasised the limited character of its monarchy buttressed and, on occasion, corrected by a virtuous nobility (or 'nobilis stoica'). In the *Historia*, it is this public-spirited nobility who carry out, at various moments in history, the people's natural right of resistance to tyranny, and who constitute a kind of balancing middle order in the constitution of the state. The ideal of Roman republican patriotism as a model for Scottish political behaviour persisted through the centuries often in partnership with the Calvinist idea of providential order in history.[35] Buchanan's classical interpretation of the Scottish polity was most influentially updated and revised in the late seventeenth to early eighteenth centuries by the radical Scottish parliamentarian and opponent of the Union, Andrew Fletcher of Saltoun. Drawing upon the intellectual resources of the civic tradition, Fletcher crusaded for an independent, politically viable, and prosperous Scotland. He ridiculed Buchanan's notion that the nobility had been or might ever become the disinterested guardians of Scottish liberty. Nevertheless, he retained and elaborated Buchanan's classical notion of liberty as the freedom to take active part in the national affairs, along with an idea that Scotland's constitution was essentially limited: 'no monarchy in Europe was more limited nor any people more jealous of liberty than the Scots'.[36] Wider and more vigorous participation, Fletcher argued, might be secured by the opportunity to serve in a Scottish militia.

Robertson would have encountered Fletcher's writings during the (unsuccessful) campaign which he and his friends waged during the Seven Years' War for the creation of a Scots militia.[37] The campaigners pressed a number of Fletcher's ideas into service – the exercise by subjects of active self-reliance in the service of their country, the abhorrent nature of standing armies, and the social and moral benefits of the martial spirit.[38] Perhaps with current militia affairs in mind, Robertson singled out Fletcher as one of the few admirable figures who had lit up the dark days of seventeenth-century Scotland (II, 258). In a more general way, Robertson's analysis of the causes of political and cultural decline in this period is deeply indebted to Fletcher. Fletcher's assessment of the stagnation of Scotland in this period centred upon the country's dependence upon the English court; the Union of the Crowns in 1603 had marked the beginning of a disastrous period of political subjection for Scotland, corrupting its aristocracy with English money and making the Scots behave like a

35 Allan, *Virtue, Learning and the Scottish Enlightenment*, chapter 3.

36 Andrew Fletcher of Saltoun, 'Speech' to the Scottish Parliament (1703) in *Selected Political Writings and Speeches*, ed. David Daiches (Edinburgh, 1979).

37 John Robertson, *The Scottish Enlightenment and the Militia Issue* (Edinburgh, 1985).

38 Robertson read over and may have contributed a paragraph to his friend Carlyle's pamphlet, 'The Question Relating to a Scots Militia Considered' (1760). However, some years later (the never entirely reliable) Carlyle complained that 'he [Robertson] took no great concern about those kind of writings' (*The Autobiography of Dr. Alexander Carlyle*, 419).

conquered people.[39] Robertson's brief survey of the hundred years or so following the Union of the Crowns adopts Fletcher's diagnosis, if not the final prescription (for Fletcher the remedy must be complete independence for Scotland). There are traces of Fletcher's classical moralist and martial rhetoric throughout this section. Robertson laments the fact that the Union of the Crowns brought about 'a total alteration in the political constitution of Scotland' by subjecting the country to the double yoke of an overbearing nobility and an absent, despotic monarch (II, 249). The rudimentary though necessary balance which had existed as an informal constitution between the (absent) king, nobility and their dependent people is now subverted, and the nobility, in losing their independent status, cease to hold self-restraining military ideas about their rights and obligations:

> the military ideas on which these rights were founded, being gradually lost, or disregarded, nothing remained to correct or to mitigate the rigour with which they were exercised. (II, 251)

By the Restoration, the nobility have forsaken all sense of responsibility and their increasing poverty 'rendered them meaner slaves, and more intolerable tyrants than ever' (II, 252). The departure of the royal court robbed Scotland of its cultural epicentre. As a symptom of this decline in virtue, Scotland's very language and culture became subject to 'new corruptions'; more diseases of dependency and the loss of national vitality soon follow (II, 259). Robertson does appear to find Fletcherian vocabulary serviceable when he comes to deplore the devaluation of national life after 1603. Although he cheerfully announces that the Union soon reversed this decline, he does not seek to contain the tragic resonances of Fletcher's lost vision of an independent Scotland. For, if seventeenth-century Scotland can be criticised as the opposite of a properly functioning state (understood in classical republican terms), it follows that Scotland once possessed the potential to become a viable state sustained by an active, participatory, virtuous and independent political class. The Union makes up for Scotland's loss of political viability. Yet, throughout the *History of Scotland*, there are traces of Buchananite, Fletcherian and classical republican vocabulary which reveal Robertson's disquiet at this loss. This is not to say that Robertson's history is either residually nationalist or nostalgic for the good old days of Scotland's martial independence. Rather, the *History of Scotland* tries to project an emotional range broad enough to encompass the sense of defeat which many of its Scottish readers, Whig, Tory and Jacobite, might have felt about their history. The classical language of Scotland's limited constitution is just one of a number of vocabularies (including the sentimental and the Protestant-providential) which Ro-

[39] Fletcher, 'An Account of a Conversation concerning the Right Regulation of Governments' (1704), *Selected Political Writings*, 115.

bertson deploys to this end. The *History of Scotland* does, of course, represent a political engagement with debates about the nature of Scotland's political history. However, it also makes extensive though unobtrusive use of literary techniques to manage the emotive elements in Scottish history to Whig-cosmopolitan ends. In this respect it has profound similarities with and was undoubtedly influenced by Hume's Stuart volumes.

One example of Robertson's management of classical-constitutional vocabulary to literary effect is his characterisation of the Scottish nobility in the medieval and early modern periods. Some elements of the Buchananite tradition go towards making up Robertson's general understanding of the unique character and functioning of medieval Scotland. The country is described as having an informal kind of military-feudal order which works somewhat like the constitution of a classical *polis*: the monarch and a virtuous, independent nobility share a loose sense of political community based on reciprocal obligations and on their joint interest in containing the threat from the English. In exchange for exemption from all taxation, the nobility (in classical terms, the political class) undertake the defence of their country without needing to have recourse to standing armies, and also regulate the activities of their vassals (the economic class). 'A feudal kingdom', Robertson explains, 'was properly the encampment of a great army' in which everyone was his own self-reliant militiaman. These military ideas would later be eroded by the Union of the Crowns (I, 13). Scotland's feudal constitution, according to Robertson, was a loose partnership between king and barons, who, being checked by each other's power, were deterred from unreasonable or tyrannical behaviour towards their vassals:

> And while the military genius of the feudal government, remained in vigour, the vassals both of the Crown and of the Barons were not only free from oppression, but courted by their superiors, whose power and importance were founded on their attachment and love. (II, 250)

The classical character of Scottish ideas of government is again in evidence when, in 1559, the Catholic Queen Regent, Mary of Guise, uses mercenary troops to put down Protestant reformers at Perth. The nobility, entering into an alliance with the Protestant reformers, who have themselves imbibed from their reading classical notions of public virtue and government, refuse to lay down their arms. Fletcher, in his reading of these events, praises the nobility for acting in the public interest by setting their face against the growing tyranny of the regent.[40] Robertson follows suit; the nobles, 'naturally free and bold', are prompted to assert their rights with more freedom and boldness than ever, and demand the expulsion of

[40] Fletcher, 'A Discourse of Government with Relation to Militias' (1698), *Selected Political Writings*, 8–9.

the mercenary troops (I, 157). At this critical juncture, the nobility and people unite, instinctively restating the first principles of their constitution. Although this alliance is short-lived, Robertson here gives additional endorsement to the Scottish Reformation through his suggestion that it is consistent with a national constitutional tradition of public virtue and independence.

Robertson's medieval and early modern Scotland does appear to contain the rudiments of a viable political community, dependent for its maintenance upon active virtue, the vigilant protection of freedoms against the encroachment of a central power, and military self-defence. He draws attention to these kinds of classical qualities in Scottish political history in ways which might appear to advance a historical basis for renewed social cohesiveness and responsible action in modern Scotland. Yet it would be erroneous to assume that this amounts to a redefinition of Scotland's ancient constitution in classical terms. Robertson is no ancient constitutionalist, in the sense that some of his contemporary English historians were. Scotland's constitution is seen as a pragmatic affair, and cannot be taken as a source of authority for absolute rights or liberties, even though it may sometimes have promoted certain codes of good behaviour – for example, the traditional indulgence of the Scots towards conquered peoples (I, 16). Robertson's occasional use of classical vocabulary to describe the successes and failures of the Scottish state before the Union is perhaps better understood in literary rather than political terms; it permits a largely aestheticised celebration of an obsolete Scottish culture not otherwise endorsed by the modern, progressive sensibility of the Enlightenment historian. The classical language of virtue, military self-reliance and heroic independence, when balanced against the language of Enlightenment modernity, captures Robertson's ambivalence towards an austere, yet heroic and quintessentially Scottish culture. The references to political notions of virtue and corruption, independence and martial vigour are part of Robertson's aesthetic recognition of the potency of Scotland's traditional history. This occasional mood of carefully contained nostalgia is also expressed, as we shall see, in Robertson's characterisation of Mary, Queen of Scots.

When writing these sections of the *History of Scotland*, Robertson had before him a good recent example of the literary appropriation of the classical, political vocabulary. His friend and fellow clergyman John Home had excited both controversy and admiration when his tragedy *Douglas* had received its first performance, on the Edinburgh stage, in 1756. There had, at the time, been some local debate as to whether clergymen had any business writing for or attending the theatre. Robertson, it should be pointed out, was among those Moderates who actively defended the right of clergymen to attend stage plays like this one, and no doubt entirely approved of the play.[41] In this blank-verse play, the naturally virtuous protagonist Norval is raised as a shepherd, and later discovers that he is of noble birth, and entitled to the name of Douglas. The play is set in a somewhat generalised early medieval Scotland. Norval hopes to serve his native land by fighting against the invading Danes, but ends up becoming embroiled in internecine quarrels with his family and fellow nobility. The presence and loss of a classical-feudal constitution in Scotland is suggested by the shape of the play which is structurally a comedy until Act III, and is then extended as a tragedy in the last two acts. Norval is attacked by his stepfather, and dies lamenting his own unheroic death: 'O had I fallen as my brave fathers fell, / Turning with fatal arm the tide of battle'.[42] Norval/Douglas exemplifies a type of Buchananite stoic nobleman eager to defend through deeds of martial valour the integrity of Scotland. His heroic aspirations are ultimately weakened and destroyed by domestic strife. In the end, it is his villainous stepfather who dies lunging at the Danish army. The play approaches medieval Scottish heroism from a unionist perspective. Scotland and England, it is implied, should unite against the external threat from the Danes instead of fighting among themselves. Home dramatises both the glory and the ironic impotence of traditional Scottish ideals of martial independence and virtue, with a forlorn yet comfortable sense of the modern Whig world which has superseded them. His play may have helped to condition the cultural response to the Ossianic poems which started to appear five years later. James Macpherson's prose 'translations' of the works of this ancient Caledonian bard would give to his Edinburgh audience similar satisfactions of nostalgia and safe sociological distance.[43] In the meantime, Robertson was probably influenced by Home's literary assimilation of the model of a (steadily deteriorating) classical republic to the early history of Scotland. His *History of Scotland* subtly mirrors Home's flirtation with patriotic or independent possibilities for Scotland, and similarly enacts their collapse.

When Robertson addresses the problem of the Union of 1707 at the end of the *History of Scotland*, what he describes is not renewal and vitality regained through public virtue and commitment, but, rather, progress through commerce, and greatly increased participation in social affairs by formerly excluded groups of people. Economic and political union with England, according to Robertson, took Scotland out of the cycles of renewal and decline under the old feudal constitution and into the linear progression of history. The Union did not resolve the old structural

[41] On the 'Douglas affair', see Sher, *Church and University*, 74–87.

[42] John Home, *Douglas* (London, 1757), 64–5.

[43] On the Scottish reception of Ossian, see Fiona J. Stafford, *The Sublime Savage: A Study of James Macpherson and the Poems of Ossian* (Edinburgh, 1988), 163–80; Sher, *Church and University*, chapter 6.

problems of Scottish society, it simply imported a new set of structures. Robertson's previous use of the classical vocabulary of traditional Scottish constitutionalism now seems like a form of nostalgia, a way of validating yet consigning forever to the past the old forms of Scottish society already destroyed by the Union of the Crowns. Like Hume in his essay 'Of Commerce' (1754), Robertson recognises the social utility of martial valour in previous eras, but indicates that governments will henceforth have to reckon with the new social expectations aroused by commerce. As a footnote on the question of national self-defence, the *History of Scotland* stands midway between Robertson's support for a Scots militia, and his historicisation of the militia issue; he increasingly came to believe that modern warfare must, regrettably, be perpetrated by standing armies. By the time he came to write *The History of the Reign of the Emperor Charles V* (1769), he had become deeply interested in the growth, from the sixteenth century onwards, of the 'science' of war – the increased taxation it entailed, its connection with the growth of royal power in Europe, and its role in the emergence of Europe as a series of militarily balanced, interconnected states.[44] As in the *History of Scotland*, he continues to attach the language of invigorating warriorship to obsolete cultures, such as the 'hardy barbarians' of early medieval Europe, including Tamerlane and his nomadic horsemen who invaded and reinvigorated states 'sunk in luxury and enervated by excessive refinements'.[45] The warrior nations of Europe were eventually replaced, and their form of warfare outmoded by the political and diplomatic growth of the 'great' European 'family'. War became harder to win, more expensive and detrimental to the liberties of the people, yet this paradoxically enhanced international stability.[46] Although Robertson rails against the growth of standing armies and the decline of militias, he does not resist the tendency of his own analysis, which is to suggest that such changes in nations' defences are the inevitable by-products of the rise of the European system of large balancing states.

Unpleasantness of the aristocratic-feudal order

Despite bouts of retrospective affection for the occasionally virtuous nobility of the medieval and early modern periods, the *History of Scotland* has many negative things to say about the feudal system from which they derived their power. Even when conceding the existence of fragile balanced constitution in Scottish history, Robertson is always careful to specify this as a feudal, rather than a civil form of social order. Like Fletcher before him, he takes Buchanan to task for failing to notice the fact that Scottish

[44] *The History of the Reign of the Emperor Charles V* (3 vols.; London, 1769), III, 430–2.
[45] Ibid., III, 431. [46] Ibid., III, 432.

society was more like an army camp than a classical city state. Blair made a similar point in the *Lectures on Rhetoric*:

Accustomed to form his political notions wholly upon the plans of antient governments, the feudal system seems never to have entered [Buchanan's] thoughts; and as this was the basis of the Scottish constitution, his political views are, of course, inaccurate and imperfect.[47]

The new understanding of the Scottish feudal system came about as a result of intensified investigation in the eighteenth century, and Whigs like Blair and Robertson now approached Buchanan with a sense of lost innocence. Robertson's Enlightenment generation, as Colin Kidd has most fully explained, 'remodelled post-Buchananite Scottish whiggism into an ideology critical of the rigidity of the Scottish feudal past'.[48] This remodelling brought with it a wholesale critique of the role of the aristocracy in Scottish history, and the dismantling of the aura of civic virtue which had hitherto surrounded them.[49] It was conducted with the aim of producing a more participatory and anglicised model for modern Scotland.

Robertson's *History of Scotland*, with its emphasis upon the exceptional resilience of the Scottish feudal system in holding back the onset of modernity, certainly participates in this general movement of scholarly anti-feudalism. The royalist emphasis, common to eighteenth-century Whig studies of the Middle Ages, combines in Robertson's work with a recognisably Voltairean *thèse royale.* At times, Robertson follows Voltaire in insisting that feudalism was really only an anarchic set of local jurisdictions incapable of generating a political community. Robertson emphasises the fact that the chief source of Scotland's ills was the exceptional stranglehold which the nobility had over the country. Not only does this form of government inhibit the growth of uniform civil justice, but it also prevents the development of a properly constituted church, whether Roman Catholic or Reformed. Despite their pragmatic alliance with the Reformers in defence of civil liberty, the nobility use their power to crush systematically the fledgling Presbyterian Church (described as their 'prey'), and starve it of funds (I, 216). 'A state of order and tranquillity', Robertson comments ruefully, 'was not natural to the feudal aristocracy' (I, 241). Feudal oligarchy was at best serviceable under pre-commercial conditions when Scotland was united by threats from England, but it quickly degenerated into anarchy. In the prefatory essay, Robertson explains the exceptional elements in Scotland's geographical and social composition which led to the entrenchment of baronial oligarchy; Scotland's kings attempted in vain to adopt the European pattern of monarchical *revanche* and establish their power on a firmer basis. Thus, in Robertson's *thèse*

[47] Blair, *Lectures on Rhetoric and Belles Lettres*, II, 284.
[48] Kidd, *Subverting Scotland's Past*, 98. [49] Ibid., 166–84.

royale, the success of the monarchy in establishing and extending its jurisdiction is identified with progress (I, 18–71).

Despite the stance of detached historical-mindedness from which he describes this process, Robertson's analysis of the decay of feudal Europe reverberates with the wider meanings which Voltaire ascribed to feudalism; it was, in essence, a system of oppression and a set of obstacles to the development of mobile, commercially active societies. Both authors evoke feudalism in terms of architectural imagery (monuments, fabrics, edifices) in order to suggest restrictiveness and rigidity, in emotive contrast to the fluidity and linear progress of the post-feudal world. The *History of Scotland* also owes a great deal to contemporary Scottish historical analyses of feudalism which were similarly inbued with moral and political significance. The Scottish studies of the feudal system were often part of a wider polemic against the country's vestiges of medieval government which, it was claimed, had survived even into the post-Union period, inhibiting progress in agriculture and commerce, and so preventing full social participation by the majority of the Scottish people.

In particular, Robertson's account of feudal government may owe something to Adam Smith, who had given public lectures on jurisprudence and other topics in Edinburgh between 1748 and 1751. Smith's biographer Duguld Stewart cites a paper by Smith, written in 1755, and then comments that the history of law and society were 'constant subjects' with Smith from that time forward.[50] It is likely that all this work formed the basis of Smith's Glasgow lectures on jurisprudence, delivered during his tenure at that university between 1751 and 1764. These are extant in the form of two student reports, and it is likely that they are expanded versions of the ideas Robertson may have gathered from Smith's public lectures in Edinburgh.[51] One somewhat unreliable witness even accused Robertson of plagiarising Smith's Glasgow lectures for the first volume of the *History of Charles V*, which may have circulated in the form of student notes.[52] The extent of the influence of Smith's Glasgow lectures upon Robertson is not known. An exposition of feudal law as it reflected and shaped medieval social development, Smith's series of Glasgow lectures on jurisprudence is also a polemic against the obstructions to commerce and social justice caused by feudalism. For Smith, as for Robertson, feudal government antedated civil government; feudalism also functioned in his discourse as a symbol of the imbalance of power and restrictions upon commerce (in the form of entails upon property, for example) which still persisted in the Scotland of their day. Like Smith, also, Robertson thought that urban

[50] Dugald Stewart, *Biographical Memoirs of Smith, Robertson and Reid*, 100.

[51] These have been reprinted in volume V of *The Glasgow Edition of the Works of Adam Smith* as *Lectures on Jurisprudence*, eds. R. L. Meek, P. Stein and D. D. Raphael (Oxford, 1978).

[52] John Callander in Edinburgh University Library, MS La. ii. 451–2.

centres, where commerce had first taken root, had formed an important political base from which feudal authority was ultimately transcended.

The *History of Scotland* explicitly acknowledges a debt to two general studies of feudal law by Robertson's friend and (since 1746) fellow Whig, Henry Home, Lord Kames. The first of these, Kames' influential *Essays upon Several Subjects Concerning British Antiquities*, was published in 1747, and emphasised the feudal origins of aristocratic privileges in both English and Scottish society and the deep psychological drives behind the formation of feudal institutions. The second, the *Historical Law-Tracts* (1758), dissected the feudal basis of Scots law. Another Scottish legal theorist, John Dalrymple, supplemented Kames' studies of the common feudal origins of English and Scottish institutions in his *Essay towards a History of Feudal Property in Great Britain* (1757).[53] Like Kames' work before and Robertson's history after it, this study militates against the inherited exceptionalist historiography of Scotland's medieval past, while at the same time exploring the reasons behind the country's failure to modernise along English lines. Robertson's account of feudal Scotland and its European context does not have the larger sociological dimension of the feudal studies of Kames, Smith or Dalrymple. However, Robertson does, at times, follow Kames and Dalrymple in presenting feudal forms of government as the product of an inner drive for power and perpetuity among aristocratic elites, or as an outcome of the irrational psychological forces at work in history (I, 20). Although Robertson's work is primarily a history rather than a sociology of medieval Scotland, there is also a distinctively Scottish reformist polemic behind his attacks on the depredations of his country's medieval past which overlaps with Voltaire's portrait of feudalism as a structure of oppression. Robertson's characterisation of feudal society as pre- or anti-modern ultimately prevails over his celebration of elements of martial independence and public virtue in Scotland's past. The Union, by giving power to the middling order of Scottish society and pointing the way towards further development, exposes as outdated the trappings of classical republicanism with which medieval Scotland was sometimes decorated. Nevertheless, Robertson never entirely resolved the tension between his two attitudes to the Scottish feudal past. As John Robertson has argued, here was a dilemma common to Robertson and his Whig contemporaries: 'Fierce critics of the feudal social system, and of aristocratic power, they yet found in the martial Scottish past values which they held worth preserving.'[54] Robertson was torn between his desire, as a Scottish patriot, to celebrate the past, and his intention, as a British Whig and cosmopolitan historian, to enact narratively the collapse into violence

[53] Dalrymple's *Essay* is dedicated to Kames, and is cited in Robertson's *History of Scotland*, I, 67.
[54] John Robertson, *The Scottish Enlightenment and the Militia Issue*, 80.

and then decline of Scotland which rendered necessary and advantageous the Union of 1707.

Mary, Queen of Scots

Robertson's aesthetic acknowledgement of Scotland's inherited classical-constitutional vocabulary gives emotional breadth to the *History of Scotland* without necessarily compromising his Whig, cosmopolitan reading of the nation's history, Robertson sought a similar literary effect when telling the story of Mary, Queen of Scots. The large section of the history devoted to the tragic queen undertakes, in a more sustained way, a comparable reconciliation of political objectives with an aesthetic sensitivity to the unique and appealing features of the national past. For Mary, a Catholic and French-born queen of dubious moral and inept political conduct, could never attract the full sympathies of an eighteenth-century Presbyterian Whig. At the time when Robertson was writing his history, there was a revival of interest in Mary's story, and she steadily grew into a potent symbol of a Stuart, independent Scotland lost after the Union and Hanoverian succession. Jacobite historians tried to instigate a sympathetic reappraisal of her life, while Whig historians found themselves defending the demonising version of her life originally set out in Buchanan's *Detectio Mariae Reginae* (1568). The debate was reopened when, in 1715, the Jacobite Thomas Ruddiman produced an edition of Buchanan's works.[55] Collections of state papers followed, arraying themselves for or against Mary, as Jacobite or Whig sympathies dictated. The English scholar Samuel Jebb produced a documentary life (*De Vita et Rebus Gestis . . . Mariae Scotorum Reginae*, 1725) in which he berated Buchanan for his unreliability. This collection, in effect, gave scholarly substance to the sympathetic, though superficial account of Mary's life to be found in *The Historie of . . . Princesse Elizabeth* (first English translation 1630) by the popular Jacobean historian William Camden. Next into the fray was James Anderson, Scottish compiler of the *Collections relating to Mary, Queen of Scots* (1727–8), a work broadly unfavourable to Mary but proclaiming its own detachment from the 'party rage' which had recently bedevilled the Marian debate.[56] This was answered by another documentary history by a Scottish Episcopalian bishop, Robert Keith who, in the *History of the Affairs of Church and State in Scotland* (1734), again attacked Buchanan and contrived a portrait of

[55] George Buchanan, *Opera Omnia*, ed. Thomas Ruddiman (2 vols.; Edinburgh, 1715). See also Mary Fearnley-Sander, 'Philosophical History and the Scottish Reformation: William Robertson and the Knoxian Tradition', *Historical Journal*, 22 (1990), 327–8. I am grateful to Howard Erskine-Hill for supplying me with a bibliography of the Marian controversy.

[56] James Anderson, *Collections relating to the History of Mary, Queen of Scotland* (4 vols.; Edinburgh, 1727–8), iii.

an innocent and victimised Mary. Another anti-Marian collection soon followed, this time from the Scottish Whig Patrick Forbes. His *Full View of the Public Transactions in the Reign of Queen Elizabeth* (1740–1) carried the story only as far as 1563, but made use of material from the Cotton library soon afterwards lost in the fire.

Robertson made use of all these collections, and would have been fully aware of the political passions which Mary's story had excited in his own century. He might also have glanced over Smollett's eloquent and sympathetic account of her story in volume III of his *Complete History of England* (1757–8). This section of the history reveals Smollett's emotional loyalties to a tragic Jacobite sense of history, and gave literary life to a biography more often mired in dry documentary controversy. Smollett was not the first to spot the literary potential of a life story later to become one of the greatest subjects of nineteenth-century historical romance. Several years earlier, Eliza Haywood had translated from a French original by Pierre Le Pesant a baroque novel of royalty, love and death entitled *Mary Stuart, Queen of Scots: Being the Secret History of her Life.* This is a simmering tale of passion ('Scacre will [Mary and Darnley's] mutual ardour give them leave to show themselves to their Subjects'), violence ('Rizo's Blood spouted upon her'), and tragic doom (Mary is said to be innocent of any wrongdoing).[57] Robertson may or may not have known this work, but he would certainly have been aware that he had an audience already receptive to literary treatments of the Mary drama. He preferred, in any case, a sentimental to a heroic presentation of Mary's tragedy, and in this his real literary tutor was Hume. Robertson certainly learned from Hume's Stuart volumes the political applications of sentiment in history, since he adapted this technique to his own treatment of the Mary story. In this way he was able to manage and soothe the emotional and political sensibilities of his readers. This literary operation was, as we shall see, conducted with such political tact that Robertson's position as a national, rather than a party historian was significantly enhanced.

Robertson understood the capacity of the language of sentiment to unite readers around a picture of misfortune while neutralising their indignation at its political causes. Like Hume, he also knew when his authorial persona might be permitted to enter into tales of misfortune, and when a more measured, stabilising voice was required. The authorial voice of the *History of Scotland* frequently aligns itself with Mary's perspective, and participates imaginatively in her suffering in order to render more convincing the measured tones of the final character appraisal with which this section of

[57] Pierre Le Pesant, *Mary Stuart, Queen of Scots: Being the Secret History of her Life*, trans. Eliza Heywood (London, 1725), 68, 75.

the *History* ends. Robertson's Mary is passive, beautiful, the epitome of gentility, and always in tears. The first time he introduces Mary, she is sailing from France to Scotland. He watches with her the French coast recede as she leaves the country of her youth for the last time, her 'eyes bathed in tears':

While the French coast continued in sight, she intently gazed upon it, and musing, in a thoughtful posture, on that height of fortune whence she had fallen, and presaging, perhaps, the disasters and calamities which imbittered the remainder of her days, she sighed often, and cried out 'Farewel France! Farewel beloved country, which I shall never more behold! (I, 225)

This account of Mary's fateful journey from France to imminent doom is very similar in tone and vocabulary to the reporting of the same incident in the history by the Jacobite Robert Keith ('she . . . still looked to the Land, often repeating these Words, *Farewell France, Farewell, I shall never see you more*').[58] Both writers are adapting a first-hand French source, but it is nevertheless noteworthy that Robertson retains the emotional immediacy of the Jacobite account. Hume writing, at the same time as Robertson, a more hostile account of Mary's life in the Tudor volumes of his history, also uses Keith's account of Mary's momentous voyage, but adds, for distancing effect, the words 'it is said' to the part about her staring longingly at the French coast (IV, 37 and note u).

When Mary is arrested in 1567 for the murder of her husband, Darnley, and paraded before hostile crowds, Robertson both censures her and imagines her as an object of common sympathy for both narrator and reader:

The Queen, worn out with fatigue, covered with dust, and bedewed with tears, was exposed as a spectacle to her own subjects, and led to the Provost's house. Notwithstanding all her arguments and intreaties, the same standard was carried before her, and the same insults and reproaches repeated. A woman, young, beautiful, and in distress, is naturally the object of compassion. The comparison of their present misery with their former splendour, usually softens us in favour of illustrious sufferers. But the people beheld the deplorable situation of their Sovereign with insensibility. (I, 367–8)

The sentimental heroine beckons her trans-historical observers to a common community of sympathy. The author participates in their compassionate response to this spectacle ('softens *us*'), and together author and reader atone for the 'insensibility' of the original audience. Even the Jacobite scholar, William Tytler, who tried to expose the factual inaccuracy of Robertson's Marian narrative the year after the *History of Scotland* came

[58] Keith, *The History of . . . Scotland* (1734), 179.

out, confessed that he was moved and impressed by this 'masterly and well painted . . . pathetic description' of Mary's humiliation.[59]

Mary's sentimental appeal reaches its greatest intensity at her trial in England. At this point, Robertson abandons his customary neutrality and angrily questions the justice of the trial (II, 135–6). Thereafter, however, he lays more emphasis upon the unchivalrousness of the English treatment of Mary than upon its illegality. Prior to her execution, Mary is ritually stripped of the trappings of royalty; the canopy of state in her apartment is 'pulled down', her guard, Sir Amias Paulet, rudely appears 'covered' in her presence, and Mary removes her outer clothes in readiness for execution (II, 141, 149). Her dignified but passive helplessness then reaches its zenith. It is not until the narrative has stripped her of all emblems of regality, deprived her of symbolic status as a Scottish queen, and robbed her of political significance, that she is finally given voice. She is magnificent in her final moments. Her Catholic piety is, finally, private and admirable, instead of public and threatening to the Scottish realm. She does not cry but recovers voice and composure at the moment of her destruction:

> Mary mounted the steps with alacrity, beheld all this apparatus of death with an unaltered countenance, and signing herself with the cross, she sat down in the chair . . . Then the Dean of Peterborough began a devout discourse, suitable to her present condition, and offered up prayers to Heaven in her behalf; but she declared that she could not in conscience hearken to the one, nor join with the other; and falling on her knees repeated a Latin prayer. (II, 148; 1794, II, 178 has the subtly more dignified 'kneeling down' for 'falling on her knees')

Robertson's account of the execution is closer in detail to Camden than to any of the other cited sources. Camden, however, has Mary in tears in her last moments: 'And now the tears trickling downe, shee bad Melvyn againe and againe farewell.'[60] By contrast, Robertson accords Mary a final moment of dry-eyed self-possession. After the execution, the tears are transferred to the spectators at Fotheringay ('the spectators continued silent, and drowned in tears'), and ultimately to the readers and to the author himself ('we are apt altogether to forget her frailties . . . and approve of our tears, as if they were shed for a person who had attained much nearer to pure virtue', II, 149, 151). Mary's lack of 'pure virtue' is never forgotten, even at this tragic moment. In this way, Robertson successfully neutralises Mary as a potentially potent political symbol for Scotland, and minimises the significance her death may have for future Scottish political

[59] William Tytler, *An Historical and Critical Enquiry into the Evidence . . . against Mary Queen of Scots* (Edinburgh, 1760), 223–4.

[60] William Camden, *The Annals and Historie of the Most Renowned and Victorious Princesse Elizabeth*, trans. R. Norton (London, 1630), 111.

debate, while bringing his audience together around a unifying symbol of compassion.

Hume, the probable author of a puff for the *History of Scotland* which appeared soon after its publication in the *Critical Review*, appreciated the conciliatory purpose of Robertson's life of Mary:

> The result is such as we might expect from an impartial enquirer. Queen Mary is presented to us, neither as a divine nor an infernal, but a human object; a woman with female failings; a character mixed with virtues and vices, such as merits, on many accounts, our condemnation, whilst there is room left for our pity in deploring her misfortunes.[61]

Hume's own narrative of the life of Mary in the *History of England* (written independently of Robertson's) is not so governed by Scottish cultural objectives, and makes very little use of the sentimental historical style which he had previously developed in the Stuart volumes. Mary's story forms, instead, a part of the larger dramatic conflict between Catholic and Protestant systems of belief which runs through the Tudor volumes. Hume stages the execution scene as a blackly comic encounter between Protestant fervour and Catholic piety. The Dean of Peterborough warns Mary at preposterous length that, unless she renounces her faith, 'she must expect in an instant to fall into utter darkness, into a place where shall be weeping, howling, and gnashing of teeth', but she remains admirably steadfast before this torrent of zeal (1983 text, IV, 250). The spectators, however, experience humane emotions which transcend the sectarian passions which had led to Mary's execution: 'zeal and flattery alike gave place to present pity and admiration of the expiring princess' (IV, 251). However dignified, Hume's Mary is essentially a Catholic bigot whose unreasoning faith had caused her to conspire with Babington against the life of Elizabeth (IV, 252). Hume splits his final judgement of Mary, unable to reconcile her winning femininity with her moral failings: 'An enumeration of her qualities might carry the appearance of a panegyric; an account of her conduct must, in some parts, wear the aspect of severe satire and invective' (IV, 252).

In Robertson's more integrated presentation, it is Mary's exquisite femininity that is the source of her moral weakness; she seems to invite empathy from female readers, and indulgent yet belittling sentiments of chivalry from the men. Robertson is working within an aesthetic, inherited from the Scottish philosopher Francis Hutcheson, which is benevolist, uniting the inner moral and aesthetic senses through feelings of sympathy. Robertson, knowing that Mary's execution was a deeply divisive event in Scottish history, and that 'the rancour' of the factions engendered by her

[61] Raynor, 'Hume and Robertson's *History of Scotland*', 61.

death 'hath descended to succeeding ages, and their prejudices, as well as their rage, have been perpetuated, and even augmented', has tried to make Scottish, and, indeed, British, readers of all political persuasions experience a recuperation of national unity through mutual sympathy. In order to indicate that Mary is marginal to the mainstream of Scottish history, and that the independent Catholic Scotland she represented can never be revived (not even by the Scottish Jacobites who had taken her as their symbol), Robertson insists upon her morally incompetent femininity, a trait which stems, it is implied, from her French connections. In marginalising Mary as a national symbol, Robertson is also putting aside France as a suitable political partner for Scotland: 'The French were, in that age, what they are in the present, one of the most polished nations in Europe. But it is to be observed ... that their manners have been remarkably incompatible with the manners of every other people' (I, 109). Scotland's destiny is English and Protestant, not French and Roman Catholic; the national destiny represented by Mary or, by implication, by Charles Edward Stuart, is unsuitable for Scotland. Robertson's anti-Jacobitism is subtle and indirect; he maintains his readers' sympathy for Mary while demonstrating that she, and the French world she embodies, have no continuing political relevance for Scotland. Both Buchanan and Fletcher had demonised Mary. Robertson, knowing that Mary was a nationalist icon to the Jacobites, merely feminises her because, as a truly national historian, he does not wish to give the appearance of being too dogmatic a Whig. Indeed, in his own life, too, he appears to have been conciliatory in his political opinions, maintaining a friendship with the Jacobite Lord Elibank, who once praised him publicly for his political tolerance.[62]

It is not surprising, therefore, to discover that Robertson evaluated and selected the factual details of Mary's career according to his own ideas of what a moderate, politically tolerant version of the story might be. His willingness to adapt the facts to the demands of his conciliatory political agenda is evident in his correspondence with Hume, who was writing his own history of the period at precisely the same time. The two historians did not collaborate. Robertson only allowed Hume to see the uncorrected sheets of his *History of Scotland* immediately prior to publication. They did swap information, however, on the much disputed questions about Mary's involvement in various conspiracies. Hume was the more assiduous researcher. His efforts were fortified by his zeal thoroughly to discredit

[62] Boswell quotes Lord Elibank's recollection of an incident in the Select Society in which Robertson is supposed to have said that he 'did not think worse of a man's moral character for his having been in the rebellion'. 'This', Lord Elibank went on to say approvingly 'was venturing to utter a liberal sentiment while both sides had a detestation of each other' (*Boswell's Journal of a Tour to the Hebrides*, eds. Frederick Pottle and Charles Bennett (New York, 1936), 384).

Mary and the type of sentimental Scottishness associated with her defenders. Hume tried to establish the authenticity of the 'Casket' letters between Mary and her lover Bothwell, and so implicate her in the conspiracy to murder her first husband Darnley. These letters provided ammunition for Whig historians who endorsed the legitimacy of Mary's deposition in 1567, and had predictably been dismissed as forgeries by Jacobite historians such as Jebb. Hume set out to convince Robertson of the authenticity of the Casket letters, and, by November 1758, Robertson seems to have acquiesced.[63] Robertson accepted that Mary did have an affair with Bothwell, and that she might have been in some way complicit in the murder of her husband. In the *History of Scotland*, this is rendered dramatically in terms of Mary's understandable distaste for her feeble and recalcitrant husband, and her female susceptibility to the 'insinuating address' of Bothwell (I, 339). Despite the narrative plausibility of his account, Robertson still found it necessary to go on the defensive in the second edition of the history. He appended a 'Critical Dissertation concerning the Murder of King Henry, and the Genuineness of the Queen's Letters to Bothwell' and, after close examination of the letters, convicts Bothwell of the deed, but neither accuses nor wholly exculpates the queen: 'Mary is not pronounced guilty of having contrived the murder of her husband, or even of having given her consent to his death; but she is not acquitted of having discovered her approbation of the deed, by her behaviour towards him who was the author of it' (II, 39). Robertson's elaborately fair judgement did not succeed in settling the issue. The year after the publication of the *History of Scotland*, Robertson received William Tytler's angry reply in the form of a treatise on Mary's innocence.

Even after they had reached agreement about the Casket letters, Hume continued to bombard Robertson with factual information discrediting every aspect of Mary's conduct. Hume and Robertson disagreed most sharply over the question of Mary's involvement in the Babington conspiracy, a Catholic plot to assassinate Elizabeth and install Mary, then a prisoner in England, in her place. Robertson maintained that Mary knew nothing of the plot, that Elizabeth's minister Walsingham forged the letters which implicated her and led ultimately to her execution, and that she was unfairly sacrificed to English political expediency (II, 125–35). Hume had been doing his own research, and became completely convinced of Mary's complicity in this plot when the Burghley State Papers were published in

[63] Hume to Robertson (18 November 1758), *The Letters of David Hume*, no. 155. On Hume, Robertson and the controversy surrounding Mary's involvement with the Darnley murder, see Lawrence L. Bongie, 'The Eighteenth Century Marian Controversy and An Unpublished Letter by David Hume', *Studies in Scottish Literature*, 1 (1963–4), 236–52. On Hume's scholarly evaluation of the Casket letters, see also Hume to Lord Elibank (1759/60), *Letters*, no. 172; Hume to Alexander Dick (26 August 1760), *New Letters*, no. 31.

1759. As soon as he saw these, Hume wrote hurriedly to Robertson, and tried to get his printer Millar to hold up publication of the *History of Scotland* so that the section on the Babington plot could be altered and Mary's guilt made plain.[64] Millar refused to stop the press, but was quite convinced that Robertson would want to make these alterations in a second edition once he saw the State Papers.[65] Robertson, however, never made the slightest alteration to his account (although he made several other minor alterations to his text as a result of Hume's researches), and never padded out the few sentences in the history on the subject.[66] When he wrote the preface to the eleventh edition of the *History of Scotland*, Robertson still was sounding somewhat defiant: 'Wherever I am satisfied that my original ideas were just and well founded, I adhere to them; and resting upon their conformity to evidence already produced, I enter into no discussion or controversy in order to produce them.'[67] The last time we hear from Hume on the matter, he is exasperated at Robertson's stubborn refusal to do any more research into the Mary question, despite all kinds of untapped available source material.[68]

Robertson, of course, had his reasons. By insinuating Mary's acquiescence in one crime and exonerating her of another, he hoped to demonstrate his own moderation and impartiality, and expected that his history would be a locus of agreement for both her partisans and detractors. His was a politic rather than a scholarly selection of the facts. Robertson demonstrated that it was possible to incorporate Jacobitism as a purely aesthetic attitude, redolent of an attractive but defeated nationalism, within a Whig and cosmopolitan sense of progress. Robertson was a good deal less interested in factual accuracy than in opening up a space for the release of national emotions not satisfied by a mere narrative of improvement. This space is subsumed within, but not annihilated by more modernising cultural priorities. So begins a long tradition of purely literary and sentimental Jacobitism in Scotland. Fourteen years after the 1745 Rebellion, Jacobitism has been made safe, and a vocabulary has been created for the reinvention of Jacobitism as an aesthetic attitude only. Robertson's immediate heir in this enterprise would be Walter Scott. Scott's Mary, Queen of Scots cuts a somewhat weak, capricious character in *The Abbot* (1820), unworthy of the young protagonists who misguidedly dedicate themselves to her service. However, in *Waverley* (1814) itself, Scott

64 Hume to Robertson (25 Janury 1759), *Letters*, no. 156.

65 Millar to Robertson (27 January 1759), NLS, *Robertson–MacDonald Papers*, MS 3942, ff. 11–12.

66 J. Y. T. Greig found a cancel on page 139 of the first edition of the *History of Scotland*. Robertson is here revising his opinion of James I's filial loyalty to Mary during her trial. Hume convinced him that James gave a fairly unconvincing performance (The *Letters of David Hume*, note to letter no. 155).

67 *History of Scotland* (2 vols.; 1787), I, ix–x.

68 Hume to Robertson (7 April 1759), *New Letters*, no. 28.

enacts a cultural process similar to that of the *History of Scotland*; a young man journeys between the two historical worlds of an obsolete but compelling Jacobite romance and a civilised but unadventurous modernity, before coming to rest in the latter. Neither Robertson nor Scott were able to halt the rise of Romantic Mariolatry, but they did secure for such ritual nostalgia a safe place in a cosmopolitan narrative of Scottish progress.

Providence and progress

The modernity of the Whig present into which the tragedy of Mary must at last dissolve is defined and guaranteed in Robertson's history by a number of key words: light, dawn and darkness, rudeness and refinement, abatement and perfection, barbarity and improvement. This vocabulary structures the text internally, and, even in the most chaotic moments of the history, preserves the outline of a linear model of historical progress. By the end, Scotland reaches the moment of fulfilment at the time of the Union, 'as commerce advanced in its progress, and government attained nearer to perfection' (II, 253). This process had started in the late seventeenth century when 'both nations [England and Scotland] were emerging out of barbarity' (II, 259). Perfection, of course, is never attained, but history moves forward along a spectrum from barbarity to relative refinement, and different nations follow this one path at different stages in their history. In England 'many causes contributed to bring government earlier to perfection' because 'the rigour of feudal institutions abated sooner' than in Scotland (I, 67). Robertson is aware that this sketchy linear narrative is imposed rather than deduced by the historian, and links this progressive vocabulary to his own cognitive procedures as a historian. The historian elucidates the historical process by shining the light of his intellect into the dark cave of the past. Scottish history, for example, becomes more transparent when the historian holds it up to the light of European history: 'many dark passages in our history may be placed in a clear light; and where the bulk of historians have seen only the effect, we may discover the causes' (I, 72). At times, Robertson blurs the distinction between the historiographical operation and the independent processes of the past; he both reveals and creates the inner order of history. This conflation is revealed, for example, in his opening remarks about the obscurity of early Scottish history: 'Truth begins to dawn in the second period, with a light, feeble at first, but gradually increasing', so hinting that there is a coincidence between the backwardness of an era and its unintelligibility (I, 5). These verbal indices of progress are too infrequent and imprecise in Robertson's first history to suggest an underlying theory of social evolution. They are tied, in the main, to Robertson's own shifting formulations of the role of the historian peering into the dark well of history.

Despite Robertson's metaphorical acknowledgements of his own ordering presence in his history, it is a measure of his intellectual immersion in his own Scottish Presbyterian tradition that he embraced the role of historian without any apparent sense of the philosophical ironies of reconstructing the past. As David Allan has shown, Robertson inherited a Presbyterian faith in the theological utility of history, and the need to investigate the past in order to understand the workings of Providence. Such a faith in the value of history might at first seem curiously at odds with the predestinarian character of Calvinist theological thinking. However, Allan has suggested that, in the historical works of seventeenth-century Scottish historians, providential determinism paradoxically led to intensified forms of empiricism; close scrutiny of the causal tissue of manifest events revealed God's will and purpose.[69] There is much to support Allan's analysis that Robertson's appropriation of this providential-empiricist sense of historical causality and purpose was relatively unproblematic. The routing of the Spanish Armada, for instance, is announced as the intervention of Providence on behalf of Protestant England (II, 166). By the early eighteenth century, when Robertson was learning his literary trade, Scottish providential history acquired a little Cartesian or Newtonian polish, and lost some of its moral austerities. After Burnet, it also learned how to perform the ideological work of whiggery. To the extent that the *History of Scotland* is an investigation of the (ultimately divine) nature of historical causation, it certainly belongs to this softened tradition of Presbyterian history. As a Presbyterian minister who subscribed without any apparent qualms to the Calvinist Westminster Confession of Faith, Robertson was able to draw upon a rich vein of historical language centred upon God's providential operations through time. His own intellectual environment made it possible for him to write histories which were at once theocentric, cosmopolitan and modernising. The relative infrequency of Robertson's direct references to Providence implies, not religious unconcern, but a belief in the existence of a sphere of constructive operation for people in history within a framework of divine provision. Robertson's direct references to Providence should not be read as merely convenient explanatory metaphors in an otherwise secular narrative. Robertson's theology of historical causation in fact drew few objections from pious contemporaries. John Wesley's attack on Robertson's lack of outward piety is untypical: 'I cannot admire ... A Christian Divine writing a history, with so very little of Christianity in it. Nay, he seems studiously to avoid saying any thing which might imply that he believes the

[69] Allan, *Virtue, Learning and the Scottish Enlightenment*, 109–43.

Bible.'[70] Robertson's evangelical opponent and generous funeral eulogist, John Erskine, did think that he might have been somewhat influenced by the Arminians: '[Robertson] adopted some of their peculiar sentiments and modes of expression, not relished by many Calvinists.'[71] However, Erskine goes on to defend Robertson as an essentially orthodox Calvinist whose intellectual tastes were merely a little more catholic than those of his stricter clerical contemporaries.

Erskine had not always been so tolerant of Robertson's intellectual activities. In the 1760s, when there was greater friction between the moderate and evangelical wings of the Church of Scotland, he took public exception to ministers devoting too much of their time to history or philosophy. Although he did not mention any minister by name, Robertson is clearly one of the intended targets of criticism: 'a teacher of Christianity ... may innocently, nay, usefully, amuse himself with them [history or philosophy]: but he cannot, without sacrilege, devote to them the greatest part of his time'.[72] 'Sacrilege' is a hard word, and Erskine evidently felt strongly that, although history may be written in ways consistent with Presbyterian orthodoxy, the activity of historical writing itself was essentially secular in its objectives. Throughout Robertson's career there would always be a (largely unacknowledged) tension between the earnest, if unobtrusive Protestant providentialism of his histories and the ecumenicalism of their cultural objectives. In his ministerial career, Robertson, like others of his moderate persuasion, tried to round off the hard sectarian edges of Scottish Presbyterianism, and refashion it as a civil religion. This moderate programme often went hand-in-hand with a more general sociological interest in the role of religion in civil society. Hugh Blair's sermon to the Society in Scotland for Propagating Christian Knowledge, delivered in 1750, praises Christianity as an agent of social improvement: 'it forms [people] for Society. It civilises Mankind. It tames the fierceness of their Passions, and wears off the Barbarity of their Manners'.[73] In Robertson's case, this sociological approach to religion would eventually lead him towards increasingly sympathetic evaluations of non-Presbyterian forms of Christianity. In later works, his ecumenical cosmopolitanism would go far beyond the cultural and ecclesiastical priorities of his moderate colleagues. Even so, he would retain his Protestant providential sense of the way things happen in history.

70 *The Journal of John Wesley; A Selection*, ed. Elizabeth Jay (Oxford, 1987), 219.

71 John Erskine, 'The Agency of God in Human Greatness' in *Discourses preached on Several Occasions* (Edinburgh, 1798), 264. See also Jeffrey Smitten, 'The Shaping of Moderatism: William Robertson and Arminianism', *Studies in Eighteenth-Century Culture*, 22 (1991), 33–67.

72 John Erskine, 'Ministers of the Gospel cautioned against giving offence' (preached 1763) in *The Scotch Preacher or, A Collection of Sermons by some of the most eminent clergymen of the Church of Scotland* (3 vols.; Edinburgh, 1776), I, 219–20.

73 Hugh Blair, *The Importance of Religious Knowledge to the Happiness of Mankind* (Edinburgh, 1750), 23.

The basic elements of Robertson's brand of Enlightenment history are already visible in his first published sermon, *The Situation of the World at the Time of Christ's Appearance* (1755). His grandnephew and biographer, Henry, Lord Brougham, went so far as to describe this sermon as a piece of Enlightenment history: 'it is admirable, as an historical composition, in that department which Voltaire first extended to all the records of past times'.[74] Robertson's colleague and fellow clergyman John Jardine gave it a laudatory notice in the *Edinburgh Review*.[75] Robertson's sermon, delivered, like Blair's, to the SSPCK, is indeed a fascinating essay on historical causation, and on the interaction between providence and social progress. In 'The Situation of the World', Robertson examines the precise confluence of historical circumstances surrounding Christ's birth, and explains why these were propitious for the spread of Christianity, as well as for the impact of Christianity upon civil life thereafter. In addition to revealing Robertson's moderate Presbyterian preoccupation with the civil aspects of the church, this sermon helps to explain the connection between his Calvinist understanding of the agency of God and his Enlightenment view of history. History, Robertson explains, is accessible to rational enquiry because God almost always acts through secondary, or efficient causes: 'The Almighty seldom effects by supernatural means, any thing, which could have been accomplished by such as are natural.'[76] There are sufficient or 'powerful unknown causes' at work in history, but since 'we are not permitted to discover' them, they do not concern him, and he does not adduce special providences or miracles to guarantee the theological significance of time.[77] Christianity is literally progress itself, and, paradoxically, even the birth of Christ is not so much the unique epiphany as the most advanced point along the 'progressive plan of providence'.[78] Robertson finds the birth of Christ continuous with natural law, and sees the progress of Christianity as gradual, linear and intertwined with the advance of culture and political institutions. His notion of Providence incorporates contemporary mechanistic ideas of nature. His God is Newton's God, operative through demonstrable secondary causes and very occasional special interventions.[79] Robertson thus marks out the coordi-

[74] Henry, Lord Brougham, *Lives of Men of Letters and Science who Flourished in the Time of George III* (2 vols.; London, 1845), I, 268.

[75] *Edinburgh Review*, (1755) i, 40–3.

[76] *The Situation of the World at the Time of Christ's Appearance, and its Connexion with the Success of his Religion Considered* (Edinburgh, 1755), 13.

[77] Ibid., 42.

[78] Ibid., 8; on the general currency of this idea, see David Spadafora, *The Idea of Progress in Eighteenth-Century Britain* (New Haven, 1990).

[79] On Newtonianism and Providence, see Jacob Viner, *The Role of Providence in the Social Order* (Philadelphia, 1972).

nates of secular history within the context of the Presbyterian form of Christianity.

By giving a detailed account of the world united and made accessible for the diffusion of a new faith under the *Pax Romana*, Robertson is able to provide a kind of sociology of the rise of Christianity. He presents a world already interconnected politically and through trade, practised in the moral virtues necessary to the maintenance of the secular state, but now corrupted by a culture which condones slavery, luxury and polygamy. It is therefore ready to receive the message of Christ, which is also a message of moral improvement through political and economic progress in the civil sphere. This aspect of Robertson's sermon has marked out ground, occupied by his later histories, for the investigation of the adaptability and effect of different forms of religion in different societies. This inquiry into the relationship between historical setting and social receptivity to religious belief would precipitate a sociological turn in Robertson's subsequent works; he remained committed to his own form of Christian belief, and yet developed an imaginative ability to transcend the sectarian idiom of Scottish Protestant history.

The development of this aspect of Robertson's thinking can be seen most clearly in his two accounts of the Reformation, the first in the *History of Scotland*, the second in the *History of Charles V*. The latter is part a narrative of European transformation in the sixteenth century, in which religious reformation is both a symptom and an agent of still wider processes of change in both Catholic and soon-to-be Protestant states. In the *History of Scotland*, the account of the Reformation is relatively traditional in Scottish terms. Mary Fearnley-Sander has demonstrated the extent to which Robertson relies upon John Knox's *Historie of the Reformation of the Church of Scotland* (1587, 1644), including the relatively secular emphasis upon the 'political motives' and 'love of civil liberty' animating the reformers (I, 129, 156).[80] There is, throughout the Reformation section of the *History of Scotland*, a generally orthodox sense of the instrumentality of individuals and peoples to the larger providential design. Intolerant figures, such as Mary of Guise and her relatives, become, by a 'singular disposition of Providence' the unwitting 'instruments' of Reformation (I, 113). Robertson overcomes his palpable distaste for the crude personality of John Knox by emphasising his instrumentality to a larger plan: 'Those very qualities, however, which now render his character less amiable, fitted him to be the instrument of providence for advancing the reformation among a fierce people' (II, 35). This sentence incorporates the idea that Knox was a sociologically appropriate specimen of a religious leader for his times,

[80] Mary Fearnley-Sander, 'Philosophical History and the Scottish Reformation', *Historical Journal*, 33 (1990), 323–38.

though the vocabulary remains essentially Calvinist. Moreover, Robertson explicitly rejects the idea – by implication entertained by historians such as Voltaire or Hume – that the Reformation was merely 'the effect of some wild and enthusiastic frenzy in the human mind'(I, 128). Robertson insists instead upon the constructive role of human agents within the larger scheme of things: 'The human mind felt its own strength, broke the fetters of authority by which it had been so long restrained' (I, 119). As well as explaining the intentional and providential nature of the Scottish Reformation, Robertson also argues that this event was a bid for civil liberty, and, as such, part of a European political response to the ideology and mechanisms of papal power.

Robertson's differs from previous accounts of the Scottish Reformation principally in its European frame of reference, and in its emphasis upon the catalytic role of religious reform in wider political progress. Robertson links these events into his structuring images of progress and enlightenment. In Scotland, the Reformation marks the beginning of a silent process of improvement. At this point Robertson's unilinear images proliferate; the doctrines of Reform were still in their 'infancy' during the Regency of Mary of Guise, but they soon 'advanced, by large and firm steps, towards a full establishment in the kingdom', and, after the 'first dawn of the new light' among Scottish priests,

> the inquisitive genius of the age pressed forward in quest of truth; the discovery of one error opened the way to others; the downfall of one imposture drew many after it; the whole fabric, which ignorance and superstition had erected in times of darkness began to totter; and nothing was wanting to compleat its ruin, but a daring and active leader to direct the attack. (I, 111)

The Reformation is thus part of the transition from 'times of darkness' to times of light. In the *History of Charles V*, it will make a second and longer appearance as a chaotic but necessary chapter in the still grander 'Progress of Society in Europe'.

For now, Robertson rewrites the Reformation as part of Scotland's Whig destiny, but also suggests that the political self-respect which was first offered at this time to the Scottish people had a wider franchise than the Protestant portion of the nation. Many of his evangelical contemporaries continued to believe in the special destiny of Protestant nations. John Witherspoon, for example, as a leader of the evangelical wing of the Kirk, and, subsequently, as President of the College of New Jersey in America, carried with him at all times a confident sense of the unique value of the uncorrupted Protestant province.[81] Robertson, who makes disparaging

81 See, Ned Landsman, 'Witherspoon and the Problem of Provincial Identity in Scottish Evangelical Culture' in *Scotland and America in the Age of the Enlightenment*, eds. Richard B. Sher and Jeffrey R. Smitten (Edinburgh, 1990).

reference to the great Covenant of 1643, does not seek to draw out of Scottish history any specific divine endorsement for the Scottish Protestant nation (II, 164). Some of Robertson's Evangelical contemporaries felt that they were purveyors of truth *contra mundum*: 'The faithful minister', preached John Erskine, 'though reviled by an ungrateful generation as a trouble of Israel, and a turner of the world upside down, is glorious in the eyes of the Lord'.[82] The traditionally minded among Scotland's clergymen extended this isolationist, exceptionalist sense of selfhood to the Scottish nation itself. Robertson's *History of Scotland* ultimately rejects this formulation of Scottish exceptionalism. Even in his first history, he attempts to represent national history from the imaginative vantage point of an internationalised sensibility. His text, in its skilful proposition of a modified form of British identity, is intended to be taken as evidence for a Scottish cultural revival of more than local importance. There are difficulties involved, of course, in attempting to pull the history of a province into the matrix of Enlightenment history. Since the province cannot enjoy, like Voltaire's France, the status of a representative and exemplary European state, it can only be endorsed within cosmopolitan historical discourse in so far as it is subsumed within the patterns of a wider European modernity. The *History of Scotland* reflects Robertson's anxiety that Scottish culture cannot sustain itself unless turned towards the wider world, but also dramatises his regret for the lost worlds of Scottish history – the medieval barons defending freedom and the borders, the traduced Scottish queen, and the obstinate heroism of the reformers. Having served his apprenticeship on the *Edinburgh Review*, Robertson set out, in the *History of Scotland*, both to explore this anxiety about the inherently provincial character of Scottish culture, and to widen the context within which that culture must be understood, and must understand itself. It was an ambitious programme which would soon come to fruition in his account of the origins of modern Europe, the *History of the Reign of Charles V*.

[82] Erskine, 'Ministers of the Gospel cautioned against giving offence', I, 209.

5

Robertson on the triumph of Europe and its empires

Ten years elapsed between the publication of Robertson's first history and the arrival of his second, *The History of the Reign of the Emperor Charles V*, and he awaited public response with some trepidation.[1] Few of his friends, least of all Hume, had greatly encouraged the project.[2] In the event, apart from a few mutterings from Horace Walpole and an anonymous unflattering article by Boswell, his fears proved groundless, and, in addition to the unusually high sum he received for the work (£3,500 in the first instance, with around £500 for subsequent editions – a considerable improvement on the £600 he received for his first work), he had the joy of a very favourable reception.[3] Robertson's French translator, Suard, thought he had found in this Scotsman a genuine *philosophe*.[4] Buoyed up by his success, Robertson went on to write a third substantial work, the *History of America*, the portion of which dealing with the Spanish colonies he published in 1777. His last work, representing yet another new departure, was an extended essay entitled *An Historical Disquisition concerning the Knowledge which the Ancients had of India* (1791).[5] All of these later histories represent, in

[1] William Robertson, *The History of the Reign of the Emperor Charles V. With a view of the progress of society in Europe, from the subversion of the Roman Empire to the beginning of the sixteenth century* (3 vols.; London, 1769). All quotations in the chapter are from this edition. It was slightly revised and altered over the course of Robertson's lifetime, and I have collated all quotations in my text with the last authorially corrected seventh edition (4 vols.; London, 1792). No significant differences have emerged, although the revisions do tend to firm up the liberal and religiously tolerant tone of the history. Felix Gilbert has also edited the introductory essay, *The Progress of Society in Europe* (Chicago, 1972). Robertson to Hume (31 January 1769) in R. B. Sher and M. A. Stewart eds., 'William Robertson and David Hume: Three Letters', *Hume Studies*, 10 (1985), 76.

[2] Hume to Robertson (Summer, 1759), *Letters*, no. 170.

[3] Walpole to Cole (20 August 1768) in Walpole's *Correspondence*, I, 152. Letters of congratulation are to be found in the National Library of Scotland, *Robertson–MacDonald Papers*, MS 3942, ff. 73–4, ff. 81–2, ff. 85–94, f. 103. Boswell wrote an article criticising Robertson's character in the *London Magazine* (April 1772, 281–3) and implying that, as a historian, he lacked the 'profound reflection and acute discrimination' of Hume (282). Among those sending letters of congratulation were Lord Lyttelton, the King, the Prince and Princess of Wales, and Voltaire. For the formal offer of payment made by Strahan, Robertson's publisher, see NLS, *Robertson–MacDonald Papers*, MS 3942, ff. 63–4.

[4] Suard to Robertson (19 January 1769), NLS, *Robertson–MacDonald Papers*, ff. 73–4.

[5] Robertson, *The History of America* (2 vols.; London, 1777); *An Historical Disquisition concerning the knowledge which the ancients had of India* (London, 1791).

different ways, an elaboration of the international themes tentatively explored in the *History of Scotland*. Robertson's cosmopolitan historical commitments were apparently unshaken by the Anglo-French hostilities of either the Seven Years' or American Revolutionary wars, and the generously international reach of his imagination appears to have been extended by the upheavals in the British Empire.

The *History of Charles V* and the *History of America* expand upon the sixteenth-century history of Robertson's first work. The *History of Charles V* recapitulates in European context the themes of the *History of Scotland*, including the erosion of the feudal order, the Reformation, the rise and fall of strong monarchies. Like *Le Siècle de Louis XIV*, Robertson's second history is about would-be universal monarchy, and how it is eventually forced to give way to a more viable system of balancing states in Europe. After the overhaul of the sixteenth century, Robertson argues, Europe achieved its distinctive identity and political shape:

> It was during [Charles V's] reign ... that the different kingdoms of Europe acquired internal vigour, that they discerned the resources of which they were possessed, that they came both to feel their own strength, and to know how to render it formidable to others. It was during this reign, too, that the different kingdoms of Europe, formerly single and disjointed, became so thoroughly acquainted, and so intimately connected with each other, as to form one great political system, in which each took a station, wherein it has remained since that time with less variation than could have been expected after the events of two active centuries. (III, 432–3)

This passage, perhaps self-consciously, echoes similar observations at the beginning of Hume's first Tudor volume:

> The European states on the continent were then hastening fast to the situation, in which they have remained, without any material alteration, for near three centuries; and began to unite themselves into one extensive system of policy.
> (III, 24)

Hume's Tudor volumes provided the retrospective European context for his earlier work, and Robertson's second history similarly supplies an international framework for his first. Scotland's turbulent sixteenth-century history can now be more clearly seen as part of this journey to stability and coming-to-political-consciousness in Europe. The eventual Union of Scotland with England may be regarded, at least at the cultural level, as its point of entry into this modern system of closely interacting states.

The *History of Charles V* is an assured and ambitious narrative which tells how the peoples of sixteenth-century Europe gradually dragged themselves towards the modernity prescribed by Providence. It is also a sociological investigation of the process of modernisation which tries to elicit general formulations about the economic and institutional causes of social change.

Robertson was one of the first narrative historians to embrace the new forms of sociological speculation pioneered by Smith, Hume and others in his home country. In his later works, two kinds of history – cosmopolitan grand narrative and sociological inquiry – by turns reinforce and compromise each other. Robertson achieves new theoretical sophistication in his narrative handling of familiar concepts such as 'feudalism' and 'civil society'; nevertheless, he does not lose his faith in the operations of Providence in history, nor in the human capacity to shape events within its larger dispensations. Robertson's new understanding of the unseen and uncontrollable economic and social processes at work in history paradoxically strengthened his commitment to the idea that human agents have some constructive part to play in their destiny.

Traditional Calvinist history, as David Allan has shown, often incorporated relatively permissive accounts of human agency in the shaping of events.[6] Robertson, who shared this sense of the constructive role of human agents within a providentially ordained history, was troubled by the secular determinism which the new Scottish science of society might be seen to entail. This conflict deepened his reflections upon the old Calvinist problem of human intention in history, while generating new problems for his historical method. The long and quickly famous introductory essay to the *History of Charles V*, 'A View of the Progress of Society in Europe', is conducted according to universal methodological principles applied to the case of social development in Europe (with the implication that similar investigations using similar conceptual tools could be conducted into, say, America or India). Portions of the essay, however, along with the rest of the *History of Charles V*, explore the creative responses of the European peoples to the tide of events which lead ultimately to the formation of a distinctive, modern European identity. Robertson does not resolve these methodological tensions in his second history, and it is uneven as a result. Hume was typical of his contemporaries in admiring the opening essay above the rest of the *History of Charles V*: 'Neither the character of Charles V, nor the Incidents of his Life are very interesting; and were it not for the first Volume, the Success of this work, tho' perfectly well writ, woud not have been so shining.'[7] Although it would be hard to disagree with Hume's view that the introductory essay is the most innovative portion of the history, it is misleading to suggest that the *History of Charles V* is primarily a biography. Robertson uses the story of Charles' itinerant life as a general structure for a wide-ranging history of sixteenth-century Europe. Ten years earlier, Hume had, in fact, tried to talk Robertson into writing a Plutarchan-style biography of some great figure in European history, and

[6] David Allan, *Virtue, Learning and the Scottish Enlightenment* (Edinburgh, 1993), 110.

[7] Hume to Hugh Blair (28 March 1769), *Letters*, no. 427.

Robertson's depiction of Charles V and François I makes some concessions to the Plutarchan 'parallel lives' style of biography.[8] Even so, Robertson does not share, in the main, Hume partly biographical fascination with the dynamic between (great) persons and things, but retains instead a Presbyterian interest in the collective lives of God's peoples.

Stadial history

Intellectual conditions in Scotland had changed since Robertson's *History of Scotland*, and would continue to develop during his later writing career. Soon after Hume published the Tudor and medieval volumes of his *History of England*, there was a great outpouring of Scottish works dealing with the historical genesis of law, and the economic and institutional development of early and advanced societies. Robertson read and cited in his works many of the major productions in this field. These included Kames' *Historical Law-Tracts* (1758) and, later, his *Sketches of the History of Man* (1774); Adam Ferguson's *Essay on the History of Civil Society*, which came out and was warmly championed by Robertson in 1767;[9] Adam Smith's *Inquiry into the Nature and Causes of the Wealth of Nations* (1776) elicited a letter of congratulation from Robertson;[10] Smith's pupil, John Millar, brought out the first edition of *Observations concerning the Distinction of Ranks in Society* (1771) in good time for Robertson to absorb it before writing the *History of America.* Although Scottish writing on civil society and law can be loosely described as a sociological project, these researches originally grew out of the traditional disciplines of natural jurisprudence and classical political theory, as recent studies have shown.[11] Although the products of this collective Scottish inquiry into the nature of society differed considerably, even fundamentally, in their objectives and chosen mode of examination, it will nevertheless be useful to point to a number of their methodological similarities, before assessing their impact upon Robertson. Robertson's later histories reveal a good deal about the transfer of method from speculative sociological and legal inquiry to narrative history.

Although the methods of social inquiry conducted in eighteenth-century Scotland did not adhere to a single scheme, it is nevertheless useful to denote the historical aspects of this social thought as 'stadial history' (i.e.

[8] Hume to Robertson (7 April 1759), *New Letters*, no. 28.

[9] Robertson to Hume (27 March 1767), *Hume Studies*, 10 (1985), 75.

[10] Robertson to Smith (8 April 1776), *Correspondence of Adam Smith*, eds. E. C. Mossner and I. S. Ross (Oxford, 1977), no. 153.

[11] Major re-evaluations of Scottish social theory in the light of new scholarship in the fields of civic humanist political thought and natural and civil jurisprudence include Donald Winch, *Adam Smith's Politics: An Essay in Historiographic Revision* (Cambridge, 1978); Istvan Hont and Michael Ignatieff eds., *Wealth and Virtue: The Shaping of Political Economy in the Scottish Enlightenment* (Cambridge, 1983).

history subdivided into 'stages'). This kind of historical thinking was originally dubbed 'conjectural' history by the Scottish moral philosopher Duguld Stewart, although the word 'conjecture' was widely rejected at the time, not least by Robertson and Ferguson.[12] In the work of Kames, Smith and Millar, stadial history was not a narrative form of explanation, but an organised system of historical reference for the study of natural law. Comparative treatment of different societies revealed the underlying principles and perversions of natural laws operative in history. Such principles could be empirically elicited, and so natural law itself took a particularly empirical and sociological turn in the hands of its Scottish practitioners.[13] Stadial history, narrowly defined, describes a natural trajectory or spiral of development in which societies undergo change through successive stages based on different forms of subsistence. Ironically, it was Robertson, a somewhat reluctant stadial historian, who provided in the *History of America* the most widely quoted definition of the stadial form of social analysis:

> In every inquiry concerning the operations of men when united together in society, the first object of attention should be their mode of subsistence. Accordingly at that varies, their laws and policy must be different. (*History of America*, I, 324)

Four economic stages – the hunter-gatherer, the pastoral, the agricultural, and the commercial – were held to represent the basic taxonomy of societies. This did not necessarily imply a determinist or materialist let alone proto-Marxist theory of history. The idea of stages was adaptively applied, and, among Scottish social scientists of the eighteenth century, only Kames, Smith and Millar, adhered to these specific categories. Smith's unpublished *Lectures on Jurisprudence* provide an especially good example of how laws may be understood historically in relation to social modalities (abbreviated as four stages of economic development), and how this may in turn lead to a comprehension of the underlying nature of law in society. Ferguson, by contrast, does not refer to 'mode of subsistence' as

[12] Robertson, *History of America*, I, 288; II, 173; Ferguson, *Essay on the History of Civil Society* (1767), ed. Fania Oz-Salzberger (Cambridge, 1995), 8. The earliest definition of 'conjectural' history was supplied by Dugald Stewart in *Biographical Memoirs of Adam Smith, L L D., of William Robertson, D. D. and of Thomas Reid, D. D.* (Edinburgh, 1811), 48–9. For more recent accounts of Scottish stadial or conjectural history, see Robert A. Nisbet, *Social Change and History* (New York, 1969); Ronald L. Meek, *Social Science and the Ignoble Savage* (Cambridge, 1976); H. M. Höpfl, 'From Savage to Scotsman: Conjectural History in the Scottish Enlightenment', *Journal of British Studies*, 17 (1978), 19–40; Knud Haakonssen, *The Science of a Legislator* (Cambridge, 1981), chapter 7; Ronald Hamowy, *The Scottish Enlightenment and the Theory of Spontaneous Order* (Carbondale, Illinois, 1987). The European background to the Scottish science of man is provided by Michèle Duchet, *Anthropologie et histoire au siècle des lumières* (Paris, 1971).

[13] On the study of natural law in the Scottish Enlightenment, see Duncan Forbes, 'Natural Law and the Scottish Enlightenment' in *The Origins and Nature of the Scottish Enlightenment*, eds. R. H. Campbell and Andrew S. Skinner (Edinburgh, 1982).

one of the variables which enable the historian to distinguish between one society and another. He divides societies into a more classical scheme according to their allocation of property and labour: the savage, the barbarian and the polished. However, there was broad agreement among Scottish social theorists that man's historical progress was essentially stadial, rather than linear, and that the earliest stage of man's development could be conjecturally reconstructed as having existed historically, rather than simply functioning as a fiction to facilitate social theory or social criticism.

All Scottish social scientists had a common book of wisdom in Montesquieu's *De l'Esprit des lois* which had opened up possibilities for the empirical study of legal patterns through the comparative evaluation of societies. Stadial history was essentially a descriptive and critical, rather than a narrative, project, as Ferguson explained: 'There is a descriptive or natural history which leads to induction and laws, but there is also a narrative history which explains men's deeds.'[14] In order to assimilate the insights and method of his Scottish contemporaries, Robertson needed to bridge this descriptive/narrative divide. The *History of Charles V*, with its opening 'View of the Progress of Society in Europe', straddles two historiographies, and a tension between narrative and descriptive imperatives is evident in the contrast between the overall title (the history of a particular reign) and the intrusion of the theoretical category of 'Society' into the sub-title of the first volume (Voltaire would have written a 'View' of the 'Progress of Europe'). Robertson only fully embraced stadial history belatedly in the *History of America*. Nevertheless, he often found the stadial conception of social evolution intractable to straightforward narrative emplotment.

In writing his histories of early modern Europe and the Americas, Robertson had available to him highly flexible models of historiographic interpretation both in the writings of his compatriots, and in the work of Voltaire and Montesquieu. Voltaire's work may well have provided Robertson with a somewhat underdeveloped model for the ways in which social analysis might be harnessed to causal explication. Voltaire had tried to gauge the pressure of laws, manners and customs on social behaviour, not only synchronically, as Montesquieu had done, but in the diachronic process of modernisation. Robertson paid a wry, but generous tribute to Voltaire in a note at the end of his 'View' of medieval Europe:

> I have not once mentioned M. de Voltaire, who, in his 'Essai sur L'Histoire Generale', has reviewed the same period, and has treated of all these subjects. This does not proceed from inattention to the works of that extraordinary man, whose genius, no less enterprising than universal, has attempted almost every different

[14] Adam Ferguson, *Institutes of Moral Philosophy* (Edinburgh, 1769), 61.

species of literary composition. In many of these he excels. In all, if he had left religion untouched, he is instructive and agreeable. But as he seldom imitates the example of the modern historians in citing the authors from whom they derive their information, I could not, with propriety, appeal to his authority in conformation of any doubtful or unknown fact. I have often, however, followed him as my guide in these researches; and he has not only pointed out the facts with respect to which it was of importance to inquire, but the conclusions which it was proper to draw from them. If he had, at the same time, mentioned the books which relate these particulars, a great part of my labour would have been unnecessary, and many of his readers, who now consider him only as an entertaining and lively writer, would find that he is a learned and well-informed historian. (I, 392)

Despite Voltaire's weaknesses as a scholar, he would have represented for Robertson the most prominent example of a historian who viewed man as the creator of his own history. Smith, Kames, Ferguson and Millar, on the other hand, tended to view the deep structure of change as in some sense natural, which is to say the product of man's instinctual and unconscious programming. This was not a biologically determinist theory of history; social institutions and cultural forms which proliferate as part of these changes are not interpreted as purely epiphenomenal since they in turn may retard or interfere with stadial progression. However, the Scottish theorists did not dissolve, as Voltaire did, the boundary between economic causes and cultural effects, or view history as man's search for aesthetic order. Voltaire's history is an assertion by the historian of civilised modernity, and the authorial self becomes a principle of identification whereby signs of modernity in history are located and endorsed. The stadial historian, by contrast, is condemned by the very logic of his history to a weakened authorial position, since stadial history, by suggesting that divided labour and specialisation are characteristics of modern economies at the most advanced stage, implies that the writer, too, is specialised, and has only partial understanding.[15] As a narrative historian, Robertson inevitably encountered the new stadial history as a problem for the writer's authority. In the *History of Scotland*, he expanded the self-confidently provincial strategies of self-presentation, adopted by his Scottish contemporaries, into a more cosmopolitan view of his own nation's history. More committed than ever, in the *History of Charles V*, to this (strenuously unironic) Europeanised authorial voice, Robertson cannot accept the weakening of his authority implicit in his espousal of a more Scottish mode of historical analysis. The maintenance of an all-embracing Enlightenment perspective, in spite of a more fractured history of stages, becomes a still greater imperative. Robertson's work brings to the fore some of the more value-laden assumptions of stadial history: that

[15] See John Barrell, *English Literature in History, 1730–80: An Equal, Wide Survey* (London, 1983), 25–31.

change is qualitative in both a moral and material sense (an idea which only Ferguson explicitly rejected), and that modern Europe, having been the first part of the world to reach the commercial stage, possesses innate cultural superiority.

The decay of the European feudal order

The central theme of Robertson's *History of Charles V* is the rise of Europe as a republic of states out of the ruins of the pre-civil feudal system. This was the subject of the opening section of the *History of Scotland*, and now appears in expanded form in the long prefatory essay, 'A View of the Progress of Society' in medieval Europe. This essay begins with a brief summary of the collapse of the Roman Empire, and the ensuing period of barbarism in Europe. Like Ferguson, Robertson sees barbarism as a distinctive social stage with its own behavioural norms ('force of mind, a sense of personal dignity, gallantry in enterprize', I, 20). The feudal-agricultural social stage which follows brings a still worse state of affairs; Europe becomes a stateless patchwork of petty military dominions. At first, the European peoples seem imprisoned in the feudal era, economically and culturally retarded by their form of society. Robertson draws (in tones strongly reminiscent of Hume's essays) the following sociological inference from the Dark Ages: 'If men do not enjoy the protection of regular government, together with the certainty of personal security which naturally flows from it, they never attempt to make progress in science, nor aim at attaining refinement in taste or in manners' (I, 18). The analysis of the feudal form of government (which 'resembled a military establishment, rather than a civil institution') owes a great deal to other contemporary Scottish re-evaluations of feudal Europe (I, 17): first, he sees feudalism as a stage, or, indeed, a somewhat prolonged sub-stage of the agricultural phase of human development; secondly, he distinguishes, as Voltaire does not, between feudalism technically defined as a system of social dominance by an aristocracy through ties of vassalage, and feudalism as an emotive eighteenth-century term used to denote all forms of seigneurial relationships and peasant subjection. Robertson sticks more rigidly in this essay than in the *History of Scotland* to the first definition, though, like Smith and Kames, he is quite convinced that post-feudal society represents a vast improvement on the feudal world. Robertson drew upon, but gives little credit to, the predominantly political and legal presentation of feudalism in the section of Hume's history on 'The Feudal and Anglo-Norman Government and Manners'. Privately, Robertson was rather dismissive of Hume's medieval work ('the last volumes are both negligent in composition, and he hath bestowed no great degree of labour in researches of any kind'), whereas Hume more generously acknowledged a debt to Robertson in this field (*History of England*, I, 455).[16]

Having described the feudal ice age, Robertson tells how it eventually came to thaw and melt. The transition from one stage to another presents him with something of a narrative problem, which he tries to resolve in a number of ways. Initially, he resorts to familiar linear images of seeds ripening: 'we must search for the seeds of order, and endeavour to discover the first rudiments of policy and laws now established in Europe' (I, 11); and darkness giving way to light:

> a more pleasant exercise begins here, to observe the first dawnings of returning light, to mark the various accessions by which it gradually increased and advanced towards the full splendor of day. (I, 22)

For Robertson, as for Hume, it is the eleventh century which marks 'the return of government and manners in a contrary direction' (I, 21). There is, Robertson explains in a deliberate echo of Hume, 'an ultimate point of depression, as well as of exaltation' (Hume writes, 'there is a point of depression, as well as of exaltation') after which human societies naturally move from one stage to another (I, 20; *History of England*, II, 519). However, the transition from the point of depression in the eleventh century to greater elevation is not subsequently narrated in chronological order, but broken down into a series of nine or so explanatory sections. Robertson's mode of analysis (which is conducted under the subheadings of the Crusades, the development of cities, changes in rural life, new adaptations of criminal, Roman and canon law, chivalry, arts and sciences, and commerce) emulates Montesquieu in its synchronic complexity, and in its emphasis upon simultaneous layers, rather than narrative lines of causality. All observations are supported by copious scholarly notes in the large and often discursive 'Proofs and Illustrations' section of the essay. Robertson's account of the decay of the feudal stage is certainly more various and elaborate than those of his Scottish predecessors. He goes beyond the usual eighteenth-century view of the Crusades as 'a singular monument of human folly', by adding a new layer of irony: 'to these expeditions, the effect of superstition or folly, we owe the first gleams of light which tended to dispel barbarism and ignorance' since they brought previously isolated Christendom into contact with the more sophisticated Greek and Muslim East (I, 25, 27). He is also innovative (in ways which would later interest Gibbon) in his use of the latest antiquarian scholarship from France to bolster an argument about the social utility of chivalry as a civilising influence on politics and manners: 'The wild exploits of those romantic knights who sallied forth in quest of adventures, are well known, and have

[16] Robertson to Eliot (8 March 1762), NLS, *Minto Papers*, MS 11009, ff. 113–14.

been treated with proper ridicule. The political and permanent effects of the spirit of chivalry have been less observed' (I, 71; note 27 cites the French medieval scholar of chivalry, La Curne de St Palaye).

Robertson's synchronic method generates a certain circularity in his reasons for the decay of feudalism, which both enhances the theoretical complexity of his social analysis, and further distances the essay from narrative form. For example, Robertson, like Hume before him, lays emphasis upon the role of commerce in ushering in more civilised forms of social and international relations:

> Commerce tends to wear off those prejudices which maintain distinction and animosity between nations. If softens and polishes the manners of men. It unites them, by one of the strongest of all ties, the desire of supplying mutual wants. (I, 81)

However, Robertson also explains that, for commerce to take place among and between nations, a degree of social refinement must already exist. Commerce is both a symptom and a cause of a society's transition from one developmental stage to the next. The most visible outcome of the end of the feudal stage is, in fact, the twin growth of civil liberty and monarchy, the interrelated products of the enfranchisement and enrichment of cities, along with the growing regularity of legal systems. The second section of 'A View' examines the changing conduct of external affairs during the late medieval period. Increases in wealth and changes in technology alter the character of warfare. Standing armies become an inevitable feature of more commercial societies, though war, paradoxically, becomes less damaging as European states come to see themselves as mutually deterrent strategic blocs and learn the pragmatic value of religious toleration. Robertson is especially interested, in this section, and throughout the *History of Charles V*, in the way in which European states evolved (or, more often, failed to evolve) modern notions of foreign policy based on quantifiable permanent interest and understood as the balance of geo-political power.

A third section of the essay examines in detail the political constitutions and 'spirit of the laws' of the principal states of Europe at the beginning of the sixteenth century. Here Robertson is mainly interested in the mechanisms for balance within each country's governmental structure. Stadial theory can account for the deep similarities between each state:

> The view which I have exhibited of the causes and effects, whose influence was universal, will enable my readers to account for the surprizing resemblance among the nations of Europe in their interior police, and foreign operations. (I, 123)

England is the only major European state not to be described. A quietly subversive note explains why:

> The state of government, in all the nations of Europe, having been nearly the same

during several ages, nothing can tend more to illustrate the progress of the English constitution, than a careful inquiry into the laws and customs of the kingdoms on the continent. (I, 393)

As well as gently subverting many of his readers' cherished beliefs about the special historical character of the British constitution, Robertson drives home a cosmopolitan point: to understand themselves English readers must understand and appreciate European history.

Robertson's description of the waning of the Middle Ages has many similarities to the one given by Voltaire in the earlier texts of the *Essai sur les mœurs*. Both writers lay peculiar emphasis upon the sixteenth century as the crucible of modernity. Like Voltaire, and, indeed, many of his Scottish contemporaries, Robertson is relatively inattentive to the role of agrarian developments in eroding feudal structures, and emphasises instead the co-operation between monarchs and municipalities in bringing feudalism to an end. Neither Voltaire nor Robertson define feudalism in exclusively juridical terms, nor even (as Robertson had done in the *History of Scotland*) as a military structure, but as a cultural and economic system. There are aspects of Robertson's exposition of the endogenous and exogenous factors behind the erosion of the feudal system which do not belong to a Humean or a stadial mode of analysis. When discussing exogenous factors, Robertson's model is a distinctively Voltairean one; Europe comes to consciousness of its own common political identity, and individual states begin to direct their recently acquired 'vigour' towards external activity:

The kingdoms of Europe [in the sixteenth century] had arrived at such a degree of improvement in the internal administration of government . . . that they were in a condition to enlarge the sphere of their operations, and to increase the vigour of their efforts.

(I, 120–1; the 1792 text added after 'operation', 'to multiply their claims and pretensions', I, 145)

Robertson, like Voltaire, dwells upon the beneficial effects of Europe's recognition of its interdependency, and sees the strategic theory of the balance of power as one outcome of this.[17] Before the sixteenth century, European states 'appear to have considered themselves as separate societies', whereas they would soon come to consider themselves, and to be considered by historians as a single entity: 'whoever records the transactions of any of the more considerable European states, during the last two centuries, must write the history of Europe' (I, 87–8).

Robertson's vision of the endogenous dissolution of the feudal order is one of human activity silently and naturally breaking down artificial constraints in the pursuit of greater liberty. This growth of personal liberty

[17] Voltaire, 'Tableau de l'Europe depuis la paix d'Utrecht jusqu'en 1750', in *Le Siècle de Louis XIV* (all editions before 1768).

is structurally linked to the transition from the medieval to the post-feudal world, in ways similar to those described in Hume's appendix on 'Feudal and Anglo-Norman Government and Manners'. Smith's *Wealth of Nations* would later emphasise this model of the internal erosion of feudalism through economic activity rather than exogenous factors. Kames, too, had much to say about the role of irrational appetites in both the internal construction and erosion of the feudal system.[18] Nevertheless, what is missing from 'A View', as a piece of Scottish stadial history, is any sense that the post-feudal sixteenth century is the unlooked-for by-product of medieval man's individual appetites and drives. Like Ferguson, whose *Essay on the History of Civil Society* he had read by this time, Robertson is a methodological collectivist. This is to say that his unit of study is not composed of individuals, but of the collective, and divinely prompted action of whole groups. Like Ferguson, too, Robertson believes that conflict, in which nations or large social groups are the collective significant actors, is a necessary force for change. He thus focuses a good deal upon those conflictual acts which are collective, such as the Crusades, and, in the rest of the *History of Charles V*, upon the violent social and religious upheavals which transformed sixteenth-century Europe.

In 'A View', the acquisition of liberty and mental emancipation are central themes, since it is by exerting their capacity for freedom and independent thought that the European peoples gradually create the conditions for their own commercial modernity. Robertson sees liberty in a natural jurisprudential light as a person's freedom from external interference, although he also links it, in a classical way, to the acquisition of citizenship (specifically a municipal phenomenon in Robertson's Middle Ages). From the eleventh century onwards, liberty's franchise is gradually broadened as commerce permits the admission of more and more people into the benefits of citizenship. Commercial interchange between the cities and the countryside stimulates rural social mobility: 'a numerous class of men, who formerly had no political existence, and were employed merely as instruments of labour, became useful citizens and contributed towards augmenting the force or riches of the society which adopted them as members' (I, 41–2). This expanded classical view of liberty as the freedom to participate in society may also owe something to Hume.[19] Robertson's chief departure from his Scottish contemporaries, and a major point of similarity with Voltaire, is his repeated insistence that liberty and the desire for justice are causal, and that history is an arena of moral choice between

[18] Henry Home, Lord Kames, *Essays upon Several Subjects Concerning British Antiquities* (Edinburgh, 1747), 127–9.

[19] On the Scottish Enlightenment adaptation of classical ideas of liberty, see John Robertson, 'The Scottish Enlightenment at the Limits of the Civic Tradition' in *Wealth and Virtue*, eds. Hont and Ignatieff.

fanaticism and reason. The rudimentary form of citizenship slowly acquired by the medieval agrarian population, for example, comes about because the rural people see the improvements in life in the cities, and demand greater liberty for themselves: 'the freedom and independence which one part of the people had obtained by the institution of communities, inspired the other with the most ardent desire to acquiring the same privileges' (I, 40). Many of the other alterations to the feudal system are also the result of deliberate human intervention. Robertson is uneasy about the moral implications of the Scottish notion of unintended consequences in human affairs. What is missing from the stadial side of Robertson's method is a thoroughgoing commitment to the notion that historical development is the outcome of man's irrational, individual appetites and activities; his is, in part, a stadial history without its motor running.

Stadial models of history do not always give entirely convincing accounts of what propels man from the bottom stage of civilisation to the outermost part of the circle. It is only with difficulty that Montesquieu's synthetic model of society as the integration of multiple causal effects can be transformed into a model of social change. To a degree, stadial history is inherently circular precisely because it does not establish the anteriority of any single cause. Robertson inevitably found himself more hidebound than contemporary social theorists by the exigencies of constructing a narrative, and his 'View of the Progress of Society in Europe' frequently sidesteps its own circularity by emphasising the role of conscious intervention by participants in history, often in the cause of liberty. The cities, for example, in seeking enfranchisement, are said to be deliberately asserting the 'unalienable rights of humanity' (I, 31). Both in 'A View' and in the rest of the *History of Charles V*, Robertson continues to make use of metonymic connectives ('progress' and 'abatement', 'light' and 'dark', 'seeds' ripening, and so on) which meet the linear demands of narrative history. The references to Providence persist, and fundamental change is accounted for at the manifest level, as well as emanating from a hidden natural trajectory. Robertson did not entirely accept the sufficiency of stadial modes of explanation to the history of the fall and rise of Europe, and here he has much in common with Voltaire and, later, with Gibbon. They all saw history as the application as well as the acquisition of ideas, and as intended as well as spontaneous order.

The vigorous Reformation

The sociological and legal–historical vocabulary, so prominent in 'A View', plays a smaller role in the main body of the narrative of the life and times of Charles V. The remainder of the work is, for the most part, a political history, structured around the parallel lives of Charles V and François I, of the triangular power struggles in the sixteenth century between the Spanish and Ottoman Empires and France. The story begins with Ximenes' Regency in Spain, and ends with the abdication and death of Charles V. The whole period is conceived as an intermediate stage in European political and social development between the feudal and modern, commercial phases. Eighteenth-century historians had no word for 'Renaissance', and this concept did not form part of their schemes of historical periodisation. However, like Voltaire, Robertson distinguishes the sixteenth century as a transitional period between medieval and the post-feudal societies (Hume had seen the seventeenth century as the more momentous period). The convulsive upheavals of the period are all occasioned by an encounter between the customary order and the new. All aspects of the church and state are caught by Robertson's narrative at this point of transition: feudal anarchy gives way to more centralised, higher-taxing monarchies which are as yet unlimited by other intermediate powers in the state; external affairs and warfare are conducted by new, more technologically sophisticated standing armies, yet without any proper strategic understanding of the balance-of-power politics which such armies necessitate; the medieval Catholic Church is at last torn apart by the Reformation yet neither side yet understands that they do not have the power to enforce their beliefs. Europe has to pass through the fire of absolutism, civil and external wars, and religious schism on its route to modernity. Robertson's idea of the sixteenth century as an interim stage hovers behind his chronological narrative, surfacing at every interpretive moment. The vast perspectives of this history, as the author surveys the continent from vantage points in Spain, Flanders, France, Italy, and England, are anchored in this unifying sense of Europe in transition.

In the *History of Scotland*, Robertson bemoaned the fact that, in the late sixteenth century, Scotland had not taken the painful but necessary road to strong, centralised monarchy. In his second history, he explains why the emancipation of the rest Europe from its medieval past was achieved only at the cost of absolute monarchy in many of its countries, and at the risk of one of those absolute monarchs, Charles V, establishing a Europe-wide imperial order. Robertson ultimately regards powerful centralised monarchies as a necessary evil in this turbulent phase of European history since some of them will eventually give way to properly constituted post-feudal political institutions. The biographical emphasis upon the lives of Charles V, François I and Henry VIII, and the portions of the history dealing with their giant, capricious squabbles, reflect no real interest in their personalities; the influence of personality on history is, for Robertson, an accidental feature of a certain stage in history, soon to be diminished by the more limited monarchies of later centuries. In any case, Robertson's Charles V, like Voltaire's Louis XIV, is a shadowy figure without any clear motivation beyond his ruling passion of 'ambition', and his private character is wholly absorbed into his public persona (II, 230). Summarising Charles' life and personality, Robertson haughtily declares his intention to dispense with private anecdotes, perhaps implicitly rebuking the more gossipy style of Hume and Voltaire ('these are not the object of history'), and judges the emperor sternly according to the public utility of his actions:

> his desire of being distinguished as a conqueror involved him in continual wars, which exhausted and oppressed his subjects, and left him little leisure for giving attention to the interior police and improvement of his kingdoms, the great objects of every Prince who makes the happiness of his people the end of his government.
> (III, 419; minor adjustments in 1792, IV, 288)

Having committed himself to a one-dimensional presentation of Charles as Ambition personified, Robertson is at a loss to explain why he eventually abdicated. He only ventures a few uncharitable remarks about Charles wanting to conceal his physical infirmities from the public eye, and a few more satirical comments about his superstitious predilection for self-mortification once in retreat (III, 352, 412).

Robertson's real interest lies behind the thin psychological covering in which he dresses his kings, in the new form of sovereignty which they represent. Absolutism is first made possible, in Robertson's (possibly) Smithian analysis, by the weakened position of the aristocracy who spend their way into comparative poverty on the luxury items produced or traded in the cities (III, 441).[20] During the transitional stage of the sixteenth century, the new monarchs are nevertheless still able to make use of the residually martial spirit of their noble subjects to aggrandise themselves and increase their territories. For example:

> The vigour of the Feudal times remained, their anarchy was at an end; and the Kings of France could avail themselves of the martial ardour which that singular institution had kindled or kept alive, without being exposed to any of the dangers or inconveniences which are inseparable from it when in entire force. (III, 439)

More technologically sophisticated warfare ('war, from a very simple, became a very intricate science'), conducted in part by standing armies necessitates higher taxes (II, 199). These changes in the political and economic order are at first experienced as a profound disruption to the customary order by Europe's poorest peoples, and in some cases the peasantry articulate their feelings of disorientation through violence:

> [Feudal] exactions, though grievous, were born with patience, because they were customary and ancient: But when the progress of elegance and luxury, as well as the changes introduced into the art of war came to increase the expence of

[20] Adam Smith, *Lectures on Jurisprudence*, eds. R. L. Meek, D. D. Raphael and P. G. Stein (Oxford, 1978), 261–2.

government, and made it necessary for Princes to levy occasional or stated taxes on their subjects, such impositions being new, appeared intolerable. (II, 256)

The Reformation, in Robertson's account, is one consequence of this social disorientation, which itself gives rise to further political change. The nature and extent of Robertson's social analysis of the Reformation has tended to go unnoticed in this century, yet it is, in many ways, his most distinctive contribution to stadial history. Robertson does provide a long and substantial 'digression' (as he calls it) on the causes and progress of the Reformation in the second book of the *History of Charles V*, although this is not his last word on the subject (II, 250–91). The digression explains the causes of the Reformation in mainly ecclesiastical and political terms – the corruptions of the Church, its exorbitant wealth, and its unwarranted interference in the operations of civil government, local state affairs in Germany, and so on. There are also more general causes, for example, the invention of printing (following Hume), and the revival of classical learning, which also form part of the account of intellectual transformation elsewhere in the history. The narrative is assimilated to the usual linear images of light and dark, and seeds growing ('the darkness which then covered the church'; '[Erasmus] first scattered the seeds, which Luther cherished and brought to maturity', II, 111, 119). It is also firmly, if unobtrusively providential. Luther, like Knox in the *History of Scotland*, is the somewhat blunt instrument of a 'peculiar providence'. Robertson is little interested in Luther's personality, although, like Voltaire, he is ill at ease with his coarseness, his 'low buffoonery', and the 'gross scurility' of his writings (II, 115); these qualities, however, fit him to his divinely ordained task (III, 67). Robertson is explicitly indebted to Gilbert Burnet's ardently providential *Historie of the Reformation of the Church of England* (1679–1715), but he places far greater emphasis than his predecessor upon the secular mediations of God's will on earth. As in *The Situation of the World* and the *History of Scotland*, Robertson shows how providence operates through secondary historical causes: 'their success was the natural effect of many powerful causes, prepared by peculiar providence, and happily conspiring to that end' (II, 120; 1792 text has 'the success of the Reformation' for emphasis, II, 160).

This 'natural effect' of all these concurrent causes is not only described in the digression on the Reformation, but integrated into the narrative of social transformation elsewhere in the history. The Reformation is both an event of unique spiritual significance, and an aspect of the stadial transition taking place in the sixteenth century. For reasons which will be given below, this stadial analysis of the Reformation is never fully worked through, but the pre- and post-Reformation periods are loosely connected with the medieval and modern periods respectively. The pre-Reformation period is predictably associated with darkness, and also with the passivity of superstition ('those dark and quiet ages, when faith was implicit, when submission was unreserved', III, 448). Medieval Catholicism, as well as the pernicious new order of the Jesuits, are appraised, with clinical detachment, in the sectarian vocabulary of superstition and corruption (II, 444–78). The Reformation itself is associated with tumultuous energy:

> The human mind ... rouzed of a sudden and became inquisitive, mutinous, and disdainful of the yoke to which it had hitherto submitted. That wonderful ferment and agitation of mind, which, at this distance of time, appears unaccountable or is condemned as extravagant, was so general that it must have been excited by causes which were natural and of powerful efficacy. (III, 445)

This passage echoes Hume on the same subject: 'men, roused from that lethargy, in which they had so long sleeped, began to call in question the most ancient and most received opinions' (*History*, III, 139). For Robertson, however, the agitation prompted by the desire for ecclesiastical reform also aims to moderate the centralised forms of government ushered in by the sixteenth century. In this destabilised post-feudal world, the people regrettably, though inevitably fall prey to fanaticism, as they struggle for access to civil liberty (for example, the insurgent Anabaptists of Münster) (II, 348). These passions, so suddenly unleashed, prove fatal, in some countries, to both the Catholic Church and the state. Throughout Europe, the spirit of the Reformation strengthens the people's resolve to acquire civil liberty. The social upheavals sponsoring or engendered by religious reform are part of a transitional phase which will eventually deliver a new stage of greater stability in Europe. The bitter division between Catholic and Protestant churches is also a characteristic of an age of transition. The violent process of emancipation from the medieval Catholicism affects the peoples of both denominations; it releases long suppressed political and intellectual energies which transform Catholic and Protestant countries alike. The Catholic Church eventually learns the lesson 'that the credulity and patience of mankind might be overburdened and exhausted' (III, 447). The old medieval Catholic world, which Robertson had unapologetically characterised as corrupt and cravenly superstitious, gives way to a modern pluralist system of interplay and constructive emulation between the denominations. The modern opposition between Catholic and Protestant churches leads to mutual improvement in many areas of religious and secular life: 'this great division in the Christian church hath contributed, in some measure, to encrease purity of manners, to diffuse science, and to inspire humanity' (III, 451; the surrounding passage in 1792, IV, 329 adds a generous reference to the particular 'moderation' and 'love of literature' of the 'Pontiffs of the present century'). After a medieval era of superstition, and a sixteenth-century interlude of religious strife, hints Robertson, comes the modern stage of harmonious Christian pluralism.

Despite the confidence expressed in the *History of Charles V* that the era of Christian pluralism had now arrived, Robertson was soon to discover, to his cost, that Scotland had not developed as rapidly as the rest of Europe in this respect. Ten years after the publication of his second history, he and his moderate colleagues in the Kirk Assembly were vilified by evangelical groups for their support of better civil rights for Catholics in Scotland. Robertson had led the campaign for the extension of the 1778 English and Colonial Catholic Relief Bill to Scotland.[21] He and his supporters were soon faced with vehement opposition (led by John Erskine) and anti-popery protest so violent that he and his family were forced to take temporary refuge in Edinburgh castle. Recognising that Scotland had not yet reached the higher stage of religious toleration, Robertson eventually backed down ('I preferred the public good to my own private sentiments').[22] Robertson's speech conceding defeat in the Assembly 'On the Penal Laws against Papists' is nevertheless revealing in the context of his view on the progress of religious ideas on Europe:

> The first intimation I had of any intention to grant relief to Papists from the rigour of penal statutes, was in the newspapers. Though I had observed, with pleasure, the rapid progress of liberal sentiments in this enlightened age; tho' I knew that science and philosophy had diffused the principles of toleration through every part of Europe; yet I was so well acquainted with the deep-rooted aversion of Britons to the doctrines and spirit of Popery, that I suspected this motion, for giving relief to Papists, to be premature. [23]

As usual, Robertson links the principle of religious toleration to a historical scheme. This principle may be for him, as it was, of course, for so many eighteenth-century writers, an absolute good, but its implementation depends upon the evolutionary readiness of a particular country. He gently insinuates that Britain, and, in particular, Scotland, is somewhat backward in this respect in comparison with the more enlightened countries of Europe. In a similar way, Robertson's ecumenicalism, in the closing pages of the *History of Charles V*, is offered as a corollary of his secular cosmopolitanism. For it is only in the modern age that Europeans attain the greater cultural diversity which is their source of strength and competitive energy: 'that wide diversity of character and of genius which . . . hath exalted the Europeans above the inhabitants of the other quarter of the globe' (III, 432; 1792, IV, 304).

For Robertson, the Reformation is part of a wider process of religious

[21] For a detailed account of these events, see Richard Sher, *Church and University*, chapter 7.
[22] Robertson's remark is reported in the *Scots Magazine*, 41 (1779), 412.
[23] Ibid., 409.

and secular modernisation, and its causes are (at one level) natural: 'it must have been excited by causes which were natural and of powerful efficacy' (III, 445). Nevertheless, Robertson's social analysis of the Reformation cannot be said to have been entirely assimilated to a stadial model of history, and, in some important respects, he resists the theoretical tendency of his own speculations. For Robertson, stadial history accords too limited a place to the role of human intervention in history. Although Robertson senses that history is altogether larger than the sum of human purposiveness, he continues to recognise the role of rational decision in the process of change. This may be contrasted with the brief account of the Reformation which Smith supplied, some years later, in the *Wealth of Nations*. Smith argued that the constitution of the Church of Rome could never have been overturned by 'the feeble efforts of human reason', but was, rather, 'by the natural course of things, first weakened, and, afterwards in part destroyed'.[24] Robertson would not have accepted the implicit opposition in Smith's interpretation between the 'natural course of things' and deliberate human intervention. In the *History of Charles V*, the Reformation is not only a transitional social stage, but the point at which many Europeans take intellectual possession of their world:

> The Reformation, wherever it was received, increased that bold and innovating spirit to which it owed its birth. Men who had the courage to overturn a system supported by everything which can command respect or reverence, were not to be overawed by any authority, however great or venerable. (II, 258)

> Mankind seem, at that period, to have recovered the powers of inquiring and of thinking, faculties of which they had long lost the use; and fond of the acquisition, they exercised them with great boldness upon all subjects. (II, 116)

The Reformation may not, in the ultimately divine scheme of things, be a matter of human intention or unintention, but there is scope for rational human agency, as a secondary cause, in the process of reform.

In order for nations to acquire properly constituted ecclesiastical and political institutions, and for those states to exist in a balanced power relation with their neighbours, the people of Europe must voluntarily transform their habits of thought. For Robertson, the acquisition of new religious and political vocabularies always precedes practical change. Toleration must be invented and learned before it can be applied; throughout most of the reign of Charles V, 'the sacred rights of conscience and of private judgement were unheard of, and not only the idea of toleration, but even the word itself, in the sense now affixed to it, was unknown' (III, 335). The same applies to improvements in foreign

[24] *An Inquiry into the Nature and Causes of the Wealth of Nations*, eds. R. H. Campbell and A. S. Skinner (Oxford, 1976), II, 802–3.

relations: 'the ideas with respect to a proper distribution and balance of power were so lately introduced into the system of European policy, that they were not hitherto objects of sufficient attention' (II, 52–3). Sixteenth-century Europeans, Robertson implies, had to make important conceptual leaps with respect to privacy, liberty, religious freedom and the international balance of power before modernisation could be achieved. These were prompted by, but also regulated, the reception of deeper economic and social transformations.

Intention

By continuing to emphasise the role of language and human initiative in history, to a degree unusual in contemporary Scottish historical writing, Robertson appears dissatisfied with stadial models of change and with the moral inferences which he felt his readers might draw from stadial history. Stadial history characterises change as the outcome of unintended consequences, thereby implying that the significance of individual action is no longer embedded in intentionality. The 'invisible hand' in Smith's *Wealth of Nations*, for example, does not reveal to the acting individual the moral logic of its operations, and so opens out possibilities for a profoundly ironic interpretation of man's condition. Hume's account of the Reformation in England, for example, is replete with consequential ironies. Good effects (such as political liberty which comes from religious enthusiasm) are derived from trivial or unplanned causes:

> there followed from this revolution [Henry VIII's break with Rome] many beneficial consequences; though perhaps neither foreseen nor intended by the persons who had the chief hand in conducting it. (*History of England*, III, 206–7)

Robertson flirts with such consequential ironies: 'It was from causes seemingly fortuitous, and from a source very inconsiderable, that all the mighty effects of the reformation flowed' (I, 79). However, this outcome can only be viewed ironically by the superficial observer, since closer inspection reveals a Calvinist hermeneutic; the 'causes' are only '*seemingly* fortuitous' to those who ignore the deeper human and divine intention behind their operation. History, for Robertson, always has at least some degree of moral transparency.

Stadial history is always overshadowed by the Mandevillan spectre of morally nihilist satire;[25] if private vices are indeed public benefits, then man has a divided self and the moral significance of his actions is denied a historical dimension. Different Scottish writers tried to contain this moral

[25] See, for example, M. M. Goldsmith, 'Regulating anew the Moral and Political Sentiments of Mankind: Bernard Mandeville and the Scottish Enlightenment', *Journal of the History of Ideas*, 49 (1988), 587–606.

problem in different ways. Kames thought that unintending man could be redeemed to history by cultivating patriotism.[26] Smith, reading Mandeville as a moral philosopher, restored man in his private setting to the status of moral agent in the *Theory of Moral Sentiments* (1759), although there are, of course, notorious generic as well as internal difficulties in reconciling this work with Smith's view of the less morally autonomous type of man who inhabits the civil and economic setting of the *Wealth of Nations*. Ferguson could not lay Mandeville's ghost to rest, and, in the *Essay on the History of Civil Society*, he placed the problem of man's divided identity at the centre of his discussion of commercially evolved societies. For him, the split between man's civic and material functions, his identity as soldier and trader, citizen and specialised labourer could only be healed by a recovery of intentionality. It is as an actor asserting his will that man redeems himself from the condition of irony.[27]

Robertson was heir to the same civic moralist tradition as Ferguson, and, in the *History of Scotland*, occasionally waxed nostalgic for the times when active participation in society had been a pre-condition of citizenship. Like Ferguson, too, Robertson thought that more recent societies could escape the condition of irony and acquire agency by becoming vigorous.[28] 'Vigour' is one of Robertson's favourite words. He always genders 'vigour' as male, as Ferguson does, and uses it in the first instance to describe the martial, active qualities of early societies that have emerged from the hunter stage (for example, *Charles V*, III, 439). Rome, in both Robertson's 'View' and Ferguson's later *History of the Progress and Termination of the Roman Republic* (1783), is said to have fallen because it exchanged its vigorous qualities for an enervated state of relaxation.[29] Robertson also suggests that 'vigour' is an attribute of post-medieval societies which have successfully integrated commerce, defence, liberty and political balance into a cultural whole (I, 121; III, 439, 441). During the age of Charles V, for example, 'the different kingdoms of Europe' are said to have 'acquired internal vigour' (III, 432). Commercial societies, then, when they lose their earlier martial character, must substitute a new kind of purposiveness or vigour. In the word 'vigour' Robertson unites social activity with its effect. Modernity, when vigorous, is not a condition of irony. Robertson's 'vigour' also embodies a residual civic moralist notion that societies, even commercial ones, must continue to be judged, in part, on the qualities of active or

[26] Kames, *Sketches of the History of Man* (2 vols.; Edinburgh, 1774), II, sketch 7.

[27] For an illuminating discussion of the problems of moral intention and unintended consequences in the eighteenth and nineteenth centuries, see J. W. Burrow, *Whigs and Liberals: Continuity and Change in English Political Thought* (Oxford, 1985), chapter 3.

[28] Ferguson, *Essay on the History of Civil Society*, 202, 204.

[29] Ferguson, *History of the Progress and Termination of the Roman Republic* (3 vols.; London, 1783), III, 574.

intentional citizenship which their members exhibit. The civic moralist tendencies, which can also be discerned in Kames and Smith, have the effect on Robertson of fortifying his resistance to a wholly stadial historical model. Despite Robertson's reluctance to subscribe completely to a theory of history based upon non-intentionality, his difficulties with the stadial mode of narrative explanation also have their roots in his desire to project as an author and instil into the reader a cosmopolitan sense of identity. Stadial history, by emphasising the impersonal and the typical in history, gives little account of regional and national uniqueness. By insisting upon the role of conscious choice in history (as he had, for example, when describing the Act of Union), Robertson places greater stress upon the uniqueness and centrality of Europe's historical experience. It is for this reason, perhaps, that Robertson brought to the stadial exploration of social development an Enlightenment historical interest in how Europe had become more civilised through a mutual process of cultural dissemination. He added to the theory of history as a succession of stages, an idea of change as it is effected by a process of transmission or imitation.

This was a point which Robertson was to develop later in his career in an unpublished sermon of 1788 commemorating the Glorious Revolution. Taking an unusually cosmopolitan approach to this supremely national event, Robertson characterises the Revolution as an affair of general European derivation and consequence. Once again, he emphasises the roles of initiative and imitation in the formation of the unique European character:

> All the civilized nations of Europe may be considered as forming one exclusive community. The intercourse among them is great, and every improvement in science, in arts, in commerce, in government introduced into any of them is soon known in the others, and in time is adopted and imitated. Hence arises (as I might easily shew were this the proper place) the general resemblance among all the people of Europe, and their great superiority over the rest of mankind.[30]

This idea of imitation and interplay clarifies both the extent and limit of Robertson's cosmopolitanism, which is at once broadly European and narrowly Eurocentric. Gibbon would follow Robertson in characterising the 'imitative spirit' of the western Europeans as the quality which ultimately ensured 'their successive improvement and present superiority'.[31] Ferguson, by contrast, is more amenable to a generalised stadial model of social development, and a greater cultural isolationist. He expressed his doubts as to 'whether we have gained more by imitation than

[30] NLS, *Robertson–MacDonald Papers*, MS 3979, f.15. This sermon is discussed by Richard B. Sher, '1688 and 1788: William Robertson on Revolution in Britain and France' in *Culture and Revolution*, eds. Paul Dukes and John Dunkley (London, 1990).

[31] Gibbon, *The Decline and Fall* (1776–88), VI, 207.

we have lost by quitting our native system of thinking, and our vein of fable'.[32] Robertson accounts for European similarity in stadial terms, but for European diversity and superiority in terms of cultural transmission. It is these shared cultural attributes and ideals, and the possession of a 'wide diversity of character and of genius' which, he tells us, 'hath exalted Europeans above the inhabitants of the other quarters of the globe, and seems to have destined the one to rule, and the other to obey' (*Charles V*, III, 432).

Imperial themes

Robertson's next project was to have been an ambitious exploration of Europe's implementation of its entitlement to rule in the new world. A history of the colonial activities of Europe, from the time of Charles V, would have been a logical extension of his investigation of the arrival and nature of the commercial stage. Voltaire had carried out a similar plan by adding substantial new chapters on the theme of new world colonisation to later revisions of the *Essai*. Among rival histories, however, only Guillaume Thomas Raynal's *Histoire philosophique des ... deux Indes* (first edition 1770, second edition 1774) had realised similarly comprehensive ambitions. Raynal's work, documenting the whole process of European discovery and colonisation in the Americas and East Indies, was written with a team of collaborators (most notably Diderot), and became a standard work of reference, not least for the North American colonists currently challenging British policy and dominion. However, this was not a work to deter Robertson, who rarely cites it in the footnotes to the *History of America*, and only ever acknowledges very local debts to his work (for example, II, 490). Raynal's politically radical work preached the universal brotherhood of nations through trade, denounced slavery, and launched an undiscriminating attack on Spanish colonial history. The massive, collaborative 1780 edition of this work would later include an up-to-date narrative of the American Revolutionary War, warmly defending the colonists' right to independence.

Robertson originally planned to produce a complete history of European colonisation in the Americas. In the event, only the part dealing with Spanish and Portuguese discoveries and colonisation was ever published as the *History of America* (1777);[33] the American Revolution put paid to the section on the North American colonies, even though composition of this section was some way advanced at the time. 'While [the British colonists]

[32] Adam Ferguson, *Essay*, 163.

[33] *The History of America* (2 vols.; London, 1777). The work went through six editions in the author's lifetime. Revisions were minor (but see note 55 below) and citations are taken from the first edition.

are engaged in civil war with Great Britain', Robertson prudently explained, 'inquiries and speculations concerning their ancient forms of policy and laws, which exist no longer, cannot be interesting' (Preface, I, v). The narrative covers the period from Columbus' first voyage to Central America, to the conquest of Mexico and Peru, and ends with an overview of the aftermath of Spanish and Portuguese colonisation to the second half of the eighteenth century. Robertson carried out a good deal of research for the *History of America*, although he remained worried by the insufficiency of accessible archival material, and daunted by the example of a newcomer to this historical scene, one Mr. Gibbon (Preface, I, ix, xv–xvi). Robert Waddilove, the chaplain to the British ambassador to Spain, procured quantities of state documents for him, a task which required great tact and diplomacy. One of his researchers, who ran up against the hostility of the Spanish authorities, explained to Robertson that Raynal had made them doubly suspicious of foreign historians.[34] In the main, however, Robertson was obliged to plunder the standard texts of the Spanish imperial historical canon (Acosta, Garcilaso de la Vega, Gomara, Antonio de Solis). Antonio de Herrera y Tordesillas' *Historia general* (1610, 1615) was his favoured guide throughout, especially when it came to weighing up the allegations of the Dominican Las Casas about Spanish depredations towards the Natives (the Black Legend). Like Herrera, Robertson incorporated and mitigated Las Casas' celebrated findings while exculpating the Spanish crown from direct involvement in the cruelty. Antonio de Ulloa's *Relación histórica de viaje a la América meridional* (1748) (with Jorge Juan y Santacilla), and his *Noticias americanas* (1772) provided the impetus for much of his assessment of the state of modern Spanish America, although the method is avowedly Smithian and much indebted to Book IV of the *Wealth of Nations*, which Robertson declared to be 'of capital importance' to his work.[35] In contrast to Ulloa, he does not paint a particularly healthy picture of Spanish colonial life and trade, nor, on the other hand, does he repeat the old *canard* about the natural laziness of the creoles. The colonies are described as languishing on account of an ill-conceived social and economic system which discourages intercolonial trade, favours large scale land ownership, and robs the creoles of all incentive to activity by restricting their access to positions of authority (II, 406–20). Robertson concedes that steps had been taken in previous years in the direction of freer trade, but this picture of modern Spanish America contains both a reverse image of the British style

[34] Letter to Robertson (31 October 1776), NLS, *Robertson–MacDonald Papers*, MS 3942, ff. 283–8.

[35] Robertson to Smith (8 April 1776), *Correspondence of Adam Smith*, no. 153. On Robertson and the imperial tradition, see D. A. Brading, *The First America: The Spanish Monarchy, Creole Patriots and the Liberal State*, 1492–1866 (Cambridge, 1991), 432–41; David Armitage, 'The New World and British Historical Thought: From Richard Hakluyt to William Robertson' in *America in European Consciousness*, ed. Karen Ordahl Kupperman (Chapel Hill, ND, 1995).

of new world colonialism, and an indirect scheme for improvements in British imperial administration should the American colonists be returned to the British fold.

The *History of America* is closer than any of Robertson's previous works to the preoccupations and methods of the contemporary Scottish stadial theory. In the celebrated fourth book on the Native Americans, Robertson supplies one of the most rigidly materialist expositions of the four stages theory to be found anywhere in Scottish writing (I, 324). Robertson's belated excursion into a kind of anthropology based upon rigid ontological propositions about man's uniform nature parallels Voltaire's move from narrative history in the *Essai* to human science in the *Philosophie de l'histoire.* The *History of America* can be seen as a popularisation of Scottish theories about the development of man in society, set within sequential narrative of conquest and discovery. Robertson, by combining the roles of social theorist and theologian, is able to make explicit the connection between stadial evolution and his idea of qualitative moral change in history.[36] Thus, despite Robertson's apparently purist stadialist commitment to describing primitive man in terms of economic and climatic variables, the description of Native Americans in Book IV, along with the account of Aztecs and Incas in Book VII, are morally normative to a degree unusual among Scottish writers.

The opening book of the *History of America* is, in essence, a recapitulation of 'A View of the Progress of Society in Europe' from the 'second infancy' of the dark ages to the onset, in the late fifteenth century, of the commercial stage bringing with it the search for overseas suppliers and markets. Like Robertson's first essay on this subject, the narrative of European revival combines stadial elements (including an analysis of changing forms of property and political institutions) with an emphasis upon intellectual emancipation. This time, however, Robertson elaborates upon the imperial consequences of the commercial stage, and incorporates an explanation for the apparent slowness of the Europeans to carry their trading activities into new or undiscovered parts of the globe: 'their progress appears to be wonderfully slow. It seems neither adequate to what we might have expected from the activity and enterprise of the human mind, nor to what might have been performed by the power of the great empires that successively governed the world' (I, 21). Robertson, therefore, develops a theory of technological retardation to account for the comparative delay in the development of the imperial potential of the commercial stage. He

[36] Nicholas Phillipson finds Robertson ill at ease with the materialist implications of stadial theory in this work. He has assessed, in an essay (in *William Robertson and the Expansion of Europe*, ed. S. J. Brown, Cambridge University Press forthcoming) entitled 'Progress and Providence in Robertson's Historical Writing', the ways in which Scottish sociology provided Robertson with a new natural theology.

gives a long overview of improvements in navigation and geographical knowledge, pointing out that they lagged behind and, for a time, impeded other areas of development. Robertson embellishes this theory of stadial delay later in the work, probably in response to the section in the *Wealth of Nations* entitled 'Of Colonies', which he read during the final stages of composition. Smith had distinguished modern European colonies from those of ancient Greece and Rome on the grounds that they had not simply been created out of necessity, even though, in many respects, they approximate to a Roman model of dependency made less harsh by the greater distances involved.[37] Robertson developed the argument further in the closing book of the *History of America*. The pre-modern world, he tells us, had developed only 'two kinds' of colony: the first were the products of 'migrations, which served to disburden a state of its superfluous subjects', such as those of the Greek republics or the barbarians who invaded Roman Europe; the second were 'military detachments stationed, as garrisons, in a conquered province', such as those of ancient Rome (II, 361). Spain had invented and 'set the first example to the European nations' of a new kind of colony, at once separate from the mother country, and yet also politically and economically dependent upon her (II, 363). This is the modern form of colony which differs fundamentally from all previous forms of imperial government. Robertson may here be indirectly suggesting that the American colonists, currently in revolt against their parent state, are mistaken when they continually invoke classical precedents as the intellectual basis for their critique of British imperial conduct in North America.

Despite this new theorisation of imperial retardation and development, Robertson once again gives priority to the role of human volition in historical change. The transition from the commercial to the imperial-commercial stage does not occur naturally once the technological resources have come into being. Instead, cultural imperatives drive the process forward: 'the spirit of discovery was connected with zeal for religion, which, in that age, was a principle of such activity and vigour, as to influence the conduct of nations' (I, 49). The European peoples have to become vigorous before they can engage in exploratory and imperial activity. In the Italian city states, for example, 'the acquisition of [liberty and independence] roused industry, and gave motion and vigour to all the active powers of the human mind' (I, 28). The first voyages of discovery rouse and embolden the Portuguese:

> Men, long accustomed to circumscribe the activity and knowledge of the human mind within the limits to which they had been hitherto confined, were astonished

[37] Smith, 'Causes of Prosperity of new Colonies', *Wealth of Nations*, eds. R. H. Campbell, A. S. Skinner and W. B. Todd (2 vols.; Oxford, 1976), II, 558.

to behold the sphere of navigation so suddenly enlarged, and a prospect opened of visiting regions of the globe, the existence of which was unknown in former time. (I, 49)

Other countries are soon captivated by this sense of excitement ('men, animated and rendered active by the certain prospect of gain', I, 52). Then, at last, Columbus reaches America, and Europe becomes the enthralled spectator of its own adventure:

an account was brought to Europe of an event no less extraordinary than unexpected, the discovery of a New World situated in the west, and the eyes and admiration of mankind turned immediately towards that great object. (I, 57)

This expansion of human capacities through discovery and encounter is, of course, supervised by God: 'At length the period arrived, when Providence decreed that men were to pass the limits within which they had been so long confined' (I, 38). Keats, responding to Robertson's breathless sense of adventure, would later write of 'stout Cortez' (in fact, Balboa, in Robertson's account) and his men, as they reached the Pacific, and 'Look'd at each other with a wild surmise – / Silent, upon a peak in Darien' (I, 204).[38]

In some respects, the rest of the *History of America* is about the cost of this excitement and adventure both to the Native American peoples and to the European migrants to the New World. To the first Spanish conquistadores and settlers, America seems fatally seductive, and awakens in them a hunger of the imagination which can never be satisfied: 'For it is observed', Robertson concludes, 'that if any person once enter this seducing path, it is almost impossible to return . . . Visions of imaginary wealth are continually before his eyes, and he thinks, and speaks, and dreams of nothing else' (II, 391). The Spanish, fired by these dreams, concentrate upon mining precious metals to the exclusion of more productive, civilising enterprises. Robertson reflects upon the economic and social stagnation of New Spain to which this pioneering spirit eventually leads them: 'No spirit is more adverse to such improvement in agriculture and commerce, as render a nation really opulent' (II, 391). Robertson is in no doubt that the Spanish colonial experiment was, in the long run, disadvantageous to the mother country and to her New World subjects. The Spanish state, 'intoxicated with the wealth which poured in', quickly became economically lazy and unable to exploit its captive colonial market. In this respect, the *History of America* is a moralised study of the dangers of cultural vigour not properly regulated by a good understanding of economic and social development. Robertson suggests that the intellectual capacities of the Spanish regime were not equal to the demands which the sudden acquisition of an imperial

[38] Keats, 'On First Looking into Chapman's Homer', lines 13–14, *Complete Poems*, ed. John Barnard (Harmondsworth, 1973), 72.

economy thrust upon it. The regime surrendered the establishment and control of new territories to privateers who inevitably failed to 'carry on any plan of regular civilisation'. The Spanish colonists prospected for gold and silver in the mountains when they should have been planting in the plains. Agriculture, which might have flourished under a system of small-holding land tenure, was smothered by a structure of quasi-'feudal jurisprudence' which confined it to a few, powerful owners (II, 364). Robertson is thinking here of Smith's analysis of the greater success of the smaller, less restricted system of land tenure in British North America. Instead of creating the conditions for the gradual stadial evolution of the New World colonies, the Spanish installed an economic system and social hierarchy which replicated the stagnant phase of the feudal stage. This persistent stagnation is compounded by the Spanish government's monopolisation of its colonial commerce and its prohibition of intercolony trade. The Spanish were wise to avoid, Robertson suggests, the setting up of monopoly trading companies (such as the East India Company). Here he briefly appropriates Smith's polemic on behalf of freer colony trade, and against the monopoly companies and navigation acts as damaging to the health of the British colonies (II, 400). In the present century, Robertson is pleased to say, the Spanish have been slowly learning the lessons of free trade (though he is far less optimistic about the health of the Spanish colonies than Smith).[39]

Stadial encounters in the New World

The *History of America* is about the failure of the Spanish to implement in the New World the phase of social improvement inaugurated by the discoveries. It is also about the catastrophic encounter between two races of people at widely differing stages of social evolution. Columbus' first interview with the natives of Hispaniola is dramatised as a (potentially tragic) meeting between representatives of incompatible stages of human development:

> The former, enlightened and ambitious, formed already vast ideas with respect to the advantages which they might derive from those regions that began to open to their view. The latter, simple and undiscerning, had no foresight of the calamities and desolation which were now approaching their country. (I, 93)

In books three and six, Robertson plays out the terrible consequences of this stadial mismatch between Spaniard and Native American. Robertson finds exaggerated Las Casas' 'black legend' of the Spanish depredations in the New World, but acknowledges that Las Casas and other Catholic

39 Smith, *Wealth of Nations*, II, 512, 574.

clergymen like him did have a mitigating influence on Spanish cruelty towards the native populations. With revisionist zeal, Robertson exonerates the Catholic Church at every opportunity from any share in the brutality. He is equally convinced that the Spanish state itself had no real part in the blame, since its legal codes made adequate provision for the security of the natives (II, 375). The local privateers and governors were the most culpable, since it was they who forced the native 'wandering tribes of hunters' and 'such as had made small progress in cultivation and industry' into a labour system badly suited to their level of development: '[the Native Americans] possessed not vigour either of mind or of body to sustain this unusual load of oppression' (II, 346).

In order to describe and account for the more primitive developmental level of the Native Americans, Robertson devotes book four of the *History of America* to a stadial analysis of their form of life. Robertson's discussion of Native Americans (excluding the more advanced Mexicans and Peruvians) can be understood as the product of the two overlapping discourses about primitive man available in the eighteenth century; the first derives from stadial theory, and the second comes from the somewhat different 'New World immaturity or degeneracy thesis' currently prevalent in France. Robertson's stadial approach is consistent with much Scottish social theory in which Native Americans are often cited as unspoilt examples of the hunter-gatherer stage with its attendant modes of social organisation. Robertson presents his natives as aspects of this stage; their identity, far from being self-fashioned or unique, being merely a function of their mode of subsistence. Following on from his presupposition that 'the progress of man hath been nearly the same' in all parts of the world, Robertson examines the physical condition, the affective and domestic relations (including the condition of women), and the mental condition of these apparently typical hunter-gatherers (I, 268). He makes no distinctions between different tribes at the same stage of development, and then discusses their common political institutions, social conventions and religious practices. This structure of analysis has much in common with John Millar's *Observations concerning the Distinction of Ranks in Society* (1771), whose influence can be seen, in particular, in Robertson's shift to methodological individualism: 'Man existed as an individual before he became a member of a community' (I, 288). Robertson's description of how societies progress from their earliest stages by seeking the gratification of their 'acquired wants and appetites' also owes something to Millar's *Observations* and Kames' *Sketches of the History of Man* (1774) (I, 314).

Before composing the *History of America*, Robertson sent out questionnaires to a number of correspondents with New World experience, including the former governor Thomas Hutchinson of Massachusetts, and the Pacific explorer Louis de Bougainville.[40] Although he sometimes ignored their findings, the questionnaires evince typically Scottish stadialist preoccupations:[41] he asks questions about ideas and distribution of property in native societies, the nature of familial relations, the type of criminal justice and so on. Other questions, however, as to sexual appetite, physical constitution, the absence of bodily hair and susceptibility to alcohol, as well as the size and strength of local animals also pertain to the separate but related French discourse of the immaturity or degeneracy of the New World. This climatically determinist thesis, which postulated that America was either a young or an ancient and degenerate continent in which plants, animals and human natives were inevitably small and feeble, enjoyed a popular currency in the Old World well beyond the circles of naturalists to whom it was originally addressed.[42] Its main scientific originator was the great French naturalist, Buffon, in whose *Histoire naturelle, générale et particulière* (1749–88) it makes a moderate and quasi-scientific appearance as the idea that America is geologically a young continent whose human inhabitants tend to be physically weak and sexually unenthusiastic, and in which European livestock tend to become unhealthy.[43] Robertson's account of America is most heavily indebted to Buffon (he begins his account of Native Americans with a Buffonesque overview of the continent's landscape and animals). Robertson also read and cited the more extreme expositions of the thesis, including Corneille de Pauw's *Recherches philosophiques sur les Américains* (1768) which argued the case for the degenerate antiquity of America's physical and human geography, and Raynal's *Histoire philosophique* which, unlike Buffon and De Pauw, placed Peruvians and Mexicans, as well as supplanted Europeans, on the list of degenerates. The cultural roots of these pseudo-scientific ideas were to be found in wider European anxieties about the New World. Such characterisations of America were, of course, hotly refuted by northern and southern colonial Americans.

Robertson was a populariser, rather than an originator, of such ideas. His Native Americans are at once Scottish exemplifications of the earliest economic stage, and biologically immature or degenerate French savages lacking procreative sexual appetite and exhibiting many other signs of 'debility', 'degradation' or 'diminution' (I, 291–2). This popularisation is especially interesting in the Scottish context, since Robertson also appears

[40] These questionnaires can be found in the NLS, *Robertson–MacDonald Papers*, MS 3954, ff. 3–93.

[41] See Mark Duckworth, 'An Eighteenth-Century Questionnaire: William Robertson on the Indians', *Eighteenth-Century Life*, 11 (1987), 36–49.

[42] On Robertson's view of South America, see also Antonello Gerbi, *The Dispute of the New World*, trans. Jeremy Moyle (Pittsburgh, 1973), 165–9; D. A. Brading, *The First America*, 432–41; Anthony Pagden, *European Encounters with the New World: From Renaissance to Romanticism* (New Haven, 1993), 99–100.

[43] On Buffon, see also Jacques Roger, *Buffon* (Paris, 1989).

to have been expressing a somewhat civic moralist distaste for what he perceives to be an inactive society. Where Adam Ferguson (always inclined to evaluate different societies on their own merits) found that Native Americans had a certain 'vigour' of their own, Robertson finds only a crude instinct for self-gratification, physical debility (their beardlessness is one of many examples of their 'defect in vigour') and an absence of that characteristically Scottish virtue, a capacity for 'sympathy' (I, 290, 406). The Native Americans are repeatedly infantilised: 'As the individual advances from the ignorance and imbecility of the infant state, to vigour and maturity of understanding, something similar to this may be advanced in the progress of the species' (I, 308). In particular, the inability of the Natives to compute time, and the fact that they exist, as it were, outside time, gives them 'the thoughtless levity of children' (I, 310).

Although he asserts that all men have the same 'capacity for improvement', Robertson lacks an adequate theory of language to explain how the Native Americans might one day come out of childhood and develop more sophisticated forms of social organisation (I, 401). The question of language is central to all eighteenth-century discussions of the development of society. Robertson shares with Smith and Rousseau the essentially Lockean idea that social institutions could not develop without the advent of abstract vocabulary to convey general ideas, and that abstract vocabulary, since all words are only symbols of ideas, can only develop as a consequence of a more complex social experience.[44] Smith's reworking of this circular set of ideas as a dialectic goes much further towards explaining contemporaneous linguistic and social development than anything attempted by Robertson.[45]

Robertson's theory of native language, such as it is, strays little beyond the traditional connection between abstract thought and Christianity. For it was generally supposed that, in order for a person to appreciate general ideas, such as 'god' or the 'divine laws', and so convert to Christianity, he must first acquire the requisite capacity for abstract thought and language.[46] Native Americans, having only concrete language capabilities

[44] Robertson's general ideas concerning language are quite consonant with the standard Lockean work on the subject, James Harris, *Hermes; or A Philosophical Inquiry concerning Language and Universal Grammar* (London, 1751). He does not appear to have been interested in the work of his countryman James Burnet, Lord Monboddo, *Of the Origin and Progress of Language* (6 vols.; Edinburgh and London, 1773–92). This was unusual in attempting a Platonic resolution to the problem of the origin of abstract ideas. See also Rudiger Schreyer, '"Pray what language did your wild Couple speak, when first they met?" Language and the Science of Man in the Scottish Enlightenment' in '*The Science of Man*' *in the Scottish Enlightenment: Hume, Reid and their Contemporaries*, ed. Peter Jones (Edinburgh, 1989).

[45] Smith, *Considerations Concerning the First Formation of Languages* (1761), ed. J. C. Bryce in volume IV of *The Glasgow Edition of the Works and Correspondence of Adam Smith* (1977).

[46] Pagden, *European Encounters with the New World*, 126–40.

(endless names for particular kinds of mountain, but no general word for them, and so on) inevitably made poor conversion material:

> The powers of their uncultivated understandings are so limited, their observations and reflections reach so little beyond the mere objects of sense, that they seem hardly to have the capacity of forming abstract ideas, and possess not language to express them. To such men, the sublime and spiritual doctrines of Christianity must be incomprehensible. (II, 385)

Outside time and unqualified for 'speculative reasoning', Robertson's Americans appear incapable of adding to their linguistic range and civilising themselves; they must choose between extermination by the conquering Spaniards or submission to their culture (I, 309). Even in its most elaborate form, the stadial side of Robertson's historical writing lacks a motor for social development. His stadial history is static, in part because it is incomplete and highly materialistic, but also because it has been moralised through contact with other historical discourses. Negative evaluations of the American Natives are reinforced by a civic moralist preference for social 'vigour', by the notion of the immaturity or degeneracy of America, and by the Enlightenment historical idea of the superiority of Europe. This is not unlike Voltaire's conflation of barbarism as a developmental stage with barbarism as a form of moral inferiority. Although Voltaire was passionate in his defence of the American Native, the discourse of the savage, in both writers, remains firmly centred upon the uniqueness and viability of modern Europe.[47]

The case is somewhat different with the altogether more sophisticated Incas and Aztecs, as Robertson explains in a second dissertation in book seven. Measured along a stadial scale of development, both nations are considerably more advanced, although, in the last analysis, 'they can hardly be considered as having advanced beyond the infancy of civil life' (II, 269). In that infancy in sixteenth-century Mexico, however, an agricultural order has been consolidated, and a process of urbanisation is well under way, although the monetary currency and communications necessary for trade have not yet been developed (II, 296). In its 'distinction of ranks', and unequal distribution of property, the Aztec empire presents 'an image of feudal policy in its most rigid form' (II, 277, 280). At the cultural level, the Aztecs have invented ways of computing time, and, more importantly, a pictographic form of writing which nevertheless reveals that their powers of abstract thought were still limited (the pictograms 'represent *things*, not *words*') (II, 288). The closing pages of this analysis downplay the extent of Aztec advancement, pointing to their savage religion as the reason why 'their manners, instead of softening, became more fierce' (II,

[47] Michèle Duchet, *Anthropologie et histoire au siècle des lumières* (Paris, 1971), chapter 2.

303). Robertson has fewer difficulties in reconciling the religious practices of the Incas to their civilisational level. Peru presents 'the idea of a society in the first stages of transition from barbarism to civilization' (II, 322). Its mild form of religious worship improves and polishes its society: 'the Peruvians ... were formed, by the spirit of the superstition which they had adopted, to a national character more gentle than that of any people in America' (II, 310). They too have a distinction of ranks, and a sophisticated kind of agriculture. However, despite Robertson's systematic application of stadial theory to the relatively complex Aztec and Inca societies before the Spanish conquest, he is at a loss to explain the profound differences between the two of them. Nicholas Phillipson has pointed out that the contrast between Aztec ferocity and Inca peacefulness undermines Robertson's general sociology of semi-civilised barbarian empires.[48] There is a further unresolved tension in Robertson's narrative between his desire to prove that these two peoples were, in their superstitious paganism, far less advanced than many historians have supposed, and his sense of their (interrupted) potential for further social evolution. Statements about the polished nature of the Incas, in particular, were often associated with a general vindication of America by Spanish creole and imperial historians alike (including Acosta, Garcilaso, and, to some extent, Ulloa). Robertson was clearly willing to make some concessions to this traditional defence of the American continent.

North America

The *History of* [*South*] *America* was to have had a counterpart piece on North America which Robertson subsequently abandoned during the American Revolutionary War. Robertson's stated reason for giving up the project was that it had become too politically sensitive for him to execute with any degree of impartiality.[49] He had little sympathy with the Revolution and suggested that, as a matter of national 'vigour', it ought to have been put down decisively from the outset: 'This [freedom] they [the American colonists] will one day obtain, but not just now, if there be any degree of political wisdom or vigour remaining.'[50] The surviving portion of the North American history, which breaks off at the time of the Interregnum (for New England) and in 1688 (for the southern colonies), suggests that he saw the history of the British colonies as one of slow consolidation and

[48] Phillipson thinks that, in this section of the *History of America*, stadial history has been subordinated to a more moralised history of superstition ('Progress and Providence in Robertson's Historical Writing').

[49] Robertson to Strahan (6 October 1775) in Stewart, *Biographical Memoirs of William Robertson*, 244–6.

[50] Robertson to Strahan, *Biographical Memoirs*, 245.

approximation to British norms.[51] There are also indirect hints, as there were in the published portion of the *History of America*, for the improvement of British colonial government in the area. The work shares many of the preoccupations of its sister history. The Virginia colony narrative, which is indebted to William Stith's competent *History of the First Discovery and Settlement of Virginia* (1747), finds that the early years of settlement were much disrupted by gold-hunting, and that social consolidation only began with tobacco planting (this, in turn was impeded by the growth of the slave labour system). Political conditions improve when the monopoly Virginia Company, which had failed 'to give vigour and stability to the colony', is dissolved, although the government's Navigation Acts, against which Robertson shows Smithian disapproval, generate a 'secret spirit of discontent' (IV, 227, 254). Robertson takes a social scientist's interest in early Virginia as an example of 'a society in the first moment of its political existence', as well as showing his usual distinctive concern with 'observing how its spirit forms in its infant state, how its principles begin to unfold as it advances' (IV, 183).

The section on the New England colonies is a highly promising analysis, at once arch and sympathetic, of the origins and effects of Puritan separatism in the laboratory of the New World. The New England colonies, Robertson concedes, are an exception to the usual European pattern, being founded not for public utility or private gain, but for the free worship of God (IV, 258). Condensing his earlier histories, and adapting Hume, he gives a brief account of the social genesis of the separatist Puritan spirit in Europe, before weighing up its benefits and disadvantages for the creation of the New England colonies. Despite his sympathy for the early settlers, Robertson sticks by his previous prescriptions for the stadial evolution of colonies. The communal property and labour systems of some of the colonists, he remarks, 'retarded the progress of their colony' (IV, 276). In general, he appears to think that crown charters for the New England colonies would, at many points in their history, have been appropriate; without them, the colony theocracies tended to become eccentric and autocratic, and arrogantly to ignore the directives of the monarch 'under whose authority they settled in America, and from whom they derived the right to act as a body politic' (IV, 284). These sentiments seem patriotic in the context of the events leading up to and including the American Revolutionary War. Robertson certainly appears to be in no doubt as to the legal entitlement of Britain to her

[51] NLS, MS 3965, printed posthumously, with minor alterations, as books IX and X of the *History of America*, (London, 1796), ed. William Robertson the Younger. See also Jeffrey Smitten, 'Moderatism and History: William Robertson's Unfinished History of British America' in *Scotland and America in the Age of the Enlightenment*, eds. Richard B. Sher and Jeffrey Smitten (Edinburgh, 1990).

colonies, whatever his criticisms of some of the mechanisms of colonial government. Quite apart from the political difficulties involved in publishing this piece, we can surmise that Robertson was obliged to discontinue his history of the British colonies, since, once they had repudiated their European identity, they no longer made up part of the story of how Europe attained the commercial-imperial stage, and how the superior European mind exported itself to other parts of the globe.

Indian explorations

Robertson's last historical footnote to his long engagement with the phenomenon of the rise of modern Europe is topical and surprisingly broad-minded. His politics appear to have undergone a certain liberalisation during his controversial and personally costly support of Catholic toleration in Scotland during the late 1770s.[52] His last work is, in many ways, a plea for tolerance. Written during the time of Warren Hastings' impeachment for alleged depredations in British East India, *An Historical Disquisition concerning the Knowledge which the Ancients had of India* (1791) is a short history of European contacts with India from biblical times to the sixteenth century.[53] The work makes a case for the antiquity, humanity and sophistication of India in the hope that this would promote toleration and benignity in the East India Company's management of the colonies there. To an extent, the work is in implicit dialogue with Burke, who was currently leading the Hastings impeachment, and was a correspondent and acquaintance of Robertson (who had entertained Burke in Edinburgh in 1785), and, previously, Robertson had sent Burke a complimentary copy of the *History of America*. Burke, who had in his youth collaborated with his cousin on a short history of European settlements in America, greeted book four of the *History of America*, in particular, with rapturous praise. His letter to Robertson is well known but worth quoting in part:

> I have always thought with you, that we possess at this time very great advantages towards the knowledge of human Nature. We need no longer go to History to trace it in all its stages and periods. History from its comparative youth, is but a poor instructour. When the Aegyptians called the Greeks children in Antiquities, we may well call them children; and so we may call all these nations, which were able to trace the progress of Society only within their own Limits. But now the Great Map of Mankind is unrolld at once; and there is no state or Gradation of barbarism, and no mode of refinement which we have not at the same instant

[52] Walpole reports Robertson in 1778 as saying that 'he himself had been born and bred a Whig, though he was now a moderate one – I believe a very moderate one' (Walpole to Mason (April 1778), *Correspondence*, XXVIII, 387).

[53] Robertson's publisher, Strahan, brought out a second edition 'with the author's last corrections and additions' in 1794. As these are fairly minor, quotations are taken from the first edition.

under our View ... You have employd Philosophy to judge on Manners; and from manners you have drawn new resources for Philosophy.[54]

Robertson may have thought Burke's report of the death of history greatly exaggerated, although he would no doubt have been flattered to have been greeted as a master of stadial theory. He would certainly have agreed with Burke that the kinds of historical vistas opened up by the conjectural reconstruction of early forms of society had the potential to enhance political understanding.

By the 1790s, Burke entirely shared Robertson's sharply critical attitude towards chartered companies such as the East India Company, especially in respect of the stranglehold they held over a colony's internal and external trade. Robertson's *Disquisition* drops few hints, of a Burkean nature or otherwise, as to how colonial government might be better supervised in India, but it does have a good deal to say about trade in the subcontinent. The first part is a brief history of India's trading relations with the world since biblical antiquity. By the time of the Portuguese conquests in the sixteenth century, India was, Robertson insists, 'highly civilised', and therefore quite capable of entering into the global network of commerce without coercion (167). The ringmaster in this trading fair was Europe:

> the commercial genius of Europe, which has given it a visible ascendant over the three other divisions of the earth, by discerning their respective wants and resources, and by rendering them reciprocally subservient to one another, has established an union among them, from which it has derived an immense increase of opulence, of power, and of enjoyments. (167)

In the modern context, Robertson implies that very little political or military intervention is really needed for India to continue to take part in this system of commercial reciprocity. Like Burke, he thinks that India's system of domestic and international trade can function naturally on its own, and appears to favour a contraction (if not an abolition) of British political control. The counter-example to sixteenth-century India which Robertson supplies is America which, at this time, had attained a far lower stage of evolution than India, and needed greater intervention to bring it into a productive relationship with Europe (170). However, Robertson is more liberal than Burke in his Smithian view that commercial reciprocity is, in the long run, the natural death of direct colonial control from the metropolis (170).

The most important section of the *Disquisition* is the Appendix on the manners and institutions of the Indian people which examines India's

[54] *The Correspondence of Edmund Burke*, ed. Thomas Copeland *et al.* (10 vols.; Chicago, 1958–78), III, 350–1.

social hierarchy, political institutions, arts, sciences and religious practices. The discussion is predicated upon the idea that all societies progress through very similar stages of development. Robertson's polemical task is to establish that India long ago reached a very advanced stage (298). At the cultural level, he shares Burke's reverence for all aspects of Hindu civilisation, and is little interested in the Mogul legacy. He also draws upon the work of the orientalist scholar William Jones, explicitly welcoming the kinds of scholarly enquiry into Bengali culture which he had fostered: 'persons who visited that country with other views ... are now carrying on scientific and literary researches with ardour and success' (310). In the *History of America*, Robertson argued that the Native Americans might have been treated sympathetically if the Spaniards been able to understand that they were several evolutionary stages behind them, and so unfit for exploitation. This humane contention had been somewhat compromised by his sense of their (seemingly permanent) incapacity for Christianity, since Robertson could not or would not explain how they were to acquire the abstract language necessary for Christian belief.[55] The *Disquisition*, resolves this dilemma by tying Christian belief more closely into the stadial scheme, and linking this, in turn, with natural theology. True religion is the offspring of reason, and only 'attains to its highest perfection in ages of light and improvement' (313). False religions belong to the early stages of all societies, and are (as Hume suggested in the *Natural History of Religion*) polytheistic in origin. These polytheistic religions tend to appeal to the senses, rather than to the intellect, as Hinduism is supposed to do, but in more advanced societies, they can be understood allegorically as aspects of the one God. Robertson thinks that the Indian Brahmin caste have reached this more advanced monotheistic stage; like the ancient Stoics, they espouse an 'active philosophy ... formed only for men of the most vigorous spirit' (300–1).

All this, of course, amounts to magnanimous excusing of Hinduism on the (perhaps dangerously relativist) grounds that God is only as advanced as our state of mind. The *Disquisition* does not escape the Eurocentrism of Robertson's earlier works. Each time Robertson supplies an instance of Indian achievement, he gives an example of a European authentication of its value (for example, the case of Indian astronomy, 307). Even so, as an example of the authentication of a non-western civilisation by a self-consciously representative European author, this is a generous piece. Robertson's cosmopolitanism is, finally, inseparable from his liberal imperialism, and in this he differs considerably from his deceased colleague

[55] In the fifth edition of the *History of America*, I, 183 Robertson added a discussion of the social genesis of false religion to meet this objection.

David Hume.[56] Robertson's last published piece is a warning against the very complacencies, whether provincial, national or imperial, from which he, as a highly successful Scottish cultural leader with admirers in England and the colonies, might have been expected to suffer. This is one of the curiously reflexive moments in the *Disquisition*:

> Men in every stage of their career are so satisfied with the progress made by the community of which they are members, that it becomes to them a standard of perfection, and they are apt to regard people, whose condition is not similar, with contempt, and even aversion. (335)

Whatever the limitations of the cultural perspectives of Robertson's last work, it is, perhaps, remarkable to find him, at the end of his life-long study of the origins of European modernity, renewing his commitment to a thoroughly self-critical form of cosmopolitanism.

[56] See Donald Livingston, 'Hume, English Barbarism and American Independence' in *Scotland and America*, eds. Sher and Smitten; J. G. A. Pocock, 'Hume and the American Revolution: the Dying Thoughts of a North Briton' in *Virtue, Commerce and History* (Cambridge, 1985).

6

Emulation and revival: Gibbon's *Decline and Fall of the Roman Empire*

Introductory

Despite the falling cadence of its title, Edward Gibbon's *The History of the Decline and Fall of the Roman Empire* (6 vols.; 1776–88) exceeds the extinction of the Roman world in the West by some three volumes, and makes frequent allusions to the secure, cultivated Europe from which it observes the unstable, crumbling antique world.[1] In Gibbon's story, the barbarian ancestors of eighteenth-century Europeans initially precipitated but ultimately broke the fall of the Roman Empire. This chapter will concentrate upon Gibbon's description, not of the decline and fall of the Romans, but the ascent and rise of those barbarians over more than a millennium of change in western Europe. For Gibbon's history is, in part, an incomplete civil history of medieval Europe to the beginning of the sixteenth century. Although not exactly a view of the progress of society in post-classical Europe, it has clear and deliberate affinities with the medieval histories of Hume and Robertson, and, to a lesser extent, of Voltaire. It tells a similar story about the formation of modern Europe, and engages profoundly, though critically, with Scottish stadial and narrative history.

A selective focus, in a study of eighteenth-century European identities,

[1] Edward Gibbon, *The History of the Decline and Fall of the Roman Empire* (6 vols.; London, 1776–88). Citations are taken from the first edition throughout. Gibbon supplied small but significant revisions to the first volume in the 1777 edition and to the 'new edition' of 1782. However, there were no revisions to the quotations from the first volume selected for this chapter. For a discussion of the revisions and other texts of the first volume, see J. E. Norton, *A Bibliography of the Works of Edward Gibbon* (Oxford, 1940), 38–9, 46–7.

Other works by Gibbon are taken from the following editions: *The Miscellaneous Works of Edward Gibbon*, ed. John, Lord Sheffield (5 vols.; London, 1814); *The Autobiographies of Edward Gibbon*, ed. John Murray (London, 1897); *Gibbon's Journal to January 28th, 1763*, ed. D. M. Low (London, 1929); *Le Journal de Gibbon à Lausanne, 1763–4*, ed. Georges A. Bonnard (Lausanne, 1945); *Miscellanea Gibboniana*, eds. G. R. de Beer, Georges A. Bonnard and Louis Junod (Lausanne, 1952); *The English Essays of Edward Gibbon*, ed. Patricia B. Craddock (Oxford, 1972). Also cited are: *The Letters of Edward Gibbon*, ed. J. E. Norton (3 vols.; London, 1956); *The Library of Edward Gibbon*, ed. Geoffrey Keynes (Oxford, 1940). Gibbon's critical biography has been written by Patricia B. Craddock in two volumes: *Young Edward Gibbon, Gentleman of Letters* (Baltimore, 1982) and *Edward Gibbon, Luminous Historian, 1772–1794* (Baltimore, 1989).

on this facet of Gibbon's narrative will inevitably fail to do justice to the scale of his work. *The Decline and Fall* was published in three instalments in 1776, 1781 and 1788: the first (volume I) moves from the age of the Antonines to about half way through the reign of Constantine, and concludes with the notorious chapters 15 and 16 on the persecutions and progress (by which Gibbon means socially damaging impact) of Christianity; the second instalment (volumes II and III) begins with the relocation of the imperial capital to Constantinople and ends, some years after Alaric's sack of Rome, with the Saxon conquest of Britain; the final and longest instalment (volumes IV, V, VI) covers the immense historical terrain of the Byzantine Empire to the time of its destruction in 1453, and, though it also sketches in aspects of the sixteenth century, carries the story of western Europe to a roughly similar date. The focus of this chapter upon the narrative of the birth of modern civil society in Europe in *The Decline and Fall* inevitably throws the burden of interpretation onto the fifth and sixth volumes – a portion of the work which is often felt to lack the literary intensity and tonal control of the rest. Gibbon certainly found himself, in these last volumes, with a great deal of historical material to dispatch, and he did so in only three years. However, even within the immense chronological reach of *The Decline and Fall*, we should not read the medieval history as a coda to the narrative of late antiquity. Gibbon declared in the prefaces to both the 1776 and 1781 instalments his intention to carry the work to 1453. Although his original plans were confined to the story of Rome itself, and though he expressed doubts as to whether he would ever complete his task, the fall of the eastern and the rise of the western empires were always to have been implicated in the structural scaffolding of the whole.[2] An emphasis, therefore, on the rise of Europe within the larger teleologies of *The Decline and Fall* may help to reorientate readings of the work away from the glittering anti-clerical ironies of the first volume. This emphasis reveals a different kind of historiographical irony in Gibbon's work at the expense of the Scottish idea of the progress of society in Europe.

Gibbon diluted the ironies of chapter 15 (in which Christianity is belatedly and dramatically identified as the slow and secret poison gnawing

[2] The prefaces to both the 1776 and 1781 instalments make mention of Gibbon's intention to go through to the revival of the western Empire. Gibbon stated that his 'original plan was circumscribed to the decay of the City rather than of the Empire', and that 'At the outset all was dark and doubtful – even the title of the work, the true aera of the decline and fall of the Empire' (*Autobiographies*, 270, 308). Gibbon admitted that he was tempted to stop after three volumes (*Autobiographies*, 325). Nevertheless, this mainly reflects Gibbon's feelings of weariness at the prospect of mastering so much Byzantine material. He had, probably around 1771, already compiled an abstract of world history from 800 to 1500, the 'Outlines of the History of the World', which Craddock has collated with the fifth and sixth volumes of the *Decline and Fall* (*English Essays*, 565–6).

at the vitals of the Empire) by absorbing them, in volumes IV, V and VI, into the unfolded story of how western Christianity in the long run adapted and protracted the Roman imperial culture which it had helped to undermine. Gibbon undoubtedly regarded early Christianity as uncivil in its tendency to generate an exclusive and finally subversive city of the godly within the imperial polity. In Gibbon's account, it saps the commitment of its citizens to the empire, and depletes its human resources and cultural vitality. Yet even the opening to chapter 15 announces the larger inevitability which encircles Gibbon's attack upon the incivility of early Christianity:

> Nor was the influence of Christianity confined to the period or to the limits of the Roman empire. After a revolution of thirteen or fourteen centuries, that religion is still professed by the nations of Europe, the most distinguished portion of human kind in arts and learning, as well as in arms. (I, 449)

The later volumes locate, in the seeming barbarousness of the early medieval period in the West, the origins and development of a classicised Christianity modified and given civilising impetus by its reappropriation of the past (for example, III, 532–3). Although Gibbon never forgets the price that has been paid for the creation of the western Catholic Church, new and reflexive ironies are generated by his observations upon the social process of adjustment to the erection of the 'banner of the cross on the ruins of the capitol' (I, 449). The ascent and rise of the Christian West, though not completed within the chronological confines of Gibbon's history (the Protestant Reformation, and then Arminian and finally sceptical revisions of Protestantism, as Gibbon points out at some length, have yet to play important parts in this process), is gradually acknowledged as the prerequisite for a historical sensibility capable of grasping the meaning of declines and falls (II, 188; V, 100; V, 538–40).

In recent years, critics and historians have started to explore the deep, though qualified admiration for modern Europe which underpinned Gibbon's great investigation of its Roman antecedent. J. G. A. Pocock has insisted that 'a vision of Europe as a plurality of interacting states and cultures was at the heart of his understanding of history'.[3] Jeremy Black has shown how this cosmopolitan vision was translated, both before and after Gibbon's stint as a member of parliament (1774–83) and on the Board of Trade and Plantations (1779–82), into an idea of British foreign policy structured in terms of a balanced 'constitution' of European states. Gibbon's idea of a civilised, multipolar Europe of mutually compatible interests was very similar to Robertson's, and it was also, as Black has explained, philosophically blind to the precarious, entirely unbalanced

[3] J. G. A. Pocock, 'Edward Gibbon in History; Aspects of Text in the *History of the Decline and Fall of the Roman Empire*', *The Tanner Lectures on Human Values*, 11 (1990), 293.

state of European relations in the 1770s and 80s.[4] Gibbon had declared in his youthful, unpublished 'Lettre sur le Gouvernement de Berne' that he preferred patriotism to hypocritical cosmopolitanism, but this was for a Swiss audience during the Seven Years' War.[5] More typical was his later insistence, in the propagandist *Mémoire justicatif* – written on behalf of the North government (in which Gibbon pragmatically served during the American Revolution) to remonstrate with France for recognising American independence – that the bonds of European trust are a precious achievement and should not be broken lightly.[6] Gibbon's cosmopolitan idealism remained unscathed by this episode, and, in 1786, after the signing of a commercial treaty between France and Britain, he expressed it again in a letter to his friend Lord Sheffield:

> As a Citizen of the World a character to which I am every day rising or sinking I must rejoyce in every agreement that diminishes the separation between neighbouring countries, which softens their prejudices, unites their interests and industry, and renders their future hostilities less frequent and less implacable.[7]

Despite the attention now paid to the political and institutional dimensions of Gibbon's interest in modern Europe, little has been written about his still more compelling sense of Europe's cultural, and, to an extent, ethnic distinctiveness. Gibbon was deeply struck by the fact that Europe was the only geographical area in which the secularisation of the civil and political spheres, and formation of modern, transnational identities had ever occurred. This was because its inhabitants had long possessed the cultural capacity and innate verve (a legacy of Gothic barbarism) to adapt and syncretise, in a constructive way, their Roman and Christian heritage. Gibbon's account of medieval Europe is more fully a cultural history than anything attempted by Hume, Robertson or Voltaire. *The Decline and Fall* coalesces around three major groups of actors, the western Romans, the Byzantines, and the northern tribes, all of whom are endowed with thickly described, differentiating characteristics. Other groups and hordes pass across Gibbon's canvas without taking on the same floodlit visibility. It is in the densely imagined cultural portraits of the northern Europeans and their Roman and Byzantine forebears, rather than in Gibbon's overt and often mischievous pronouncements on the subject, that we may find a veiled narrative of the rise of the modern West.

At the beginning of *The Decline and Fall*, we are introduced, during the

[4] Jeremy Black, 'Gibbon and International Relations' to be published as part of the proceedings of the Royal Historical Society's bicentenary conference on Gibbon, eds. Roland Quinault and Rosamund McKitterick (Cambridge, forthcoming).

[5] 'La Lettre de Gibbon sur le Gouvernement de Berne' , *Miscellanea Gibboniana*, 123.

[6] *Mémoire justicatif pour servir de réponse à l'Exposé, &c. de la cour de France* (1779), *Miscellaneous Works*, V.

[7] Gibbon to J. B. Holroyd, Lord Sheffield (20 January 1787), *The Letters of Edward Gibbon*, no. 642.

fortunate and prosperous period of the Antonine peace (AD 98–180), to a people and an empire trapped in the atrophy of stability. Already poised on the territorial borders of the Roman imperial 'race of pygmies', are the Germanic barbarians, or 'fierce giants of the north', who soon after 'broke in', as Gibbon puts it, 'and mended the puny breed'; he continues: 'They restored a manly spirit of freedom; and after the revolution of ten centuries, freedom became the happy parent of taste and science' (I, 59). The mythological imagery of 'giants' and 'pygmies' hints at some kind of ethnic difference between Romans and Germans, and the abrupt prolepsis of 'freedom became the happy parent of taste and science' establishes the political and cultural superiority of a future which will, in the end, only be glimpsed over the horizon of six volumes of ensuing narrative. Meanwhile, the Gothic theme slowly moves to the centre of Gibbon's story of the continuation of the Roman Empire by other means. As the Roman Empire perpetuates the forms without the substance of the Roman Republic, so the Roman imperial heritage is steadily transformed by both its eastern heir, the Byzantine Empire, and its northern successor dominions of Ostrogoths, Visigoths, Alamanni, Franks, Saxons, and Angles: the former evolves into a culture of ostentation which stifles and extinguishes the very life of the empire it had tried to preserve; the latter constructs its own syncretic western culture, at once Germanic, Christian, and classical, which, beyond the limits of Gibbon's story, will finally supersede and, in some respects, surpass, its Roman ancestor. In its last two volumes, *The Decline and Fall* ranges across the territory previously traversed by Scottish Enlightenment writers, investigating the economic and social structure of primitive societies, and the growth and erosion of Gothic feudalism. Here the western portion of Gibbon's narrative yields up, under the pressure of conflicting explanatory strategies, a vision of modern Europe in the making. Europe's dynamism and homogeneity are the outcome of similar ethnic origins, processes of political development and mutual economic interdependency, and yet are also the achievement of cultures uniquely capable of forging a new identity out of their Roman inheritance. The sweep of time after the extinction of the Roman Empire in the West, from the reign of Theodoric in Italy (493) to the fall of Constantinople in 1453, is organised into two imaginative blocs, East and West, while other worlds – Persian, Arab, Mogul, and, finally, Ottoman – are illuminated as they intersect and impinge upon them. The East is a static culture of ostentation which mimics rather than imitates its Athenian and Roman parents; the West is barbarian, unstable and benighted, yet it exhibits, in its propensity to imitate and emulate other cultures, a capacity for regeneration. The East is characterised by its rigidity and its creation, out of the raw materials of Platonic myth, of a fixed Christian theological and linguistic system; the West improvises new political structures to fill the vacancy left by the old empire, and translates or mistranslates Latin and Greek with erroneous and creative results. Behind them both lies the Roman Empire, which is flexible, adaptive and customary rather than creative, and, still more deeply embedded in the Empire, the political and cultural forms of the Republic.

The West observed

Gibbon's double sense of the interdependency as well as the cultural and political dissimilarity between the Roman world and modern Europe is given full, if not entirely satisfactory, expression in a sub-section at the end of the second instalment entitled 'General Observations on the Decline of the Empire in the West'. This essay was almost certainly first drafted several years earlier, and is often dismissed by critics as a disappointing relic from a less mature stage of Gibbon's thinking.[8] The 'Observations' are inserted after passages on the Frankish conquest of Gaul in the late fifth century, and on the barbarian king Odo(v)acer's seizure of the exarchate in Italy. Gibbon's answer to the big question ('why did the Roman Empire fall?') is disarmingly brief: 'The story of its ruin is simple and obvious; and instead of enquiring *why* the Roman Empire was destroyed, we should rather be surprised that it subsisted so long' (III, 631). The rest of the discussion is given over to the reasons why modern western European states and their empires are unlikely to succumb to calamities similar to those which afflicted ancient Rome. Barbarian invasion is now, Gibbon argues, technologically preventable and geographically unfeasible. In addition, the modern European empires, which are all overseas, would afford a refuge in the event of an invasion: 'Europe would revive and flourish in the American world, which is already filled with her colonies and institutions' (III, 637). This somewhat bizarre scenario was, perhaps, originally suggested or brought back to mind by the American Revolutionary War. In his letters, Gibbon ruefully associated the 'conquest' of America (as he often styled it) with the completion of the first volume of *The Decline and Fall*:[9] 'having supported the

[8] Craddock thinks that the 'General Observations' were completed in 'some form no later than July or August 1773' (*Edward Gibbon, Luminous Historian*, 8). Peter Ghosh dates them to 1772 and thinks that 'cheekily and culpably' they were 'inserted as a spice at the end of the third volume' ('Gibbon's Dark Ages: Some Remarks on the Genesis of the *Decline and Fall*', *Journal of Roman Studies*, 73 (1983), 18). J. G. A Pocock also finds them disappointing ('Between Machiavelli and Hume: Gibbon as a Civic Humanist and Philosophical Historian' in G. W. Bowersock, John Clive and Stephen R. Graubard eds., *Edward Gibbon and The Decline and Fall of The Roman Empire* (Cambridge, MA, 1977), 295).

[9] 'The *Conquest* of America is a *great* Work', Gibbon to Holroyd (31 October 1775), *Letters*, no. 326; 'America is not *yet* Conquered', Gibbon to Holroyd (2 December 1777), *Letters*, no. 404. J. G. A. Pocock has offered one explanation as to why Gibbon would not have seen the decline of Rome and Britain's loss of the American colonies as comparable: 'Rome had suffered the loss of the institutions of the *res publica* in the attempt to control provinces, and Britain was about to lose her

British I must destroy the Roman Empire' ... 'it became necessary to finish my book and to subdue America'.[10] The scenario ultimately derives, however, from a passage in the first Stuart volume of Hume's *History of England* in which he reflects upon the benefits of American colonies to England as a potential means of rescue from a fate similar to that of Rome:

The seeds of many a noble state have been sown in climates, kept desolate by the wild manners of the antient inhabitants; and as asylum secured, in that solitary world, for liberty and science, if ever the spreading of unlimited empire, or the inroad of barbarous nations, should again extinguish them in this turbulent and restless hemisphere.[11]

The 'General Observations', taking this initial cue from Hume, announce the structural dissimilarity between the Roman and British Empires in terms which both simplify and diminish the enormous cultural subtleties and cultivated causal agnosticism of the rest of volumes II and III. Gibbon prefaces his remarks with a passage of unmistakable Robertsonian triumphalism:

It is the duty of the patriot to prefer and promote the exclusive interest and glory of his native country: but a philosopher may be permitted to enlarge his views, and to consider Europe as one great republic, whose various inhabitants have attained almost the same level of politeness and cultivation. The balance of power will continue to fluctuate, and the prosperity of our own, or the neighbouring kingdoms may be alternately exalted or depressed; but these partial events cannot essentially injure our general state of happiness, the system of arts, and laws, and manners, which so advantageously distinguish, above the rest of mankind, the Europeans and their colonies. (III, 633–4)

The making of this great European republic is one important subject of *The Decline and Fall.* Nevertheless, the history stops far short of the modern epoch it prescribes, leaving its readers with a lingering image of the city of Rome in a state of political stagnation and physical decay. Gibbon was always and increasingly reluctant to submit the story of the decline of Rome to the kind of causal schematisation previously applied in one of the most important eighteenth-century accounts of the decline of Rome, Montesquieu's *Considérations sur les causes de la grandeur des Romains et de leur décadence* (1734). I shall argue that, particularly in the later volumes, Gibbon became, for similar reasons, suspicious of the Scottish analysis of the rise of Europe; a unique and complex historical phenomenon could not

American provinces rather than modify her political and ecclesiastical institutions to accommodate them' (*The Varieties of British Political Thought, 1500–1800*, eds. J. G. A. Pocock, Gordon Schochet and Lois Schwoerer (Cambridge, 1993), 278).

10 Gibbon to Holroyd (15 May 1775), *Letters*, no. 303; Gibbon to Deyverdun (7 May 1776), *Letters*, no. 341.

11 Hume, *History of Great Britain*, ed. Duncan Forbes, (Harmondsworth, 1970), 243.

readily be surrendered to an explanatory scheme which might also serve for other states in other continents and hemispheres.

Debts

In his *The Transformation of The Decline and Fall of the Roman Empire*, David Womersley has explained how Gibbon, as he became ever more alert to the intractable individuality of the past, interrogated Montesquieu's laws of causality to the point where they yield no meaning except, perhaps, the banality of sociological explanation itself.[12] An additional reason which may be offered for this is Gibbon's ever more insistent refusal, as his history approaches the cultural revival of the West, to yield his sense of the unique history and identity of Europe to a general sociology of the decay and rise of republics, monarchies and empires. Where other, non-western empires were concerned, Gibbon did not altogether jettison the convenient, sociological 'case history' approach. Unlike Voltaire, Gibbon did not find Montesquieu unduly unempirical as a historian or social philosopher, and pointed out in his first published work, the *Essai sur l'étude de la littérature* (1761), how well Montesquieu understood the limits to the explanatory extent of his theories of general causation.[13] Gibbon makes the story of Christian Byzantium structurally dependent upon a larger, encompassing narrative of decline and partial recovery as a way of indicating its inferiority to the western Roman Empire (V, 422). These chapters (50–52) have the explanatory cogency of Montesquieu's account of the Roman Republic as a polity which derived its initial coherence from a public-spirited commitment to expansion, but was driven to over-extensive conquest by its own dynamism, and corrupted by the concentrations of wealth garnered from those conquests. Inevitably, perhaps, Gibbon does not accord an equal measure of uniqueness and complexity to all non-western national and imperial histories. This Montesquieuan abbreviated mode of analysis would never do for the Roman Empire or its European successor states. In this, he faces, on a far greater scale, problems of focus and narrative intelligibility similar to those encountered by Voltaire in the *Essai sur les mœurs*.

It is usual, these days, to emphasise Gibbon's debt to Hume, rather than to Voltaire or Robertson. At the deepest level, there is a recognisably Humean dimension to Gibbon's sense of the way in which events are propelled by the beliefs which people hold about their society and governments – beliefs sometimes creatively, sometimes disastrously, out of kilter with the unheeded historical currents swelling beneath them. Even

[12] David Womersley, *The Transformation of The Decline and Fall of the Roman Empire* (Cambridge, 1988).

[13] Gibbon, *Essai sur l'étude de la littérature* (London, 1761), 109.

so, Gibbon is inevitably forced to engage more directly with Voltaire and Robertson than with Hume by virtue of the greater degree of overlap between their chosen historical ground and his. The precise nature of Gibbon's debt to Voltaire is difficult to ascertain. Gibbon, as his early comments on the *Siècle de Louis XIV* suggest, found him irritatingly unscholarly yet supremely eloquent:

when he treats of a distant period, he is not a man to turn over musty monkish writers to instruct himself. He follows some compilation, varnishes it over with the magic of his style, and produces a most agreeable, superficial, inaccurate performance.[14]

Gibbon's residual affection for Voltaire's plays, and his acerbic asides throughout *The Decline and Fall* on his bigotry and haughtiness suggest the conscious superiority of a former admirer who feels he has to dismantle the Frenchman's reputation in order to clear space for his own. Beyond emulating and surpassing his stylishness, the footnotes to the penultimate and last volumes of *The Decline and Fall* refer explicitly to the *Essai sur les mœurs* at the points where these two world histories, from the time of Charlemagne onwards, have major interpretative issues to address (the Crusades, the spread of Islam, the rise of the Ottoman Empire).[15] Gibbon's campaign of attrition against Voltaire's *Essai* should not blind us to broad similarities in their interpretation of the western Middle Ages. There is, in *The Decline and Fall*, the same emphasis upon urban incorporation, technological development and commerce as key factors in the erosion of feudal structures; these are causally linked to the increasing, voluntary capacity of the human mind to grasp and manipulate reality, and eventually shape it into a common European civilisation.

[14] Gibbon's library contained editions of Voltaire's works (dated 1768–77 and 1780–1) and a copy of *Le Siècle de Louis XIV* (London, 1752). See Keynes ed., *The Library of Edward Gibbon.* Gibbon's journals show him to have been reading the *Essai sur les mœurs* before 1763 (*Le Journal de Gibbon à Lausanne*, 133). Gibbon's critique of *Le Siècle de Louis XIV* as a superficial and oddly arranged, though entertaining performance appears in *Gibbon's Journal to January 28th, 1763*, 129. Other asides, such as Gibbon's reference to Voltaire's 'magisterial haughtiness' are typical of his early attitude to the French historian ('Index Expurgatorius' in *English Essays*, 116). Nevertheless, a number of critics have sensed in Gibbon, as I do, a significant early stylistic debt to Voltaire, including Craddock in *Young Edward Gibbon*, 66. Michel Baridon has pointed out the echoes and similarities between the *Essai sur les mœurs* and *The Decline and Fall* (*Edward Gibbon et le Mythe de Rome* (Paris, 1977, 438–9). G. Giarrizzo has also pointed these out (*Edward Gibbon e la Cultura Europea del Settecento* (Naples, 1954), 303–7), and elsewhere engages fully with the question of the relationship between Voltaire and Gibbon). The echoes of Voltaire's *Essai* in chapter 15 of *The Decline and Fall* have often been noted, for example by Robert Shackleton, 'The Impact of French Literature on Gibbon' in *Edward Gibbon and the Decline and Fall of the Roman Empire*, eds. Bowersock, Clive and Graubard, 214.

[15] Among the fuller references in Gibbon's notes to Voltaire's *Essai* and other works are: V, 138, 146 (on Charlemagne); V, 239, 251, 418, 437 (on Islam and the Arab empires); VI, 58, 117, 202, 210 (on the Crusades); VI, 295, 352 (on Timur Lane); VI, 495, 511 (on the Turks). 'In his way Voltaire was a bigot, an intolerant bigot', VI, 442.

Gibbon's debt to Robertson, a historian with whom he was associated by warm ties of mutual admiration, is more straightforward.[16] Gibbon referred to Robertson as a 'master-artist' in the preface to the fourth volume of *The Decline and Fall*, and a small piece of ammunition, which he brings out in his *Vindication* of chapters 15 and 16 against outraged Anglican opinion, is the observation that he has 'a right to name Dr. Robertson for his friend'.[17] Gibbon kept first editions of the *History of Scotland* (which he cited in an early unpublished essay on feudal government) and the *History of Charles V* in his library, and was presented with a copy of the *History of America* by Robertson himself.[18] He described Robertson as an 'animal of great, though not perhaps of equal and certainly not of similar merit' to Hume, and, although he looked up to Hume, it was to Robertson that he claimed, with faint self-mockery, to belong as a 'disciple'.[19] Robertson is a constant presence in the footnotes to the last two volumes of *The Decline and Fall*, and provides, along with Hume and Voltaire, a substantial part of the matrix within which episodes such as the Crusades and the Reformation are interpreted in Gibbon's incomplete narrative of the rise of European civil society.

Apprenticeship

Gibbon's first published appearance, in the *Essai sur l'étude de la littérature* (1761), was as a literary critic seeking (somewhat belatedly) to offer an exposition of and reply to the ancient/modern debate.[20] The *Essai* reflects upon a series of topics, including the neglect of classical learning, the problem of pyrrhonism and the history of religious belief. It embraces a broad conception of criticism as a philological, historical, and interpretive

[16] Robertson praised volume I (*Edward Gibbon, Luminous Historian*, 69), appeared to be even more enthusiastic about volumes II and III (Gibbon to Suzanne Necker (1 June 1781), *The Letters of Edward Gibbon*, no. 501), and was also complimentary about volumes IV, V and VI (Gibbon to Thomas Cadell (11 February 1789), *The Letters of Edward Gibbon*, no. 721).

[17] *A Vindication of Some Passages in the Fifteenth and Sixteenth Chapters of the History of The Decline and Fall of the Roman Empire* (1779), *English Essays*, 232.

[18] 'Du Gouvernement féodal, surtout en France' (*c.* 1767), *Miscellaneous Works*, III, 189. Robertson to Gibbon (14 July 1777), *The Letters of Edward Gibbon*, no. 389.

[19] Gibbon to J. B. Holroyd (7 August 1773), *The Letters of Edward Gibbon*, no. 227. 'The candour of Dr. Robertson embraced his disciple; a letter from Mr. Hume overpaid the labour of ten years' (*Autobiographies*, 311–12). See also Gibbon and Deyverdun's literary journal *Mémoires littéraires* (1767), I, 29, in which Robertson and Hume are praised highly. Gibbon even left Robertson 100 guineas in his will (*Autobiographies*, 422). Robertson is, of course, a frequent guest in the footnotes to the later volumes of *The Decline and Fall* (for example, V, 138; VI, 210, 614). Gibbon, perhaps unconsciously, directly echoes Robertson when he describes the era from Domitian to Commodus as the most happy and prosperous of all eras. See John W. Oliver, 'William Robertson and Edward Gibbon', *Scottish Historical Review*, 26 (1947), 86.

[20] For details of the extant drafts and composition of the *Essai*, see *Edward Gibbon, Luminous Historian*, 117–20, 126–31, 152–4. On Gibbon and the ancient/modern debate, see Joseph M. Levine, *Humanism and History: Origins of Modern Historiography* (Ithaca, NY, 1987).

activity in the manner of late seventeenth-century polymaths such as Pierre Bayle and Jean Le Clerc.[21] The unifying theme of the *Essai* is the search for a properly critical approach (or *esprit philosophique*) which will deliver both history and literary history from the banal dismissiveness of the French moderns, and the prolix antiquarianism of the ancients. As an example, Gibbon attempts a set-piece contextual reading of Virgil's *Georgics*. He then goes on to tackle the knotty problem of veracity in history, making reference to the Académie Royale des Inscriptions' debate as to how to guarantee reasonable probability in the presentation of history. Gibbon conjectures how a properly 'philosophical' historian would locate, among his data, the springs ('ressorts') of action, and how these might be integrated into a synthetic account of cause and effect. Even so, he cautions against the overly systematic mentality of historians of general causes ('causes determinées mais générales') who try to yoke them to grand theories of historical necessity ('l'enchaînement qu'ils aiment').[22] Montesquieu is specifically exempted from these strictures.

Gibbon's culture is strongly (though by no means exclusively) French at this stage and, like Voltaire before him, he reaches the case for reasonable probability in history by way of a rejection of pyrrhonism. Like Voltaire also, Gibbon develops a notion of the philosophical spirit in historical writing by analogy, not only with contextualising methods in literary criticism, but also with the procedures by which poets themselves select material from history and mould it into a new whole. Gibbon's recognition of the literariness of the historical operation at its most basic cognitive level thus grows out of a broad reappraisal of the ancient/modern debate. To Voltaire, who made similar elisions between the problems of literary criticism and the problems of historical epistemology, this literariness presented great stylistic opportunities; to Gibbon, it was a source of anxiety. One of Gibbon's most revealing early pieces, an attempt to date and sort out the dynastic structure of the Median Empire entitled 'Mémoire sur la Monarchie des Mèdes' (*c.* 1765–70), shows him worrying away at the paradox of historical creativity. He is unhappy with the way in which historians tend to press the stamp of their *esprit philosophique* on their material, and in which, as in the case of Voltaire, this self-ratifying *esprit* traps them in the circularity of their own imaginings.[23] This point is made with particular reference to Xenophon:

> Un esprit philosophique se plaît à suppléer tous ces termes intermédiaires; et à tirer du vrai, le vraisemblable et le possible. S'il donne à ses réflexions la forme

[21] For Le Clerc's definition of criticism, see his *Ars Critica* (2 vols.; Amsterdam, 1697), I, 5.

[22] *Essai sur l'étude de la littérature*, 108.

[23] 'Mémoires sur la Monarchie des Mèdes, pour servir de supplément aux dissertations de MM Fréret et de Bougainville', *Miscellaneous Works*, III, 128. For the dating of this work, see Craddock, *Young Edward Gibbon*, 251.

d'une histoire, il est obligé de prendre un ton plus ferme. Ses hypothèses deviennent des faits, qui semblent découler des faits généraux et avérés.[24]

In the *Essai*, Gibbon embarks on a sophisticated critique of the problem of historical representation; the linking terms ('termes intermédiaires') which the historian supplies to generate intelligible narrative inevitably usurp the status of the factual. The task of the historian, armed with an *esprit philosophique*, is not to prevent altogether this usurpation, but to try to limit the distortions of these extraneous explanatory connectives. The problem, set out in the *Essai*, of bringing classical poets to life in the present without co-opting them to contemporary concerns ('Horace et Plaute sont presqu'inintelligibles à quiconque n'a pas appris à vivre et à penser comme le peuple Romain') has become a paradigm for the issue of historical representation in general.[25]

Gibbon's preferred resolution to the paradox that history must be distorted in order to be represented entails a revision of Aristotle's theory of poetic mimesis (on the way in which poetry selectively imitates nature and human action). Aristotle dismisses history as conveying a lower order of knowledge than poetry. André Dacier, the editor of the French edition of the *Poetics* owned by Gibbon, reinforces this point in his running commentary: 'la *Poësie*, dit-il, *est plus grave & plus philosophique que l'Histoire*, car c'est le terme dont il se sert [Aristotle uses the word 'philosophoteron']. En effet, l'Histoire ne peut instruire qu'autant que les faits qu'elle rapport.'[26] Gibbon parts company with Aristotle (and Dacier) by suggesting, in the *Essai*, that history does, in fact, engage in a process of selective imitation of human culture, and that, despite the epistemological liabilities entailed, it is upon this very analogy between artistic and historical imitation that historical writing grounds its claims to be 'philosophical'.

Gibbon's defence of history as a branch of *studia humanitatis* equal in value to literary study belongs, in part, to a tradition of historical apologetics developed by seventeenth- and early eighteenth-century scholars based in The Netherlands. These scholars had developed a distinctive, neo-Aristotleian brand of historical scholarship and theory.[27] The praise accorded in the *Essai* to Gerardus Vossius, Justus Lipsius, Isaac Casaubon and Jean Le Clerc demonstrates Gibbon's early familiarity with this intellectual culture. In particular, Gibbon may have known Vossius' *Ars Historica* (1623) which attempts an alignment between history and Aristo-

[24] 'Mémoires sur la Monarchie des Mèdes' in ibid., III, 128–9.

[25] *Essai sur l'étude de la littérature*, 28.

[26] André Dacier, *La poëtique d'Aristote ... Traduite en francois avec des remarques critiques sur tout l'ouvrage* (Paris, 1692), 137.

[27] On historical thought and writing in The Netherlands, see A. C. Duke and C. A. Tamse, *Clio's Mirror: Historiography in Britain and the Netherlands* (Zutphen, 1985). On its influence in England, see J. W. Johnson, *The Formation of English Neo-Classical Thought* (Princeton, 1967).

tle's theory of poetry in order to dignify history as a literary art while retaining its status as a branch of scientific knowledge. Gibbon appears to have admired Vossius, whose *Opera in Sex Tomos Divisa* (1695–1701) and other studies of Greek and Latin histories are well represented in his library. The third volume of Vossius' complete works contains a highly influential discussion of poetics, including a dissertation on imitation ('De Imitatione, cum oratoria, tum praecipue, poetica, liber de que recitatione veterum', originally published in 1647) which may have helped the young Gibbon to make the connection between the problem of artistic representation and the problem of how artists paradoxically derive originality from imitating the productions of the civilisations which have preceded them. Vossius divided imitation into childish or slavish and manly or liberal types ('Modus imitationis est duplex: puerilis, & virilis'), and celebrated a particularly creative form of liberal imitation which he called 'imitatio ingenua' ('Ingenuam imitationem appello, quando non verbum verbo reddimus; sed sic aliena tractamus, ut non in alterius possessionem irruisse, sed jure nostro venisse, credamur').[28] Shortly after the publication of the *Essai*, Gibbon again ruminated upon the issues of imitation and originality when he wrote out a critical abstract of Richard Hurd's edition and commentary on Horace's *Epistola ad Pisones* (the *Ars Poetica*). Hurd had extrapolated from Horace the notion that similarities between ancient and modern poets largely resulted from their imitation of nature, and that, given the common basis of art in fixed nature, originality is not possible. Gibbon counters Hurd's poetics with a more dynamic, historically minded model of his own. He argues that most modern art takes as its starting-point the imitation of classical writers ('If habit was not sufficient, to dispose us to imitate the ancients, authority founded on reason, would oblige us to do it'), but that its original component derives from the fact that the writer is embedded in and draws upon the manners of his age: 'It is the manners, the government, the religion of that age and country, he is to study, and ... they will always make him an original.'[29] Gibbon, then, emerges from the ancient/modern debate with a well-exercised theory of artistic development which postulates a dynamic process of transmission, and which emphasises the interactions between inherited culture and the present in the production of works at once imitative and original.

Custom and imitation

By the time he came to write *The Decline and Fall*, this model of artistic production seems to have suggested to Gibbon ways of thinking about the

[28] Gerardus Vossius, *Opera in Sex Tomos Divisa* (6 vols.; Amsterdam, 1695–1701), III, 177.
[29] 'Hurd on Horace' (1762) in *English Essays*, 47, 50.

larger processes of cultural transmission from the ancient to the modern world. He applies his model of artistic originality to the manner in which the Germanic inheritors of the Roman Empire imitate their Romano-Gallic forebears while drawing upon the inner resources of their own civilisation. A synthetic balance between these two components is not achieved by these Germanic peoples within the chronological confines of *The Decline and Fall*, but Gibbon frequently contrasts their long-term potential for self-renewal with the cultural bankruptcy of Byzantium, which seems doomed to mimic the Roman Empire until it is simply taken over by the Ottomans. The westerners will ultimately demonstrate a lively capacity for Vossius' 'imitatio ingenua' whereas the East can engage only in 'imitatio puerilis'.

The revival of the West depends upon the continuation and reinfusion of practices and ideas (about law, liberty, a notion of citizenship wider than ethnic or geographical boundaries, freedom of intellectual inquiry) derived from the Roman Empire, though often of older Greek ancestry. For Gibbon, the object of imitation, the Roman Empire, is not a coherent or monolithic entity, but a cumulative set of practices and histories deposited over a long period of rise and decline. For this reason, Gibbon finds the *Corpus Juris Civilis* – the monumental compilation and codification of Roman jurisprudence undertaken by the emperor Justinian in the second quarter of the sixth century – the most satisfying image of the totality of Roman history. Chapter 44 (the fruit, as Gibbon recalls in his memoirs, of a 'laborious winter') reads the Codes, Pandects and Institutes, as it were, geologically, finding layer upon layer of laws and customs, silted down from the earliest years of the Republic, and deposited in the strata of a rock which can no longer be mined.[30] The whole legal enterprise steadily becomes, in Gibbon's account, a metaphor for the sedimentary, rather than organic, nature of the faintly legible monument of the Roman Empire. Despite the pristine wisdom of the Republic's original twelve tables, Roman laws have come, by the time of Justinian, to purport despotism in their (literally) Byzantine complexity:

> In a period of thirteen hundred years, the laws had reluctantly followed the changes of government and manners; and the laudable desire of conciliating ancient names with recent institutions, destroyed the harmony, and swelled the magnitude of the obscure and irregular system. (IV, 415)

The laws, which retain enough of their origins to enable Gibbon 'to breathe the pure and invigorating air of the republic', disclose how the forms and fictions of the Roman Republic were protracted and then slowly expunged by the formation of an obscurantist, monarchical jurisprudence

[30] *Autobiographies*, 326.

(IV, 334). Roman law may originally have been based upon principles of natural law, but its true character was flexible and customary ('positive institutions are often the result of custom and prejudice; laws and language are ambiguous and arbitrary'), and custom, as it proliferates, often disables the state (IV, 354). Chapter 44 distils Gibbon's image of the Roman Empire as a world steadily debilitated by the weight of its own history, engaged in a customary prolongation of the legal, political, and religious forms of the Republic, and yet unable to revive them. The Roman people are 'less attached indeed to speculative opinion, than to ancient custom', and their 'Pagan worship', as Gibbon reiterates in the *Vindication* of chapters 15 and 16, 'was a matter, not of opinion, but of custom' (II, 310).[31]

Gibbon's reservations about the customary legal and cultural reflexes of the Roman Empire are consistent with his views on the customary basis of English law. Unlike his acquaintance and fellow parliamentarian Edmund Burke, Gibbon specifically rejects the notion that England (whose total severance in the fifth century from the Roman world and its laws he records in chapter 38) derives its vigour from the customary heritage enshrined in its common law. Burke's refurbishment of the common-law view of Britain's constitutional heritage as part of a more dynamic, evolutionary doctrine of prescription appears to have excited little interest in Gibbon.[32] In an earlier abstract of William Blackstone's *Commentaries on the Laws of England*, he explicitly takes issue with the common-law view of the English constitution:

> Mr Blackstone speaks with uncommon respect of the Old Common Law, which the generality of Lawyers highly prefer to the Statute Law. He will find it however difficult to persuade an impartial reader, that old customs (begun in barbarous ages and since continued from a blind reverence to Antiquity) deserve more respect than the positive decrees of the Legislative power. I can indeed suspect that a general rule which is gathered only from a rude and prodigious mass of particular examples and opinions will easily acquire an obscurity, a prolixity and an uncertainty which will at last render the priests of Themis the sole interpreters of her oracles. [33]

To the common lawyers' notion of a customary, immemorial British Constitution slowly deposited into history by legal precedent, Gibbon prefers the flexible energies of statute law.[34] By analogy, the codes of the

[31] *English Essays*, 285.

[32] On Burke and the common law, see J. G. A. Pocock, 'Burke and the Ancient Constitution: A Problem in the History of Ideas' in *Politics, Language and Time: Essays on Political Thought and History* (London, 1971) and Paul Lucas, 'On Edmund Burke's Doctrine of Prescription: or, an Appeal from the New to the Old Lawyers', *Historical Journal*, 11 (1968), 35–63.

[33] 'Abstract of Blackstone' (*c.* 1765–6) in *English Essays*, 63.

[34] *English Essays*, 63.

Roman Empire, lacking the transparency of the English forms of statute law, fall victim to emperors who conceal their growing despotism behind a customary fabric of (originally republican) jurisprudence which simultaneously extends and disables their dominion. The Republic casts its shadow over the Empire. Like Tacitus' *Annals*, *The Decline and Fall* opens with a discussion of the preservation of 'the *image* of a free constitution' (my italics) by Augustus, who meanwhile artfully assembles a principate (I, 1). For Tacitus, this moment marks the transition between the valid world of the Republic and a morally dubious era of dictatorship. In Montesquieu's interpretation there occurs, at this point, a decisive downturn of the Polybian wheel of political forms from republic to monarchy. Gibbon, however, is less pessimistic; Augustus, 'sensible that mankind is governed by names', inaugurates a fictitiously republican brand of politics through which, at least until the death of Commodus in 192, 'the dangers inherent to a military [as opposed to a militia-based republican] government were, in a great measure, suspended' (I, 73, 74). Despite occasionally breathing its purer air, Gibbon does not give in to Whig hankering after the 'stern and haughty spirit' of the laws of the Roman Republic (IV, 384). He had previously demonstrated the limits of his nostalgia for the Republic in a revisionist piece in which he discussed the (in his view, much overrated) character of Caesar's assassin Brutus.[35]

The empire of republican forms

Gibbon, then, is mainly interested in the Republic as an agency within the Empire (rather than as a prior political stage) which, in its customary legitimation of the Roman state, helps to explain why indeed the Empire 'subsisted so long' (III, 631). Gibbon's elaboration of the precise nature of this republican legacy is highly, even polemically senatorial. Until the reign of Diocletian, Gibbon observes, 'the model of ancient freedom was preserved in [the senate's] deliberations and decrees; and wise princes, who respected the prejudices of the Roman people, were in some measure obliged to assume the language and behaviour suitable to the general and first magistrate of the republic' (I, 386). Gibbon's interest in the senate as the key component in the protracted myth of the Republic causes him to take the somewhat unusual step of identifying Septimius Severus (AD 193–211), who broke with tradition by no longer restricting the command of the Roman legions to senators, as 'the principal author of the decline of the Roman empire' (I, 129).[36] The senate had, in fact, exercised very little influence upon public affairs since Caesar's time, but Gibbon (with the

[35] 'Digression on the Character of Brutus' (n.d.) in *English Essays*, 96–106.

[36] On this subject, see Mortimer Chambers, 'The Crisis of the Third Century' in *The Transformation of the Roman World: Gibbon's Problem after Two Centuries*, ed. Lynn White (Berkeley, 1966), 43–5.

British constitution in mind) wishes to stress the continuing legitimacy of this separate, representative tier of Roman government. For Gibbon, as for Montesquieu, the origins of limited monarchy are to be found in the attempts by aristocracies to curtail the executive power of their ruler. 'In France,' Gibbon mentions in passing, 'the remains of liberty are kept alive by the spirit, the honours, and even the prejudices, of fifty thousand nobles' (IV, 367). In a similar vein, much earlier in his writing career, Gibbon had made a Montesquieuan case for the need for intermediate powers in the state in an unpublished piece on the government of the Pays de Vaud in Switzerland.[37] On one occasion in *The Decline and Fall*, at the end of chapter 31, Gibbon even comes quite close to identifying, as a major cause of decline, the absence of stabilising, intermediate representative bodies in the empire. In one instance, he describes how the emperor Honorius, in an attempt, in 418, to improve the administration of Gaul, drew up a plan for summoning an annual representative assembly of governors, landowners and bishops of seven of its provinces to discuss and regulate local affairs; in the event, hardly anyone turned up, indicating to Gibbon that the 'health and life' of the Empire had been 'exhausted' beyond recovery (III, 280). Gibbon points out, however, that had such an assembly been convened during the reign of the Antonines or earlier, the outcome for the empire might have been very different: 'under the mild and generous influence of liberty, the Roman Empire might have remained invincible and immortal' (III, 279–80). In fact, Honorius' edict was little more than a device for solidifying the loyalty of local elites to the emperor, but Gibbon over-interprets the document in order to make a larger point about the potential role of intermediate, representative bodies in integrating institutional forms of liberty with the structures of empire.[38] The British Empire in both America and India cannot have been far from his mind.

Gibbon's empire of republican forms can be loosely divided into two stages of decay. The first stage, to the reign of Septimius Severus, is characterised by the persistence of republican customs and habits, which are less and less synchronised with the despotic institutions of the regime. The second phase, beginning with Caracalla (211–17) and culminating with Diocletian (284–305), marks the slow and sporadic transformation of the Empire from a customary culture to a display culture ('Ostentation was the first principle of the new system instituted by Diocletian') in which the memory of the Republic becomes a theatrical resource (I, 389). Gibbon denotes the process by which the traditions of the Empire are absorbed into a set of theatrical conventions as 'easternisation', pointing to the

[37] 'La Lettre de Gibbon sur le gouvernement de Berne' (1763–4) in *Miscellanea Gibboniana*, 123–41.

[38] See Bury's note to this section in *The History of the Decline and Fall of the Roman Empire*, ed. J. B. Bury (7 vols.; London, 1897–1900), III, 377, note 197. See also, John Matthews, *Western Aristocracies and Imperial Court, AD 364–425* (Oxford, 1975), 334.

presence of eunuchs, elaborate court ceremonials, and other oriental hallmarks. The emperor Elagabalus (218–22), with his extravagant taste for female costume, his eunuchs, his insatiable sensual appetites, and his profane idolatry, soon raises the visibility of this easternising process: 'Rome was at length humbled beneath the effeminate luxury of oriental despotism' (I, 148). Diocletian's centralising administrative reforms deliver the death blow to the senate, and usher in a new eastern despotic politics of display:

> Like the modesty affected by Augustus, the state maintained by Diocletian was a theatrical representation; but it must be confessed, that of the two comedies, the former was of a much more liberal and manly character than the latter. It was the aim of the one to disguise, and the object of the other to display, the unbounded power which the emperors possessed over the Roman world. (I, 389)

Julian the Apostate's (360–3) endeavour to revive some of the ceremonies, institutions, and religious practices of the Republic meets with genuine, if diluted, praise from Gibbon. Julian's republican gestures are at once generous, knowing, and perversely self-abnegating and ascetic. One example will suffice to show how Gibbon detects a note of desperation and melodrama in Julian's playing of the role of *princeps* of the Republic. In the following episode, Julian welcomes two new consuls to his palace:

> As soon as he was informed of their approach, he leaped from his throne, eagerly advanced to meet them, and compelled the blushing magistrates to receive the demonstrations of his affected humility. From the palace they proceeded to the senate. The emperor, on foot, marched before their litters, and the gazing multitude admired the image of ancient times, or secretly blamed the conduct which, in their eyes, degraded the majesty of the purple. (II, 349)

Julian, Gibbon informs us, 'solicited, with equal ardour, the esteem of the wise, and the applause of the multitude' (II, 414). Yet here his republican antics are subtly preposterous – embarrassing, perhaps even intimidating to the consuls whose esteem he exacts, and bewildering to the multitude whose applause he stirs. Julian's theatrical re-enactment of the forms of the pagan Roman Republic is thus, in part, an index of the irreversibility of their decay from custom to comedy.[39] Roman republican culture proves too permeable and flexible to regenerate itself once it has been superseded by new despotic forms of power. By an analogous process, paganism, with its 'loose and careless temper' and its basis in 'imitation and habit', is so

[39] For a marvellous essay on Gibbon's sense of the eventual depletion of the 'tissue of prejudices and interests' that made up Roman society, see Peter Brown, 'Gibbon's Views on Cultures and Society in the Fifth and Sixth Centuries' in *Society and the Holy in Late Antiquity* (London, 1982). For Gibbon's interpretation of the main source for Julian's life, Ammianus Marcellinus' *Res Gestae*, as well as his rejection of unthinking *philosophe* adulation of Julian, see Womersley, *The Transformation of The Decline and Fall*, chapters 10 and 11.

enmeshed with the customary culture of the Empire that it too succumbs to the organisational and doctrinal rigidities of Christianity (III, 90, 93).

The inferiority of Christian Byzantium, as Gibbon sees it, to the western Roman Empire is further signalled by the structural dependency, within *The Decline and Fall* as a whole, of its history upon a larger encompassing narrative of decline and partial recovery: 'the fate of the Byzantine monarchy is *passively* connected with the most splendid and important revolutions which have changed the state of the world' (V, 4). Byzantium is from the outset presented as a parasitical state, erected at the expense of other parts of the Roman Empire, and fed by the African bread-basket provinces. As an example of the difference between the western and eastern phases of the Empire, Gibbon mentions that both Rome and, later, Constantinople hosted an annual public ceremony in which slaves were manumitted by the consuls. 'The public festival was continued during several days in all the principal cities', Gibbon adds, 'in Rome, from custom; in Constantinople, from imitation' (II, 28). The government of Constantinople is, like that of its Roman predecessor, a form of theatre, staged at a still greater remove from the traditions which it tries to represent. Constantinople is a place of palace intrigue, spies, and luxurious display funded by heavy taxation. Some Roman republican forms are incorporated into this new pageant which overwhelms and depresses the subjects by its capacity for seemingly endless proliferation. Laws (set down in Justinian's Codes), emperors (the whole unmemorable succession of them wearily enumerated in chapter 48), luxuries and eunuchs multiply like locusts. For Gibbon, as for Hume, complex governments are the most despotic. The Empire, having lost the original simplicity of its administrative union, seems like a vast and dangerous entanglement of boundless peoples and places. Gibbon, on one occasion, likens this imperial miscegenation to an all-pervasive miasma:

> No restraints were imposed on the free and frequent intercourse of the Roman provinces: from Persia to France, the nations were mingled and infected by wars and emigrations; and the pestilential odour which lurks for years in a bale of cotton, was imported, by the abuse of trade, into the most distant regions.
>
> (IV, 330)

The most memorable symbols of Constantinople's stunted culture are the eunuchs who swarm the palaces 'like insects of a summer's day' (II, 341). As well as being emblematic of the easternisation of the Roman Empire, the eunuchs embody the Empire's incapacity to regenerate itself; like the powerful late fourth-century *castrensis* Eutropius 'who so perversely mimicked the actions of a man', they symbolise the extent to which the eastern Empire is a mimic culture (Gibbon borrows his invective against Eutropius from Claudian's *In Eutropium*, III, 285). Like the Byzantine

Empire itself, eunuchs seek perverse and instant forms of gratification in the absence of a capacity for creativity. The ostentatious luxury of the court provides one such source of gratification. Unlike the economically beneficial consumption of modern society (which Gibbon repeatedly differentiates from that of the ancient world), this luxury is the result of thoughtless present-mindedness leading to gratification in the absence of productivity: 'A long period of calamity or decay must have checked the industry, and diminished the wealth, of the people; and their profuse luxury must have been the result of that indolent despair, which enjoys the present hour, and declines the thoughts of futurity' (III, 67).[40] Gibbon has to make an exception of Justinian's admirable, emasculated general, Narses, but his exceedingly frequent references to eunuchs continue to evoke the wider pathology of the mimic easternised Empire.

Eastern Christianity

As it develops in its eastern orthodox form, Christianity, in the *Decline and Fall*, seems to intertwine ever more closely with the easternising Empire, replicating and reinforcing its fixity and sterility. The reign of the emperor Julian (which is described in chapters carefully interleaved with sections on the conversion of Constantine and the Arian controversy) does nothing to unravel, and quite possibly compounds, this close relationship between Christianity and the static Empire. Julian's pagan monotheism is, at bottom, the superstition of a neo-Platonic fanatic whose behaviour partakes of the same vocabulary of zeal and enthusiasm as Christianity. Julian is at once a Christian and Pagan apostate, and, as such, has no real chance of regenerating the Empire to whose debased mental level he has already sunk ('[he] did not escape the general contagion of his times') (II, 355). After Julian's death, the Christian Church returns to mirror and reinforce Byzantium's rigid and complex political structure. Like Montesquieu before him, Gibbon is unable or unwilling to recognise that the Byzantine Church was also a supplementary ecclesiastical polity, separate from and capable of constraining the secular component of government.[41] Gibbon is more interested in Byzantine Christology than ecclesiology, and devotes a number of chapters to the great theological controversies of the eastern church. The first of these, the Trinitarian debate over the question

[40] A similar distinction between 'vicious' and 'beneficial' or 'innocent' luxury is made in Hume's essay 'Of Refinement in the Arts' (1754).

[41] For the sources and nature of Gibbon's limited understanding of Byzantium, see Steven Runciman, 'Gibbon and Byzantium' in *Edward Gibbon and the Decline and Fall of the Roman Empire*, eds. Bowersock, Clive and Graubard. On Gibbon's history of religion, see J. G. A. Pocock, 'Superstition and Enthusiasm in Gibbon's History of Religion', *Eighteenth-Century Life*, 8 (1982), 83–94.

as to what degree the Father and Son can be said to be 'of one substance', is set out in chapter 21, and demonstrates the extent to which Gibbon felt that Church Christology was a means to replicate and strengthen the hold of the Empire over its ethnically and culturally diverse subject peoples. Later, the (sometimes violent) Arian dispute about the nature and divinity of Christ is temporarily resolved at the ecumenical Council of Nicaea (325) with the signing of a creed which, according to Gibbon, 'essentially contributed ... to maintain and perpetuate the uniformity of faith, or at least of language'(II, 253–4). It is significant that the word 'language' overbalances the word 'faith' in the final cadence of this sentence; the Nicaean creed is seen to complete an essentially *linguistic* process by which the Church claims fixity of meaning in words which, it argues, give body to the essence of abstract things: 'The loose wanderings of the imagination were gradually confined by creeds and confessions; the freedom of private judgement submitted to the public wisdom of synods' (II, 246). Gibbon's ultimate preference for Athanasius over the defeated Arius is more pragmatic than doctrinal; orthodoxy entails less violence than heresy. Both Arius and Athanasius are equally guilty of Platonic mystification with regard to language. This yoking together of a Platonic, essentialist view of language with a centrist and intolerant ecclesiology proves understandably unacceptable to many separatist North African, eastern and finally western churches.

Gibbon connects closely the problems of ecclesiastical unity and orthodoxy to the paradoxical fact that the early church grew up in multilingual communities and yet remained committed to a Platonic, essentialist view of language. He is thus particularly drawn to the second great church contest for control over theological language, the Incarnation controversy between Cyril of Alexandria and Nestorius and their followers, which took place in the second and third quarters of the fifth century. At stake was the question as to whether Christ incarnate has two distinct natures, a human and a divine, which together form a single person (the Chalcedonian orthodoxy), or whether there is a duality between the humanity of Christ and the eternal Word (the Monophysite interpretation). The issue was hammered out in successive councils, and a partial resolution was draw up in 482 in the form of the 'Henoticon' or formula of union. This resulted in a precarious conciliation between the Egyptian and Syrian Monophysite congregations, but precipitated a thirty-year schism between the eastern and western churches. Gibbon's approach to the whole dispute is to emphasise the linguistic roots of the ultimately separatist tendencies of the Monophysite Syrian, Coptic and Armenian churches, often at the expense of the national and secular causes of the schism.[42] The whole wretched

[42] See Miriam Lichtheim, 'Autonomy versus Unity in the Christian East' in White ed., *The Transformation of the Roman World.*

dispute seems to him to exemplify a descent from properly theological to analogical reasoning: 'The poverty of ideas and language tempted them to ransack art and nature for every possible comparison, and each comparison misled their fancy in the explanation of an incomparable mystery' (IV, 545). Nestorius is especially prone to this form of theology by weak analogy: '[he] was exasperated ... to draw his inadequate similes from the conjugal or civil partnerships of life, and to describe the manhood of Christ as the robe, the instrument, the tabernacle of his Godhead' (IV, 552–3). The consequence of this reduction of belief to the politics of language is division and schism:

> Language, the leading principle which unites or separates the tribes of mankind, soon discriminated the sectaries of the East, by a peculiar and perpetual badge, which abolished the means of intercourse and the hope of reconciliation. (IV, 591)

Gibbon is unconcerned by the gradual dissolution of the church into a multiplicity of local jurisdictions and orthodoxies. He ironically welcomes the inelasticity of the Latin language of the western church in response to the Platonisms of the Greek:

> The Latins had received the rays of divine knowledge through the dark and doubtful medium of a translation. The poverty and stubbornness of their native tongue, was not always capable of affording just equivalents for the Greek terms ... and a verbal defect might introduce into the Latin theology, a long train of error or perplexity. (II, 258)

A long and unregretted process of separation of the eastern and western churches begins after Nicaea and culminates in the iconoclasm of the first half of the eighth century when 'the liberty of Rome' is 'rescued' as the Latin church decides to retain its images in defiance of the emperor (V, 111).[43] Gibbon finds primitive and superstitious the religious use of images and relics. However, as the finely balanced section in chapter 28 entitled 'Revival of Polytheism' indicates, he does recognise that such forms of image worship represent a syncretic fusion of paganism with Christianity which enables the new religion to establish itself among the uneducated without doing violence to their dispositions and habits.

By contrast, the eastern church achieves orthodoxy only at the cost of the loss of the basis of linguistic meaning in social consensus. Its inflexibility replicates the political structures of the eastern-based Roman Empire, and its dissolution into a number of divergent churches is ultimately unavoidable. Although the gradual achievement of orthodoxy in large parts of the eastern church effects and preserves a degree of unity and civility in the empire, it is bought at the high price of compounding its incapacity to

[43] On the iconoclasm in Gibbon, see Timothy Peters, 'A History of Images: Christianity and Historiography in the Later *Decline and Fall*', *Studies in English Literature*, 30 (1990), 503–15.

respond flexibly and creatively to its own traditions. Summarising the state of the Greek Empire in the tenth century (now severely contracted after successive Arab conquests), Gibbon suggests that the fossilised state of the Greek culture and church is intimately bound up with a loss of dynamism and historical sensitivity in the use of the Greek language. The Byzantine Greeks fail to draw upon the cultural resources of ancient Greece: 'They held in their lifeless hands the riches of their fathers, without inheriting the spirit which had created and improved that sacred patrimony' (V, 515). By the tenth century, the Greek Empire has become so isolated culturally that it is no longer even capable of *imitatio puerilis*: 'Not a single composition of history, philosophy, or literature, has been saved from oblivion by the intrinsic beauties of style or sentiment, of original fancy, or even of successful imitation' (V, 515–16). At the end of this section on the long-term cultural failure of Byzantium, Gibbon supplies a summary passage in which he ventures a general explanation as to why some cultures are capable of self-renewal and creativity while others languish in a state of decline. The motor of cultural and political self-renovation, he assumes, is 'emulation', a term which signifies the process by which some peoples seek to surpass others through selective imitation of their most admirable or successful characteristics. Such emulation requires certain political preconditions unavailable to the Byzantines but now ripe in contemporary Europe:

> In all the pursuits of active and speculative life, the emulation of states and individuals is the most powerful spring of the efforts and improvements of mankind. The cities of ancient Greece were cast in the happy mixture of union and independence, which is repeated on a larger scale, but in a looser form, by the nations of modern Europe: the union of language, religion, and manners, which renders them the spectators and judges of each others merit: the independence of government and interest, which asserts their separate freedom, and excites them to strive for pre-eminence in the career of glory ... The empire of the Caesars undoubtedly checked the activity and progress of the human mind; its magnitude might indeed allow some scope for domestic competition; but when it was gradually reduced, at first to the East and at last to Greece and Constantinople, the Byzantine subjects were degraded to an abject and languid temper, the natural effect of their solitary and insulated state. (V, 517)

The loss of the cosmopolitan awareness enforced by large empires and encouraged by the looser cohabitation of modern states finally deprives Byzantium of the cultural stimulus of competitive emulation.[44] Like most of the reasons which Gibbon offers for the stagnation and contraction of the eastern Empire, this final idea of 'non-emulation' is also an indirect

[44] On the uses of the vocabulary of 'emulation' in the eighteenth century, see Howard D. Weinbrot, *Britannia's Issue: The Rise of British Literature from Dryden to Ossian* (Cambridge, 1993), 99–113.

way of writing about the converse success of the West. Despite the preponderance of chapters in the later volumes dealing with eastern affairs, Gibbon once again indicates the subordination and structural dependence of the eastern story upon a larger western narrative whose chronological compass will exceed *The Decline and Fall*.

The slow reawakening of the West

The sections in the last three volumes which deal with western affairs document the slow construction of the political and cultural preconditions for historical developments which are to occur beyond the scope of Gibbon's narrative. Gibbon emphasises how long it will be before these seeds of modernity in the West will come to their fruition. The Roman Empire, however, reaches a point of irreversible decay early in the narrative, and the third volume brings to an end the story of the collapse of the Roman Empire in the West in 476 (or 480), at the point at which the barbarian general, Odo(v)acer, pensions off the emperor at Ravenna and declares himself king of Italy. Since the Renaissance, this moment had been regarded as the final disaster of the Roman Empire. Gibbon, however, without departing altogether from established historiography, goes to some lengths to mitigate the suddenness and calamitousness of this episode. He restates his case that the destruction of Rome itself was started sooner and finished long after this barbarian political takeover: 'the destruction which undermined the foundations of those massy fabrics, was prosecuted, slowly and silently, during a period of ten centuries' (III, 457). He dates the disaster (if disaster it was) at least as far back as 364 when the Empire was divided permanently (except for brief periods in the fourth and sixth centuries) into eastern and western halves. Rome then sunk to a point of self-indulgent degeneracy which rendered it incapable of running the western Empire some time before the sacking of the city in 410 by Alaric and his Gothic confederacy.[45] The western Roman Empire had passed beyond redemption at this point, though not on account of any single moment of disaster.

Gibbon had long held the view that the extinction of the Roman Empire was merely hastened, rather than effected, by the invasions of Alaric, Attila and the Huns (defeated in 451), and Genseric and the Vandals (who sacked Rome in 455). Back in 1763 Gibbon had composed an elegant practical criticism of a poem by a pagan Gallic nobleman, Rutilius Namatianus, entitled *De Reditu Suo*. The poem recounts a journey made by sea from Rome to southern Gaul six years after Alaric's sack of Rome. The most

[45] Womersley shows how Gibbon subtly altered his source, Ammianus Marcellinus' *Res Gestae*, to sensationalise the magnitude of the decay of Rome shortly before Alaric's invasion. See *The Transformation of The Decline and Fall*, chapter 11.

appealing part of the poem is the long exordium addressed to Rome which expresses, through images of healing wounds, spring, rising stars, and so on, the poet's confidence in the imminent rejuvenation of the Roman Empire after all its ills ('ordo renascendi est crescere posse malis').[46] Gibbon's response to this exordium is sharply critical. He complains that Namatianus' yearning for a revived Rome would have seemed somewhat sentimental at a time when the city had ceased to have any symbolic resonance for most of the citizens of its crumbling Empire.[47] The Roman Empire, Gibbon unsympathetically remarks, had long since gone into a decline, and, by this time, it was losing even its symbolic potency:

> Ce n'etoit pas sous le regne d'Honorius qu'il falloit peindre la force de l'Empire Romain. Ses forces l'avoient abandonné depuis longtems; Mais son antiquité et son etendue, inspiroient une sorte de veneration et meme de terreur à ses voisins et le soutinrent encore. Cette illusion s'etoit enfin dissipée. Peu à peu les Barbares le connurent, le mepriserent et le detruisirent.[48]

Despite the aesthetic appeal of his poem, Namatianus was wrong to suppose that the sack of Rome was merely an aberration from which the city would one day recover.[49] Namatianus is cited several times in the footnotes to the relevant portions of *The Decline and Fall* which also insist that no single event or sudden cataclysm was alone responsible for the demise of the Roman Empire.

Volume III ends with a series of events which would, indeed, plunge Europe into an extended period of darkness: the subjugation of Gaul by Clovis and the Franks, the conquest of England by the Anglo-Saxons, and the consolidation of Visigothic rule in Spain. Nevertheless, even in these closing chapters, there are signs of modulation to a new key. Gibbon anticipates the establishment of the Ostrogothic kingdom in Italy under Theodoric, a ruler whom he greatly admires for his (sometimes excessive) *romanitas* (III, 504; IV, 21). Furthermore, whereas Gibbon had previously remarked that successive barbarians had invaded the Empire 'without imitating the arts and institutions, of civilised society', he now acknowledges that it is the conversion, around the fifth century, of many of the barbarian tribes to Christianity which finally gives them a point of access to a Roman heritage (III, 251). The literacy which the Christian faith often fostered also brought the Franks, Celts and Goths into contact with classical Latin masterpieces. Thus, in turn, 'the emulation of mankind was encouraged by the remembrance of a more perfect state; and the flame of

[46] Rutilius Namatianus, *De Reditu Suo* (416) in *Minor Latin Poets*, eds. J. Wight Duff and Arnold M. Duff (London, 1934), line 140.

[47] *Le Journal de Gibbon à Lausanne*, 178–9.

[48] Ibid., 178.

[49] Gibbon preferred this poem to Horace's 'Journey to Brundisium' (*Satires*, I, v): 'I would not hesitate to pronounce that the almost unknown journey of Rutilius is superior to that of Horace in point of description', *Miscellaneous Works*, IV, 345.

science was secretly kept alive, to warm and enlighten the mature age of the Western world' (III, 533). Like ancient Rome before and modern Europe after it, the developing Christian Church supplied the network of transnational contacts and cosmopolitan atmosphere necessary for a thriving culture of 'emulation' (V, 517 quoted above):

> The perpetual correspondence of the Latin clergy, the frequent pilgrimages to Rome and Jerusalem, and the growing authority of the Popes, cemented the union of the Christian republic: and gradually produced the similar manners, and common jurisprudence, which have distinguished, from the rest of mankind, the independent, and even hostile, nations of modern Europe. (III, 533)

Although sixteenth-century Europe will ultimately dismantle much of the power of the Roman Church, Gibbon readily concedes that the Christian republic, as the bearer of the classical heritage, is to be the precursor of civil society in Europe.

The barbarians' access to classicised western Christianity is initially retarded by the 'Teutonic idiom and pronunciation', as well as by their widespread adherence to the Arian heresy (III, 605). However, the lineaments of the future face of Europe are already visible in the settled states of the Franks, Goths and Saxons. Gibbon is therefore able to set the 'General Observations' at the end of the third volume in a sharper key by examining, not so much why the Roman Empire fell, as why barbarian incursions into Europe on the scale of those of the fourth and fifth centuries are never likely to be repeated. Gibbon had, on a number of occasions, identified, as the major exogenous pressure on the security of the Roman world the structural problem of there being nomadic, primitive peoples hovering on the borders of a commercial and luxury-producing empire. Barbarians such as the Huns with an 'eager appetite for the luxuries of civilized life' are irresistibly drawn towards the superior wealth of the Empire (III, 355). The relative, if not absolute stability of the modern European republic of states is, Gibbon suggests in the 'General Observations', a consequence of their having developed in tandem the 'complex machinery' of civil governments, commerce and manufacture of luxuries (III, 639). This level of advancement is achieved and consolidated through 'emulation' and 'the mutual influence of fear and shame' over an area still wider than that controlled by the Romans (III, 636). In the coda to the collapse of the Roman Empire in the West, Gibbon brings into clearer focus the theme of the eventual rise of a new Latin West out of its ruins.

Gibbon's Middle Ages

The first three volumes of *The Decline and Fall* initiate, and the last three elaborate, a familiar Scottish narrative of the imposition and erosion of the feudal 'system' in western Europe which inaugurates the transition from pre-civil to civil society. Gibbon had sketched out this narrative in his 'Outlines of the History of the World, 800–1500', which probably dates from 1771, and which can be correlated quite closely with the final instalment of *The Decline and Fall*.[50] In both works, Gibbon follows Robertson in designating the eleventh century as a major turning point in the history of Europe, and implicitly neglects Hume's citation of the twelfth century as the era in which the rediscovery of Justinian's Codes led to important new developments in civil law (this is, of course, consistent with Gibbon's idea that the Pandects encode a Byzantine system of despotism) (VI, 209). Prior to this, Gibbon parts company with Robertson and Hume, and, indeed, with Voltaire, when he ascribes to the Germanic warlords a generosity and freedom of spirit which infuses energy into societies formerly fatigued by Roman domination. Although Gibbon was critical, in the first volume, of the type of sentimental Gothicism derived by eighteenth-century political oppositions and others from Tacitus' *Germania*, he never entirely discards his original image of the independent, masculine Germanic (or Frankish, or Saxon) barons at the starting-line of the race towards European freedom: 'The persons of the Germans were free, their conquests were their own, and their national character was animated by a spirit which scorned the servile jurisprudence of the new or the ancient Rome' (V, 162).[51] He sets up a dichotomy between the Germanic tribesmen's impulsive freedom of spirit, which is diffused down the social scale and animates the common people, and their anarchic rejection of all civil government, which leads their magnates to fracture their states into a thousand separate jurisdictions ('a monster', as Gibbon describes it 'with an hundred heads') (V, 164). Gibbon's account of the Middle Ages aligns itself at various points with a Montesquieuan *thèse nobiliaire*; the libertarian habits of the barons are said ultimately to lay the foundations for limited monarchies. At other times, however, the liberty of the Germanic barons is seen to be in conflict with civil liberty, and the origins of invidious distinctions of ranks are located in their 'pride and prejudice' (III, 597). From the moment when Europe begins to recover from stagnation, Gibbon adopts a distinctively Scottish (and partly Voltairean) narrative of the endogenous erosion of feudalism through the break-up of the great baronial estates and fortunes, and through the development of incorpo-

[50] *English Essays*, 565–6.

[51] On Gibbon's critical reappraisal of Tacitus' *Germania*, see Womersley's *The Transformation of The Decline and Fall*, chapter 6. On Gibbon and eighteenth-century Gothic theory, see R. J. Smith, *The Gothic Bequest: Medieval Institutions in British Thought, 1688–1863* (Cambridge, 1987), chapter 3. The picture is a complex one. In his review of Adam Ferguson's *History of Civil Society* in the *Mémoires Littéraires de la Grande Bretagne*, I (1768), 54, Gibbon reproaches Ferguson for his excessive regard for barbarian eras ('un peu trop ami des siècles barbares').

rated cities ('one of the most powerful' causes of the liberation of 'the plebeians from the yoke of feudal tyranny') (VI, 70). Gibbon observed in the 'Outlines' that, by the fourteenth century, 'a more diffusive Commerce began to connect the European Nations by their mutual wants and conveniences', heralding the development of a more interdependent, socially participatory western world.[52] The growth of personal liberty (accorded a Humean welcome) which results from these changes eventually instigates a degree of emancipation from the superstitious fetters imposed by the Catholic Church, and leads to the cultural flowering of the sixteenth century: 'In Europe, the lower ranks of society were relieved from the yoke of feudal servitude; and freedom is the first step to curiosity and knowledge' (VI, 417).

Despite the clear affinities between Gibbon's Middle Ages and the Scottish narrative, made familiar by Hume, Robertson, Kames and Millar, of the rise of civil society out of the ruins of the feudal system, the *Decline and Fall* also embarks upon a critique of his contemporaries' methodology and modes of analysis. As we have already seen, elements of Montesquieuan and Whig constitutionalism disturb the Scottish vision of the decay of feudalism as the outcome of spontaneous activity from the lower orders. Gibbon finds in the Middle Ages only a faint pattern of development where Robertson discerns a clear line. For example, and by way of correcting Robertson, Gibbon feels that the Carolingian Empire, for all its political and cultural achievements, was largely dependent upon the genius of one unusual man, and did not herald the birth of regular government (here Gibbon takes the unusual step of recommending Voltaire's (non-celebratory) account of Charlemagne) (V, 146, note 116).[53] Gibbon's uneasy history of the progress of society in Europe is compromised but not overwhelmed by his intuitive sense that European society stumbled forward in an irregular and unpredictable way; its apotheosis is glimpsed but emphatically postponed beyond the chronological limits of the *Decline and Fall*, and its progress is sometimes halted or reversed: 'if the ninth and tenth centuries were the times of darkness, the thirteenth and fourteenth were the age of absurdity and fable' (VI, 209).

Gibbon's fullest exposition of his doubts about 'the progress of society' mode of analysis is to be found in the long section on the Crusades. The Crusades are the occasion of a spectacular encounter, in the wide dimension of the *Decline and Fall*, between the 'stationary or retrograde' state of

[52] 'Outlines' in *English Essays*, 187.

[53] Gibbon's remarks on the failure of the Carolingian Empire to consolidate a political infrastructure after extensive conquests (V, 159) echo exactly those made earlier in 'Du Gouvernement féodal, surtout en France' (*c.* 1767) in *Miscellaneous Works*, III, 195. On Gibbon's view of early medieval Europe, see also Jeffrey B. Russell, 'Celt and Teuton' in White ed., *The Transformation of the Roman World*.

Greek civilisation and the barbarous yet 'active spirit' of the Latin interlopers who finally turn against them (VI, 207, 209). There are localised engagements with Voltaire's and Hume's versions of these events (when Gibbon mentions that the crusading urge spread like an 'epidemical disease', for instance, or when he discusses their conflicting accounts of the aftermath of the first capture of Jerusalem in 1098–9) (VI, 17, 61). Inevitably, though, it is Robertson's revisionist interpretation of the Crusades as a vital factor in the progress of Europe which commands the fullest attention. For Robertson, the Crusades were the 'first event that rouzed Europe ... from lethargy' by precipitating a sudden widening of geographical and cultural horizons, and a major shift in the balance of property away from the feudal magnates who dissipated their fortunes in new and chivalrous enterprises of eternal glory.[54] Robertson's thesis of the 'accidental benefits of the Crusades' was initially parroted by Gibbon in the 'Outlines': 'the first Crusade ... rouzed Europe from its long and profound Lethargy, and was productive of much unforeseen benefit to the Popes, the Kings of France and the commercial State of Italy'.[55] However, in the mature work of *The Decline and Fall*, although a summary section on the 'General Consequences of the Crusades' continues to award the Crusades 'a conspicuous place' among 'the causes that undermined that Gothic edifice', there is a clear departure from Robertson in Gibbon's judgement that, on balance, the principle and consequence of the Crusades was a 'savage fanaticism' (VI, 210, 209). Although the Crusades present the Latins with a precious opportunity to vent their doughty spirits, their failure to overcome 'the difference of language, dress, and manners, which severs and alienates the nations of the globe', and so learn from and emulate the Greeks and Arabs, indicates that, after all, these events belong primarily to the Dark Ages (VI, 126).

Gibbon's account of the evolution of commercial, participatory, partially urbanised societies during the European Middle Ages is further complicated by his sense of the way in which old attitudes and forms constrict and even asphyxiate the life of the new. In general (and in ways more like Voltaire than Robertson), Gibbon's progress of western society takes place within a larger drama of tensions between secular and ecclesiastical powers. The closing chapters of *The Decline and Fall* cover the enormous struggles between the Italian cities, the Papacy, and the Holy Roman Empire. Like Voltaire, Gibbon is reluctantly an admirer of the medieval Catholic Church and its papal monarchy. He venerates the Church as the chief preserver of antique civilisation, finding even Gregory the Great's hostility to classical learning less significant than the classical spirit of his

[54] Robertson, 'A View of the Progress of Society in Europe' in *The History of the Reign of the Emperor Charles V*, I, 26.

[55] 'Outlines' in *English Essays*, 171.

reformist management of church and civil affairs (IV, 454–5). The revival of the West, and its attainment of theological and political autonomy from the stagnating eastern Empire is, Gibbon freely acknowledges, crucially dependent upon the consolidation of the temporal power of the Papacy from the eighth century onwards. The coronation of Charlemagne by Pope Leo III, by cementing a partnership between the western spiritual and temporal powers, signifies the triumphant expropriation of a Roman heritage unmediated by the East. This far outweighs in importance the fact that this partnership derived its appearance of legality from the 'Donation of Constantine' (which purported to show that Constantine had given his dominions in Italy to the Bishop of Rome), and that this document was later famously exposed as a forgery. In connection with the Donation, Gibbon permits himself the brief Humean reflection that the truth of an idea may be less important than its political consequences: 'This fiction was productive of the most beneficial effects . . . the edifice has subsisted after the foundations have been undermined' (V, 125–6, 127). The partnership between Papacy and empire is again revived in the late tenth century when Otto the Great reunites the German and Italian crowns, and lays the foundations of the Holy Roman Empire after a papal coronation. This alliance, however, soon outlives its usefulness. Gibbon's closing chapters document the struggle for imperial dominion in Italy, and record, with obvious approbation, the concurrent development of the Italian city republics and the power and prestige of the Papacy. The latter may be invidious, but its legitimacy always depends, he remarks with Humean emphasis, 'on the force of opinion' (VI, 613).

Reformation

Gibbon takes his leave of the western Europeans as they stand on the brink of the Reformation and the Renaissance. He looks forward to these events with undisguised relish:

> In the reformation of the sixteenth century, freedom and knowledge had expanded all the faculties of man; the thirst of innovation superseded the reverence of antiquity, and the vigour of Europe could disdain those phantoms which terrified the sickly and servile weakness of the Greeks. (V, 100)

In his early essay, 'Du Gouvernement féodal', Gibbon had given a recognisably Humean account of the ways in which the medieval church tried to set limits to the jurisdictions of the barony and to infuse a spirit of legality into civil transactions.[56] In *The Decline and Fall*, this idea is partly qualified by the story of how the Church facilitates political revival in the

[56] *Miscellaneous Works*, III, 198.

West at the cost of stunting the mental growth of its flock. Some of the flock, in turn, draw upon their Germanic stocks of vigour to modify or transform the Roman heritage which the Church has preserved for them in ways which the Church itself had never envisaged. This relatively familiar version of events, elaborated within a knotted texture of ironies and false starts, includes a celebration of a recovery of mental initiative through renewed access to the classical past. Robertson's own celebration of the Reformation as a broad process of intellectual transformation in Europe provides a starting-point for Gibbon's considerations of these events. He follows Robertson in characterising this change as a distinct stage in the development of European civil society in both Protestant and Catholic countries which supplements personal freedom (the chief gain of the late Middle Ages) with intellectual freedom. However, for Gibbon, as for Hume, this freedom did not originally feature in the calculations of the reforming enthusiasts: 'The chain of authority was broken, which restrains the bigot from thinking as he pleases, and the slave from speaking as he thinks ... This freedom however was the consequence, rather than the design, of the reformation' (V, 538). Gibbon unfolds his interpretation of the Reformation as a stage releasing other stages of development in a digression in volume V on the 'Character and Consequences of the Reformation'. The Reformation is an on-going process: 'Since the days of Luther and Calvin, a secret reformation has been silently working in the bosom of the reformed churches'; it is intertwined with the development of 'manly reason' in Protestant societies, and leads them towards toleration, Arminianism and, finally, moderate scepticism ('the articles of faith, are subscribed with a sigh or a smile by the modern clergy') (V, 539).

Gibbon's Reformation appears to be more limited in its social impact than in Robertson's, since it does not securely install theological and ecclesiological principles compatible with modern civil government; but it does signal the eventual capacity of at least some post-classical European societies for robust innovation, despite the fact that the reformers themselves often claimed that they were seeking to revive original Christianity:

> The protestants of France, of Germany, and of Britain, who asserted with such intrepid courage their civil and religious freedom, have been insulted by the invidious comparison between the conduct of the primitive and of the reformed Christians. Perhaps instead of censure, some applause may be due to the superior sense and spirit of our ancestors, who had convinced themselves that religion cannot abolish the unalienable rights of human nature. (II, 188)

Here, with insidious mock earnestness, Gibbon turns traditional Protestant historiography against itself; unlike the earliest Christians, the reformers were pioneers of liberty often in spite of their own and their historians' beliefs to the contrary.[57]

Renaissance

Reviewing the general state of the Latins at the end of the crusading era, Gibbon again remarks upon the innate and acquired developmental capabilities of European societies, and contrasts them with the stalled or declining societies of the East:

Their successive improvement and present superiority may be ascribed to a peculiar energy of character, to an active and imitative spirit, unknown to their more polished rivals, who at that time were in a stationary or retrograde state. (VI, 207)

In the remainder of the volume, we learn that the Reformation is one consequence of this active European spirit, and the revival of learning (or Renaissance) in the fourteenth to sixteenth centuries is another, although Gibbon does not link the two events as closely as Robertson does.[58] The business of revival is recounted in chapter 66 in a section subtitled 'Curiosity and Emulation of the Latins'. Numerous visits to the West by Greek emperors and their subjects, followed by the arrival of Greek refugees after the fall of Constantinople, give the Latins access to the 'golden key' to Greek classical philosophy, science and literature which Byzantium had been powerless to unlock (VI, 414). At first western scholars are hindered by an excess of 'classic enthusiasm', and their efforts take the form of *imitatio servilis*: 'However laudable, the spirit of imitation is of a servile cast' (VI, 432). Eventually, however, they learn to improve upon what they have extrapolated from Greek and Roman antiquity; emulation, in other words, succeeds imitation: 'the classics of Athens and Rome inspired a pure taste and a generous emulation; and in Italy, as afterwards in France and England, the pleasing reign of poetry and fiction was succeeded by the light of speculative and experimental philosophy' (VI, 433). Without the recollection and refashioning of the classical past, the energy of the societies conquered by the Germanic barbarians cannot be released. This, as one of the infrequent passages on the author's home country at the end of chapter 38 illustrates, poses peculiar problems for Britain which (except for Wales and Cornwall) had been so thoroughly Teutonised by the Angles and Saxons as to sever it completely from its Roman past: 'the limits of science as well as of empire, were contracted. The dark cloud which had been cleared by the Phoenician discoveries, and

[57] See Owen Chadwick, 'Gibbon and the Church Historians' in *Edward Gibbon and the Decline and Fall of the Roman Empire*, eds. Bowersock, Clive and Graubard.

[58] Robertson, *The History of . . . Charles V*, II, 287.

finally dispelled by the arms of Caesar, again settled on the shores of the Atlantic, and a Roman province was again lost among the fabulous Islands of the Ocean' (III, 625).[59] After this point, Britain disappears into the remote vistas of legend ('the haunt of seals, and orcs, and sea-mews clang', as Milton might have put it), and is rarely again mentioned in the text. We are left to presume that Britain will, in time, reappropriate from books and from the continent the classical heritage which it cannot draw out of the resources of its own customs.

Gibbon and Scottish thought

Like the *History of Charles V*, and, to some extent, *Le Siècle de Louis XIV*, *The Decline and Fall* incorporates a polemic against universal monarchy in Europe. To an imperial super-state on the Charles V or Louis XIV model, Gibbon prefers a collective and diverse European civilisation constantly reinforced and improved by the presence of a large number of state boundaries across which Europeans may admire or cajole. He combines the Scottish commendation of the extended European citizenship conferred, at the commercial stage, by national interplay and economic interdependence with an emphasis upon the civilising effects of raised cultural self-consciousness: 'In a civilized state, every faculty of man is expanded and exercised; and the great chain of mutual dependence connects and embraces the several members of society' (I, 224). Since the Reformation, 'the mind has understood the limits of its powers, and the words and shadows that might amuse the child can not longer satisfy his manly reason' (V, 539). This self-awareness entails an appreciation of the multiplicity in unity of those cultures which have reached the higher level of refinement, whereas 'uniform stability' of 'manners' is characteristic of homogeneous, primitive societies (II, 564). Modern self-consciousness, for Gibbon as for many Scottish writers, is the mind's response to its encounter with the greater plurality of objects placed before it by a mobile, trading society. Gibbon, however, transforms this Scottish idea of consciousness into one of imaginative capacity and limitation by implicitly linking it to his own visual range as a historian. Antonine Rome, unlike modern Europe is, as the historian can see, doomed from the moment when its peoples lose the desire to imagine time or change: 'This long peace, and the uniform government of the Romans, introduced a slow and secret poison into the vitals of the empire. The minds of men were gradually reduced to the same level, the fire of genius was extinguished, and even the military spirit evaporated' (I, 57).

[59] For a fine study of Gibbon's vistas and long views, see W. B. Carnochan, *Gibbon's Solitude: The Inward World of the Historian* (Stanford, 1987).

In his account of consciousness, as at many other points in *The Decline and Fall*, Gibbon's engagement with the Scottish history of civil society in Europe is at once deep and critical. Gibbon's pre-history of modern Europe is, in any case, narrated with a degree of sensitivity to the past quite beyond the emotional register of these Scottish texts, and, in general, Scottish social theory does not ultimately win out against Gibbon's reluctance to surrender the story of a unique Roman and European history to generalised stadial history. Nor does social theory supplant the need for a continuing assault upon the false dichotomies of the civic moralist understanding of history (ancients versus moderns, civic virtue versus luxury, vigorous barbarians versus effete Romans, the Roman Republic versus the Augustan monarchy, and so on). The courting and criticism of Scottish theory is most in evidence in the chapters which examine primitive societies. The first of these, chapter 9, on the state of the Germanic peoples before the time of Decius, revises Tacitus' account of their ambiguous virtues by making use of a methodology and vocabulary strongly reminiscent of Hume's *Essays* as well as of Buffon's work on the American Natives. The chapter is conducted as a case study of the nature of the 'infancy' of nations at a pre-agricultural, pre-civil stage (I, 220). Explanatory factors such as climate, technology religious beliefs, and the form of government are listed, but Gibbon's eye is really drawn to the narrow range of experience which limits the Germans' desires, encourages their oscillation between indolence and violence, and conditions their monotonous human homogeneity (I, 224–5). There are probably echoes here of Hume's essay, 'Of Refinement in the Arts', which associates the arts and industry with the process by which the 'mind acquires new vigour; enlarges its powers and faculties' and loses 'the relish of indolence'.[60] However, this theoretical, Humean mode of analysis does not stand alone, but is absorbed into a double polemic: the first part of which is to demonstrate that the Germanic peoples were too aimless and feeble to have been the sole cause of the destruction of the Roman Empire in the West; the second part is to attack the kind of vulgar Whig Gothic theory which used Tacitus, somewhat perversely, to create a myth of Britain's virtuous Germanic ancestors as the founders of a free ancient constitution.[61]

The second major examination of primitive societies occurs in chapter 26 in the section on the Hun, Tartar and Scythian pastoral nations. Gibbon had read Robertson's *History of America* by this stage, and had singled out for praise the fourth book on the state of the American

[60] Hume, 'Of Refinement in the Arts' (1754, under the title 'Of Luxury') in *Essays Moral, Political and Literary*, 270.

[61] See S. J. Kliger, *The Goths in England* (Cambridge, MA, 1952) and R. J. Smith, *The Gothic Bequest.*

Natives.[62] The section follows a broadly Robertsonian taxonomy, examining, in succession, physical environment and diet, followed by forms of government and economic activity, and the functional relation of all these factors to the general stage of society. Once again, however, the concerns of the moralist intrude, and Gibbon's inquiry also appears to be impelled by an anti-primitivist desire to prove that 'the pastoral manners, which have been adorned with the fairest attributes of peace and innocence, are much better adapted to the fierce and cruel habits of military life' (II, 564). Elsewhere, Gibbon's unwillingness to allow his story to be subsumed within a stadial theory of social development is indicated with a lighter touch. There is the mildly facetious expression of hope that New Zealand may one day reach a sufficient stage of refinement to produce a 'Hume of the Southern Hemisphere' (II, 531). There are a number of asides about Adam Smith's *Wealth of Nations*, including one near the end where Gibbon is describing the softening of the manners of the powerful Italian families in the late Middle Ages: 'This gradual change of manners and expence, is admirably explained by Dr. Adam Smith ... who proves, perhaps too severely, that the most salutary effects have flowed from the meanest and most selfish causes' (VI, 615, note 92). The word 'perhaps' encapsulates Gibbon's reluctant relationship with the Scottish theoretical enterprise. He cannot fully acknowledge a general trajectory of social development to be the outcome of undirected, multiple economic activity. He hesitates over the idea of a universal state of savagery:

> The discoveries of ancient and modern navigators, and the domestic history, or tradition, of the most enlightened nations, represent the *human savage*, naked in both mind and body, and destitute of laws, of arts, of ideas, and almost of a language. From this abject condition, perhaps the primitive and universal state of man, he has gradually arisen to command the animals, to fertilise the earth, to traverse the ocean, and to measure the heavens. (III, 638)

Once again, in the word 'perhaps', Gibbon communicates his unwillingness to universalise patterns of historical evolution, to abdicate entirely the historian's prerogative as moral arbitrator between good and bad nations, or to subordinate the immense histories of ancient and modern Europe to a larger, repeatable history of civil society. Some savages (the Africans he describes in chapter 25, for instance) are, in Gibbon's view, incapable of arising out of their destitute state; other peoples, like the fused Germanic and Romanised societies of post-imperial Europe, have a unique gift for self-improvement.

[62] Gibbon to Robertson (14 July 1777) in *The Letters of Edward Gibbon*, no. 389. See J. G. A. Pocock, 'Gibbon and the Shepherds: The Stages of Society in the *Decline and Fall*', *History of European Ideas*, 2 (1981), 193–202.

An unfinished history of Europe?

If Gibbon had written a history of Europe from the time of the Reformation after he had completed *The Decline and Fall* – an expanded version of his unfinished work on the House of Brunswick, for instance – he would have presented this process of self-improvement as a faltering, contingent and uncertain business.[63] That his French translator Guizot was also the author of an uninhibited national history of the providential progress of liberty and constitutional monarchy in France is an irony that would not have been lost on Gibbon. As it was, Gibbon concluded *The Decline and Fall* with a group of three chapters (69–71) on the fortunes of the city of Rome from the twelfth to the fifteenth centuries, stopping chronologically short of the revival of learning in the sixteenth century anticipated in chapter 66. The final chapter, entitled the 'Prospect of the Ruins of Rome in the Fifteenth Century', adopts the perspective of a fifteenth-century archaeological commentator Poggio Bracciolini to survey the remains of the imperial city before conjecturing, with unemotional thoroughness, the causes of its ruin.[64] The prospect takes place from the old Capitol, which at the time looked down towards the imperial fora before it was remodelled by Michaelangelo and turned to face the modern city. Gibbon imaginatively intercepts the Renaissance in order to deliver this final elegy to an unimproved Rome – a gesture he would later repeat when he recollected in his memoirs sitting 'amidst the ruins of the Capitol while the barefooted fryars were singing Vespers in the temple of Jupiter', even though, as many critics have noted, the Capitol was no longer ruined at this time.[65] Gibbon's enumeration of the reasons for the city's architectural decay is both rigorous and inconclusive, an exercise more in the consolations of precision than in the diagnosis of causes.[66] Gibbon's sense of the causes of the decline of the Rome has become infinitely complicated by this point, and this chapter exposes the shallow picturesque behind the kind of philosophic perspective which might attempt to bring all of Roman history simultaneously under its gaze. Viewed from the perspective of a single spectator, the city does not finally give up its secrets or reveal the 'real or

[63] Gibbon's project for compiling the antiquities of the House of Brunswick (*c.* 1789–92) is reproduced in *English Essays*. See David Womersley, 'Gibbon's Unfinished History: The French Revolution and English Political Vocabularies', *Historical Journal*, 35 (1992), 63–89.

[64] I have given a fuller account of these last chapters in an essay entitled, 'Gibbon's Prospects: Rhetoric, Fame and the Closing Chapters of *The Decline and Fall*' to appear, along with much new work on Gibbon, in the proceedings of a bicentenary conference, ed. David Womersley (Oxford; The Voltaire Foundation, forthcoming).

[65] *Autobiographies*, 302. For example, Patricia B. Craddock, 'Edward Gibbon and the "Ruins of the Capitol"' in Annabel Patterson ed., *Roman Images* (Baltimore, 1984).

[66] The phrase 'consolations of precision' is W. B. Carnochan's in an essay entitled 'Gibbon's Feelings' for the volume cited in note 64.

imaginary connection' between the triumph of barbarism and religion and the ruin of ancient Rome (VI, 626).

Beside Gibbon's own unobtrusive voice, modern Europeans appear in the closing chapter in the guise of grand tourists on pilgrimage to the shrine of the Roman Empire:

> The map, the description, the monuments of ancient Rome, have been elucidated by the diligence of the antiquarian and the student; and the footsteps of heroes, the relics, not of superstition, but of empire, are devoutly visited by a new race of pilgrims from the remote, and once savage, countries of the North. (VI, 645)

These pilgrims, reassured by their affecting rite of homage to an empire more heroic, and, therefore, less durable, than their own, belong to the 'safer and more enlightened age' promised by Gibbon a few pages before. To the readers of this enlightened age, Gibbon's history might have seemed, at its close, to beckon towards Robertson's *History of Charles V* as its logical sequel: Gibbon takes his leave of a moribund papal Rome soon to be shaken to its foundations by the religious and military upheavals described by Robertson. Yet the early modernity which Robertson announces is, by the inward turn of these final chapters back to the ailing city of Rome, quietly postponed. Like Hume at end of the *History of England*, Gibbon does not project from the past the inevitability of the present inhabited by his readers. Like Hume also, he does not promise his readers that the world of modern commerce will deliver them from every evil. In the last page, Gibbon's viewpoint is gently disengaged from that of the over eager, mildly ridiculous 'pilgrims' who 'devoutly' revisit the theatre of Roman history. It is they who, by an ironic inversion of perspective, step out of the 'remote', and once again unfamiliar 'countries of the North'. Not for the first time, Gibbon's persona ironises the modernity in which it is secured, and conveys a sense of loss not readily assimilated to the confidences of Enlightenment history.

7

David Ramsay's sceptical history of the American Revolution

All the histories so far discussed seek, in various ways, to project a cosmopolitan cultural awareness as a corrective to the political and religious habits of thought of their local readerships. This awareness often extends to the imperial edges of the eighteenth-century world, although, so far, only Robertson can be said to have given detailed consideration to synchronicities and disjunctures between European and colonial patterns of history. In the unpublished portion of his *History of America*, Robertson started to explore the ways in which British North American history, viewed as a process of steady anglicisation, might be assimilated to a historiographical model of European convergence and development. Although this particular work remained in manuscript until well after the American Revolutionary War, Robertson's project – the application of a narrative of European distinctiveness and civilisation to its colonial settlements – was echoed in a number of North American colonial histories as well as some early national historical writings in America. This chapter investigates the viability of Enlightenment forms of historical narrative for American writers addressing the colonial and revolutionary experience in their country. It focuses upon one of the first American historians of the American Revolution, David Ramsay, a Pennsylvanian writer of Scottish ancestry, although it also has something general to say about later eighteenth-century American historical writing.[1] Ramsay was one of the few post-Revolutionary historians who tried to fit American history into the moulds made by Robertson, Hume and Voltaire. An American patriot, Ramsay nevertheless mistrusted his own subject-matter, and a form of Humean sceptical cosmopolitanism is generated in his work by his anxieties

[1] David Ramsay, *The History of the American Revolution*, ed. Lester H. Cohen (2 vols.; Indianapolis, 1990). This reproduces the first and only edition of Ramsay's text and will be cited throughout. Although secondary material is in short supply, a full intellectual biography has recently added considerably to our knowledge of Ramsay: Arthur Shaffer, *To be an American: David Ramsay and the Making of the American Consciousness* (Columbia, SC, 1992). Shaffer's reading of *The History of the American Revolution*, however, differs considerably from my own. For Ramsay's letters and some of his shorter writings, see Robert L. Brunhouse, 'David Ramsay, 1749–1815: Selections from his Writings', *Transactions of the American Philosophical Society*, 55 (1965), part 4 (hereafter cited as *Selections*, with letters cited by number and other writings cited by page).

about the cultural differences between America and Europe. He was not a writer of the first rank, and is, despite the great topical interest of his work, somewhat out of place in company such as Hume's. For this reason, the awkwardness of American Enlightenment history, best exemplified by Ramsay, is one underlying theme of this chapter.

American cultural contexts

Any argument about the impact of European Enlightenment history in America, and, in particular, any claim that an American Enlightenment historian such as Ramsay was unusual for his time, must inevitably engage with modern debates about the nature and tone of intellectual life in eighteenth-century America. Many recent studies of the fate of European ideas in late eighteenth-century America have emphasised the increasing intellectual convergence between the two continents.[2] In this scheme, the appearance of a Humean historian in America, even after the Revolution, would seem, at first sight, to confirm the persistence there of ingrained, old world habits of historical thought. In practice, however, most of the early histories of the Revolution draw upon the resources of a distinctively American dissenting historical tradition; a sectarian Protestant idiom (of the kind popularised in America by Catharine Macaulay) everywhere underwrites an exceptionalist national history of liberty.[3] Moreover, the evidence for the genuinely wide currency of Enlightenment histories in colonial and early national American literary society is difficult to decipher. On the one hand, Americans of this period were, without doubt, avid readers of histories. The works of Voltaire, Hume, Robertson and Gibbon are everywhere present in American public and private libraries, and in booksellers' catalogues. Frequent attempts were made by American printers to issue cheap, local editions of these works, although finely bound European editions remained desirable prestige objects for any American gentleman's library shelf.[4] On the other hand, many studies of colonial and

[2] Henry Steel Commager, *The Empire of Reason: How Europe Imagined and America Realized the Enlightenment* (New York, 1977); Henry F. May, *The Enlightenment in America* (New York, 1976); J. R. Pole,'The American Enlightenment' in *The Enlightenment in National Context*, eds. Roy Porter and Mikulas Teich (Cambridge, 1981); most recently Robert A. Ferguson's helpful essay on 'The American Enlightenment, 1750–1820' in *The Cambridge History of American Literature, Volume I, 1590–1820*, ed. Sacvan Bercovitch (Cambridge, 1994). Jack P. Greene's 'America and the Enlightenment' in *Imperatives, Behaviors and Identities: Essays in Early American Cultural History* (Charlottesville, VA, 1992) suggests a new interpretive framework.

[3] On the nature and political agency of this tradition on both sides of the Atlantic, see J. C. D. Clark, *The Language of Liberty, 1660–1832: Political Discourse and Social Dynamics in the Anglo-American World* (Cambridge, 1994). For a very different portrait of America in culturally exceptionalist terms, see Jack P. Greene, *The Intellectual Construction of America: Exceptionalism and Identity from 1492 to 1800* (Chapel Hill, NC, 1993).

[4] On the presence of Enlightenment histories in eighteenth-century America, see Mary H. Barr,

early national American literary culture reveal a people little susceptible to the cosmopolitan and sceptical tones of the newer European publications. The most comprehensive study of intellectual exchange between America and Europe, Henry May's *The Enlightenment in America*, has noted the relatively low purchase obtained by what he calls the 'Skeptical Enlightenment' (including writers such as Voltaire, Hume and Gibbon) upon educated Americans, even before the French Revolution rendered such authors utterly repugnant to them. The enduring and warm receptivity of America to productions from Scotland was based upon the shared status of the two countries as provinces of the English metropolis, and Robertson remained for many years a popular and esteemed author on both sides of the Atlantic.[5] In addition, more radical Americans already had available to them a European history of America of a rather different cast, Raynal's *Histoire philosophique et politique des établissements et du commerce des Européens dans les deux Indes* (1770, 1774, 1780). This work imaginatively embraced the peoples of Europe and the colonies in a cosmopolitanism of a universal (rather than a cultural) kind; united in brotherhood, the oppressed of the world (including, in later editions, the rebelling American colonists) were urged to shake off their shackles and take control of their own political destinies.

Most studies of eighteenth-century American culture have emphasised the growing importance of the repertoire of British 'commonwealth' literature (the updated and moralised forms of republican writing generated by the opposition to Walpole or to the ministries of George III), as well as the continuing potency of the Puritan apologetics, conversion narratives and sermons which had structured American thought since the seventeenth century. The Enlightenment histories examined so far in this study all emphasise the necessity for modern societies to subjugate at least some aspects of traditional church power to civil authority. This emphasis is generally taken in surveys of the period to represent a defining characteristic of the European Enlightenments. The occasionally anticlerical tone of Voltaire's histories, which at times masks similarities between his works and those of his British counterparts, is his response to

Voltaire in America, 1744–1800 (Baltimore, 1941); H. Trevor Colbourn, *The Lamp of Experience: Whig History and the Intellectual Origins of the American Revolution* (Chapel Hill, 1965), appendix 'History in Eighteenth-Century American Libraries', 197–232; Giles Barber, 'Books from the Old World and for the New: The British International Trade in Books in the Eighteenth Century', *SVEC*, 151 (1976), 185–224; Edwin Wolf II, *The Book Culture of a Colonial American City: Philadelphia Books, Bookmen and Booksellers* (Oxford, 1988), chapter 3. The Philadelphia bookseller Robert Bell was a notable purveyor and reprinter of Enlightenment histories, including Robertson's *History of Charles V* and Hume's *History of England.* His numerous catalogues and pamphlet proposals for new books are housed in the Library Company of Philadelphia.

5 Andrew Hook, *Scotland and America: A Study of Cultural Relations* (Glasgow and London, 1975). Pages 78–90 give details of the interest in Scottish historical works in America.

the perceived failure of the French state to follow the British example, and bring religious institutions under greater state control. In a far less strident manner, Robertson's histories are also concerned with the proper relationship between the sacred and secular powers in civil society. In this key respect, American institutional history was bound to differ. The 'American Enlightenment', which is to say the intellectual changes which preceded or resulted from the Revolution, brought about no serious conflict between churches and states, and none is recorded, for example, in Ramsay's history. Observance of Protestant worship remained steady, and, if anything, continued to intensify in North America throughout the eighteenth century.[6] Behind the consciousness of most American writers of the exceptional nature of their history lay a Protestant sense of their nation's special piety and destiny, and a moralised, 'commonwealth' understanding of politics. A cosmopolitan history of European political and cultural evolution was not, therefore, a particularly suitable paradigm for American historians eager to provide their readers with an enabling myth of national unity and uniqueness.

Ramsay's *History of the American Revolution* (1789) was almost the first and very probably the best of the many histories of the American Revolution and Federal Constitution published in the immediate aftermath of those events. As a conservative work, unusually sceptical in tone and cool in its assessment of the viability of the newly constituted American state, it has generally been passed over by studies of the cultural work performed by American literature during the early national period. The publication of a recent edition of the *History*, as well as the first critical biography of Ramsay, have rendered him once again accessible, and a reinsertion of his work (albeit as a complicating factor) into the canons of eighteenth-century historical writing can now more easily be attempted. Ramsay was directly involved in the political events of the 1780s, and his *History of the American Revolution* mirrors in narrative form the quest, at that time, of the nation's leaders for a descriptive vocabulary adequate to their invention of new American politics. For this reason, Ramsay, once a neglected figure, has excited some interest in recent years in the context of debates about the nature of American politics in the early republic. His *History of the American Revolution* has been seen as standing at the intersection of two conflicting views of politics in the 1780s: traditional classical republicanism, which enjoins the values of active, patriotic citizenship, frugality and self-sacrifice; and the newer liberalism, which finds a role for government in the enforcement of natural rights, but otherwise stipulates that individuals should be free to pursue happiness and generate their own harmonious

[6] See Patricia U. Bonomi, *Under the Cope of Heaven: Religion, Society and Politics in Colonial America* (Oxford, 1986).

society through the acquisition of property. Opinion is further divided among modern historians as to whether either political philosophy can be said schematically to characterise proponents or opponents of the Federal Constitution drawn up in 1787, or, subsequently, the Federalist party administration of the 1790s and the Democratic–Republican opposition which eventually replaced it.[7]

In so far as Ramsay can be co-opted into this modern debate, he might be said to evince a liberalism of analysis but not of creed; he was worried that the existence of uninhibited acquisitive individualism in America would not necessarily guarantee a harmonious social order. He welcomed the fact that Americans enjoyed greater political freedom than Europeans, but feared that, like the seventeenth- and eighteenth-century Englishmen of Hume's *History of England*, his own people might demand a degree of liberty inconsistent with public safety. Whatever its place in the development of early American liberalism, Ramsay's *History* supplies twentieth-century critics with a significant early reading of the Federal Constitution, alongside Hamilton, Madison and Jay's *Federalist Papers*. Ramsay's *History* and his other writings show him to have been a Federalist during the late 1780s, and subsequently a Federalist party supporter. His vision of a commercially developed, internationally respectable America after independence paradoxically precluded a full recognition of his country's potential for westward, agricultural expansion in ways which would differ from the usual patterns of recent European history. His cautious sensibility, and his lack of confidence in a unique path for future American history enhanced his susceptibility to the influence of French and British styles of history. Ramsay's engagement with models of history not native or congenial to colonial and post-colonial American literary traditions raises larger questions about the relationship between the American, British and French Enlightenments. His concern to enhance America's cultural status after independence precipitates a revealing encounter between American and European forms of self- and national presentation.

Literary critics have generally agreed that American literary works written in the immediate aftermath of the Revolutionary War and ratification of the Federal Constitution were engaged in a secondary process of nation building. The epic and prospect poems, the novels and literary

[7] On 'commonwealth' ideas in America, see note 28 below. On liberal political thought after the Revolution, see Louis Hartz, *The Liberal Tradition in America: An Interpretation of Political Thought since the Revolution* (New York, 1955); Joyce Appleby, *Capitalism and a New Social Order: The Republican Vision of the 1790s* (New York, 1984) and her *Liberalism and Republicanism in the Historical Imagination* (Cambridge, MA, 1992); John Patrick Diggins, *The Lost Soul of American Politics: Virtue, Self-Interest and the Foundations of Liberalism* (New York, 1984); James T. Kloppenberg, 'The Virtues of Liberalism: Christianity, Republicanism and Ethics in Early American Historical Discourse', *Journal of American History*, 74 (1987), 9–33; Isaac Kramnick, *Republicanism and Bourgeois Radicalism: Political Ideology in Late Eighteenth-Century England and America* (Ithaca, NY, 1990).

letters of the period are seen as participating in a collective effort to generate new modes of self- and social representation as a literary correlative to the expanded political representation ushered in by the states' and federal constitutions.[8] In this interpretative matrix, contrasts are frequently drawn between the American writers' quest for national identity, and their besetting fears that post-colonial America may be fractured by social and regional diversity, and morally compromised by slavery and the continuing expropriation of native lands. Considered within this matrix, histories of the Revolution and its aftermath can be seen as an integral part of this narrative formation of America. Critics of the literature of the early republic have explored its dependence upon styles and genres of European importation, noting the often awkward fusion between distinctively American cultural priorities and formal literary appropriations of neoclassical poetics, pre-Romantic Miltonics and the Richardsonian novel. Studies of the histories written in this period have similarly emphasised their roots in European philosophical or Enlightenment history, as much as in domestic colony histories and New England providential narratives.[9] The explanatory framework in both cases is one of European components and Americanised end results. However, I shall argue that Ramsay's *History of the American Revolution* poses a challenge to this American exceptionalist literary framework by presenting itself as a part of a cosmopolitan European historical tradition – a choice of literary position which correlates with Ramsay's belief that the United States of America have no future historical destiny over and above the norms of European political and cultural patterns of development.

Ramsay's *History of the American Revolution* begins with an overview of the original settlement of the colonies, proceeds to a full account of the events leading up to and including the Revolutionary War, gives an extended analysis of the later 1780s, and ends, in 1789, with the inauguration of Washington as president. Like all the early histories of the Revolutionary

[8] For example, Mark R. Patterson, *Authority, Autonomy and Representation in American Literature, 1776–1865* (Princeton, 1985); Thomas Gustafson, *Representative Words: Literature, Politics and the American Language* (Cambridge, 1990); Larzer Ziff, *Writing in the New Nation: Prose, Print and Politics in the Early United States* (New Haven, 1991). However, a significant alteration in this literary paradigm, in which the medium of print rather than the content of printed texts is seen as the primary carrier of incipient nationalist meaning, has been made in Michael Warner's *The Letters of the Republic: Publication and the Public Sphere in Eighteenth-Century America* (Cambridge, MA, 1990)

[9] Arthur H. Shaffer, *The Politics of History: Writing the History of the American Revolution* (Chicago, 1975); Lester H. Cohen, *The Revolutionary Histories: Contemporary Narratives of the American Revolution* (Ithaca, NY, 1980); Michael Kraus and David D. Joyce, *The Writing of American History* (revised edn, Norman, Oklahoma, 1985). For studies of colonial American historical writing, see Richard S. Dunn, 'Seventeenth-Century English Historians of America' in *Seventeenth-Century America: Essays in Colonial History*, ed. James H. Smith (Chapel Hill, NC, 1959); Lawrence H. Leder ed., *The Colonial Legacy* (2 vols.; New York, 1971); George Athan Billias and Alden T. Vaughan eds., *Perspectives on Early American History in Honor of Richard B. Morris* (New York, 1973).

War, it plays down the extent and significance of loyalism among colonial British Americans, but is otherwise the least celebratory of the first patriot histories of the Revolution. It is informed by an identifiably southern perspective, and places itself at an oblique angle to the sense of providential fulfilment or secular millennialism characteristic of other national narratives of this period. For Ramsay, the legitimate repudiation of British administration by the colonies did not, in itself, provide an adequate basis for American nationhood. The Revolution united the colonies in a common experience of war, but national disunity was one major outcome of its violence. The institutional resolution to this disunity would soon be, in Ramsay's account, the Federal Constitution; the generic resolution would be the incorporation of American history into the norms of European time by way of a narrative which owes more to British historians such as David Hume or William Robertson than to distinctively American historians such as the great New England writers Cotton Mather or William Bradford. Nevertheless, it is a history which lacks the courage of its sceptical, conservative convictions; as such, it represents not so much an alternative narrative of the Revolution as the delayed Americanisation of American history.

Ramsay's apprenticeship

David Ramsay (1749–1815) was born in the Pennsylvania backcountry to parents of Scottish descent. He graduated from the College of New Jersey (Princeton) in 1765, and then studied medicine at the College of Philadelphia where he met the physician, philosopher and philanthropist Benjamin Rush who became his mentor and friend. Having completed the greater part of a thesis on 'white diarrhoea', he moved down to Charleston, South Carolina in 1774 where he combined the roles of doctor, and active local politician and assemblyman. During the Revolutionary War, he became a member of the prestigious South Carolina Council, and after the fall of Charleston he was imprisoned by the British army for a time at St Augustine in Florida. After his release, he was elected, in 1782, as a delegate to the Continental Congress where he served periodically until 1786. He also made use of this time to examine congressional papers as part of his research for his *History*. He spoke briefly in favour of the Federal Constitution at the South Carolina state ratifying convention.[10] Ramsay liked to represent himself to his northern correspondents as an exile in a sultry southern climate, even though, very soon after his move down to Charleston, he began speaking of southerners in the first person plural.

[10] Jonathan Elliot ed., *The Debates in the Several State Conventions on the Adoption of the Federal Constitution* (4 vols.; Washington, DC, 1836), IV, 286.

However, his opposition to slavery, which had always qualified his position as a naturalised South Carolinian, probably did cost him the election he sought in 1788 to the new federal House of Representatives, and he was never again as prominent even in local politics. His career as a historian, however, continued unabated, and he produced a *Life of George Washington* in 1807, and an excellent *History of South Carolina* in 1809. His literary career as pamphleteer, historian and compiler was only finally interrupted by his murder by a deranged former patient in 1815, and his *History of the United States* was published shortly after his death.

Ramsay's surviving correspondence shows him to have had an extensive network of contacts among many of the prominent figures of his time, including Thomas Jefferson, John Adams, John Witherspoon his sometime father-in-law and president of Princeton, and numerous New England divines. His most successful bid for entry into the South Carolina elite was his marriage to Martha Laurens, daughter of the distinguished and wealthy patriot politician Henry Laurens. His *History of the American Revolution* also gained him wide credibility, if not revenue from sales. Unlike most other histories of the Revolution, this history conveys a sense of the regional diversity of contemporary America, as well as its social and financial instability. This originated in Ramsay's own experience as an ambitious, but financially insecure, and incompletely assimilated, southerner.

Ramsay's reading of American history was grounded to a significant degree in his experience of events and politics in South Carolina. His first historical production was a *History of the Revolution of South-Carolina* published in 1785.[11] His presentation, in the *History of the American Revolution*, of the colonial era as something of a golden age, is redolent of the exceptional stability of his adoptive state during the 1770s. His account of the horrors of the Revolutionary War and its depraving effect upon American citizens is also influenced by South Carolina's exceptionally bitter war experience (the up-country western areas of the state witnessed especially savage internecine conflict between Whigs, Loyalists, the British and their Cherokee allies). His representations of America as fissured between the seaboard and the West, and his descriptions of the savagery of the backcountry, have their origins in the metropolitan sensibility of South Carolina's low-country rice planter, merchant and professional elites of which Ramsay was a part.[12] This sensibility was especially characteristic of

[11] David Ramsay, *The History of the Revolution of South-Carolina, from a British Province to an Independent State* (2 vols.; Trenton, NJ, 1785).

[12] On these aspects of the South, see especially Robert M. Weir, *'The Last of American Freemen': Studies in the Political Culture of the Colonial and Revolutionary South* (Macon, Georgia, 1986). Other important studies of South Carolina include George C. Rogers, *Charleston in the Age of the Pinckneys* (Norman, Oklahoma, 1969); Jerome J. Nadelhaft, *The Disorders of War: The Revolution in South Carolina* (Orono, Maine, 1981); Michael O'Brien and David Moltke-Hansen eds., *Intellectual Life in Antebellum Charleston* (Knoxville, Tennessee, 1986); Rachel M. Klein, *Unification*

Charleston, a city which more readily identified itself with Boston, Philadelphia, Paris and Edinburgh, than with the relatively underdeveloped rural parishes further inland. Ramsay interpreted the revolutionary republicanism of many of the southern planters as the nationalist result of a very specific local culture centred upon their conception of freedom as a form of rank and privilege. He had also inherited the South Carolinian individualistic interpretation of republicanism, and he liked to emphasise the roots of American political culture in 'personal independence' within 'communities of separate individuals'.[13]

During this early stage of his career, however, Ramsay had no interest in placing his talents as a historian at the service of an embryonic southern sectional identity, and he was profoundly worried by its emergence in the later years of his life. His historical writing in any case antedates the sectionalist forms of southern consciousness which were to begin to characterise the region during the early decades of the nineteenth century. After the Revolutionary War, Ramsay joined the race between American writers to publish the first properly national history of the Revolution. In the event, he came in a disappointing second to an eccentric and less than talented New England minister, William Gordon.[14] Gordon's *History of the Rise of ... the United States of America*, which carried the story as far as 1783, came out in 1788, boasted an illustrious list of subscribers (including Thomas Jefferson and Catharine Macaulay), and had the advantage of access to the private papers of Washington and the former governor of Massachusetts, Thomas Hutchinson. Despite all the publicity, Gordon turned out to be as lack-lustre a writer as he was a presumptuous and ridiculous correspondent, and his poorly crafted compilation in epistolary form falls far short of Ramsay's achievement.[15] Ramsay exchanged some factual information with Gordon, but gained far more from his own researches among the archives of the Continental Congress and other state papers, as well as the questionnaires which he sent out to correspondents such as Benjamin Rush.[16] Having lost the race, Ramsay then delayed

of a Slave State: The Rise of the Planter Class in the South Carolina Backcountry, 1760–1808 (Chapel Hill, 1990); David R. Chestnutt and Clyde N. Wilson eds., *The Meaning of South Carolina History* (Columbia, SC, 1991).

13 Ramsay, *The History of the Revolution of South-Carolina*, I, 7; I, 9.

14 William Gordon, *The History of the Rise, Progress and Establishment of the Independence of the United States of America: including an Account of the Late War and of the Thirteen Colonies, from their Origin to that Period* (4 vols.; London, 1788); Robert L. Brunhouse, 'David Ramsay's Publication Problems, 1784–1808', *Papers of the Bibliographic Society of America*, 39 (1945), 51–67.

15 Some of Gordon's letters are reprinted in *The Proceedings of the Massachusetts Historical Society*, 63 (1931). Other unpublished letters can be found in the Houghton Library, Harvard University and the Historical Society of Pennsylvania (in the *Hazard Family Papers*, the *Society Collection, English Clergyman* and the *Dreer Collection*).

16 Ramsay to Gordon (23 June 1784), *Selections*, no. 56. Ramsay to Rush (13 April 1786), *Selections*, no. 103.

publication of his *History of the American Revolution* until he was able to add on a passage about the inauguration of the new federal government in order to provide a relatively happy ending to his story of the American quest for a unified identity after the Declaration of Independence in 1776.

Historical traditions

The most notable feature of Ramsay's *History* is the way in which his analysis of the development of an independent American identity is rhetorically constituted outside the available idioms of American political discourse. The work shows little inclination to adapt traditional American republican and providential vocabularies to a grammar of unifying nationalism. *The History of the American Revolution* conveys a dynamic, linear and occasionally fractured sense of time which probably derives from the British historical works that made up part of Ramsay's reading. He certainly knew the works of Hume and Robertson, may well have read Gibbon, and had ready access through the local library of which he was a member to Voltaire's major historical works.[17] This kind of philosophical narrative history had long been familiar to American readers and historians, who nevertheless retained deep memories of the historical mentality which the first Puritan settlers carried with them to Plymouth and Massachusetts Bay. The settler sense of time was of a drama of sin against virtue endlessly re-enacted until it might one day be resolved into the stasis of perfection. The New England settlements were created as a static 'city upon a hill', as John Winthrop famously explained to the men and women about to land at Massachusetts Bay, which would enter the historical world of narrative only if its inhabitants deviated from righteousness: 'if wee shall deale falsely with our god in this worke wee have undertaken, and soe cause him to withdrawe his present help from us, wee shall be made a story and a by-word through the world'.[18] As decades went by, New England

[17] Ramsay wrote to Rush in 1786 saying that he had taken his advice to read Hume's *History of England* (*Selections*, no. 106). This is surprising, because, while in Edinburgh in the 1760s, Rush had moved in evangelical circles and had been suspicious both of Hume, whom he regarded as impious, and of Robertson, whom he described as a 'haughty prelate'. See David Freeman Hawke, *Benjamin Rush: Revolutionary Gadfly* (Indianapolis, 1971).

Ramsay was a member of the Charleston Library Society which contained an extensive selection of European historical works. See *A Catalogue of Books Belonging to the Charlestown Library Society* (Charleston, SC, 1770–2) which lists works by Voltaire, including the *Essai* and *Le Siècle de Louis XIV.* Ramsay was sufficiently committed to the institution to become its vice-president in the 1790s, and to order books from London for the collection; see, for example, Ramsay to John Stockdale (29 July 1791), *Charleston Library Society MS Letterbook*, Charleston Library Society, Charleston, SC. See also Shaffer, *To be an American*, 133–9. Ramsay certainly read William Robertson's *History of America* (1777) which he paraphrased in a letter to Thomas Jefferson (*Selections*, no. 106), and very probably read Robertson's *History of the Reign of the Emperor Charles V* (1769), the subject of which he mentions in *The History of the American Revolution*, I, 112.

[18] G. W. Robinson *et al.* eds., *Winthrop Papers* (5 vols.; Boston, 1929–47), II, 295.

Puritan narratives of events in America incorporated into this grand model of extra-temporal providential fulfilment the idea of the agency of individuals as secondary or 'efficient' causes in history. There is, for example, a pronounced sense of the moral agency of the first New England settlers in Cotton Mather's epic narrative of the history and moral decline of his New England people, the *Magnalia Christi Americana* (1702). This would have been alien to William Bradford's more humbly providential history *Of Plymouth Plantation* (written 1630–50) only half a century before.[19]

Adaptations of the Puritan-providential tradition continued throughout the eighteenth century, often in conjunction with new sociological methodologies of contemporary Scottish history. The most accomplished New England historical productions by Ramsay's contemporaries were Jeremy Belknap's *History of New Hampshire* (1784–92), and Mercy Otis Warren's *History of the ... American Revolution* (completed around 1791 and published in 1805).[20] These histories dramatised human activity within a well defined providential arena. They laid the foundations for a full-blown, seamless nineteenth-century American narrative of Puritan settlement, Revolution and constitution-making in which the disruptive and unexpected nature of American history would be shaded out by the idea of the national destiny of the settlers and their descendants.[21] Ramsay's *History of the American Revolution* is relieved, though not structured, by occasional references to the guiding hand of Providence. He refers to 'the special agency of providence', and even remarks that 'the Governor of the Universe' by 'a secret influence on their minds, disposed [the colonists] to union' (I, 112, 134). There is no reason to suppose that such references, issuing from the pen of a committed Congregationalist, have no literal referent.[22] Like Robertson's providence, Ramsay's theological framework is overlaid with other kinds of causal explanation, but persists as a kind of ironic commentary on human intentionality. Like Robertson also, Ramsay develops a tolerant, ecumenical religious idiom which circumvents the anti-episcopalian and anti-

[19] On Puritan historical writing, see note 9 above, and also Peter Gay, *A Loss of Mastery: Puritan Historians in Colonial America* (Berkeley, 1966); Anthony Kemp, *The Estrangement of the Past: A Study in the Origins of Modern Historical Consciousness* (Oxford, 1991).

[20] Mercy Otis Warren, *History of the Rise, Progress and Termination of the American Revolution*, ed. Lester H. Cohen (2 vols.; Indianapolis, 1988); Jeremy Belknap, *History of New Hampshire* (3 vols.; London, 1784–92).

[21] On nineteenth-century historical writing in America, see David Levin, *History as Romantic Art: Bancroft, Prescott, Motley and Parkman* (Stanford, 1959); Lawrence Buell, *New England Literary Culture: From Revolution through Renaissance* (Cambridge, 1986); John P. McWilliams, *The American Epic: Transforming a Genre, 1770–1860* (Cambridge, 1989).

[22] Lester Cohen provides a different account in *The Revolutionary Histories* chapter 1, of the reduction of the idea of providence to metaphorical status in this period. However, Nathan O. Hatch has argued that the conception of providence as the agency of a secular millennium was, in fact, revived during the revolutionary era: *The Sacred Cause of Liberty: Republican Thought and the Millennium in Revolutionary New England* (New Haven, 1977).

Catholic polemics of many of his contemporary historians. At the narrative level, Ramsay's *History* is organised around the idea of discontinuity; the American colonists are propelled into a disorientating and not readily interpreted modernity by a mixture of chance and geographical (but not moral) inevitability.

American Protestant thinking in the seventeenth century embraced the notion that God occasionally makes certain chosen peoples instrumental to his purpose, and that the New England Congregationalists were one such people. This had acquired wider currency in the eighteenth-century colonies in the modified formulation that the Protestant province had a special place as the exemplar and bearer of Christian virtues uncontaminated by the British metropolis.[23] Ramsay's *History*, however, projects a cosmopolitan vision of America earning her right to membership in the international republic of civilised states through the acquisition of credible, centralised government and sound finance. He anticipates, not the universalisation of America, but the subjugation of America's peculiarities to international norms. During the early stages of the Revolution, Ramsay had proclaimed America, in a pro-Independence oration, as the universal type for future societies: 'the cause of America is the cause of Human Nature . . . the American editions of the human mind will be more perfect than any that have yet appeared'.[24] This self-consciously echoes Tom Paine's radical vision of America, as it was set out in the most influential of all the anti-British pamphlets of the American Revolution, *Common Sense* (1776). By the late 1780s, however, Ramsay's suspicion that the states had relapsed into faction and self-interest had cured him of such moral utopianism. The idea of America as a universal possibility for mankind persisted as a radical political vision in the early republic, if not in Ramsay's thinking. It was the 1780 edition of the Raynal/Diderot *Histoire philosophique des deux Indes*, with its added section on events in North America since 1763, which first celebrated American political ideals as promises made to all mankind. Later, the Painite New England writer Joel Barlow gave the first sustained literary treatment to the idea of a universalised America prefiguring a secular millennium. His Miltonic epic *The Columbiad* (1807), and the less grandiose *Vision of Columbus* (1787) which preceded it, prophesy the moral transcendence of North American history beyond the European and American particularities which initially shaped its course. Taking his cue from Mather's Virgilian enunciation of the universalised symbolic resonance of American history, Barlow figures epic as the genre within which American history is to be rendered intelligible. Ramsay's history, by contrast, implicitly avoids the epic universalisation of

23 See especially Susan Manning, *The Puritan-Provincial Vision: Scottish and American Literature in the Nineteenth Century* (Cambridge, 1990).

24 Ramsay, 'An Oration on the Advantages of Independence' (1778) in *Selections*, 188–9.

America which was to characterise the nineteenth-century American historical works by such writers as Francis Parkman, John Motley and William Prescott. The closing passage of the *History of America* (which Ramsay in fact asked Rush to write for him) are hortatory rather than anticipatory, and envisage only a partial resolution to a history without epic possibilities.[25]

The seventeenth-century New England historical tradition available to Ramsay had, then, been mediated in the eighteenth century through epic poetry, through (slightly more) secularised historical narratives, and through the political idiom of the republican tradition. Recent New England colonial historians such Thomas Prince, William Douglass and Thomas Hutchinson both exemplified and accelerated the great receptivity of the colonies to European histories of a more secular and rationalist type.[26] Despite their concern with the growth of constitutional and legal structures in British North America, most of these colonial histories lacked a sophisticated grasp of historical issues and method. They were generally more concerned to document the extension of the British experience in America than to describe a uniquely American experience. However, there were some historical writers and thinkers who had concerned themselves with distinctively American historiographical problems, most notably the nature and plight of the Native Americans. Cadwallader Colden's fascinating history of the Iroquois in the 1720s, and Jeremy Belknap's 1784 article, 'Has the discovery of America been useful or hurtful to mankind?', for example, belong to this strand of historical interest in exclusively American concerns.[27]

In America, the eighteenth century also witnessed a long and fruitful marriage between the language of Puritanism and modified republican (or 'commonwealth') forms of political articulation. The imported literature of the British 'country' or 'commonwealth' tradition (including Trenchard and Gordon's *Cato's Letters*, Catharine Macaulay's *History of England*, Bolingbroke's *The Craftsman*, and the works of Molesworth, Burgh and others), with its emphasis upon the imperative need to reinvigorate and

[25] The Library Company of Philadelphia holds a copy of *The History of the American Revolution* which belonged to Rush's son James, and contains a handwritten note that 'this closing address was written by Dr Benjamin Rush' on p. 354 of the second volume (corresponding to II, 665–7 of Cohen's edition). Brunhouse noted this, Cohen and Shaffer did not. Also see Rush to John Adams (12 February 1812) in L. H. Butterfield ed., *The Letters of Benjamin Rush* (2 vols.; Princeton, 1951), II, 1126, note 15.

[26] Thomas Prince, *The Chronological History of New-England in the Form of Annals* (Boston, 1736); William Douglass, *A Summary, Historical and Political, of the First Planting, Progressive Improvements, and Present State of the British Settlements in North-America* (2 vols.; Boston, 1749–50); Thomas Hutchinson, *The History of the Colony of Massachusetts Bay* (1764–1828), (3 vols.; New York, 1972). William Robertson reviewed Douglass' book (favourably) for the *Edinburgh Review*, ii (1755–6), article 11.

[27] Cadwallader Colden, *The History of the Five Indian Nations Depending on the Province of New-York* (1727); Jeremy Belknap in the *Boston Magazine*, 1 (1784), 281–5.

restore the British Constitution, gave political precision to Puritan ideas about generational decline and the recovery of primitive Christianity.[28] In the American pulpit and pamphlet literature of the mid- to late eighteenth century, these notions were redramatised as a threat of imminent social decay and a crisis in the history of liberty brought about by ministerial corruption in the metropolis. The Puritan quest for extra-temporal stasis overlapped with the republican desire for a stable *polis* immunised against historical decline by the active virtue of its citizens. By the time of the Revolution, clergymen were able to place Puritan-country eschatology at the service of the patriot cause.

Protestant American historical thinking of the revolutionary era characterised the past as a repository of instructive examples within a structure of endless repetition. John Adams' *A Defence of the Constitutions of Government of the United States of America* (1787) exemplifies this idea of repetition by presenting, not so much the history, as the phenomenology of republican governments; in order to vindicate the new states' constitutions after independence, Adams places them beside numerous examples of previous republican thought and practice in a timeless political pantheon. Ramsay's earliest historical production, *The History of the Revolution of South-Carolina* (1785) also articulates this sense of history as deviation from, and then repetition of, the perfect state of republican equilibrium. A narrative of events in the state from the Stamp Act to the cessation of hostilities in 1783, Ramsay's first history is organised around simple metaphorical cycles of light, dark and light again, farmers metamorphosed into soldiers and then into farmers once more. At the beginning of the story, the South Carolinians appear as an ideal republican community of independent yeomen: 'they were not led by powerful families, or by great officers in church or state. Luxury had made but very little progress among their contented unaspiring farmers'; at the end, they are on the point of returning to their former condition: 'nothing is now wanting but the smiles of Heaven, and their own good conduct, to make them a great and happy republick'.[29] Although this history provides a graphic account of the collapse of civil order in the state into internecine conflict, it is in no sense the story of the transformation of a region by war. Stasis is regained at the end when the independent yeomen of the state resume their southern pastoral.

[28] On this literature, see Caroline Robbins, *The Eighteenth-Century Commonwealthman: Studies in the Transmission, Development and Circumstance of English Liberal Thought from the Restoration of Charles II until the War with the Thirteen Colonies* (Cambridge, 1959); H. Trevor Colbourn, *The Lamp of Experience*; Bernard Bailyn, *The Ideological Origins of the American Revolution* (Cambridge, MA, 1967); J. G. A. Pocock, *The Machiavellian Moment: Florentine Political Thought and the Atlantic Republican Tradition* (Princeton, 1975).

[29] *The History of the Revolution of South-Carolina*, I, 11; II, 387.

Ramsay's *History of the Revolution of South-Carolina* partly exemplifies the Protestant-republican emphasis upon the moral immanence rather than the narrative order of history. Nevertheless, at no stage does he adopt a recognisably American 'country' account of the origins of the Revolutionary War in the corrupt, liberty-threatening behaviour of British ministers and colonial officials. In this respect, the histories of Warren and Belknap are more conventionally 'country' in their dramatisations of the conflict of liberty and corruption on a providential stage. In the case of Warren, an opponent of the Federal Constitution (or 'anti-federalist'), this conflict is said to have been continued and internalised in the post-war history of America in the disputes in the 1780s between Federalists and anti-federalists, and, in the 1790s, between the Federalist party and the Jeffersonians. In far more complex and subtle ways, Ramsay's *History of the Revolution of South-Carolina* and *The History of the American Revolution* deploy, criticise and finally undermine the country and providential narrative characterisation of American history as a simple contest between the colonial defenders of liberty and the British proponents of arbitrary power. The Revolutionary War, in Ramsay's account, temporarily creates, but then rapidly moves beyond, the political conditions under which disinterested self-sacrifice on behalf of liberty might be effective in the struggle for national liberation. Although the American actors in this struggle initially have the sense that they are taking part in a drama of disinterested liberty against arbitrary power, Ramsay's narrative of the war exposes the simplicity of such schemes of action.

The transformations of war

At the beginning of the war, in *The History of the American Revolution*, Ramsay declares himself impressed by the self-denying willingness of the colonists to join the militia, their readiness to make financial sacrifices, and, under the Articles of Confederation (which created a coalition of the separate states), to recognise and obey a central authority which had no real power to coerce. He concedes that all of the actions are evidence for the mobilising effects of virtuous patriotism: 'A noble strain of generosity and mutual support was generally excited. A great and powerful diffusion of public spirit took place' (I, 135). Even so, Ramsay accentuates the irrational origins of the colonists' republican activism: 'The eagerness for independence resulted more from feeling than reasoning' (I, 316). His favourite metaphor, to encapsulate simultaneously the republican ardour of the colonists and the presence of forces beyond their control, is fire (for example, I, 58; I, 111). From the moment he introduces images of fire, Ramsay begins to downplay the importance of the colonists' republican virtue as an agency in events. The experience of war proves the initial idealism of the colonists to be impracticable. The narrative is no longer ordered around the contest between American liberty and the British determination to enforce arbitrary parliamentary sovereignty. Instead, the colonists appear to act out of the exigencies of self-defence. By the time his narrative approaches the end of the war, Ramsay has extended his scepticism to the very idea that republican idealism might form a reliable basis for a new kind of nationality. Even the 'lovers of liberty and independence', Ramsay remarks, 'began ... to fear that they had built a visionary fabric of government, on the fallacious ideas of public virtue' (II, 653).

Similarly, the Continental Congress finds, in Ramsay's account, that it has erred in basing policy decisions upon assumptions about public self-sacrifice – as, for example, when a persistent crisis in financial confidence is precipitated by Congress' overreliance on the public trust required to underpin its excessive issuing of paper money (Appendix 2, 'Of Continental Paper Currency', II, 460). Ramsay regularly criticises Congress for engaging in abstract, speculative politics at the expense of responsible pragmatism, as, for instance, when its theoretical hostility to standing armies (a traditional shibboleth of republican politics) impedes the efficient functioning of the army under Washington's command: 'daily occupied in contemplating the rights of human nature, and investigating arguments on the principles of general liberty', America's leaders:

> trusted too much to the virtue of their countrymen, and were backward to enforce that subordination and order in their army, which, though it intrenches on civil liberty, produces effects in the military line unequalled by the effusions of patriotism, or the exertions of undisciplined valor. (I, 309)

Ramsay's *History of the American Revolution* is as much a sociology as a celebration of the actors in the patriot cause, and its American brand of revisionist whiggery owes a considerable debt to Hume's *History of England* (Ramsay closely echoes Hume's *History* on one occasion).[30] Like Hume's, Ramsay's history is a detached rumination upon the character of a society propelled by events into a modernity inexplicable within the framework of its own historiographical traditions. This also has affinities with Robertson's account of European turbulence during the Reformation, although, unlike Robertson, Ramsay does not suggest that major events can be accounted for in terms of collective intentionality. Despite the fact that Ramsay separates American federated modernity from the logic of its

[30] Compare Hume, *History of England*, II, 519: 'But there is a point of depression, as well as of exultation, from which human affairs naturally return in a contrary direction, and beyond which they seldom pass, either in their advancement or decline'; Ramsay, *History of the American Revolution*, I, 295: 'but there is in human affairs an ultimate point of elevation or depression, beyond which they neither grow better nor worse, but turn back in a contrary course'.

history, he suggests that the impulse to independence was, in part, the natural and unintended outcome of a geographically inspired colonial political culture:

> The distance of America from Great Britain generated ideas, in the minds of the colonists, favourable to liberty. Three thousand miles of ocean separated them from the Mother Country ... In large governments the circulation of power is enfeebled at the extremities. This results from the nature of things, and is the eternal law of extensive or detached empire ... The wide extent and nature of the country contributed to the same effect. The natural seat of freedom is among high mountains, and pathless deserts, such as abound in the wilds of America. (I, 28)

Ramsay's colonial Americans absorb naturally a distinctive and inherently separatist political culture long before they ever start to question their obligations to their mother country:

> They looked up to Heaven as the source of their rights, and claimed, not from the promises of Kings but, from the parent of the universe. The political creed of an American Colonist was short but substantial. He believed that God made all mankind originally equal. (I, 30)

The colonists, as it were, imbibe naturally Locke's second *Treatise of Government.*

During the eighteenth century, the idea of natural rights had entered into and started to reshape legal discourse in the colonies. British common-law rights were steadily reinterpreted by colonial writers as natural entitlements, for example, in John Adams' *Dissertation on the Canon and the Feudal Law* (1765), and James Wilson's *Considerations on the Nature and Extent of the Legislative Authority of the British Parliament* (1774).[31] Ramsay adopts this American idea that the privileges of British subjects were really natural rights, but he gives it a characteristically Humean twist by insisting that natural rights were always a matter of habit and feeling for Americans, not of metaphysical speculation. The Revolution is therefore presented as the transformation of a nation through experience, and the Declaration of Independence is mainly discussed in terms of its practical implications rather than, as so often since, as an event in the history of abstract ideas (I, 317–23). Ramsay's account of the series of crises, from the Stamp Act to

[31] 'Let it be known ... That many of our rights are inherent and essential, agreed on as maxims and establish'd as preliminaries, even before a parliament existed', *The Papers of John Adams*, eds. Robert J. Taylor *et al.* (Cambridge, MA, 1977–), I, 127; 'if we shall be reinstated in the enjoyment of those rights, to which we are entitled by the supreme and uncontrollable laws of nature, and the fundamental principles of the British constitution, we shall reap the glorious fruit of our labours', *The Works of James Wilson*, ed. Robert Green McCloskey (2 vols.; Cambridge, 1967), II, 722. On notions of natural rights in America, see John Dunn, 'The Politics of Locke in England and America in the Eighteenth Century' in John W. Yolton ed., *John Locke: Problems and Perspectives* (Cambridge, 1969); Isaac Kramnick, *Republicanism and Bourgeois Radicalism*; J. C. D. Clark, *The Language of Liberty*, 100–110.

Lexington and Concord, which lead to the Revolution has something of the flavour of Hume's account of the Civil War in the *History of England*. For, like Hume before him, Ramsay stages the clash, not of theoretical notions of virtue and arbitrary power, but of two types of sensibility locked into separate constructions of the world and incapable of reconciliation. The American colonists act out of the imperatives of their own environment and libertarian instincts. Similarly, the British, 'too highly impressed with ideas of their unlimited authority', are trapped by their own habits of imperial self-definition (I, 145). Once the war gets under way, Ramsay's Americans are further politicised and led to an understanding of their common identity by painful experience:

> What the warm recommendations of Congress, and the ardent supplications of general Washington could not effect, took place of its own accord, in consequence of the plunderings and devastations of the royal army. (I, 305)

Moreover, as a consequence of this emphasis upon experience, Ramsay's descriptions of the war take a new aesthetic turn when he abandons the usual neoclassical decorousness of history in favour of vivid and detailed catalogues of horrors: infants sucking at the breasts of their dead mothers, bones 'whitening in the sun', mangled limbs strewn over the battlefield, and soldiers' torn feet leaving blood tracks in the snow (II, 601). These more sensational moments signal Ramsay's stylistic departure from his European predecessors.

After the war: a liberal America?

Although Ramsay's Revolutionary War teaches the colonists practical lessons in common identity and interests, it proves to be, in the end, an event too violent and dislocating to engender a lasting basis for post-war American community. The national war effort paradoxically releases an individualist spirit of enterprise: 'the young, the ardent, the ambitious and the enterprising', Ramsay points out, 'were mostly whigs', and qualities of 'personal independence' were often the real spur to patriot exertion (II, 629). The social mobility, financial liquidity and instability, along with the creation of new forms of political participation necessitated by the Revolution simultaneously release and disrupt a society previously deferential, filial and hierarchical. In modern terminology, Ramsay might be said to be welcoming the birth of a liberal capitalist society out of the ruins of classical republican politics. However, particularly when Ramsay starts to discuss the debtor crises and increasingly decentralised politics of the early to mid-1780s, he takes issue with the 'liberal' idea of society based upon individual pursuits of self-interest and minimally regulated by government. Ramsay accepts that post-independence American society may be (what we would now call) liberal–capitalist in character, but he does not believe that its competing interests will be productive of a harmonious, pluralist social order, or that any kind of invisible hand will regulate the economy to service the needs of all members of the public. Like Hume, he fears that the commitment to liberty characteristic of Protestant societies may not be entirely compatible with stability and justice. Energetic and independent America is brought, in the 1780s, to the brink of social disintegration. The repudiation of public and private debts is one outward sign of a wider collapse in the moral economy: 'The non-payment of public debts, sometimes inferred a necessity, and always furnished an apology, for not discharging private contracts. Confidence between man and man received a deadly wound. ... From this failure of public justice, a deluge of evils overflowed' (II, 650–1).

Ramsay's reading of the 1780s as a period of crisis is, of course, a polemical federalist response to perceived increases in social mobility and excesses of democracy or even demagogy in the decentralised states' governments. The 1780s was a period of debtor crises, bad harvests and social disruption in South Carolina, as in most other states. Although the state's political leaders were able to contain popular dissatisfaction, often by means of debt relief legislation, Ramsay felt that the basis in trust of the continental economy was being undermined, and said so to the state Assembly.[32] He had told the Continental Congress that the assumption by central government of responsibility for the debts it had incurred during the Revolutionary War was nothing less than a matter of the strictest justice.[33] Ramsay felt that public and private justice could only be secured if it was also observed by central government: 'The failure of national justice, which was in some degree unavoidable, increased the difficulties of performing private engagements, and weakened that sensibility to the obligations of public and private honor, which is a security for the punctual performance of contracts' (II, 637). For Ramsay, the coincidence of the monetary and the moral economy can only be guaranteed by strong, exemplary government, since men are too depraved to generate, without assistance, a spontaneous social and moral order. Ramsay thus implicitly rejects the famous liberal distinction, made in Tom Paine's *Common Sense*, between civil society and government ('the former promotes our happiness positively by uniting our affections, the latter negatively by restraining our vices').[34] By the late 1780s, Ramsay was calling for a Federal Constitution

[32] Minutes of the South Carolina State Assembly in *The City Gazette and Daily Advertiser* (Charleston, SC) for 23 February 1788. See also Ramsay's remarks on money lenders and instalment laws in the same newspaper for 15 January 1788.

[33] *Journals of the Continental Congress*, ed. J. C. Fitzpatrick (34 vols.; Washington, DC, 1904–37), (27 January 1783), XXV, 869.

[34] Thomas Paine, *Common Sense* (1776), ed. Isaac Kramnick (Harmondsworth, 1976), 65.

to heal the breach in the moral economy of America. The new liberal individualist order had turned out to be kinesis without regulation, society without government.

Space and history

Paine's optimism about the happiness-enhancing civil sphere in America was grounded in the knowledge that the country had one unique property unavailable to Europeans: space. Independence, along with the earlier expulsion of the French from most of North America, put an end to the British limitations upon westward expansion. To the political theorist, the West represented a practical restraint upon the power of the government, since the citizen could always travel beyond its grasp. To the historian, the West would come to challenge traditional images of the nation state; it was disorientating to imagine a political and legal entity that could seep out at the edges. The new political situation of the confederated states after the war required an imaginative readjustment of ideas of nation and space which Ramsay, as we shall see, was ultimately unwilling to make. He envisioned instead a cosmopolitan, urbanised America of the eastern seaboard, with its cultural face turned towards Europe, and its back defensively to the West. Ramsay had no confidence in the self-regulating potential of a society steadily moving westwards, and no faith in the moral properties of space in America. In his writings, he characterises the western regions of the country as a savage wilderness, and dwells on the barbarity of the Native Americans (despite a sympathetic evaluation of their plight) as a symbol of the uncivilising effects of the untamed landscape (e.g. II, 471). He shows a Charlestonian patrician contempt for the backsettlers who, in his view, tend to regress to the evolutionary state of the native savages in the western mountains (e.g. II, 441–2; II, 627). Before the war, Ramsay observes, 'the western wilderness ... afforded an asylum for the idle or disorderly, who disrelished the restraints of civil society' (II, 441). When describing the violent phase of the war in the South, he constantly overestimates the extent of loyalism in the backcountry, as though respectable revolutionary whiggism were the sole preserve of urban professionals, intellectuals and old southern planter families (II, 627).

Ramsay's tendency to see the West, not as the future of America, but as an outlet for its unruly elements, sets him apart from the strong strain of expansionist optimism in contemporary American thought. This strand of environmental optimism was most prominently represented by Jefferson, whose *Notes on the State of Virginia* Ramsay read in 1786, and with whom he corresponded. 'The state of society has an influence not less than climate', he pointed out in a letter to Jefferson disagreeing with the pastoral tendencies of the *Notes*, 'Our back country people are as much savage as the Cherokees'.[35] The opening sections of Ramsay's *History of the American Revolution* have much in common with previous colony history narratives of migration and settlement in British America which relied heavily upon charters and other founding documents in order to emphasise the legality of the acquisition of native American land.[36] For Ramsay, too, British America was a matter of the legal imposition of society upon an alien wilderness. To a degree, Jefferson's *Notes* also follow the procedure of these colony histories by describing Virginia's flora, fauna, the state of the natives, and the legal framework of the immigrant society. Jefferson wrote the *Notes* in response to a series of questions set for him by a member of the French delegation in America. However, it is significant that he reordered the original questions in order to provide a sequence of notes which suggest that the structural basis of Virginian society is not so much legally imposed upon, as derived from, the natural landscape itself. The benign natives, especially, appear to derive their pre-legal society, based upon the regimen of the internal moral sense rather than upon external rules, from the regulating power of the natural world. The *Notes* put to the test in a Virginian laboratory the traditional natural jurisprudential tenet that positive laws do or should have their ethical foundation in natural laws and rights.[37] In Jefferson's reading of the American environment, the pastoral basis of the social will endure as long as there are sufficient western lands to provide an outlet for migrant populations. The propensity of time to produce discord or decay can be checked by the properties of space.[38]

Although Ramsay originally observed that the American continent held out the promise of natural republican liberty by virtue of its distance from Great Britain, he could not repose any Jeffersonian confidence in the redemptive possibilities of its open spaces, and was deeply fearful of the threats of regional disunity and social degeneration which it seemed to offer to the immigrant society imposed upon it. After completing the *History of the American Revolution*, he continued to be worried by the baleful influence of the backcountry and the centrifugal pull of the regions. He struck a note of warning in a July 4th commemorative oration in 1794:

35 Jefferson's *Notes* were first published in a private edition of 1785. Ramsay to Jefferson (3 May 1786), *Selections*, no. 106.

36 In addition to those histories mentioned in note 26, Ramsay (who does not footnote his sources) probably made use of such informative colony histories as Robert Beverley, *History and Present State of Virginia* (1705, 1722); William Stith, *History of the First Discovery and Settlement of Virginia* (Williamsburg, 1747); William Smith, *The History of the Province of New York* (London,1757); Samuel Smith, *The History of the Colony of Nova-Caesaria, or New Jersey* (Burlington, NJ, 1765); Alexander Hewatt, *An Historical Account of the Rise and Progress of the Colonies of South Carolina* (2 vols.; London, 1779), all of which give details of founding charters and laws.

37 For this reading of the *Notes*, see Robert Ferguson, *Law and Letters in American Culture* (Cambridge, MA, 1984).

38 On the political ramifications of this aspect of Jefferson's thinking, see Drew McCoy, *The Elusive Republic: Political Economy in Jeffersonian America* (Chapel Hill, NC, 1980).

'We should, above all things, study to promote the union and harmony of the different states. Perish the man who wishes to divide us into back country, or low country, into a northern and southern, or into an eastern and western interest.'[39] Ramsay's American continent is both the 'natural seat of liberty' and the source of regional divergence between North and South whose differences, he claimed, 'arose, less, from religious principles, than from climate and local circumstances' (I, 28; I, 23). Ramsay's fears that American sectionalism was the likely result of its diverse environment are particularly evident in his discussion of slavery. He was always opposed to slavery, and still more to the slave trade, and one reason for his support of the Federal Constitution was its stipulation that the whole question of the trade should be reviewed in 1808. Although, in the pamphlet he wrote in support of the Federal Constitution, he carefully seeks to allay southern fears that the North would flex the muscles of the federal government to put a stop to the slave trade, privately he hoped that this would prove the case, and he deplored the reopening of the trade after the war.[40]

Ramsay abhorred slavery partly as a moral evil, but still more as a sign of environmentally derived difference in America. Unlike Jefferson, who thought that slavery arose from an essential or taxonomic difference between blacks and whites, Ramsay, who held more conventionally Christian beliefs about the created equality of all members of the human family, looked for the origins of slavery in the regional differences of the American continent. Jefferson's theory of humankind inclines to 'polygenesis', that is, a belief in the separate origins of different human 'varieties' within the species of man. The 'difference', Jefferson pointed out, between blacks and whites 'is fixed in nature', and such 'distinctions' are 'real', which is to say, not an accident of environmental circumstance but a reflection of biologically different roots.[41] Voltaire had expressed similar ideas in his *Singularités de la nature* (1768). Ramsay, by contrast, believed in the monogenesis of the human species, and in this he followed Christian teaching, the researches of Buffon, and the influential work on the subject of his one-time brother-in-law Samuel Stanhope Smith. Smith was an anti-

39 Ramsay, 'An Oration ... in Commemoration of American Independence' (Charleston, 1794) in *Selections*, 195. Sectional differences of these kinds had first surfaced at the Constitutional Convention of 1787. See Jack P. Greene, 'The Constitution of 1787 and the Question of Southern Distinctiveness' in *Imperatives, Behaviors and Identities*.

40 Ramsay, 'An Address to the Freemen of South Carolina, on the Subject of the Federal Constitution' (1787) in Paul Leicester Ford ed., *Pamphlets on the Constitution of the United States* (Brooklyn, NY, 1888), 378. Ramsay to Rush (22 August 1783), *Selections*, no. 48. Ramsay may also have been the anonymous author of a pamphlet entitled *Observations of the Impolicy of Recommending the Importation of Slaves* (Charleston, 1791). See *Selections*, 229.

41 Thomas Jefferson, *Notes on the State of Virginia*, ed. William Peden (New York, 1972), 138. The classic study of race in early America is Winthrop Jordan, *White over Black: American Attitudes Toward the Negro, 1550–1812* (New York, 1968). More recently, see Dana D. Nelson, *The Word in Black and White: Reading 'Race' in American Literature, 1638–1867* (Oxford, 1992).

slavery advocate and critic of Jefferson. His celebrated *Essay on the Causes of the Variety of Complexion and Figure in the Human Species* (1787) – almost certainly known and endorsed by Ramsay – defends scientifically a Christian position, and asserts that human variety is accidental, not taxonomic, and due to external factors in nature and the social environment. Like Smith, Ramsay regarded racial variety in America as an accidental and soluble problem. He formulated his objections to the *Notes on the State of Virginia* in a letter to Jefferson himself:

> I admire your generous indignation at slavery; but think you have depressed the negroes too low. I believe all mankind to be originally the same and only diversified by accidental circumstances. I flatter myself that in a few centuries the negroes will lose their black color. I think now there are less blacks in Jersey and Carolina. Their [lips] less thick – their noses less flat. The state of society has an influence not less than climate. Our back country people are as much savage as the Cherokees.[42]

This contains elements of Scottish stadial theory taken to its racial–environmental extremes; since America contains simultaneously all the different stages of social development, Americans of any race may be metamorphosed upwards or downwards on the civilisational scale.

It is, perhaps, no coincidence that both Ramsay and Smith subsequently became supporters of the Federalist party in the 1790s; they saw America's future as belonging to the already cultivated East, and agrarian westward expansion did not captivate their imaginations as it did those of their opponents, the Jeffersonians. Ramsay's fearful environmentalism led him into further contradictions. The most alarming aspect of slavery for Ramsay was that it might itself turn out to be, after all, a pre-condition of civilisation in the Southern seaboard. He felt obliged to acknowledge, in his history, that slavery may have been necessitated from the outset by the malarial, marshy character of the southern landscape:

> It is certain, that a great part of the low country in several of the provinces must have remained without cultivation, if it had not been cultivated by black men. From imagined necessity, founded on the natural state of the country, domestic slavery seemed to be forced on the Southern provinces. It favoured cultivation, but produced many baneful consequences. (I, 23)

In private, Ramsay was even willing to uncouple 'imagined' from 'necessity'; 'I have long considered their [the slaves'] situation', Ramsay told a correspondent in 1788, 'but such is our hard case here to the Southward that we cannot do without them. our lands cannot be cultivated by white men'.[43] His *History of South Carolina* (1809), although critical of the feckless

[42] Ramsay to Jefferson (3 May 1787), *Selections*, no. 106. Ramsay's *History*, however, does echo the *Notes* word for word in its description of the alleged 'greater degree of transpiration' in slaves which 'renders [them] more tolerant of heat'. Compare the *History*, I, 23 with *Notes*, 139.

[43] Ramsay to John Eliot (26 November 1788), *Selections*, no. 161.

mores of the southerners, barely alludes to slavery. Before this defeated silence, Ramsay's discussions of slavery may be read as an index of the conservative, apprehensive, even self-defeating character of his environmental republicanism. The old American Puritan dialectic between the self and the wilderness is replaced, in Ramsay's *History*, by a self socially, even physiologically, implicated in an environment which urgently needs to be brought under control. Ramsay's (and Smith's) synthesis of Lockean epistemology, Buffonesque monogenesism and Christian creationism gives rise to the hope that all Americans will eventually prove susceptible to natural and social improvement, as well as to the profound fear that their interaction with the American continent may precipitate their biological and social decline.

Environmental empiricism

The historical importance which Ramsay attaches to the 'natural state of the country' is consistent with new and widespread forms of environmental empiricism in late colonial and early republican American thinking. This strand in Ramsay's historical thought probably owes something to Robertson's *History of America*, but otherwise marks an unacknowledged break between British and American historical practice. Ramsay derived many of his environmental ideas from Benjamin Rush. He particularly admired Rush's *Enquiry into the Influence of Physical Causes upon the Moral Faculty* (1786), a fairly extreme essay in environmentalist behavioural science which claims that deviant moral and social behaviours are the result of physical causes such as climate, diet, disease and uncleanliness. Rush's Christian environmentalism is based on the idea of man's original sin, and the possibility of his social redemption through the manipulation of political, social and physical settings. By reading this work, Ramsay came into contact with a new, American formulation of stadial history as social policy. The *Enquiry*'s materialist implications worried its author, but do not appear to have troubled Ramsay who wrote back to Rush promptly after receiving his complimentary copy to say that he felt inspired to compose an inquiry of his own, along the same lines, into 'the nature and effects of the climate and soil of Carolina on the inhabitants'.[44]

Rush's optimistic social science of redemption represents in part an American answer to the European 'immaturity' or 'degeneracy' thesis of American nature. Colonial and post-colonial Americans understandably resented the derogatory, if not always deliberate implications of the writings of Buffon, Raynal and Robertson for the physical and moral

[44] Ramsay to Rush (12 April 1786), *Selections*, no. 102.

health of transplanted Europeans.[45] Buffon's *Histoire naturelle* and Robertson's *History of America* were nevertheless widely purchased and read. One Philadelphia bookseller tried to generate support for a reprinted edition of Robertson's work, and Ramsay himself took issue with it in a letter to Jefferson.[46] These European ideas were, of course, hotly refuted, although they continued to undermine the confidence of some Americans in their own continent. Given the widespread republican interpretation of history as a process of cyclical decay and renewal, the degeneracy thesis could sound to Americans dangerously like an environmentalised reworking of this tradition. Rush proclaimed the possibility of redemption from biological history through scientific means – a formulation which implicitly rejects the notion of a benign American nature, and the accompanying forms of Jeffersonian politics. This redemption, Rush argued, would also necessarily involve the agency of the inner moral sense (another idea which he derived from Scottish philosophers such as Francis Hutcheson). Among the exhortations which Rush added to the closing section of *The History of the American Revolution*, is his characteristic instruction to the readers to be 'particularly careful that your own descendents do not degenerate into savages' (II, 667).

The spectre of biological, moral or social degeneration haunted the literature of the early republican period. In one of most memorable literary treatments of this theme, the aristocratic French immigrant J. Hector St John de Crèvecoeur articulated the possibility of human metamorphosis in the New World either up or down a stadial scale of civilisation. His *Letters from an American Farmer* (1782) extol the potential of the American new man to 'finish the great circle' of western civilisation, and yet the work also incorporates, as a model for American history, an environmentalised version of republican declension.[47] At the end of the *Letters*, Crèvecoeur's protagonist, James, has to face the terrifying prospect of downward metamorphosis from farmer to hunter when he decides to take refuge from the Revolutionary War by joining the natives. The Lockean promise in America of a personal identity endlessly remade in encounters with new environments goes on to become, in the novels of Charles Brockden Brown (*Wieland*, 1798, *Edgar Huntly*, 1799 and *Arthur Mervyn*, 1799–1800) a gothic nightmare of an identity bifurcated and transformed with no possibility of external confirmation. This nightmare held special terrors for adoptive

[45] On the 'degeneracy' debate, see chapter 4, note 42, and also P. J. Marshall and Glyndwr Williams, *The Great Map of Mankind: British Perceptions of the World in the Age of Enlightenment* (London, 1982).

[46] Ramsay to Jefferson (3 May 1786), *Selections*, no. 106. On interest in Buffon in America, see Paul M. Spurlin, *The French Enlightenment in America* (Athens, Georgia, 1984), chapter 5. Robert Bell advertised a forthcoming (never-to-appear) reprint of Robertson's *History of America* in his edition of *The History of the Reign of the Emperor Charles V* (3 vols.; Philadelphia, 1770).

[47] J. Hector St John de Crèvecoeur, *Letters from an American Farmer*, ed. Albert E. Stone (Harmondsworth, 1981), 70.

southerners like Ramsay, since it was a commonplace in the North that the sultry ease of the southern climate had a degenerative effect upon the culture and morals of its inhabitants. As Jedidiah Morse, author of the (quickly standard) *American Geography* (1789), remarked: 'in a climate which favours indulgence, ease, and a disposition for convivial pleasure, they [southerners] too generally rest contented with barely knowledge enough to transact the common affairs of life'.[48] Like Morse, Ramsay is, at times, unable to resist the alarming tendency of the environmentalism through which he tries to define the American national character in the absence of tradition; the very diversity of geography raises the spectre of the moral and even physical decay of man when displaced from his European home.

Rush had attended the medical school of the University of Edinburgh, and Ramsay imbibed under his tutelage a distinctively Scottish brand of medical theory which emphasised the unitary character of diseases, their varied manifestations being generally the result of local environmental factors. This approach to medicine had been established in Charleston by another Scottish-educated doctor before Ramsay arrived.[49] Ramsay's own numerous publications on medical subjects, from the 1790s onwards, show him to have been preoccupied with the question of the relationship between health and environment. He was a founder member of the South Carolina Medical Society whose minute book reveals him to have been a consistent, public-spirited advocate for the collection of information about local climatic conditions in order to ascertain their effect upon the spread of infectious diseases.[50] Ramsay thus derived from his medical training and activities a highly empirical approach to the analysis of external variables, and a sense that physiological history could be arrested by altering environmental arrangements. Out of this medical training, Ramsay developed his own brand of scientific politics. He told Rush that he had written about the 'predisposing' causes of the Revolution in 'the medical stile', and welcomed both the states' and federal constitutions as examples of the new 'science of politics' (I, 331). [51] This constitution-making took Hume's

[48] Jedidiah Morse, *The American Geography; Or, A View of the Present Situation of the United States of America* (1789), 433.

[49] The doctor in question, Lionel Chalmers, wrote *An Account of the Weather and Diseases in South Carolina* (London, 1776). He corresponded with Rush. Ramsay wrote to Rush soon after his arrival in Charleston hinting that he needed a letter of introduction to Chalmers (27 July 1776), *Selections*, no. 8. See in general Joseph I. Waring, *A History of Medicine in South Carolina, 1670–1825* (Spartanburg, SC, 1964). Also, on Scottish medicine in America, see Lisa M. Rosner, *Medical Education in the Age of Improvement: Edinburgh Students and Apprentices, 1760–1829* (Edinburgh, 1991); Andrew Cunningham and Roger French eds., *The Medical Enlightenment of the Eighteenth Century* (Cambridge, 1990).

[50] See, for example, the entry for 30 January 1790, *South Carolina Medical Society*, MS Minute Book (South Carolina Historical Society). For a list of Ramsay's many medical articles, see Shaffer, *To be an American.*

[51] Ramsay to Rush (6 August 1786), *Selections*, no. 114.

project of reducing politics to a science one stage further by placing it, according to Ramsay, 'on a footing with the other sciences' (I, 331). This, as his pamphlet in defence of the Federal Constitution makes clear, was to spell the end of all older forms of politics.[52] The new scientific politics might then prescribe a remedy for the disease of social disunion, and bring about artificially a sense of the communal life in the nation since, Ramsay believed, the shared purposiveness of wartime had not lasted. The task for the 1780s, Ramsay remarked in a particularly revealing passage, was to '*reproduce* a spirit of union and that reverence for government, without which society is a rope of sand' (II, 637; my italics).

The Federal Constitution

Like James Madison, who noted that the Federal Constitution would have 'no parallel in the annals of human society', and like many of the other delegates to the convention in Philadelphia entrusted with the business of framing the constitution, Ramsay insisted that the new era of scientific politics was to be discontinuous with everything that had preceded it (I, 332).[53] Thus America's new political constitution would have to be open to the future, and capable of renewing itself by a process of constitutional amendment, rather than by repeated returns to the republican first principles buried in the resources of its history. This was also true, Ramsay felt, of the states' constitutions:

> It is true, from the infancy of political knowledge in the United States, there were many defects in their forms of government. But in one thing they were all perfect. They left the people in the power of altering and amending them, whenever they pleased. In this happy peculiarity they placed the science of politics on a footing with the other sciences, by opening it to improvements from experience, and the discoveries of future ages. (I, 331)

Ramsay's notion of a historical and epistemological break as the prerequisite for American modernity is grounded both in his polemically federalist reading of the 1780s as a period of chaos, and in his rejection of the idea of immanent moral meaning in American history and geography. Ramsay hoped that the renegotiation of American politics during the 1780s would open up the country to the norms of linear time. Like Voltaire's France after Louis XIV, Robertson's Scotland after the Union, and Hume's England after the negotiated settlement of 1688, Ramsay's United States accedes to a modernity which only comes after a rupture between the past and the present. The new republic, as Ramsay understood it, would have nothing in common with its classical predecessors; its immunity from

52 'An Address to the Freemen of South Carolina', 379.
53 Garry Wills ed., *The Federalist Papers* (New York, 1982), 67.

collapse into despotism would be secured by an inbuilt capacity for self-renewal, a reliance upon the 'selfish passions' rather than civic virtue as its actuating principle, and a new mechanism of representation to secure allegiance. (Ramsay, as Gordon Wood has pointed out, was among the first to appreciate the novelty of the American idea of representation as the delegation of power to rulers by the people.[54]) Instead of a narrative of national self-realisation to the point of fulfilment in 1787, Ramsay undertakes a generic recasting of American history as an interlude of disorder prior to the establishment of the civilised European norm of the centralised state. America's point of access to this historical genre is its Federal Constitution. Ramsay's thinking had always been centrist. While Chairman of Congress in 1785, he had been able to watch the erosion of the prestige of the federal tier of government from a ringside seat, and had tried to warn the states governors of the 'Anarchy or intestine wars' that might result from the collapse of the confederation.[55] He later told Rush that he would delay publication of his history until the event of the new Constitution, since 'the revolution cannot be said to be compleated till that or something equivalent is established'.[56] Ramsay regarded the Constitution as the best guarantor of modernity and civility, the most likely security for America from the violence of its history, and an innovation necessitated by its difficult past.

In Ramsay's view, the main purpose of the Federal Constitution, supported as it was by those with 'an honest ambition to aggrandize their country', was to deliver a regular and prestigious form of government (II, 655). It 'promises', Ramsay noted in a letter to Rush, 'security at home and respectability abroad'.[57] He warned his fellow South Carolinians, in his pamphlet on the Constitution, to ratify promptly lest 'without it independence ... prove a curse'.[58] Perhaps the fact that anti-federalist sentiment in South Carolina was often the result of fears about northern interventions in the slave trade caused him unfairly to characterise anti-federalists as either self-interested or dishonest (II, 655).[59] Whatever the case, Ramsay appeared to be greatly preoccupied with America's need to regain prestige in the international community:

54 Gordon S. Wood, *The Creation of the American Republic, 1776–1787* (reprinted New York, 1972), 601.

55 Circular 'To the Governors of Certain States' (31 January 1786), *Selections*, no. 96.

56 Ramsay to Rush (17 February 1788), *Selections*, no. 149.

57 Ramsay to Rush (10 November 1787), *Selections*, no. 141.

58 'An Address to the Freemen of South Carolina', 380.

59 For example, the comments of Rawlins Lowndes in the South Carolina state ratifying convention to the effect that the constitution was a northern plot designed to interfere with the slave trade (Elliot, ed. *Debates*, IV, 273). See also Robert M. Weir, 'South Carolina: Slavery and the Structure of the Union' in *Ratifying the Constitution*, eds. Michael A. Gillespie and Michael Lienesch (Kansas, 1989).

Time and experience only can fully discover the effects of this new distribution of the powers of government; but in theory it seems well calculated to unite liberty with safety, and to lay the foundation of national greatness, while it abridges none of the rights of the States, or of the people. (II, 656)

He later came to fear that this respectability abroad might be compromised by the rise of sectional divisions between the different regions. As he warned his audience in his 1794 oration: 'Forming one empire, we will be truly respectable, but divided into two, or more, we must become the sport of foreign nations.'[60] His ambitions for the new American nation had much in common with Alexander Hamilton's vision in the *Federalist Papers* of 'one great American system ... able to dictate the terms of the connection between the old and the new world'.[61] In many respects, Ramsay's cosmopolitanism was of a Hamiltonian kind (Ramsay supported the Federalist party throughout the 1790s). At this stage, both men acknowledged the economic importance of the West as well as fearing its potential as the locus for sectional strife, and yet both drew for themselves an imaginary proclamation line somewhere along the Appalachian mountains. Hamilton shared Ramsay's vision of an urbanised, developed United States of the eastern seaboard. 'I believe', Ramsay remarked to Jefferson, 'in opposition to Dr Robertson that were it not for the commercial cities on the sea coast even the use of a plough would far to the westward be forgotten'.[62] This is a cautious revision of Robertson's idea of stadial history; the transition from the pastoral to the agricultural and commercial stages cannot, it seems, occur spontaneously, but must be stimulated by eastern political leadership. For Ramsay, the West delays the onset of civilisation in America, as each newly inhabited western area has to be brought within the governance of Europeanised eastern norms.

The spatial correlative of this conservative, Federalist understanding of American history is thus a vision of America as a delimited land.[63] Ramsay's subsequent work as a distinguished local historian of South Carolina follows on from this historical vision which has no literary analogies in prospect or epic poetry, and which is not founded in a pastoral comprehension of American nature. Local history, as Ramsay explained to a correspondent shortly after reading Jeremy Belknap's fine *History of New Hampshire* (1784–92), is an important means of facilitating mutual understanding in the nation as a whole: 'The History of New Hampshire is really a valuable work. I wish we had such a one of every state in the union. We are too widely disseminated over an extensive country and too much diversified by different customs and forms of government to feel as one

[60] 'An Oration ... in Commemoration of American Independence', *Selections*, 195.
[61] *The Federalist Papers*, 55.
[62] Ramsay to Jefferson (3 May 1786), *Selections*, no. 106.
[63] On the Federalist landscape sensibility, see Larzer Ziff, *Writing in the New Nation*, chapter 7.

people which we really are.'[64] Nineteenth-century American historians dispensed with Ramsay's sceptical patriotism, and his notion that there had been moments of crisis and hiatus in American history. The Constitution, in particular, was absorbed into the continuities of Bancroft's national history which begins by celebrating the innately separatist and liberty-loving character of the first colonists. The epic universalisation of the American experience in Bancroft, the inscription of liberty as kind of metaphysical agent in the New World dialectic of Catholicism and Protestantism in Parkman, and the prefiguration in South America of the rise of North American civilisation in Prescott – all of these represent the marriage of New England historiographic traditions with new wisdom from Germany.[65] It was German historical thought which, from Bancroft onwards, permitted a further Americanisation of American history; national spirit could now acquire the status of historical agency instead of remaining, as in Ramsay's account, the product of delicate negotiations between history and geography. If Ramsay had an heir in the nineteenth century, it was Richard Hildreth, whose self-consciously sceptical and non-mythic *History of the United States of America* (1849–53) acknowledges Ramsay as a source. Hildreth's admiration of Hamilton, his conviction that the Constitution was invented, at least in part, to regularise debt repayments, his hostility to slavery, and his depiction of the colonists as only last-minute and reluctant revolutionaries all have similarities with Ramsay's interpretation.[66] Nevertheless, there is an important sense in which Ramsay's *History of the American Revolution*, coming, as it does, in the final moments before the French Revolution, represents not the first of the American historical epics but the last of the American Enlightenment histories.

[64] Ramsay to John Eliot (11 August 1792), *Selections*, no. 203.

[65] George Bancroft, *History of the United States from the Discovery of the American Continent* (10 vols.; Boston, 1834–75); Francis Parkman, *France and England in North America*, ed. Allan Nevins (9 vols.; New York, 1965); William Hickling Prescott, *History of the Conquest of Mexico* (3 vols.; New York, 1843).

[66] Richard Hildreth, *The History of the United States of America from the Discovery of the Continent to the Organization of Government under the Federal Constitution*, (3 vols.; New York, 1850). Ramsay always insisted that only properly constituted central government in North America could adequately and fairly service public debt. Ramsay therefore welcomed the Federal Constitution as an economically centrist device for putting public credit on a credible footing. See his comments made in the South Carolina House of Representatives in *The City Gazette and Daily Advertiser* (Charleston, SC) for 25 January 1788.

Afterword

Malcolm and Frere, Colebrooke and Elphinstone,
the life of empire like the life of the mind
'simple, sensuous, passionate', attuned
to the clear theme of justice and order, gone.

(Geoffrey Hill, 'A Short History of British India, III')

None of the historians discussed in this book anticipated that Europe, a civilised place of cultural interplay and mutual strategic restraint, could ever again fall prey to universal monarchy. Only Ramsay lived long enough to witness the rise and defeat of Napoleon. To Lord Byron, wandering in the persona of Childe Harold across the war-torn landscape of the continent, history seemed to mock such dreams of a common European civilisation. Travelling along the shores of Lac Leman, he was reminded of two of the locality's most famous inhabitants, one of whom, Voltaire, 'was fire and fickleness, a child, / Most mutable in wishes, but in mind / A wit as various', the other, Gibbon, 'the lord of irony', sapping 'a solemn creed with a solemn sneer'.[1] Byron mocks and admires the lonely satiric superiority of their 'gigantic minds' to all beneath them, and imaginatively assimilates their vision of the past to the exilic cosmopolitanism of Harold; like Harold, they were Europe's internal exiles, and like Harold, also, standing where Gibbon stood amidst the ruins of Rome, they were 'orphans of the heart' repatriating themselves in the bosom of European history.[2] The imaginative homelessness which Byron finds in the titanic historians of the eighteenth century is a retrospective creation, a dissociation of the historical from the cosmopolitan sensibility which either leaves history with 'but one page' or renders it complicit with the enduring corruptions of Europe's *anciens régimes*.[3] His choice of an exiled form of European identity remotely recalls and counteracts Burke's culturally grounded position of address, in the *Reflections on the Revolution in France*, as a

[1] Byron, *The Complete Poetical Works*, ed. Jerome McGann (7 vols.; Oxford, 1980–93), II, book III, stanzas 106–7.

[2] Ibid., book IV, line 695.

[3] Ibid., book IV, line 999.

European lamenting the destruction of the 'mixed system of opinion and sentiment' which had 'given its character to modern Europe' and 'distinguished' it above nearly all other ancient and modern civilisations.[4] Yet, as the complexity of Byron's own reading of post-Napoleonic Europe makes us aware, it would be wrong to assume that the cosmopolitan self-consciousness of the eighteenth century simply fractured into a universal radical language of reform and a conservative language of reverence towards tradition. In Britain, at least, a cosmopolitan tone in historical writing persisted and evolved throughout the nineteenth century, contextualising and qualifying the enabling certainties upon which new national narratives were built. Macaulay's *History of England*, in particular, is imbued with a Robertsonian sense of the nation's place within a common and developing European civilisation, and structured, in part, by an underlying notion of the progress of society.[5] John Burrow has explained how the eighteenth-century Scottish cosmopolitan idea of the progress of society combined with and modulated the Burkean notion of change-in-continuity in Macaulay's and in other nineteenth-century Whig histories of Britain.[6] Hume's *History* is thus a continuing presence in these historical works, as is John Millar's more politically radical and boldly cosmopolitan *Historical View of the English Government* (1787). In Macaulay's work, the Scottish analytical categories of social development are integrated, as they were in Hume, Robertson and Gibbon, with an ideal of greater cultural convergence in Europe. In the work of some other nineteenth-century historians, however, these analytical categories are applied in more schematic ways which detach them from and render less visible the cultural and moral programme which they were originally designed to serve. There was a tension, particularly in Gibbon's *The Decline and Fall*, but also in the narrative portion of Robertson's *History of Charles V*, between the abstract and universally applicable idea of history as a succession of stages and a sense of the unique and uniquely valuable nature of European civilisation. The strategic corollary of this idea of Europe as a dynamic site of cultural reciprocity and emulation was, as I have previously noted, a preference for a system of strong, autonomous balancing states. Both Hume and Gibbon were aware that this geo-political model was at odds with the drive of contemporary foreign policy towards continental and imperial competition with France – it expressed their unease, in other words, with Britain's

[4] *The Writings and Speeches of Edmund Burke*, volume VIII, ed. L. G. Mitchell (Oxford, 1989), 127. J. G. A. Pocock has commented on the way in which Burke's '"view of the progress of society in Europe" constitutes a significant revision of the Scottish perception of history' in 'The Political Economy of Burke's Analysis of the French Revolution', *Historical Journal*, 25 (1982), 347.

[5] John Clive has discussed the early influence of Scottish Enlightenment history upon Macaulay in *Thomas Babington Macaulay: The Shaping of the Historian* (London, 1993), 119–20.

[6] *A Liberal Descent: Victorian Historians and the English Past* (Cambridge, 1981).

pursuit of a maritime empire. Robertson, on the other hand, fashioned cosmopolitan history into an ideological approach to the question of empire. Empires, particularly territorial empires, he suggests, grow out the encounter between peoples at higher and lower stages of social evolution, but only modern Europeans are equipped to temper the rigour of this encounter with a flexible economic, political and cultural response to other civilisations. Robertson did not explain how his idea of mitigated imperialism was to be made consistent with his commitment to the notion of a balance of power in Europe.

Robertson's *History of America* was not the only influential cosmopolitan-imperial history in the eighteenth century, but it made the most satisfactory historical case for a minimally interventionist and free trading (rather than monopoly company) British Empire. Raynal's *Histoire philosophique des deux Indes* (1770) started out as a cosmopolitan survey of Europe's trading and colonial settlements, but dissolved, in the later editions to which Diderot contributed, into a vision of a universal society united by commerce. An originally cosmopolitan notion, embedded in the earliest text of this work, of Europe's extension of freedom and commerce to barbarous portions of the globe became, in later editions, the universal and politically radical idea of a fraternity of nations united in their struggle against despotism. The passages inserted by Diderot in support of the American revolutionaries make it clear that it is Europe which should seek inspiration from the new world, and not the other way around:

> Dieu a imprimé au coeur de l'homme cet amour sacré de la liberté; il ne veut pas que la servitude avilisse et défigure son plus bel ouvrage. Si l'apothéose est due à l'homme, c'est à celui sans doute qui combat et meurt pour son pays.[7]

At moments like these, the local histories recorded in the *Histoire des deux Indes* are resolved into a universal history of liberty. Robertson was anxious that his own underlying scheme of the progress of society was susceptible to a similarly abstract and politically enabling philosophical resolution; partly for this reason, his *Historical Disquisition* on India, like Gibbon's *Decline and Fall*, promotes and explores a certain disjuncture between his interpretive schemes and his cultural material. The dangers, in an imperial context, of slippage between historical categories and general, political prescription soon manifested themselves in one of the most sophisticated histories written in the early nineteenth century, James Mill's *History of British India* (1818). Mill was born in Scotland and studied under Dugald Stewart at Edinburgh University, and his history combines a rigorously stadial account of Hindu society with a new mode of evaluating political establishments (in India and at home) according to a criterion of utility. The results

[7] *Histoire philosophique et politique des établissements et du commerce des Européens dans les deux Indes* (4 vols.; Geneva, 1780), IV, 42.

of his early ruminations on political utility, on the progress of society, and on the best means of governing India were first seen in an article printed in 1810 in the *Edinburgh Review*:

What, then, is to be done? Is a legislative assembly to be convoked in India? Certainly not. The stage of civilization, and the moral and political situation in which the people of India are placed, render the establishment of legislative assemblies impracticable . . . A simple form of arbitrary government, tempered by European honour and European intelligence, is the only form which is now fit for Hindostan.[8]

The *History of India* follows suit, and opens with an overview of Hindu society, assimilating it to a conjectural history of rude and pastoral societies, noting the division of ranks imposed by the caste system, and suggesting reasons why it may have been held up by its system of laws (just as Europe was once slowed down by feudalism) at a point of transition between the pastoral and agricultural stages. The Hindu peoples, Mill concludes, 'have in reality made but a few of the earliest steps in the progress of civilisation'; the imperial logic of this statement points towards better and more efficient British administration without, Mill hopes, the undesirable effects of direct colonisation or commercial monopoly.[9] The *History of British India* became, as Javed Majeed has shown, a standard textbook for East India Company officials and shaped, in a more general way, 'a theoretical basis for the liberal programme to emancipate India from its own culture'.[10] Of this programme Robertson would never have approved. Mill's separation of the methodology of eighteenth-century histories of European civilisation from their cosmopolitan cultural commitments exerted an influence even over those later imperial histories which rejected his anglicising policy conclusions. One final example is the popular mid-nineteenth-century *History of British India* by the Scottish scholar, colonial theorist and governor of Bombay, Mountstuart Elphinstone. This work pits the voice of personal experience against Mill's philosophical approach to an India known only through translated documents. The result, however, is a history manifestly ill at ease with, but unable to transcend the sociological vocabularies of the Scottish Enlightenment; 'it is impossible', Elphinstone remarks after lengthy reflections on the lack of 'vigour' in modern Hindu culture,

[8] *Edinburgh Review*, 16 (1810), 155.

[9] *History of British India* (3rd edn, 1826), II, 190. Mill cites Millar as a source of theoretical inspiration throughout this work. See also, Duncan Forbes, 'James Mill and India', *Cambridge Journal*, 5 (1951–2), 19–30, and Jane Rendall, 'Scottish Orientalism from Robertson to James Mill', *Historical Journal*, 25 (1982), 43–69 which tells the intellectual story of the nineteenth-century 'orientalist' heirs of Robertson's *Historical Disquisition* on India.

[10] Javed Majeed, *Ungoverned Imaginings: James Mill's The History of British India and Orientalism* (Oxford, 1992), 127.

not to come to a conclusion that the Hindus were once in a higher condition, both moral and intellectual, than they are now; and as, even in their present state of depression, they are still on a footing of equality with any people out of Europe, it seems to follow that, at one time, they must have attained a state of civilisation only surpassed by a few of the most favoured of the nations, either of antiquity or of modern times.[11]

The history then proceeds to a routine account of the rise and fall of the Mogul Empire, finding 'points of depression' and economic indicators of the 'state of civilisation' along the way, right up to the point when, at the end of the Seven Years' War, the British are poised to inherit its ruins. Here, Elphinstone briefly undertakes an effort of imaginative alienation from his authorial position amid the imperial successors of the Moguls. As he surveys the decline of the Mogul Empire, he half remembers the end of the *Decline and Fall*, the ruined capital of the Roman Empire, and the 'new race of pilgrims' who visit the city from the remote and once savage countries of the north:

Its territory is broken into separate states; the capital is deserted; the claimant to the name of emperor is an exile and a dependent; while a new race of conquerors has already commenced its career, which may again unite the empire under better auspices than before.[12]

The disingenuous indefinite article ('*a* new race of conquerors') refers the historical specificity of the British Empire to a universal genealogy of conquest and reconquest. Here at the end of this history of the Mogul Empire, as at the close of *The Decline and Fall*, another empire is anticipated and postponed. To his own way of thinking, Elphinstone has already accepted, on behalf of the British Empire, the cultural responsibilities demanded by his own scheme of social analysis. Yet, to a nineteenth-century sensibility, the literary transposition of the past into narrative no longer complicates or compromises those responsibilities, as much as it did for an earlier race of cosmopolitan historians.

[11] Elphinstone, *History of India* (2 vols.; London, 1841), I, 384.
[12] Ibid., II, 688.

Bibliography

Selected secondary studies of individual historians

Voltaire

Brumfitt, J. H., *Voltaire Historian* (revised edn, Oxford, 1970).

Diaz, Furio, *Voltaire Storico* (Turin, 1958).

Rihs, Charles, *Voltaire: Recherches sur les origines du matérialisme historique* (revised edn, Paris, 1977).

Rosenthal, Jerome, 'Voltaire's Philosophy of History', *Journal of the History of Ideas*, 16 (1955), 151–78.

Sakmann, Paul, 'The Problem of Historical Method and of Philosophy of History in Voltaire', *History and Theory*, Beiheft 11 (1971), 24–59.

Hume

Burke, John J., 'Hume's *History of England*: Waking the English from a Dogmatic Slumber', *Studies in Eighteenth-Century Culture*, 7 (1978), 235–50.

Capaldi, Nicholas and Livingstone, Donald W., *Liberty in Hume's History of England* (Dordrecht, 1990).

Forbes, Duncan, 'Introduction' to Hume *History of Great Britain* (Harmondsworth, 1970).

Hume's Philosophical Politics (Cambridge, 1975).

Giarrizzo, G., *David Hume politico e storico* (Turin, 1962).

Hilson, J. C., 'Hume: The Historian as Man of Feeling' in *Augustan Worlds: Essays in Honour of A. R. Humphreys*, eds. Hilson, M. Jones and J. Watson (Leicester, 1978).

King, James T. and Livingstone, Donald W., *Hume: A Re-evaluation* (New York, 1976).

Meyer, Paul H., 'Voltaire and Hume as Historians: A Comparative Study of the *Essai sur les mœurs* and the *History of England*', *Publications of the Modern Language Association*, 73 (1958), 51–68.

Mossner, Ernest Campbell, 'Was Hume a Tory Historian? Facts and Reconsiderations', *Journal of the History of Ideas*, 2 (1941), 225–36.

'An Apology for David Hume, Historian', *Publications of the Modern Language Association*, 56 (1941), 657–90.

Norton, D. F. and Popkin, R. H. eds., *David Hume: Philosophical Historian* (Indianapolis, 1965).

Okie, Laird, 'Ideology and Partiality in David Hume's *History of England*', *Hume Studies*, 11 (1985), 1–32.

Phillipson, Nicholas, *Hume* (London, 1989).

Trevor-Roper, Hugh, Lord Dacre, 'Hume as Historian' in *David Hume: A Symposium*, ed. D. F. Pears (London, 1963).

Wertz, S. K., 'Hume, History and Human Nature', *Journal of the History of Ideas*, 16 (1975), 481–96.

Wexler, Victor G., *David Hume and the History of England* (Philadelphia, 1979).

Whelan, Frederick G., 'Robertson, Hume and the Balance of Power', *Hume Studies*, 21 (1995), 315–32.

Robertson

Armitage, David, 'The New World and British Historical Thought: From Richard Hakluyt to William Robertson' in *America in European Consciousness*, ed. Karen Ordahl Kupperman (Chapel Hill, NC, 1995).

Duckworth, Mark, 'An Eighteenth-Century Questionnaire: William Robertson on the Indians', *Eighteenth-Century Life*, 11 (1987), 36–49.

Gilbert, Felix, 'Introduction' to Robertson, *The Progress of Society in Europe* (Chicago, 1972).

Humphreys, R. A., *William Robertson and his History of America* (London, 1954).

Raynor, David, 'Hume and Robertson's *History of Scotland*', *British Journal for Eighteenth-Century Studies*, 10 (1987), 59–64.

Sher, Richard B., *Church and University in the Scottish Enlightenment* (Princeton, 1985).

'1688 and 1788: William Robertson on Revolution in Britain and France' in *Culture and Revolution in Britain and France*, eds. Paul Dukes and John Dunkley (London, 1990).

Smitten, Jeffrey, 'Robertson's *History of Scotland*: Narrative Structure and the Sense of Reality', *Clio*, 11 (1981), 29–47.

'Impartiality in Robertson's *History of America*', *Eighteenth-Century Studies*, 19 (1985), 56–77.

'Moderatism and History: William Robertson's Unfinished History of British America' in *Scotland and America in the Age of the Enlightenment*, eds. Richard B. Sher and Jeffrey Smitten (Edinburgh, 1990).

'The Shaping of Moderatism: William Robertson and Arminianism', *Studies in Eighteenth-Century Culture*, 22 (1991), 33–67.

Whelan, Frederic G., 'Robertson, Hume and the Balance of Power, *Hume Studies*, 21 (1995), 315–32.

Womersley, D. J., 'The Historical Writings of William Robertson', *Journal of the History of Ideas*, 47 (1986), 497–506.

Gibbon

Baridon, Michel, *Edward Gibbon et le Mythe de Rome: Histoire et Idéologie au Siècle des Lumières* (Paris, 1977).

Bond, H. L., *The Literary Art of Edward Gibbon* (Oxford, 1960).

Bowersock, G. W., Clive, John and Graubard, Stephen R. eds., *Edward Gibbon and the Decline and Fall of the Roman Empire* (Cambridge, MA, 1977).

Burkhalter, F., Ducrey, P. and Overmeer, R. eds., *Gibbon à la lumière de l'historiographie moderne* (Geneva, 1977).

Burrow, J. W., *Gibbon* (Oxford, 1985).

Craddock, Patricia B., *Young Edward Gibbon, Gentleman of Letters* (Baltimore, 1982).

'Edward Gibbon and the "Ruins of the Capitol"' in *Roman Images*, ed. Annabel Patterson (Baltimore, 1984).

Edward Gibbon, Luminous Historian (Baltimore, 1989).

Ghosh, Peter R., 'Gibbon's Dark Ages: Some Remarks on the Genesis of *The Decline and Fall*', *Journal of Roman Studies*, 73 (1983), 1–23.

Giarrizzo, G., *Edward Gibbon e la Cultura Europea del Settecento* (Naples, 1954).

Gossman, Lionel, *The Empire Unpossess'd: An Essay on Gibbon's Decline and Fall* (Cambridge, 1981).

Johnson, J. W., *The Formation of English Neo-Classical Thought* (Princeton, 1967).

Jordan, David P., *Gibbon and his Roman Empire* (Illinois, 1971).

Labiola, Albert C., 'Enlightenment History and Gibbon's Decline and Fall', *Enlightenment Essays*, 5 (1974), 44–9.

Lutnick, Solomon, 'Edward Gibbon and the Decline and Fall of the First British Empire: The Historian as Politician', *Studies on Burke and his Time*, 10 (1967–8), 1097–112.

Pelikan, Jaroslav, *The Excellent Empire: The Fall of Rome and the Triumph of the Church* (San Francisco, 1987).

Pocock, J. G. A., 'Gibbon and the Shepherds: The Stages of Society in the *Decline and Fall*', *History of European Ideas*, 2 (1981), 193–202.

'Superstition and Enthusiasm in Gibbon's History of Religion', *Eighteenth-Century Life*, 8 (1982), 83–94.

'Gibbon's *Decline and Fall* and the World-View of the Late Englightenment' in *Virtue, Commerce and History* (Cambridge, 1985).

'Gibbon and the Idol Fo: Chinese and Christian History in the Enlightenment' in *Skeptics, Millenarians and Jews*, eds. David S. Katz and Jonathan I. Israel (Leiden, 1990).

Porter, Roy, *Edward Gibbon: Making History* (London, 1988).

Watson Brownley, Martine, 'Appearance and Reality in Gibbon's History', *Journal of the History of Ideas*, 38 (1971), 651–66.

White, Lynn, ed., *The Transformation of the Roman World: Gibbon's Problem after Two Centuries* (Berkeley, 1966).

Womersley, David, *The Transformation of The Decline and Fall of the Roman Empire* (Cambridge, 1988).

'Gibbon's Unfinished History: The French Revolution and English Political Vocabularies', *Historical Journal*, 35 (1992), 63–89.

Ramsay

Brunhouse, Robert L., 'David Ramsay's Publication Problems, 1784–1808', *Papers of the Bibliographic Society of America*, 39 (1945), 51–67.

Kornfeld, Eve, 'From Republicanism to Liberalism: The Intellectual Journey of David Ramsay', *Journal of the Early Republic*, 9 (1989), 289–313.

Shaffer, Arthur H., 'David Ramsay and the Limits of Revolutionary Nationalism' in *Intellectual Life in Antebellum Charleston*, eds. Michael O'Brien and David Moltke-Hansen (Knoxsville, TN, 1986).

To be an American: David Ramsay and the Making of the American Consciousness (Columbia, SC, 1992).

Smith, Page, 'David Ramsay and the Causes of the American Revolution', *William and Mary Quarterly*, 17 (1960), 51–77.

Selected general studies of historical writing in the eighteenth century

Baridon, Michel, 'Les historiens des Lumières et leur problematique', *Studies on Voltaire and the Eighteenth Century*, 264 (1989), 963–82.

Black, John Bennett, *The Art of History: A Study of Four Great Historians of the Eighteenth Century* (London, 1926).

Braudy, Leo, *Narrative Form in History and Fiction: Hume, Fielding and Gibbon* (Princeton, 1970).

Breisach, Ernst, *Historiography: Ancient, Medieval and Modern* (Chicago, 1985).

Burrow, J. W., *A Liberal Descent: Victorian Historians and the English Past* (Cambridge, 1981).

Butterfield, Herbert, *Man on his Past: A Study of the History of Historical Scholarship* (Cambridge, 1955).

The Whig Interpretation of History (Harmondsworth, repr. 1973).

Cassirer, Ernst, *The Philosophy of the Enlightenment*, trans. Fritz Koellin and James Pettegrove (Princeton, 1951).

Cohen, Lester, *The Revolutionary Histories: Contemporary Narratives of the American Revolution* (Ithaca, NY, 1980).

Collingwood, R. G., *The Idea of History*, ed. T. M. Knox (Oxford, 1946).

Essays in the Philosophy of History, ed. W. Debbins (New York, 1985).

Damrosch, Leo, *Fictions of Reality in the Age of Hume and Johnson* (Madison, 1989).

Douglas, David, *English Scholars, 1660–1730* (second edn, London, 1951).

Duchet, Michèle, *Anthropologie et histoire au siècle des lumières* (Paris, 1971).

Flint, Robert, *History of the Philosophy of History* (Edinburgh , 1893).

Fueter, Edvard, *Histoire de l'historiographie moderne*, trans. Emile Jeanmaire (London, 1962).

Gay, Peter, *Style in History* (London, 1975).

Gearhart, Suzanne, *The Open Boundary of History and Fiction: A Critical Approach to the French Enlightenment* (Princeton, 1984).

Grafton, Anthony, *Defenders of the Text: The Tradition of Scholarship in an Age of Science* (Cambridge, MA, 1991).

Hay, Denys, *Annalists and Historians: Western Historiography from the Eighth to the Eighteenth Century* (London, 1977).

Kendrick, T., *British Antiquity* (London, 1950).

Kenyon, J. P., *The History Men: The Historical Profession in England since the Renaissance* (London, 1983).

Knowles, David, *Great Historical Enterprises: Problems in Monastic History* (London, 1963).

Kramnick, Isaac, 'Augustan Politics and English Historiography: The Debate on the English Past', *History and Theory*, 6 (1967), 35–67.

Kraus, Michael and Joyce, Davis D., *The Writing of American History* (revised edn, Norman, Oklahoma, 1985).

Levine, Joseph, *Humanism and History: Origins of Modern Historiography* (Ithaca, NY, 1987).

The Battle of the Books: History and Literature in the Augustan Age (Ithaca, NY, 1991).

Manuel, F. E., *Shapes of Philosophical History* (London, 1965).

Megill, A., 'Aesthetic Theory and Historical Consciousness in the Eighteenth Century', *History and Theory*, 17 (1978), 29–62.

Meinecke, Friedrich, *Historism: The Rise of a New Historical Outlook*, trans. J. E. Anderson (New York, 1972).

Momigliano, Arnaldo, *Studies in Historiography* (London, 1966).

Essays in Ancient and Modern Historiography (Oxford, 1977).

Nadel, G. H., *Studies in the Philosophy of History* (New York, 1965).

Piggott, Stuart, *Ruins in a Landscape: Essays in Antiquarianism* (Edinburgh, 1976).

Pocock, J. G. A., *The Ancient Constitution and the Feudal Law: A Study of English Historical Thought in the Seventeenth Century: A Reissue with a Retrospect* (Cambridge, 1987).

Preston, Joseph H., 'Was there a Historical Revolution?', *Journal of the History of Ideas*, 38 (1977), 353–64.

Preston Peardon, Thomas, *The Transition in English Historical Writing: 1760–1830* (New York, 1933).

Ranum, Orest, *National Consciousness, History, and Political Culture in Early Modern Europe* (Baltimore, 1975).

Artisans of Glory: Writers and Historical Thought in Seventeenth-Century France (Chapel Hill, 1982).

Schlereth, Thomas J., *The Cosmopolitan Ideal in Enlightenment Thought: Its Form and Foundation in the Ideas of Franklin, Hume and Voltaire, 1694–1790* (Notre Dame, Indiana, 1977).

Shaffer, Arthur H., *The Politics of History: Writing the History of the American Revolution* (Chicago, 1975).

Smith, R. J., *The Gothic Bequest: Medieval Institutions in British Thought, 1688–1863* (Cambridge, 1987).

Spafadora, David, *The Idea of Progress in Eighteenth-Century Britain* (New Haven, 1990).

Trevor-Roper, Hugh, Lord Dacre, 'The Historical Philosophy of the Enlightenment', *Studies on Voltaire and the Eighteenth Century*, 24 (1963), 1667–88.

Vyverberg, Henry, *Historical Pessimism in the French Enlightenment* (Cambridge, MA, 1955).

White, Hayden, *Metahistory: The Historical Imagination in Nineteenth-Century Europe* (Baltimore, 1973).

Woolf, D. R., *The Idea of History in Early Stuart England* (Toronto, 1990).

Index

CAMBRIDGE STUDIES IN EIGHTEENTH-CENTURY ENGLISH LITERATURE AND THOUGHT

General editors

Professor HOWARD ERSKINE-HILL LITT.D., FBA, *Pembroke College, Cambridge*

Professor JOHN RICHETTI, *University of Pennsylvania*

1 *The Transformation of* The Decline and Fall of the Roman Empire
by David Womersley

2 *Women's Place in Pope's World*
by Valerie Rumbold

3 *Sterne's Fiction and the Double Principle*
by Jonathan Lamb

4 *Warrior Women and Popular Balladry, 1650–1850*
by Dianne Dugaw

5 *The Body in Swift and Defoe*
by Carol Flynn

6 *The Rhetoric of Berkeley's Philosophy*
by Peter Walmsley

7 *Space and the Eighteenth-Century English Novel*
by Simon Varey

8 *Reason, Grace, and Sentiment*
A Study of the Language of Religion and Ethics in England, 1660–1780
by Isabel Rivers

9 *Defoe's Politics: Parliament, Power, Kingship and* Robinson Crusoe
by Manuel Schonhorn

10 *Sentimental Comedy: Theory and Practice*
by Frank Ellis

11 *Arguments of Augustan Wit*
by John Sitter

12 *Robert South (1634–1716): An Introduction to his Life and Sermons*
by Gerard Reedy, SJ

13 *Richardson's* Clarissa *and the Eighteenth-Century Reader*
by Tom Keymer

14 *Eighteenth-Century Sensibility and the Novel*
The Senses in Social Context
by Anne Jessie Van Sant

15 *Family and the Law in Eighteenth-Century Fiction*
The Public Conscience in the Private Sphere
by John P. Zomchick

16 *Crime and Defoe: A New Kind of Writing*
by Lincoln B. Faller

17 *Literary Transmission and Authority: Dryden and Other Writers*
edited by Earl Miner and Jennifer Brady

18 *Plots and Counterplots*
Sexual Politics and the Body Politic in English Literature, 1660–1730
by Richard Braverman

19 *The Eighteenth-Century Hymn in England*
by Donald Davie

20 *Swift's Politics: A Study in Disaffection*
by Ian Higgins

21 *Writing and the Rise of Finance*
Capital Satires of the Early Eighteenth Century
by Colin Nicholson

22 *Locke, Literary Criticism, and Philosophy*
by William Walker

23 *Poetry and Jacobite Politics in Eighteenth-Century Britain and Ireland*
by Murray G. H. Pittock

24 *The Story of the Voyage: Sea Narratives in Eighteenth-Century England*
by Philip Edwards

25 *Edmond Malone, Shakespearean Scholar: A Literary Biography*
by Peter Martin

26 *Swift's Parody*
by Robert Phiddian

27 *Rural Life in Eighteenth-Century English Poetry*
by John Goodridge

28 *The English Fable: Aesop and Literary Culture, 1651–1740*
by Jayne Elizabeth Lewis

29 *Mania and Literary Style*
The Rhetoric of Enthusiasm from the Ranters to Christopher Smart
by Clement Hawes

30 *Landscape, Liberty and Authority*
Poetry, Criticism and Politics from Thomson to Wordsworth
by Tim Fulford

31 *Philosophical Dialogue in the British Enlightenment*
Theology, Aesthetics, and the Novel
by Michael Prince

32 *Defoe and the New Sciences*
by Ilse Vickers